DAILY LIFE IN ANCIENT INDIA

Jeannine Auboyer was curator of the *Musée Guimet*, Paris. She was born in Paris in 1912 and became interested in the East soon after leaving school. In 1931 she was appointed '*chargée de mission*' and afterwards received diplomas from the *Ecole du Louvre* and from the *Ecole des Hautes Etudes* at the Sorbonne. From 1942–46 she was attached to the Cernuschi Museum and from 1946–52 was an assistant at the Department of Asiatic Art of the National Museums. Between 1956 and 1962 Jeannine Auboyer went on several expeditions to India and Cambodia. She was also an acting professor of the *Ecole du Louvre*, a corresponding member of the *Ecole française d'Extreme-Orient*, a member of the *Société des Gens de Lettres de France* and of the *Syndicat de la Presse artistique*. In 1958 she was elected a member of the French Commission for Unesco and in 1963 of the National Committee of Scientific Research. She was a *Chevalier* of the Legion of Honour, of the Monisaraphon and of the *Ordre des Arts et des Lettres*. Jeannine Auboyer died in 1990.

OTHER TITLES IN THE PHOENIX PRESS DAILY LIFE SERIES

Life and Leisure in Ancient Rome by J.P.V.D. Balsdon

Daily Life of the Etruscans by Jacques Heurgon

Daily Life of the Aztecs by Jacques Soustelle

Daily Life in Greece at the Time of Pericles by Robert Flacelière

Daily Life in Palestine at the Time of Christ by Henri Daniel-Rops

DAILY LIFE IN ANCIENT INDIA

From 200 BC to 700 AD

Jeannine Auboyer

Translated from the French by
Simon Watson Taylor

PHOENIX
PRESS

5 UPPER SAINT MARTIN'S LANE
LONDON
WC2H 9EA

A PHOENIX PRESS PAPERBACK

Originally published in France in 1961 under the title
La Vie quotidienne dans l'Inde ancienne
First published in Great Britain
by Weidenfeld & Nicolson in 1965
This paperback edition published in 2002
by Phoenix Press,
a division of The Orion Publishing Group Ltd,
Orion House, 5 Upper St Martin's Lane,
London WC2H 9EA

A CIP catalogue record for this book
is available from the British Library.

Printed and bound in Great Britain by
Clays Ltd, St Ives plc

ISBN 1 84212 591 5

CONTENTS

ILLUSTRATIONS

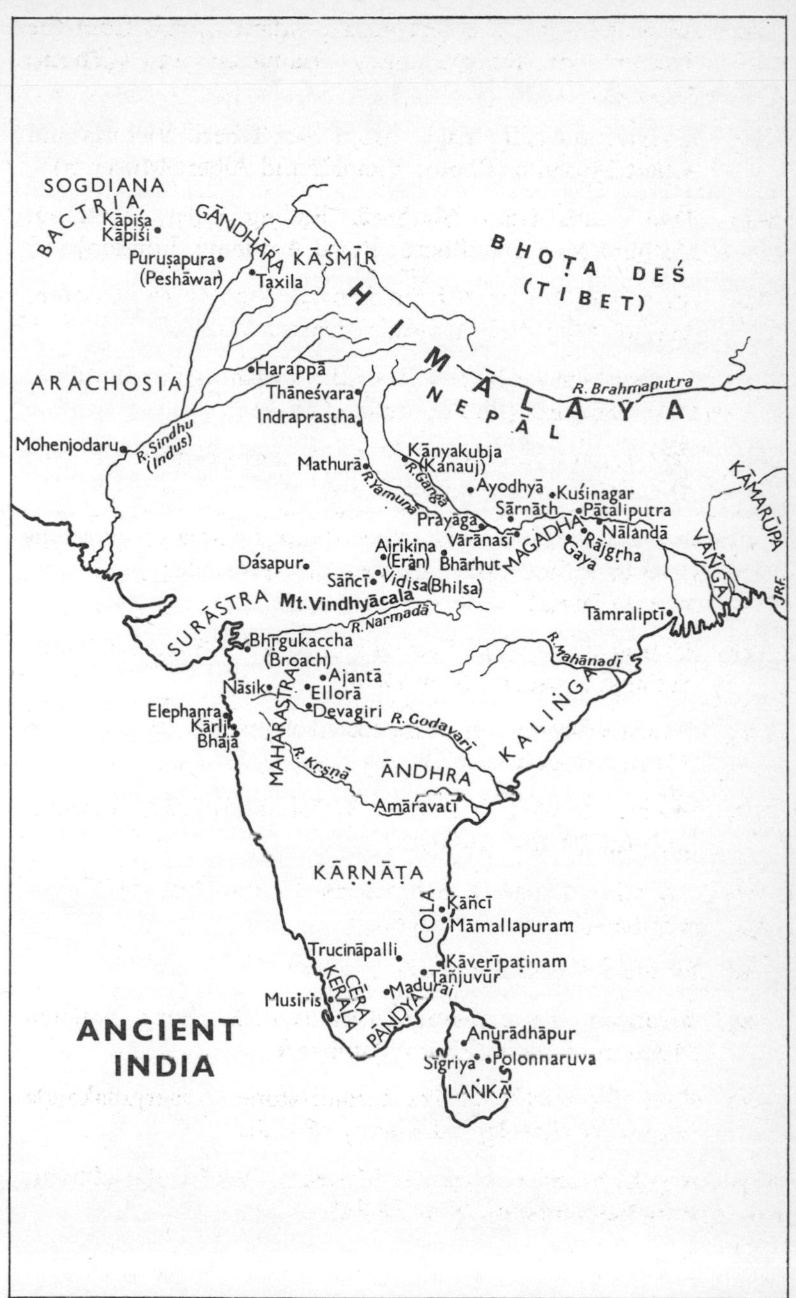
SOGDIANA
BACTRIA
Kāpiśa
Kāpiśi
GĀNDHĀRA
KĀŚMĪR
Puruṣapura
(Peshāwar)
Taxila
BHOṬA DEŚ
(TIBET)
HIMĀLAYA
Harappā
ARACHOSIA
Thāneśvara
Indraprastha
NEPĀL
R. Brahmaputra
Mohenjodaru
R. Sindhu
(Indus)
Kānyakubja
(Kanauj)
Mathurā
R. Gaṅgā
R. Yamunā
Ayodhyā
Kuśinagar
Sārnāth
Pātaliputra
Prayāga
Nālandā
Vārānasī
MAGADHA
Rājgṛha
Gaya
KĀMARŪPA
VAṄGA
Airikina
(Eran)
Bhārhut
Dásapur
Sāñcī
Vidisa (Bhilsa)
SURĀSTRA
Mt. Vindhyācala
R. Narmadā
Tāmraliptī
Bhṛgukaccha
(Broach)
R. Mahānadī
Ajantā
Nāsik
Ellorā
MAHĀRĀSTRA
KALIṄGA
Elephanta
Kārli
Bhāja
Devagiri
R. Godavarī
R. Kṛṣṇā
ĀNDHRA
Amāravatī
KĀRṆĀṬA
COLA
Kāñcī
Māmallapuram
Trucināpalli
Kāverīpaṭinam
Tañjuvūr
CĒRA
KERALA
Madurai
Musiris
PĀNDYA
ANCIENT INDIA
Anurādhāpur
Sīgriya
Polonnaruva
LAṄKĀ
J.R.F.

TRANSLATOR'S NOTE ON PRONUNCIATION

The following notes provide a rough guide for the general reader in the pronunciation of the Indian alphabet.

The vowels *ā*, *ī*, *ū*, *e*, *ai*, *o*, *au* are long, and equivalent to the vowels in the English words *palm*, *machine*, *rule*, *prey*, *lime*, *go* and *cow*, respectively. *A*, *i*, *u* are short, and equivalent to the vowels in the English words, *but*, *bit* and *bush*. The *a* is never pronounced as in English *bat*: for example, the Sanskrit *sama* is pronounced like the English *summer*. *Ṛ* is classed as a short vowel, and is pronounced as *ri* in *rich*.

The aspirated consonants *th* and *ph* must be pronounced as in English *pothole* and *shepherd*, never as in *thin* and *phial*. *C* is pronounced as *ch* in *church*. *Ś* and *ṣ* are both generally pronounced as English *sh* in *shape*. The distinction between the other sub-dotted 'retroflex' consonants (*ṭ*, *ṭh*, *ḍ*, *ḍh* and *ṇ*) and the dentals, without dots, is not important to the general reader.

Readers requiring a more comprehensive knowledge of Indian phonetics are referred to A. L. Basham, *The Wonder that was India* (Sidgwick and Jackson, London, 1954), App. X, pp. 506–8.

PREFACE

Modern India is perhaps unique, historically, in that its twentieth-century existence is still fashioned on traditions laid down thousands of years ago. Yet it has by no means been trapped in the rigid mould of an archaic civilization; in fact, its present evolution in the industrial field shows to what an extent its national equilibrium and coherence are based on an admirable continuity. This is a remarkable phenomenon for a civilization as rich and as complex as that of India, since one might well have expected the fountain of inspiration of her thinkers and artists to dry up, her innovators to be paralysed by a deadening ultra-conservatism, and all efforts at reform rendered nugatory by a rapid impoverishment of ideas. Yet none of these effects was experienced, at least in a degree sufficient to hinder the development of Indian civilization. On the contrary, India has derived from this special condition the affirmation of its own genius and the strength necessary to communicate the principles of it to the countries surrounding her. The slow pace at which changes of all kinds have taken place in India is the necessary accompaniment of this continuity, and reflects accurately the rhythm of rural life, which has always provided the essential framework of the country's structure.

These two factors are compounded by a strange disdain for history resulting directly from the fact that Indian philosophy has always emphasized the Absolute at the expense of contingency. Even the kings of India, in the inscriptions engraved in stone which often included their own panegyric, usually omitted to report the historical events of their reign with any great precision. During the entire period of ancient history, royal and local chronicles, when they exist, repeatedly convert historical facts into myth and legend. This complicates considerably the task of the modern historian and occasionally reduces him to the expedient of basing his hypotheses upon deductions alone.*

* One can gain some idea of the extent of these difficulties, when one reads in one of the most recent studies devoted to India the

There is another strange fact which still remains largely unexplained. This is that although India was in possession of its basic sacred literature in oral form long before the Christian era, and although there is no doubt about the historical existence of the Buddha in the sixth century BC, yet the first archaeological monuments whose dates we are able to establish go back no further than the third and second centuries BC. In consequence, the true historical period begins very late, although we cannot really call the previous period protohistoric, for it possessed a written language, although the writing has, unfortunately, defeated all efforts so far at interpretation.

The persistence of traditions and the slowness with which they evolved has meant that, even today, certain national characteristics exist which were already typical of Indian civilization before the third and second centuries BC. This is not to say that no changes have taken place in the social structure: it is certain that institutions have evolved over the centuries, the society has never became a static entity, and customs changed gradually. But the essential fact is that many of these transformations occurred almost imperceptibly, without sudden shock or violent revolution, and our lack of precise historical information serves to accentuate this impression, so it makes it almost impossible to determine accurately the dates of a reform or the application of a new measure. As a result, we are confronted with a juxtaposition of customs belonging to different levels of evolution, in which the most ancient customs survive alongside the most recent without mutual hostility.

For all these reasons we have been obliged to choose an exceptionally lengthy period, almost a thousand years, in order to give the necessary breadth of detail to the present study. There has been no escaping these extended time limits in this instance: any attempt to shorten the period under review or to concentrate upon one single reign would have resulted inevitably in an incomplete impression of daily life in ancient India. This period of nine centuries (roughly the second century BC to the seventh century AD), despite its length, is in fact entirely reasonable; in

---

following remark: 'The historians of India (fourth century BC) are reduced to the expedient of constructing its history on a foundation of grammatical examples!' (J. Naudou, *Histoire universelle*, I, p. 1454.)

particular, it covers the era during which, historically, India experienced on two occasions the political unification of the greater part of her territory, a fact which presupposes the growth of well-defined administrative organization and centralization. In the sphere of religion, Brāhmaṇism and Buddhism were both flourishing. In the artistic field, it was India's richest and busiest era, during which her most beautiful sanctuaries and monasteries were founded, schools and styles began to proliferate, and secular literature assumed its essential character. It is on these elements that medieval India later based her whole structure. This great and fruitful epoch of history has always been justly celebrated in Indian writings, and was made the ideal of many sovereigns, who liked to refer to the events of the period in the elaboration of their own panegyrics.

Many precious sources are available to us as the basis for our study of daily life during this era: a whole series of technical or descriptive texts, storied monuments, the discoveries of archaeological excavations, numismatics, epigraphy; and, in addition, contemporary chronicles by foreigners, mostly Greek, Latin and Chinese. These various documents clarify each other reciprocally; the bas-reliefs and mural paintings illustrate splendidly certain texts which, in their turn, facilitate a better reading of the former. Among the most useful texts should be mentioned the *Gṛhya Sūtras*, of Vedic origin (*c.* 400–200 BC) which describe the domestic religious ceremonies; a reading of these texts reveals the remarkable fact that these ceremonies have changed but little during the entire history of Indian tradition. One of the most entertaining sources is certainly the collection of *Jātakas* or 'previous lives' of the Buddha, a work which carries the same interest for ancient India as do France's fabliaux for our Middle Ages. The date of composition of the *Jātakas* remains uncertain, but the texts are at least contemporary with the bas-reliefs which serve as illustrations to them from 200 BC onwards. As far as elegant social life and amatory conventions are concerned, the celebrated *Kāmasūtra* is a basic document; its date of composition has been variously estimated, within the period fourth or fifth century and seventh century AD. The most useful source of information concerning the royal court, government and administration, military theory, and so on, is the *Arthaśāstra*, which may well have been written as early as 400 BC, although it is possible that it was composed at an appreciably later date; yet, after thirty years of research, we still do not know whether this important and unusual work, composed as a prince's handbook, summarizes the ideal elements of an imaginary constitution or, in fact, describes faithfully the structure of a real State. As far as secular literature is concerned, the best-known author of the period is Kālidāsa, poet and dramatist, who probably lived during the fourth or fifth century, or even perhaps as late as the sixth century. But India's literary heritage is so great that we shall not attempt to list any further works at this stage; the necessary references will be found during the course of this narrative.

One remark, however, is necessary: it is possible that the Western reader may find the portrait of India which emerges from this documentation to be idealized rather than realistic. It would be wrong, however, to jump too hastily to the conclusion that the contents of this book are no more than a theoretical reflection of what really existed; rather one must bear in mind the essentially traditionalist character of Indian civilization. Because of this special character, the division between the real and the conventional is finely shaded, to say the least. The Indian mental outlook has always been strongly affected by a spirit of conformism; in ancient times, especially, the Indians possessed an irresistible predilection for codification and classification in every field and a positive incapacity to deviate from the norm defined by tradition.

Furthermore, it did not seem illogical to a chronicler to describe a known town, an eminent or even historical personage, a given situation, a remarkable happening, even feelings and opinions, not according to the reality that confronted him but, rather, in conformity with a predetermined type duly standardized by tradition and corresponding to carefully established ritual prescriptions. Which is not to say that Indian writers lacked the gift of observation. Many poets and dramatists have proved that they were fully capable of noting realistic details and making deliberate use of them; if, for instance, an author had delighted in enumerating in a purely conventional manner the splendours of an imperial capital, he would very probably have indicated also, perhaps in a single phrase, that in the adjacent villages the sides of the streets were muddy. The anonymous authors of short verse-tales, stories and anecdotes were naturally more inclined to embellish their material with all sorts of images taken from life. To these sources must be added the accounts of what they themselves had seen and heard written by Chinese pilgrims, chronicles made quaint by their mixture of precise detail and moralizing; their importance lies in the fact that the information they contain often accords with that drawn from Indian sources.

So we are able to refashion an ancient India which is not so very different from the one that we know today, a country made up simultaneously of theories, principles and realities, in which the human presence is constantly visible through the tangle of rules and rites. Even though Indians' gifts of observation have, more often than we would have wished, been deflected from the particular to the general, and though India has not produced true chronicles in the Western sense of the word, still the reader may be assured that the India which we shall now try to present in its most everyday aspect conforms to the image of itself that it has transmitted to us over the centuries: a conventional image, certainly, but also an arresting one because of its multiple facets, and one that is enhanced here and there by picturesque details that add colour to the traditional pattern.

Laly-Les Tourelles, 1959–60

Part One

AN INTRODUCTION TO INDIAN LIFE

CHAPTER ONE

THE GEOGRAPHICAL AND HISTORICAL BACKGROUND

The physical conditions (of India) have been successfully exploited by mankind, since a population of 465 million souls has emerged from the morphological and climatic limitations imposed by nature a population, moreover, endowed with a certain number of traits of civilization in common, which are to be found from one end of India to the other, under climates as different as those of the Punjab and of Travancore.

PIERRE GOUROU, *L'Asie*, p. 374.

India extends from the thirty-seventh parallel (latitude of Seville) to the eighth parallel (latitude of Sierra Leone): this fact alone shows that India is more a sub-continent than simply a country. The climates are varied in this immense territory, ranging from eternal snows to torrid jungles; the fauna and flora are diverse for this same reason, while the numerous races and languages bear witness to very early settlement and successive invasions and infiltrations.

Protected in the north by the impassable barriers of the Himālayas and the Karākoram, bound by immense lengths of often inhospitable coast, the Indian peninsula would have been fated to suffer terrible isolation were it not that the great breach formed by the Indus valley kept it open to the world in the north-west. In addition, India could never have acquired a flourishing culture if nature had not endowed it with the tropical world's vastest recent alluvial plain, the Indo-Gangetic plain, the object of the greed of all the invaders, and the cradle of the truly Indian civilization. Finally, India would inevitably have consisted largely of desert tracts had it not been subjected climatically to the inexorable rhythm of the monsoons which bring it life by favouring the cultivation of crops. Its very vastness has proved to be not only a factor in its political fragmentation but also a guarantee for the security and originality of its institutions. A closed world in appearance but not in reality, India is blessed with a kind of spiritual 'magnetization' which indianizes everything from abroad which installs itself within its boundaries.

Archaeological excavations so far undertaken, even though insufficient in number, have revealed the existence, throughout the Indus valley, of highly developed urban agglomerations related to those of Afghānistān and Balūchistān, and indicating connections with Mesopotamia and Susiana around 2000 BC and earlier. The connections with India proper are still more or less hypothetical. The Āryans must have appeared towards the end of this period (*c.* 1500?), and their activities were destined to have momentous consequences for India since they brought her Sanskrit, the Vedic religion and the principal elements of her historical culture.

It is only several centuries later that precise historical facts become available to us; thenceforward, we are able to trace the establishment – by force – of the new tribes on Indian soil, then their progression eastwards and their installation in the Gangetic plain. Simultaneously, the huge mass of Vedic texts was gradually built up that has continued to provide the essential basis for Indian thought right up to the present day: its affinities were undeniably Iranian, but it drew apart little by little and its emphasis on cosmogony was gradually superseded by an increasing preoccupation with metaphysical speculation.

During the so-called Vedic era (*c.* 1500–500 BC), the Veda, 'knowledge', from which Vedism takes its name, was an impressive array of texts, which can be divided into four principal types of literary form: strophes recited during the sacrificial ceremony, sacrificial formulas (sometimes with commentary), sacred melodies and magical formulas. These texts were invariably attributed to legendary sages and were transmitted orally by priests and brāhmaṇs and by professional bards (the *sūtas*, formerly royal coachmen). They are mostly doctrinal in form, and many contain esoteric allusions. Sacrifice is the principal theme, and this consists essentially in a libation of *soma*, a vegetable liquor whose name is close enough to the Iranian *haoma* to indicate some degree of common ancestry. Similarly, the Vedic pantheon included yet other names very similar to those of the Iranian *Avesta*: Varuṇa corresponds to Ahura Mazdāh, Mitra to Mithra,

Vāyu to Vayu, Vṛtrahan to Verethragna, and so on. Nevertheless, the Vedic cycle also contained certain popular cults, such as that of Rudra-Śiva, which eventually achieved enormous success. The Vedic gods were imagined as active and impassioned, and could be made to yield to human beings through the magical power of the sacred utterance (*brahman*); they personified the forces and phenomena of nature, and since everything was a subject of fear or admiration, everything had its divine essence: fire, the dawn, the stars and the sun, water, the sky, the earth, thunder, the winds, etc. Demons, still lumped together at that stage under the generic name *asura* (cf. the *ahura* of Iran), were the enemies of the gods and of mankind, intervened in everyday life and necessitated prayers and magical practices. If the shades of ancestors were not suitably propitiated they would turn into ghosts.

One of the central concepts of Vedism was that the universe was divided into three zones – earth, 'intermediary' space, and sky, and this continued to be accepted over a long period of time. But the teachings concerning the genesis of the world were rather imprecise, although it was generally considered to have been a magical operation carried out in successive stages by the creator – the *Puruṣa*, universal body, higher 'Self' – who was still only a vaguely conceived entity at that time. The concept of the individual soul had not yet achieved the importance it was to have later in the Vedic commentaries which, in their turn, were destined to give birth to the religion's powerful new impulse known under the name of Brāhmaṇism. A hell was deemed to exist as a counterpart to the deceased's survival in the stars or elements; as for the celestial abode, it was 'the path leading to the gods', reserved for those who had undertaken pious works (asceticism, sacrifice, charity, etc.). But we do not know whether primitive Vedism had any dogma concerning the divine reward of virtue, divine judgment or penalties after death.

At a period which it is difficult for us to determine, Vedism found it necessary to elaborate a series of commentaries because of its ever-growing hermetism, and these commentaries, the *Brāhmaṇas*, the *Upaniṣads* and the *Āraṇyakas*, together constituted a new Veda, the *Vedāṅgas*. From that time onwards, Vedism became archaic and gave birth to a new form, Brāhmaṇism, a fundamental Indian religion. Sacrifice was superseded by religious services, and the fate of the individual soul became a dominant preoccupation. At this stage, too, was first posed the great problem of the individual soul and its relationship to the universal 'Self', a theme which was to haunt Indian thinkers in all subsequent ages and to which every Indian religion, indeed every sect, has tried to find a solution. This was also the moment when the domestic rituals were elaborated, when individual life appeared at last as a reality, when rules of conduct – morality or asceticism – were proposed as remedies against the consequences of the concept of the transmigration of souls, *saṃsāra*, which is common to all Indian faiths. While Indian philosophy was thus sowing the first seeds of its later greatness, the common folk continued to lead their modest lives in the peaceful manner typical of rural life everywhere. The daily ritual, working the earth, caring for the cattle, festivals and seasonal rites formed the regular rhythm of their lives; they could always invoke magical formulas to help them surmount the irrational fears of those who are affected by natural phenomena without knowing the true causes and who have every reason to fear nature's redoubtable powers. They were born, they worked and they died according to their humble condition, careful only to preserve themselves from the anger of the gods, and to guard against dearth and sickness. They already drew strength from the solidarity of family, clan or caste; later, they were to draw additional strength from the trade-guilds.

Probably about 800 BC, the Āryans' thrust eastwards along the Gangetic plain removed the centre of gravity of the conquered lands from the Panjāb to the Doāb; this last was the region between the Ganges and Jumnā, fertile and strategically important, and destined to become one of India's most constantly disputed territories over the centuries. From this time onwards it seems possible to speak of Āryan kingdoms, whose gradual establishment throughout northern India led to attempts at hegemony on the part of some of the last territories to be conquered. One of these, Magadha (southern Bihār), made a bid for supremacy as early as 600 BC.

Magadha, less thoroughly Āryanized than those kingdoms which had been conquered earlier, and considered semi-barbarian by the Āryans, became the birthplace of India's first great autochthonous empire, that of the Mauryas. To the spirit which dominated these recently conquered regions can, it seems, be attributed the blossoming, from the beginning of the sixth century onwards, of a whole series of religious and social reforms. The Āryans had apparently attempted to impose Brāhmaṇism wherever they had established themselves. Now, since its inception, Brāhmaṇism had gradually stiffened into a formalism which the intransigeance of the brāhmaṇs had finally ossified. In addition, an increasingly strict partitioning of society into castes was producing a rigid framework of impermeable compartments. Finally, orthodoxy was menaced by the liberalism of these new subject peoples. So a wind of revolt began to stir in this imperfectly Āryanized society, to bring suppleness to the social structure and suggest a new outlook; it was a human and heartfelt reaction against the brāhmaṇs' desiccating formalism.

Two men became the champions of this liberating movement. They were Vardhamāna, of the Licchavi clan (north across the Ganges from Magadha), who founded the Jain religion (under the names of Mahāvīra, 'Great Hero', and of the *Jina*, 'the Conqueror'); and Siddhārtha, 'Aim-achieved', a prince of the Śākyas (who were found on the northern borders of ancient Magadha), the founder of Buddhism under the name of Śākyamuni, 'the monk of the Śākyas', more generally known as the Buddha, 'the Awakened', 'the Enlightened' (by spiritual knowledge). Although they were both members of the warrior caste, they aimed to bring an entirely pacific solution to bear upon the increasingly acute problems that faced their society. The doctrine of Mahāvīra is founded on asceticism, and on the theory and practice of *ahiṃsā*, the prohibition of harmful activity, a philosophy of non-violence very similar to that which Gandhi preached with such authority. But it was the doctrine of the Buddha which was destined for the greatest fame and glory, first of all in India, then in the rest of Asia.

The teaching of this master is based on the affirmation that all life is suffering, and that this suffering can be put an end to only through the extinction of desire, the source of life and of pain. It preaches charity towards all beings and the equality of individuals among themselves. It condemns both asceticism and epicurism as being baneful excesses, and advocates moderation in all things, what it calls the 'middle way'. A moral system rather than a religion, ancient Buddhism remained within the traditions of Brāhmaṇism, accepting both a part of its pantheon and the fundamental conception of the transmigration of souls with its various consequences. Buddhism, at this early stage, contented itself with promising the virtuous being an amelioration in the conditions of his successive rebirths, until he finally achieved the supreme state of *nirvāṇa*, the final and complete liberation from the cycle of rebirths. When he died at the age of about eighty, the Buddha bequeathed to Gangetic India the foundations of a Buddhist Church and community animated by a universalist spirit, whose expansion was to be facilitated by several political and historical factors, and whose consequences were to be of the greatest range and importance.

This spiritual revolution did not, however, take place in isolation, among only the least Āryanized sectors of society; it was, rather, the crystallization of a great general effervescence, and reforms were carried out in the very heart of Brāhmaṇism which was forced, in order to survive, to admit cults that were more clearly personified than those of Vedism, most of these new cults being of popular and aboriginal origin: Śiva, Skanda, Viṣṇu, Kṛṣṇa, Agni, the hero Rāma, and many others opened the way to theism, which became gradually more and more powerful during the ensuing centuries.

This, then, briefly, was the situation at the time of the Buddha (*c.* 558–478 BC). On the political plane, Gangetic India was still fragmented in numerous more or less extensive kingdoms. Magadha was one of the most powerful of these, though its kings, converted to Buddhism by the Buddha himself, did not yet possess sufficient territory to form an empire. Available historical records give us no information about developments in southern India during this epoch. On the other hand, north-western India was experiencing a fresh foreign invasion of its soil; the might of Achaemenid Iran had reached the gateways of India, had conquered Bactria, Gandhāra and Arachosia and had turned these provinces into satrapies. The Emperor Darius I invaded the valley of the Indus and set up one of his satrapies there (518–515); he was thenceforward in a position to make use of the Indian Ocean (517–516); India paid him a heavy tribute in gold.

While the Indian kingdoms of the north-east were engaged in a struggle for supremacy, and Buddhism was instituting its reforms there, the West was being subjected to Persian influences. Although we are not yet in a position to measure exactly the strength of these influences, there is no doubt that they left durable traces in various fields such as administration, the system of measurement, script and, in particular, architecture. For two centuries Darius's Indian possessions remained within the imperial patrimony of Iran; this explains why designs typical of Achaemenid art passed into the plastic repertory of northern and central India. Buddhist artists adopted, for instance, Persepolitan capitals for the commemorative pillars they designed. The reputation of Persepolis penetrated as far as the chief town of Magadha, Pāṭaliputra, where the palace is said to have been inspired by that of Darius I.

In 331 BC, Alexander the Great of Macedonia defeated Darius III and proceeded to conquer the ancient Persian empire, region by region. When he finally reached the banks of the Jhelum (then the Vitastā), almost exactly two centuries after Darius I, he found himself face to face with the impressive army of an Indian sovereign, Pōros (Pūru in Sanskrit), who probably reigned in the Panjāb. At the same time, an ambitious and fiery young general of eastern India, who had rebelled against his own sovereign (of the Nanda dynasty, in Magadha), sought the support of the Greek conqueror in his plan to overthrow his master, the King of Magadha. This at least is the account given by Plutarch (*Alex.*, LXII). Numerous reasons prevented Alexander from undertaking this tempting enterprise, which would have opened up to him the access to Gangetic India, and the Māgadhī general had to do without the aid of the invaders. Known by the Greeks under the names of Androkottos, Sandrokottos or Sandrokuptos, he was to play a considerable role in the destiny of India. Was it Alexander's refusal which turned him to violent opposition? Whatever the reason, immediately after the great Macedonian's death in 323 he assumed the role of 'champion of liberty'. Alexander's prefects were put to death and his lieutenants forced to retreat (317–316). Three years later, in 313–312, Sandrokottos mounted the throne of Magadha, putting an end to the Nanda dynasty and inaugurating, under the Sanskrit name of Candragupta, that of the Mauryas. And when, shortly before 305, Seleucus Nicator, founder of the Seleucid empire and era, arrived in the Panjāb after traversing the same route as Alexander, Candragupta was already in possession of a real empire, stretching from the Indus to the Ganges, commanding the deltas of both rivers, and backed up by an imposing army. The administrative apparatus seems to have been extremely well organized, supervised by imperial inspectors whose duties were facilitated by the good state of the roads, the upkeep of which was one of the sovereign's main preoccupations. Seleucus had no choice but to accept an alliance with so powerful a monarch; he abandoned to him all the territories of the Indus basin and, it is said, bestowed upon him the hand of a Greek princess in marriage. From this moment India joined the ranks of the great powers of the age; her capital, situated at Pāṭaliputra in Magadha, was for several decades the seat of a Greek embassy made illustrious by the qualities of the ambassador, Megasthenes, whose account is very valuable even though it has only come down to us in secondary transcriptions.

Candragupta's territorial conquests seem to have been maintained under the reign of his son Bindusāra, about whom, however, we know very little. But it was one of his sons, the celebrated Aśoka, who raised the dynasty to the height of its power; Greek sources are silent about him, and Buddhist tradition has preserved only a vague image. Fortunately, this emperor took the trouble to have edicts engraved and set up throughout the territories he governed, thanks to which we are in a position to reconstruct his personality and also to examine the form of his imperial propaganda.

Aśoka seized power about 264 BC, and may have been crowned in 260. Eight years later, having conquered the powerful kingdom of Kaliṅga (which stretched from the delta of the Mahānadī to that of the Godāvarī) in a particularly brutal manner, he expressed his regrets and repentance in his thirteenth rock edict, in the following terms:

> . . . One hundred and fifty thousand persons were carried away captive, one hundred thousand were slain, and many times that number died. . . . The Beloved of the Gods, conqueror of the Kaliṅgas, is moved to remorse now. For he has felt profound sorrow and regret because the conquest of a people previously unconquered involves slaughter, death, and deportation. But there is a more important reason for the King's remorse. The Brāhmaṇas and Śramaṇas [the priestly and ascetic orders] as well as the followers of other religions

> and the householders – who all practised obedience to superiors, parents, and teachers, and proper courtesy and firm devotion to friends, acquaintances, companions, relatives, slaves, and servants – all suffer from the injury, slaughter, and deportation inflicted on their loved ones. Even those who escaped calamity themselves are deeply afflicted by the misfortunes suffered by those friends, acquaintances, companions and relatives for whom they feel an undiminished affection. Thus all men share in the misfortune, and this weighs on the King's mind. . . . Therefore, even if the number of people who were killed or who died or who were carried away in the Kaliṅga war had been only one one-hundredth or one one-thousandth of what it actually was, this would still have weighed on the King's mind. . . .[1]

This bloody conquest seems to have provoked a moral crisis in Aśoka and determined his conversion to Buddhism, a fact which was to have incalculable consequences for India. In the words of the same edict, Aśoka declared his desire that in future there should be 'security, mastery of the senses, equanimity and gentleness in the hearts of all beings'; the victory which he 'considers to be the greatest of all is the victory of the Law'. This law is equally his law as king, and the law of Buddhism and of Brāhmaṇism: it is the Indian *dharma*, which is at once law, religion and moral order. Finally, he advised his successors not to think of new victories but, on the contrary, to prefer to such ideas 'patience and the mild application of power'.

Aśoka was not content simply to have these counsels engraved 'on mountains and on stone columns'. He commanded that they should be proclaimed to the entire population, the proclamation to be preceded by the beating of a drum. During the thirty-six (or thirty-seven) years of his reign, he instituted throughout his empire a closely knit administrative organization whose functions seem to have been both social and religious. His officers were not spared the tasks of delivering criticism and moral lectures, and were ordered to keep a close watch even on his own harem. He himself constantly undertook pilgrimages to the holy places of Buddhism, and also organized regular tours to propagate the doctrine. These tours served also as means of checking on the satisfactory state of administrative affairs. His zeal for Buddhism did not prevent him, though, from preaching mutual tolerance between the different sects and even from giving them practical assistance at times. He also became famous for his charity towards animals, and after renouncing personally the pleasures of the chase he ordered that the slaughter of animals destined for the kitchens of the imperial palace should be reduced. Instead of killing 'several hundred thousand' every day, only three were to be killed, two peacocks and one gazelle, and even then, a gazelle was not to be killed 'every day'. Later, he completely abolished the service of meat at his table.

His empire encompassed the whole of northern and north-west India, including part of Afghānistān (one of his inscriptions was discovered recently in Kandahār), and extended south as far as the land of Āndhra (the lower valleys of the Godāvarī and the Kistnā). He maintained diplomatic relations with Syria, Cyrenaica, Egypt, Macedonia and Epirus or Corinth. The political unification which Aśoka promoted so vigorously stimulated the economic development of the entire country, and he was responsible for the widespread diffusion of Buddhism as a civilizing influence, perhaps in Kashmīr, certainly in the Greek colonies on the upper Indus and as far as Ceylon where, tradition holds, he sent his son as a missionary. Simultaneously, the plastic arts sprang into vigorous life and, it seems, started using long-lasting materials for the first time.

After his death, his empire was carved up. Magadha, Mālava and the Ayodhyā region passed into the hands of the Śuṅgas (*c.* 176–64 BC), then the Kāṇvas (*c.* 75–30), and the centre of gravity moved westwards. This coincided with serious political developments in the north-west which were to have profound repercussions throughout the rest of India. From *c.* 250 BC onwards, Indo-Greek kingdoms had sprung up in Bactria, in Gandhāra (Peshāwar), in Kāpiśa (Kābul) and other places. These minor potentates were constantly engaged in waging war against each other, when they were not resisting attacks from the Iranians and the Parthians. One of the Bactrian kings, Demetrius, undertook the conquest of India about 189, and he may have reached as far as Pāṭaliputra. His successor, Menander, was forced to retreat from that city in *c.* 168, but preserved a kingdom in the Panjāb, and from this time onwards, the region of Cambay and Broach formed part of the regular Greek commercial itinerary. It seems that the first of the Śuṅgas, Puṣyamitra (*c.* 176–140), drove back the invaders, though it remained to his grandson to repel them finally to the other side of the Indus.

The importance of the Śuṅgas and the Kāṇvas should not be minimized, despite the fact that they were unable to hold together the Maurya empire. Their administration was less spectacular than that of Aśoka, but there is no doubt that they maintained a high cultural and artistic tradition in the regions that they dominated. It was during their epoch that the most beautiful grottoes of ancient times were excavated and decorated; and many monuments (*stūpas*) were erected, including the famous ones of Bhārhut and Sānchī, whose historiated reliefs illustrate so perfectly the literary descriptions of life at that time.

On the other hand, Buddhism was making great progress evangelistically, since it had not only spread its doctrine throughout India, including the southern regions (especially around Amarāvatī), but it had also reached the Indo-Greeks as far as Bactria. King Menander, for instance, has remained famous in the Buddhist tradition for the 'questions' he posed to the master Nāgasena, whose answers are a eulogy of Buddhism.[2] Brāhmaṇism, too, was evolving – towards an increasingly pronounced theism and, at the same time, towards an epic tradition that corresponded precisely with India's martial structure at that time. More and more different sects were founded during this era: worshippers of Śiva, who were soon to be organized by the master Lakulīśa; worshippers of Viṣṇu, who had become the mystical symbol of spiritual peace; worshippers of his incarnation, the bucolic god Kṛṣṇa, whose followers took the name of *Bhāgavatas*; and of his other incarnation, Rāma, the hero of the great epic poem, the *Rāmāyaṇa*. That this affective form of Indian religion was capable of attracting the Western mind is proved tangibly by the pillar, adorned with Viṣṇu's mythical bird, Garuḍa, and dedicated to Vāsudeva-Kṛṣṇa, which was set up around 100 BC, not far from Vidiśā in Besnagar, by the Greek Heliodorus, a native of Taxila and ambassador of King Antialkidas at the court of the Śuṅga king.

About 80 BC, the Indo-Greek kingdom collapsed definitively under the increasing pressure of semi-nomads from central Asia who had themselves been driven out of that region by the advance of a branch of the Hūṇas from inner Mongolia. Among these newcomers, Scythian tribes whose Parthian overlords had planted in them the seeds of Iranian and Greek culture invaded western India; these invaders were known by the Indians as the Śakas. Simultaneously, the Āndhras, whose power was continuing to grow in the Deccan, were exerting pressure on the Śuṅga kings. In vain, the latter gave way to the new Kāṇva dynasty; it, in its turn, soon collapsed, leaving Gangetic India in the same state of political fragmentation from which the Mauryas had rescued it. But a new force, which was to play an important role in northern India, was in the process of consolidating itself in the north-western regions: that of nomadic tribes whose language (originating in Khotān, central Asia) shows affinities with that spoken in eastern Iran. Based at first in Bactria, and known as Kuṣāṇas, they built a vast empire which stretched from the Oxus to the Ganges plain, thus uniting under their authority most of the ancient possessions of the Indo-Greeks and the Śuṅgas. Their third sovereign, Kaniṣka,[3] represented the apogee of this dynasty, and his authority was recognized both in Mathurā in northern India and Kāpiśī (north of Kābul). Although the Kuṣāṇas had been installed in northern India for more than a century by the time that Kaniṣka appeared on the scene, this monarch had himself depicted as wearing an Iranian tunic, with a Scythian cap on his head and a nomadic horseman's heavy boots on his feet. However, he gave proof of a wide eclecticism. A convert to Buddhism, he was the first to feature the image of the Buddha on his coins, although he also depicted the Iranian divinities; he protected Jainism and Brāhmaṇism impartially; he adopted, at one and the same time, the Indian imperial title *mahārāja* ('great king'), the Parthian title which in Sanskrit was *rājātirāja* ('king of kings') and the Chinese title which in Sanskrit was *devaputra* ('son of Heaven'). Kaniṣka's empire was centred upon the crossroads of the busiest commercial routes of his time, and he united under his single rule regions permeated for centuries by Hellenism and by Iranian influences side by side with Indian traditions; he was the ruler of a great variety of differing populations who were habituated to the idea of cosmopolitanism, and his strong personality is strikingly recorded in Indian, Tibetan, Chinese and Mongol tradition.

It was an epoch entirely dominated by international exchanges, both commercial and intellectual. In the commercial field, the activities of Rome and China were of equal importance. The 'silk routes' crossing the Eurasiatic continent from one end to the other carried a constant stream of slowly moving caravans, and were responsible for a great increase in the traffic of luxury articles and raw materials along their path. At the same time, navigation across the open sea became possible by using the rhythm of the monsoon's winds. Roman *emporia* were even established at various points along the Indian coast, the most important one being situated not far from where Pondicherry now stands. India benefited from these various factors, exporting and importing both by sea and overland, and enriching herself greatly; so much so that an edict of the Emperor Vespasian (69–79) forbade the export of gold to India to put a halt to the severe drain on the empire's treasury. Eventually, India set up her own trading posts in countries bordering the southern seas, and, somewhat later, reached the extreme limits of her expansion towards south-east Asia (Borneo and the Celebes).

In this atmosphere of opulence and incessant travel, the religious and literary evolution of India continued to develop. If the northern part of the country enjoyed the advantages of the political unification established there by the Kuṣāṇa dynasty, the south did not profit less. It saw the establishment of powerful kingdoms such as those of the Pāṇḍyas (in the Madurai region), the Sātavāhanas (of the Deccan), the Keralas (in Travancore), and Coḷa, on the coast of Coromandel, with Tanjore for its capital. Thenceforward the whole of the Indian subcontinent contributed its share to the intellectual glories of this brilliant epoch.

A great literary and artistic burgeoning ensued: the *Rāmāyaṇa* was probably completed some time during this era, as was the compilation of the *Mahābhārata*, and the *Bhagavad Gītā*'s texts were assembled during this same period. And Aśvaghoṣa – who is supposed by Buddhist tradition to have been one of Kaniṣka's ministers – wrote his dramatic and edifying works, ancient fragments of which have been discovered in the sands of central Asia. Finally, Sanskrit, the ancient sacred language of the Vedas, became a living tongue and was popularized to the extent of serving official, literary, secular and scientific needs, and was used both by the Buddhists and by the followers of Brāhmaṇism.

Buddhism continued to evolve and to spread ever further afield. Generations of Indian monks followed each other in China and

Turkestan to complete the work, which had been proceeding continuously since perhaps the first or, more probably, the second century AD, of translating its canonical works and the principal texts of dogma and exegesis. Its doctrine had undergone important changes, and a more mystical tone was evident; the faithful were exhorted to adore creatures of charity called *Bodhisattvas*, some of whom fulfilled a messianic function. A schism occurred between the ancient and new doctrines, provoked, no doubt, by the various influences – Greek, Semitic, Iranian, even Christian and subsequently Manichean – which were vying for attention in the north-west.

The final break occurred, quite pacifically, during the second century: the Theravāda remained faithful to the original rules, while the Mahāyāna or 'Great Vehicle' adopted an attitude of negativist dogmatism and relied on a strict dialectic of which Nāgārjuna (first half of second century?), a native of the central Deccan, became the dedicated proselyte. At the same time, mutually syncretic tendencies became apparent in Buddhism and Brāhmaṇism. In both religions, sects multiplied and mysticism increased: the brāhmaṇic theory of *bhakti* ('trustful adoration') was elaborated, while a reaction against the confusion resulting from the philosophical effervescence of the moment led to the gradual foundation of the *darśanas* or orthodox 'systems' of Brāhmaṇism.

During this epoch, a flowering of the arts occurred throughout India. In the north-west, there were the Greco-Buddhist and Irano-Buddhist styles, the inheritors of Hellenism; in the north, the school of Mathurā, despite the Iranian influence of the Kuṣāṇas, remained fully Indian in style, in the tradition of Bhārhut and Sānchī; in the south-east and in Mahārāṣṭra the Āndhra styles were refined and sumptuous. Buddhist art was in full bloom everywhere, preserving its narrative character, so invaluable for any study of the epoch. Brāhmaṇic art, hitherto almost non-existent, made its appearance, especially in Mathurā, and Jain art, too, began its career. Secular art of this period, of which we still know very little today, is represented, however, by the admirable specimens of sculptured ivory discovered in Afghānistān by Joseph and Ria Hackin between 1937 and 1940, on the site of ancient Kāpiśi, the summer capital of the Kuṣāṇas.

This brilliant era was followed by political dismemberment

and the intellectual upsurge seems to have lost momentum. Around 320, a new hegemony, that of the Guptas, took shape: as previously with the Mauryas, the movement came into being in Magadha, the holy ground of Buddhism and the old imperial capital Pāṭaliputra became the centre of the new empire. Little is known of the new dynasty's first sovereign, Candragupta, except that he must have extended his conquests far enough afield to warrant his assuming the title of emperor (*mahārājādhirāja*). His reign was the first in a line of warriors who were to give rise to a true golden age of Indian civilization.

Candragupta's son, Samudragupta (335–*c.* 375), added fresh territories, practising shrewdly the feudal Indian method which consisted in attaching the conquered monarchs to himself as vassals by personally restoring them to their respective thrones. He annexed thirty-five States and his power extended over the greater part of northern and central India, reconstituting practically the whole of Aśoka's empire, the memory of which was still very much alive. The Guptas were perfectly deliberate in imitating their glorious predecessor, and it is doubtless no coincidence that their first emperor bore the same name as Aśoka's grandfather, the founder of the Maurya dynasty. Similarly, Samudragupta's motives were quite clear when he chose one of the columns erected by Aśoka in order to engrave on it his own panegyric and an enumeration of his conquests. Despite the passing of the centuries, the evidence of this 'great century' is still visible, in particular in Aśoka's palace in Pāṭaliputra which was not destroyed until 411. It is perfectly natural for ambitious monarchs to claim kinship in this manner with India's most splendid reign, but at the same time it emphasizes the desire for a well-established continuity in the traditional line of Indian civilization; it is surely symptomatic that, 1600 years later, we find the modern Indian Republic adopting for the device of its coat-of-arms the capital of the celebrated Aśokan column at Sārnāth with its frieze featuring Wheels of the Law supporting three rampant lions.

The Gupta empire expanded still more under the reign of Candragupta II (*c.* 375–414), known as the 'Sun of Heroism' (*Vikramāditya*), with conquests westward (Mālava, Gujarāt, Kāthiāwār) and southward (beyond the Narmadā). In addition, he annexed Bactria in the north-west and Bengal in the east. His reign marked what was certainly the most brilliant period of classical Sanskrit literature, represented by Kālidāsa, whose plays have been widely translated. The plastic arts had attained an extreme refinement and a remarkable unity of style; one of the most precious artistic achievements of the era is the series of mural paintings with which the Vākāṭaka kings, vassals of Candragupta (and even related to him by marriage), decorated some of the Buddhist monasteries of Ajantā in Mahārāṣṭra (fifth to sixth centuries). Religious tolerance permitted all the sects to flourish. Buddhism was ripe for the philosophical development represented by the two masters Asaṅga and Vasubandhu (fourth or fifth century). Commerce was at its height in the southern seas, preparing the way for an expansion overseas of Indian culture which, in the succeeding centuries, provided the cultural basis for Indochina's and Java's most advanced civilizations.

The dynasty reached its supreme point of power under the reign of Kumāragupta I (*c.* 414–455), the son and successor of Candragupta II. But unhappily a new menace had appeared at the north-western frontiers of the empire: the Hūṇas. Kumāragupta's son, Skandagupta (*c.* 455–467), succeeded in holding them back. It seems that thereafter a certain confusion reigned in the imperial family, possibly entailing a new territorial dismemberment. When the barbarian hordes, after building up a redoubtable armed force, started moving towards the Ganges valley soon after 485, the Guptas were unable to halt their ravaging advance despite personal acts of courageous sacrifice.

The next fifty years were ones of horror and terror: in the north-west, the Buddhist monasteries and universities which constituted the glory of Indian civilization were razed to the ground, and the monks were persecuted; deportations and murders were counted in thousands. The Emperor Budhagupta (*c.* 475–494) was driven out of Mālava, and the terrible invaders, led first by their chief Toramāṇa and then by his son, the cruel Mihirakula (*c.* 500–540), are said to have reached as far as Magadha, leaving a trail of ruin and disaster in their wake. The Gupta dynasty survived these reverses, but in so diminished a state that its princes were now no more than local chieftains.

While the Guptas were suffering the persecution of the Hunnish barbarians, the kingdoms of the Deccan continued to flourish, particularly the Pallavas in the Tamil country (Kāñcīpuram), one of whose kings, Viṣṇugopa, was contemporary with Samudragupta, and the western Cālukyas (Bādāmi) who perpetuated in Mahārāṣṭra, especially in Ajantā, the cultural and artistic heritage of the Vākāṭakas. The enfeeblement of the Guptas provided an opportunity for the northern and central states to consolidate their own power, among others, the State of Valabhī in the west (Kāthiāwār and at times the Surāṭ and Broach regions), and that of Thāneśvar, of which Kanauj became the capital, situated at the western tip of the Doāb, this latter being a territory much coveted by neighbouring states throughout history.

It fell to a Thāneśvar prince, Harṣa (605–647), to regroup northern and central India under one single power, for the last time before the medieval epoch. His personality is better known than that of the other Indian sovereigns, thanks to the accounts about him that the Chinese pilgrim Hsüan-Ch'uang has left us. He emerges from these portraits as a man wholly in the traditional Indian mould: eclectic and tolerant in matters of religion, a protector of spiritual culture and, it is said, himself the author of several plays and two exquisitely constructed Buddhist hymns. Bāṇa, the last of the great writers of Sanskrit poetic prose, was his court-poet, his favourite and his bard. In the administrative field, Harṣa perpetuated Aśoka's traditions, thus ensuring that continuity of Indian civilization which had remained unbroken since its historical beginnings. However ephemeral it may have been – a mere forty years or so – this final political and cultural revival, before the impending collapse, effectively set the seal on the enduring fame of the brilliant Gupta culture, not only throughout India but also in countries overseas where the Gupta style exercised a lasting influence. Harṣa successfully maintained the diplomatic relations his predecessors had established with China and central Asia. Foreign monks came to India to visit the sacred places of Buddhism, and to study or to teach in the universities restored after the passage of the Hūṇas. Commerce found a new impetus. In fact, the grandeur of imperial India was restored.

But it was only a brief renaissance: immediately following Harṣa's death, his empire was cut up into fragments, this time irretrievably. A page of history had been turned; and this is why our study of daily life in ancient India goes no further than 650. Not because Indian civilization ceased to exist temporarily, but because from then on, the absence of a central power makes it no longer possible for one to speak of a single India. The subsequent history of India is on a local plane, and from this time onwards it is necessary to speak of 'Indias' rather than 'India'.

Nevertheless, society continued to retain the essential character established more than a thousand years previously: if we examine documents going back to the Śuṅga era, the Gupta era or the Middle Ages, we find the same feudal basis, the same divisions into castes and guilds, the same domestic rituals. The main differences reside in modes of dress, a certain number of popular customs, and religious and legislative habits and methods. All the rest adheres to the traditional line: the figure of the king, the pomp surrounding him, his duties and his pleasures, the descriptions of various capital cities, the mentality of individual people, all seem identical with those of former times. How could it be otherwise, when orthodox brāhmaṇ families are living in the twentieth century on the same principles which have inspired their ancestors from time immemorial? Far from having to be considered archaic, these principles have shown themselves to be the surest guarantee of the perennial nature of Indian civilization, despite the vicissitudes to which it was subsequently subjected.

CHAPTER TWO

THE SOCIAL STRUCTURE AND ITS RELIGIOUS PRINCIPLES

Those who do not execute the labours appropriate to their caste are called destroyers of works by those who live within the law of 'the stages of life' (āśramas).

Vāyu Purāṇa, VIII.

Although it is true that the political history of India is made up of territorial conquests and alternating periods of anarchy and imperial unification, it is impossible to dissociate from it the religious evolution which has been such a vitally important factor in the country's general outlook. In probably no other civilization has religion been so intimately bound up not only with the conduct of public affairs but also with human behaviour. In ancient India it constituted the very basis of the social structure and the foundation of the Indian community.

The period which concerns us had long outgrown the Vedic age, when sacrifice had been religion's primordial manifestation and ritual error took the place of mortal sin. Already for several centuries, Indian society had possessed in common the great principles of Brāhmaṇism, to which Buddhism had brought the corrective of a morality based on human considerations. These principles were based on the notion of the drama in which the individual soul (*ātman*) was plunged. Although the concept of soul was subject to numerous variants, according to the school of thought, it was envisaged, ever since the *Upaniṣads*, as being of the same nature as the universal 'Self'. This essential revelation set in motion all the subsequent speculation. By simplifying somewhat, we can say that this individual soul is drawn along inexorably in a cycle of successive rebirths (*saṃsāra*), this cycle being determined by the act (*karma*). *Karma* is conceived as the effect of former deeds on one's present and future condition; it attaches itself to the soul and provokes joys and sufferings in it, leading it towards reward or punishment. A meritorious deed diminishes the total of rebirths to come; a bad deed increases that total. This principle has been accepted by all the philosophical systems of India and expounded unceasingly ever since. Each school has tried to put forward a solution to this law, some proposing the acquisition of spiritual knowledge, others asceticism or mysticism, still others moral conduct, but most of them emphasizing charitable gifts. Buddhism, in particular, claimed to be a doctrine of salvation, maintaining an original attitude which denied the reality of the *ātman*, while still preserving the notion of *karma* whose working affected the individual only on the occasion of each rebirth of a living being. From this it drew its theories of causality according to which suffering can be abolished solely by the suppression of desire, which is the genesis or maintenance of the *karma*.

The consequences of the *karma* are not limited to the moral or eschatological order, but apply to the entire universal order or *dharma* and, consequently, to the social structure of the Āryan world which reflects this universal order and which is based upon a division into castes. This notion does not appear in the most ancient Vedic texts, but there is no doubt that the Āryans imposed it gradually by codifying it to an ever greater extent, with the object of maintaining a racial – one might even say racist – distinction between their own supposedly pure race and that of the populations whose territories they had invaded. This theory seems borne out by the name *varṇa*, colour, which was used to designate the groups catalogued in this way.

During the epoch of 'classical' Brāhmaṇism, Indian society regulated itself according to *dharma*, which was at once statute, law, ethics and religion, drawing its authority from the Veda. From that period onwards, the division of society into castes acquired a rigidity to which the notion of *karma* added a formidable, almost heart-breaking character, for the effect of a man's *karma* was to subordinate him to a precise caste and, as a result, to compel him to perform the functions and accept the obligations inherent in that caste. The consequences of such a law were sometimes very grave for the affected individual, and it was precisely against these repercussions that the humanitarian views of Buddhism were directed, opposing to such *de facto* classification the value of purity of heart and nobility of feeling. This was, in effect, to preach nothing less than social revolution and to invite changes which inevitably appeared fatal and detestable in the eyes of orthodox Hindus. For the Buddhist attitude not only menaced the social order by showing up the disparity between the privileged and the disinherited, but, what was worse, overthrew the most deeply embedded doctrines of racial purity and, thereby, the very concept of sacerdotal dogmatism.

Traditionally, the castes were four in number: the brāhmaṇs or priests, the *kṣatriyas* or warriors and nobles, the *vaiśyas*, merchants or peasants, a kind of *bourgeoisie*, and the *śūdras* or servile class. The first three had the right to read the Veda, a right which was denied to the *śūdras*, although they, like the others, came within the scope of *dharma*. The brāhmaṇs and *kṣatriyas* constituted the two ruling classes and divided between them the spiritual and the temporal sovereignty. All those who did not belong to any of these four castes were automatically banned from any participation in this system and had, so to speak, no social existence at all. Each caste was assigned well-defined functions: the brāhmaṇs were to teach the Veda and to perform sacrifices; the *kṣatriyas* to protect the common people and to study the Veda; the *vaiśyas* to work; the *śūdras* to serve. Contacts and marriages between members of different castes were prohibited. But, as in so many other fields, there was a wide gulf between theory and practice, and it appears that brāhmaṇic India never succeeded in maintaining these principles in all their rigour and was constantly obliged to come to terms with reality.

THE BRĀHMAṆS

By definition, to 'possess the *brahman*', that is to say, the sacred power deriving from the ritual formula (*brahman*) was the prerogative of the brāhmaṇs, priests who had studied the Veda, the source of all knowledge. Authorized in Vedic times to conduct sacrifices, they still had the privilege during the 'classical' era of celebrating religious services for themselves and for others. At the same time, they were presumed to be endowed with the power to combat effectively any malefic influence caused by a ritual error, however venial. Consequently, they were qualified to teach the Veda, to make gifts and to receive them (see the *Mānava Dharma Śāstra* or Code of Manu, I, 88, seq.). Briefly, they were destined to lead a religious, intellectual and saintly life, surrounded by respect, full of the dignity of a pure ancestry, and theoretically absolved from the necessity of gaining a living. There was no question of their having to remain celibate – on the contrary.

The sacred nature of their functions allowed them to benefit – even in predominantly Buddhist territories – from a great number of prerogatives and exemptions. In particular, they had the privilege of receiving, individually or collectively, gifts or estates which were sometimes extremely valuable. It is important to understand that in ancient India donation was an immemorial institution which ensured for the donor a definite reward both in this life and in subsequent lives; it was considered not only an obligation but also the supreme way of acquitting the debt which every human being contracted with the gods by the very reason of his birth. It goes without saying that the brāhmaṇs were never slow in pointing out the virtue of making gifts. But, prudently, the law usually laid down that it was not permissible for a donor to disinherit his family totally for the benefit of the brāhmaṇs. Even so, the latter received very substantial benefices, among which the 'gift of land' was considered the best of all, since it 'liberated from all sin'. In this way, the brāhmaṇs acquired possession of vast estates and received their revenues; they were entitled to have these lands cultivated by slaves and serfs. They also became the recipients of public and private buildings, even of entire villages. On top of all this, they were exempt from taxes since they were deemed to have discharged such debts through 'acts of piety'.

Being sacrosanct, the brāhmaṇs might neither be sentenced to death, nor to any kind of torture or corporal punishment. The heaviest penalty which could be applied to one was the cutting off of his coil of hair, an act which was by no means a cruel joke but, rather, a symbolic gesture of profound significance. This coil of hair, which they wore knotted on the top or at the side of their head, was the visible sign of their brāhmaṇic initiation and they preserved it intact throughout their life from the moment when they had undergone, at the age of three, the ritual tonsure (called *cūḍākaraṇa*: see p. 164). The removal of this topknot was thus equivalent to proclaiming their exclusion from the brāhmaṇic caste, and the penalty entailed dreadful consequences, since this excommunication condemned the victim to the life of an outlaw: torn for ever from his surroundings, expelled from every community, rejected by all castes, he had no alternative but to leave the country. It was a social as much as a moral death.[1] On the other hand, any harm or annoyance caused to a brāhmaṇ was punished with great severity.

Many brāhmaṇs were worthy of the respect with which they were surrounded; they led a simple and pious existence, disdaining material profits and fulfilling the duties of their caste with piety. They acted as village schoolmasters, or taught in the universities. Sometimes they withdrew to a forest-bound hermitage, where they would live in humble bamboo huts and devote themselves to their religious duties, to meditation and teaching, enjoying in all simplicity the charms and austerities of a frugal but poetic existence, surrounded by the wild animals which their gentleness had tamed. But, by the side of these brāhmaṇs who fulfilled their caste obligations quietly and obscurely, with a genuine purity of heart, literary sources depict an altogether different type of brāhmaṇ, who was far less respectable. These made blatant use of the knowledge of magic acquired through a study of certain Vedic or brāhmaṇic texts, and did not hesitate to exploit the credulity and superstitious spirit of the masses, and earned their living by telling fortunes or practising sorcery. These were real charlatans, thriving most often in country districts, and though they were despised more or less openly, there is reason to think that they were feared as well.

Between these two extremes were to be found a great variety of brāhmaṇs exercising trades or professions unconnected with their priestly character; these might be actors, owners of gaming houses, quacks, tax collectors, army commanders, managers of transportation concerns,[2] spies, or even hired servants. There even exist references to brāhmaṇs who were labourers or butchers, although both these activities were disapproved by brāhmaṇic orthodoxy, involving as they did the destruction of life of animals or insects.[3] It is also possible that such individuals engaged in occupations incompatible with the purity of the brāhmaṇic caste because they lived in a society of mainly Buddhist persuasion and were forced to earn their living without hoping to receive the traditional donations. In this they would have been authorized by the law that each caste was able to apply in case of 'distress', a law that permitted individuals to practise professions normally disapproved of. It is equally possible that the Buddhist accounts were exaggerated in their criticisms and were simply giving free reign to their prejudice against a caste which was abhorrent in Buddhist circles. Nevertheless, the failings of the less deserving brāhmaṇs were, no doubt, not unconnected with the unfavourable opinions that were held about them; their arrogance, due to pride in the purity of their caste, the hypocrisy and the shady dealings of which they were sometimes guilty, the immunity they enjoyed even in the courts of justice, all these factors combined to attract the jealousy of the other castes and to arouse the censure of sincerely virtuous men. These critics have left us some splendidly racy anecdotes[4] which should not, however, make us forget those great brāhmaṇs whose intellectual worth and high morality honoured Indian society and helped to maintain its exalted traditions. Some of these played an important role in the conduct of the kingdoms, occupying high posts in the court and acting, from one reign to another, as royal chaplains (*purohitas*), even under Buddhist sovereigns.

THE WARRIOR-NOBLES

The second caste performed the functions of government. It constituted a genuine aristocracy, sometimes wealthy, sometimes not, which had taken the place of the old nobility of clan descent. This caste was, perhaps, originally limited to the king himself, his family, his suite and his vassals, but during the period with which we are concerned the name *kṣatriya* was applied to a far wider circle and was no longer reserved strictly for those who carried arms and were the professional warriors. But this essentially military character still persisted in the education given to them since, besides a knowledge of the Veda, they were taught the use of weapons and their hereditary aptitude for command was cultivated. Their whole upbringing was designed to fit them for such elevated posts as that of governor, general, administrator or high civil servant.

The king usually belonged to this caste, and was then the supreme *kṣatriya*, ruler and governor, conqueror and maintainer of order. The *kṣatriya* caste was considered pre-eminent, especially in Buddhist circles; it was, in fact, in rivalry with the brāhmaṇic caste, but its members generally recognized the superiority of the brāhmaṇs because of their priestly character.

Although the king's suite was, quite naturally, recruited from among the *kṣatriyas*, and the army was largely composed of members of this caste, many of these nobles did not exercise a military calling and were authorized to gain their living in various other ways, by taking up some trade or craft. These latter still retained the privileges attaching to their caste, the most typical of which were, perhaps, the two forms of marriage which were their special prerogative: the form which consisted in carrying off the bride – a remote survival of the forcible seizure of women during military campaigns; and that in which the union was concluded with whoever proved the victor of a competition in which the chief element was an archery contest.

THE *VAIŚYAS*

Although the *vaiśyas* shared the right of the brāhmaṇs and *kṣatriyas* to be taught the Veda and were, consequently, integrated into the system of *dharma*, they were still considered definitely inferior. Originally they had formed the agricultural community, and it was no doubt this humble character which singled them out for the drudgery of such tasks as tallage and statute labour. By the beginning of the classical era their lot had improved greatly. From being small farmers many of them had become powerful landlords, while others followed occupations that were both lucrative and honourable, often as experts in precious stones and metals, woven materials, spices or perfumes, whose knowledge was held in high esteem by the *kṣatriyas* themselves.

The social reforms set in motion by Buddhist concepts favoured the development of the *vaiśyas*, because their concepts permitted them to rise above the disdain with which they were regarded by the two ruling classes and soon to form a sort of *bourgeoisie*; furthermore, Buddhism recruited its most zealous partisans from among this group. As a class, they amassed huge fortunes, gained mostly in trade by sea and by caravan; and they set up guilds (*śreṇi*) with which the State and the administration had to reckon.

Several members of the *vaiśya* caste were, at one time or another, appointed to important posts, and it was by no means rare for a king to choose his counsellor from among them. But something of their origin still remained: just as in previous centuries it had fallen to them to perform the statutory labour, now they had to pay heavier taxes and duties than any other class. So in this way they were fulfilling their original function, that of working and earning money to maintain the priestly caste, which was exempted from working on the land (deemed impure), and the warrior caste, which was preoccupied with territorial conquest. Thus forced to support part of the population as well as their own families, their aptitudes developed and enabled them to achieve fortune and respect. It was thanks to them that the State's treasury was able to make up for the inroads on its funds caused by donations to the brāhmaṇs and the expenses of State administrtion and royal and religious ceremonies.

THE SERVILE CLASS

Born, or rather 'reborn', to serve the three other classes, the *śūdras* were burdened by a very marked social and religious inferiority. Their caste, in Vedic times, seems to have included the dark-skinned aborigines conquered by the Āryans, to whom were added later some of the poorer Āryans themselves and certain other people who had forfeited their rights for one reason or another. They were therefore not only despised from the earliest times, but also considered impure. They nevertheless took part in the *dharma*; but their benefits therefrom were limited to seeking redress under the law, and, under certain conditions, the opportunity to study the sacred texts of Hinduism, namely the *Purāṇas* and the Scriptures known as the *Tantras*, to take part in private but not public rites. This was the limit of their rights.

Their duties far outweighed these rights, for they had no possibility of freeing themselves from the servitude which was theirs by reason of birth. This is where the theory of *karma* assumed its full significance: since being born into a particular caste was considered the fruit of acts accomplished in previous existences, it was quite clear that the *śūdras* had to their debit a heavy load of evil deeds from their past lives. Since this debt ruled the condition of the individual throughout his present life and could only be modified at the next rebirth, the clear implication was that there was no hope of their improving this situation during their lifetime. They had one single means of achieving rebirth in a superior class, and that was to perform their allocated duties conscientiously. This idea was responsible for an understandable feeling of inferiority on the part of this underprivileged caste, more especially as the whole concept was carefully maintained by the ruling classes, and showed itself in the behaviour of everyone throughout India.

We lack much information about the composition of this caste, but it appears to have included servants of all sorts, wage-earners, workmen, labourers and minor functionaries. To these were added small clerks, tradesmen and craftsmen; some of the latter, however, were able to exercise relatively lucrative trades and crafts, and even practise husbandry. On the whole they were too conscious of their despicable situation to make any attempt to escape from it, but it must not be assumed that they therefore led an unbearable existence. Many of them worked for wealthy tradesmen and landlords, were paid a regular wage, fed, lodged (sometimes on the employer's premises, sometimes outside) and received further benefits in kind; agricultural workers, for example, were paid a fifth of their wages in goods and produce if they were fed and lodged, or a third if not. They remained attached to the same family, from father to son. Their low status compelled them to eat only the remnants from the master's table, to wear his cast-off clothing and to make use only of discarded objects. The employer was supposed to treat them decently, and they were in fact protected, to some extent, by the law; he was obliged to make a contract with them, a document enumerating the two parties' respective rights and duties, and setting down the names of all the employee's dependents. While the *śūdra* was expected to give proof of zeal and professional competence, his master was in his turn obliged to furnish him with the instruments necessary for his work and to replace those which were worn out or defective. The contract laid down the number of hours to be worked and the wages to be paid, and specified the goods and produce which would normally be provided over and above the wages. If the wages were not paid or if the contract was unjustifiably terminated, the employer was liable to prosecution.

The *śudras* were subjected to what seems a relatively light taxation. On the other hand, they were subject throughout the year to perform forced labour for the State consisting of one or two days' work a month. Those particularly affected by this law were the workers who processed rice, flour, oil or sugar, and those who worked in spinning or weaving mills, and in factories making arms and military supplies. This forced labour could sometimes be avoided by paying a sum of money.

But the servile class was not homogeneous since, even here, distinctions were made between the 'pure' or 'unexcluded' and the 'excluded'. The latter were practically identical with the 'outcastes' ('untouchables').

THE 'OUTCASTES'

Because of its very unworthiness, this segment of the population was only sketchily described in the sacerdotal texts, which referred to its members as 'last-born', 'low-born' or 'those who may not approach the (sacred) vessels'. These are the people whom we designate, in modern times, by the term 'pariah' or 'untouchable'. They comprised a series of sub-castes among which that of the *caṇḍālas* is the one most frequently mentioned. The outcastes all had trades or crafts which were despised, or even condemned, by religious orthodoxy, either because their work involved the taking of human or animal life, or because their functions involved some ritual defilement. Included in these two categories were hunters, fishermen, butchers, curriers, executioners, gravediggers, undertakers, those who sold liquor, sweepers, and, during certain historical periods, basket-makers and wheelwrights.

Among all these, the situation of the *caṇḍālas* was the worst; in later ages they were given the name of 'untouchables' because of their impurity. They lived in isolated villages or in quarters outside the town limits, and spoke a debased tongue which was almost a dialect.[5] They were supposed to dress in clothes stripped from corpses (for they often acted as public executioners or undertakers); they were permitted to eat only from cracked bowls and dishes, and iron was the only metal they might use for ornaments and jewellery. A brāhmaṇ who killed one of them incurred the same penalty as for killing a dog.

Regarded by society as the vilest dregs of the human species, they had to be most careful to avoid polluting members of the castes by any kind of contact or even coming within their sight. For this reason, they never moved outside their villages or quarters without striking a pair of clappers together to warn people of their approach. When a man of caste chanced to glance at one of them, he was bound to carry out rites of purification. When he learnt that he had beheld a *caṇḍāla*, even unconsciously, his first action was to turn away as quickly as possible; then he would bathe his eyes with perfumed water so as to avert ill fortune; he had then to abstain from food and drink for the rest of the day.[6] His fear of defilement was so great that he dreaded the idea even that the breeze which touched him might previously have passed over a *caṇḍāla*'s body,[7] or again, that the shadow of one of these unfortunates might have come between his own person and the sun. As far as the *caṇḍāla* was concerned, he was held responsible for having provoked such a defilement of a man of caste, even if the offending action had been quite involuntary. In fact, he was well advised to make every effort to avoid such incidents, since the wrathful men of caste would certainly have him beaten unconscious. Even worse, he could be quite sure that, as a result, he would be reborn in the body of an animal, and so the moment when he would be freed from the transmigration of the soul (however unlikely such a prospect for him, in any case) would be put back even further.[8] It went without saying that a man of caste might not share a *caṇḍāla*'s food, even if he were dying of hunger.[9]

Foreigners were placed in the same category as the outcastes, but were not subjected to the same indignities even though they were 'untouchable' by the very fact of not belonging to the *dharma* and not being initiated into the Veda. They were called *mleccha*, a term which means literally 'jabberer' and was used to designate all 'barbarians'. Many of these foreigners were ordinary travellers, others were enterprising traders or adventurers in search of fortune; but the term was applied equally to ambassadors and official delegates, as well as to monks and scholars and men of letters who had come to India either to teach or to study, mostly in the Buddhist universities. The term *mleccha* was applied more specifically to invaders, and since most of these penetrated into India through the north-western passes, it was traditional in iconography to represent them dressed in the style of the 'cold' regions, that is to say, like the Parthians who were under Iranian or Hellenistic influence. In the same way, they were depicted with pronounced features intended to make clear their distant origin.

Although foreigners of noble rank were treated with appropriate honour and respect, it was still impossible for certain essential rules to be broken on their behalf: when they were received in the home of a brāhmaṇ family, for instance, the rites of hospitality could never be carried out fully (see pp. 197–8), and no man of good caste could take a meal in their company. But a special annual feast-day was reserved for the *mlecchas*, on which they all assembled together, a fact which leads us to suppose that many of them must have been long-established residents. It was, also, by no means unknown for foreigners to be absorbed into Hinduism, introduced into an appropriate caste, sometimes a high one, and assimilated into Indian society.

Finally, ascetics were classed among the outcastes because their complete detachment from society made the term 'without caste' perfectly applicable to them. They were greatly respected.

But these were only exceptions. The disinherited caste of untouchables was composed overwhelmingly of poor devils upon whom abuse and indignities were heaped and who were permitted social contact only with those of 'mixed' origin.

THE 'MIXED' CLASS

The statute of castes (*varṇadharma*) could never really be applied strictly enough to prevent mixed marriages, and the lawgivers had, from a very early date, to face up to the facts and make the system somewhat more flexible. Although it was more or less admitted that legitimate unions between those of different castes might in fact take place, the children issuing from these unions, whether legitimate or not, were considered to have forfeited their rights because they did not belong definitely to a particular caste. Polygamy certainly aggravated this situation by multiplying such births. The opprobrium attaching itself to those of 'mixed' origin extended to two generations. But the discredit thrown upon them did not prevent them obtaining honourable posts or exercising well-esteemed professions such as that of bard, herald, equerry, physician or scribe. This brought them much closer to the 'pure' *śūdras* than to the 'excluded' classes or the 'untouchables'.

THE SLAVES

Megasthenes asserted that slavery was unknown in the India of the Mauryas. In fact, it undoubtedly did exist then, just as it did in later eras; but it did not take the same form as in Greece, so that his statement is only partly incorrect.

This class included very different types of persons. In the first category are distinguished those 'born in the house', who were practically members of the family in which they were servants. Having been bought, or received as a gift, they were then inherited along with the goods and chattels. Their purchase price was comparatively modest, and consequently slave-owning was widespread. The royal palace set the example in the practice of buying slaves: these were young women destined for the harem, brought (probably from Greece) by trading vessels, often by the merchants who traded between India and Africa, and made optimistic claims as to the girls' noble birth and their talent in the arts of song and music. In the same way, a female militia, charged with guarding the harem, was also composed entirely of slaves; they could be seen mounting guard on the ramparts or at the doors of private apartments, armed with a pike and wearing a helmet.[10] Their Western origin seems proved by the use of the term *yavanī* ('coming from Ionia') to describe them. It is worth noting that their costume changed over the centuries, being Greco-Roman in style until the third century or thereabouts, and then Iranian during the fourth and fifth centuries: we know this because there is evidence to show that, after the fall of Rome, this social group was reluctant to abandon this mode of dress and appealed for sartorial assistance to regions which had inherited Hellenistic traditions. Other classes of slaves in the royal and princely households were the hunchbacks and dwarfs whose job was to act as jesters and clowns, and the nurses who breast-fed the noble offspring of these households.

The living and working conditions of these slaves did not differ greatly from those of the *śūdras*, which is probably what misled Megasthenes. In a certain sense they were better off than the *śūdras*: they received no wages and so could more easily avoid the necessity of working when they were sick, since they were not dependent upon wage earnings for their daily bread.

Existing sources of information differ considerably in their evaluation of the slaves' living and working conditions. Pāli texts emphasize the hard labour often imposed on them, such as the transportation, morning, noon and evening, on the man's (or woman's) back, of the water needed each day by the entire household, and this throughout the year, even in winter when it was necessary to wade waist-high in icy water. These same texts state that corporal punishment was inflicted on slaves who neglected their duties, that they were beaten, even mutilated, sometimes killed. The threat of such punishment constrained them to obey at all costs, and kept them in a state of constant fear. It was not unusual to see them pursuing their tasks with tears streaming down their faces. As for the master, he appears to have complained frequently about his slaves' lack of interest in their work and the resulting inconveniences for himself. To believe him, very few of them showed themselves conscientious and vigilant, and most of them waited impatiently for nightfall to give them temporary relief from their duties. Worse than that, when in his presence the slaves appeared zealous and submissive, assuring him repeatedly of their devotion; yet, the moment his back was turned, they no longer cared about anything, allowing provisions to spoil and even going so far as to give vent to rancorous remarks directed against him.[11]

It seems, from allusions in certain narratives, that slave rebellions occurred on several occasions. But, on the other hand, Hindu legislation and the injunctions attributed to the Buddha himself were designed to make the slaves' existence bearable. If we are to believe these latter sources, they were relatively well fed and well treated. Though the master had the right to beat them, he might strike them only on the back, never on the head, and if he treated them too cruelly they would be withdrawn from his service.

Sometimes they were authorized to earn money freely during their spare time and to keep the whole amount; it was also possible for a female slave to receive permission to marry a free man outside her master's house, on the condition that she returned each day to perform her duties as a slave. The law protected a pregnant girl, and she could be neither sold nor given away during her pregnancy. If she had been seduced by the master, and had had a child by him, the master was bound to pay her an indemnity and to free her and her new-born child. Ordinarily, children remained in slavery, as did their parents. As for old people, they were kept on in the master's house until their death, even when they could no longer work; if they left no descendants, their funeral expenses were paid by the master who undertook to carry out the commemorative rites for the well-being of their souls. There was a special annual festival allocated to slaves, in which they took an active part.

It would appear, then, that the lot of these slaves was not altogether harsh, especially if one compares their conditions with those generally imposed in ancient civilizations. Apart from the brutal separations which were inevitable when they were sold or exchanged,[12] they sometimes led a less arduous existence than an ordinary labourer, especially when their master endeavoured to be just and pious. There is even a case on record of a slave inheriting his master's estate.

The law specified that slaves should have a chance to recover their freedom: they had the right to escape, but once only. If they successfully avoided recapture they could rejoin their caste (if they had one) and enjoy the condition of a free man. Those who had managed to save money from the wages they had earned freely while off-duty, could buy their freedom if the sum was sufficient. Their liberation involved a small ceremony during which a special formula was pronounced; at the same time, the fortunate individual was sprinkled with water from a ewer which was then broken into pieces. His forehead was ceremonially washed, symbolizing that he was authorized now to rejoin his caste. If he entered a religious order he was allowed to change his name, so that nobody might reproach him with his servile past.

Slaves were not only bought. Many individuals fell into slavery for a variety of reasons: those convicted under the common law and sentenced to purge their offence by a term at forced labour; debtors who had been unable to repay their creditors and so entered their service, the creditors being then obliged to provide them with food and lodging; individuals who had pledged themselves as surety in a contract, a lawsuit or a bet. There were also prisoners of war, or those who had been taken as booty. Their eventual liberation depended upon the category to which they belonged and the resultant conditions of servitude: convicts were freed when their sentence was completed, debtors when they had managed to pay off their debt, and the others when the contract they had guaranteed was fulfilled, or when they had contrived to pay a sufficient forfeit. Prisoners of war were kept in slavery only for a limited period of time, usually one year.

These, then, are the various modalities with which the 'statute' (*dharma*) of Indian society conformed. As we have seen, they were extremely complex, for the precise terms qualifying each caste embraced realities that were far more gently graduated if not, indeed, hesitant at times. India's eternal paradox is reflected in them and transforms a dry enumeration of functions, rights and duties into a living, suffering human mass. The established rules were flexible or strictly enforced according to the particular era and the comparative influence of Brāhmaṇism or Buddhism. Buddhism quite naturally brought moral and spiritual comfort to those who had the most to endure from the effects of a disadvantageous *karma*. It preached the abolition of social classes; and, in basing its principles of rewards for deeds performed on virtue rather than on birth or fortune, it promised deliverance from the cycle of 'rebirths' to the 'excluded' as much as to the others, on condition only that they should be pure of heart and honest in purpose. But no rule was strict enough to embrace this whole human mass in well-defined categories, even in brāhmaṇic circles where ideology might be supposed to be more rigorously applied. There was never a time when the rules were not broken. The existence of mixed classes, marriages between different castes, the occupations which brāhmaṇs and *kṣatriya* were able to follow with impunity, all proved that facts were more powerful than theory.

The sources available to us give us little indication of what the feelings of the individuals themselves may have been, because according to Indian tradition what matters is the definition of types, not of particular cases. It seems probable, nevertheless, that the situation created by the division into castes was taken for granted by individuals and aroused no spirit of revolt or even of reflection. Accepting the theory of *karma* (just as Roman Catholics accept the theory of original sin) they doubtless found it natural to endure the consequences. Their behaviour was governed by pre-established rules, transmitted from father to son, which decreed that the most important objective was to conform to a particular rule of life which could alone bring the remedy of a happier rebirth. So, for thousands of years, the mass of Indian society learnt to perform to the best of its abilities the duties incumbent upon it in its particular sphere.

However, the division into castes was not the only social structure operating in ancient India. Clans, guilds and family groupings were at least as important, both in social and private life, and these categories fulfilled the same need for classification which the Indian mentality demanded: to exist socially, the individual had to be included in a definite category. Very often, membership of a trade-guild was more important than belonging to a particular caste, especially where Buddhist influence was uppermost, and a man's social status was determined less by his caste than by his profession. So, too, it was very important to belong to a clan or to be able to boast a long line of ancestry (*gotra*, see pp. 159–60). The guilds (*śreṇis*) offered their members the backing of powerful organizations that were more closely defined than those of the castes and were backed by special tribunals and well-defined regulations. Their modalities are dealt with in the subsequent section of this book concerned with economics (see pp. 102–6). But, before this, it is necessary to give some account of how Indian society was normally governed and administered, what collective rules were imposed upon it, and the extent to which the penal code succeeded in ensuring law and order.

CHAPTER THREE

THE POLITICAL AND ADMINISTRATIVE STRUCTURE

I consider that my duty is the good of the whole world.

AŚOKA, *Edict on rock VI.*

The principal source of our information in this sphere is the *Arthaśāstra* or 'Science of Polity', attributed to Kauṭilya who is said to have been the minister of the founder of the Maurya dynasty, Candragupta (fourth century BC). But, as we have already suggested, this text may well be purely theoretical. Sometimes it agrees with, at other times it differs from, such sources as the chronicles of Megasthenes (ambassador at the court of this emperor), the inscriptions of Aśoka, certain passages of the *Mahābhārata* and the *Rāmāyaṇa*, and also several political treatises written probably during the period of the Gupta dynasty (fourth to fifth centuries). The *Arthaśāstra* must be considered, then, as an idealized view which needs to be approached critically and collated with other texts.

THE STATE AND THE KING

The essence of the State was the person of the king. But although this axiom held true during periods when power was effectively centralized, there were also eras when it masked very diverse realities. It would have been unthinkable in ancient India that a State should find itself without a king, for this would inevitably have given rise to anarchy, an intolerable situation from the Indian point of view. Nevertheless, until the fifth century at least, quasi-republics did exist in certain clans and tribes. Anarchy raged on several occasions during the thousand years with which we are concerned: its consequences are described lyrically in the *Rāmāyaṇa* (II, 57) where we are informed that the rain ceased to fall and no longer made the earth fertile, the son no longer honoured his father, nor the wife her husband, men no longer gathered together in public meetings, the rich were no longer protected against theft, peasants kept their doors bolted, and the whole country resembled a river without water, a forest without greenery, a flock of sheep without a shepherd.

Nevertheless, whenever a central power existed, the king was not only the living symbol of the State's rights and powers but also the controller of the weather and the soil's abundance. 'Weather maker', likened to the sun itself, he was obliged to submit himself to a strict schedule so as to maintain the regularity of the cosmic order. In the same way, to make arable land fertile the king was accustomed to supervise, in springtime, the first movements of the plough throughout his domains; he participated personally, gripping the handle of one of the ploughs in his left hand while guiding the team with the aid of a gold-handled goad which he held in the other hand. In this way, he traced the first furrow of the future harvests of his entire kingdom, and his ceremonial breaking of the soil was at once imitated by his court officials and by his own agricultural workers.[1] There was a direct link between the king and agriculture in the popular mind, and poor crops were blamed on the sovereign's injustice.[2] Collective prosperity, then, depended upon the excellence of his government and his personal conduct. In fact, a more or less explicit contract required that he should deserve to occupy his throne because of his own qualities and should desire, above all, to please his people by applying the law. The very thorough education he had undergone was supposed to predispose him to this and also to make him a conqueror, the ideal role for every Indian monarch. We must suppose that this ideal was not always perfectly realized, since various sources (not, unfortunately, historical) mention cases of bad kings who were lecherous, plunderers and thieves, who habitually broke their word, or were completely under the thumb of their courtiers or their own family. But it seems that, in general, moderation prevailed and that the average monarch was good-natured rather than despotic, strove to be even-tempered and acted above all as the protector of his people.

The monarchy was usually hereditary, although kings were sometimes elected. In either case, the kingship was conferred on the prince due to mount the throne by a solemn ritual designed to assure him sovereignty, political stability, fruitfulness and riches, which also made of him an incarnation of the king of gods among mankind. It was generally believed that the king was a predestined being, even if his succession to the throne had been hereditary. His divine right was never questioned, especially during the imperial eras, but it was modified by two factors: the acknowledged pre-eminence of the priestly caste of brāhmaṇs, and the correct application of the law to all the people, as was their right. Furthermore, no matter how great may have been the prestige of royalty at any one period in India, divine right never led to real theocracy. It is worth emphasizing, indeed, that absolute monarchy never seems to have existed in India and that the fact of a supreme ruler holding power centrally did not deprive the vassal kings of their sovereign and divine qualities in their respective territories. The situation was simply that the emperor enjoyed an even greater sovereignty and divine nature, and the imperial ceremonies and rites executed by most emperors were doubtless intended to emphasize their superiority over the kings whom they had subjected to their authority.

However, although order and prosperity were symbolized in the essential element of the State, the king, he did not possess (at least, in theory) discretionary powers, since he was unable to govern without the support of his ministers and the assembly representing his people and his functionaries. Although their voice was entirely consultative, they must have possessed, on occasions, sufficient weight and influence to depose a sovereign considered bad or inefficient. The Buddhist tales included in the *Jātakas* make repeated allusions to such incidents; although these stories are not in the least historical, there can be no doubt that they do reflect factual situations as they actually occurred in northern India during pre-Christian times.

The functions of a monarch comprised obligations and duties in several spheres: he was to protect the kingdom against all armed aggression, and to protect equally the life of his subjects, their property and traditional customs; to maintain the purity of the castes and the integrity of the family; to assure the welfare of widows and orphans; to suppress banditry and root out oppression; to ensure that the land was well irrigated and that economic life was developed efficiently; to combat famine; and to give proof of generosity and tolerance towards all religious orders. Briefly, the ideal king was at the service of his people, and their happiness should constitute his own happiness. Historical evidence indicates that most Indian rulers did their best to live up to this ideal. Aśoka had shown the way with his statement: 'All men are my children. Just as I seek the welfare and happiness of my own children in this world and the next, I seek the same things for all men.'[3]

To carry out this programme, the king was expected to possess well-defined qualities and to be capable of surrounding himself with capable counsellors. He was the supreme head of the army, and was supposed to be as well versed in military science as in diplomacy. To maintain order, he was to render justice promptly and to keep himself personally informed of everything that went on in his States; to ensure this he maintained 'spies' who sent or brought back regular reports from their respective territories. Aśoka allowed these 'spies' access to him at any hour of the day. In one of his famous edicts, he states:

> In the past, state business was not transacted or reports made at all hours of the day. I have therefore made arrangements that officials may have access to me and may report on the affairs of my people at all times and in all places – when I am eating, when I am in the harem or my inner apartments, when I am attending to the cattle, when I am walking or engaged in religious exercises. I now attend to the affairs of the people in all places. And when a donation or a proclamation that I have ordered verbally, or an urgent matter which I have delegated to my high officials, causes a debate or dispute in the Council, this must be reported to me immediately, at all hours and in all places. These are my orders.[4]

In fact, royal emissaries were given priority in securing access to the king wherever he might be. To ensure this, they were accustomed to clear a passage for themselves by shouting: 'Messenger! Messenger!', a formula which made the crowd draw back immediately and attendants open the doors promptly.[5] Their arrival in the palace was a frequent sight, and was often described in contemporary literature. Bāṇa, for instance, describes one such messenger:

> . . . his legs tired and heavy with the long journey, with his tunic girt up tightly by a mud-stained strip of cloth, the knot

> hanging loose and fastened up by a ragged clout swinging behind him, and having his head wrapped with a bundle of letters, which had a deep division pressed into it by a very thick thread that bound it . . .[6]

Kings and governors were able to communicate regularly almost only through the efforts of these courageous couriers, thanks to whom news could be exchanged with the least possible delay, allowing them to follow the most advantageous course in internal and external politics.

THE ADMINISTRATIVE ORGANIZATION OF THE KINGDOM

The king did not rule his territories single-handed. As we have already mentioned briefly, he governed with the assistance and advice of his ministers and of a political assembly of the people. Although such assemblies existed already in Vedic times, we know little about the way they were constituted, although they seem to have varied a great deal from one period to another, and appear sometimes to have been little more than a privy council. But it seems that matters involving important decisions were nearly always resolved through the convocation of a great consultative assembly, composed specifically for the occasion or according to local traditions; it was in this way, for example, that the crown was offered to King Harṣa, during the seventh century, by a council of nobles. The political formula of assemblies was nevertheless applied throughout the provinces, and the king was bound to call notables and guild-masters into consultation with him to discuss any important judicial or administrative matters. The capital itself was administered in a special manner, being ruled by four commissioners, each of whom was allocated a quarter of the population (in accordance with the theory of the four cardinal points), by a prefect, by a group of administrative officials, and by a municipal council headed by the chief representatives of the merchants, bankers, and scribes and clerks. At the bottom of the city's administrative ladder were junior stewards responsible for anything from ten to forty families each.

Central power, held by the king and applied by his ministers, was not easily imposed directly upon the provinces. Many factors combined to make the rural regions partially autonomous: the great distances separating the capital, the seat of government, from the different parts of the kingdom, the resulting slowness of communications, and the isolation of the country districts during the rainy season which lasted for four months each year and made travel almost impossible. For these reasons, the king delegated some of his powers to the local authorities, while maintaining contact with them through frequent tours of inspection, conducted by himself or by specially appointed royal emissaries (*grāma-bhṛtaka* or *gameyika*).

Unfortunately, it is difficult to build up a precise picture of the organization of a typical Indian kingdom, since the terms used in description are often very vague, and its features varied from one age to another. However, we can at least admit a general structure consisting of a kingdom composed of a certain number of provinces, to the heads of which the king placed governors who belonged mostly to the royal family; these ruled by hereditary succession and often carried the title of viceroy, holding court in their locality as did the king in his capital. The capital was the seat of government and the site of the Treasury and the different State secretariats.

Each province was divided into several districts, administered by special deputies who assumed both administrative and judicial functions. These were appointed by their immediate superior, the governor of the province. They were aided by a local council, were responsible for seeing that local affairs progressed satisfactorily, and never had recourse to the royal authority except in cases of absolute necessity. The council was composed of the chiefs of the principal craft-guilds established in the district.

Finally, the district contained a number of villages (*grāma*) or small towns, whose number and importance varied from one period to another and from place to place. Each village or town was administered by a chief (*grāmika* or *gāmabhojaka*) and by a council under his leadership. The conduct of local affairs was in the hands of the councils, but the personality of the chief was an important factor since it was he who had the final decision in cases of disagreement. Everything depended, ultimately, upon his character and behaviour. Generally speaking, he occupied this post because he was one of the town's richest peasants and also because his family had held the post before him for several generations; as village chief, he was used to travelling to the capital or, at least, to receiving royal emissaries, or even the king himself during one of his tours of inspection. The cities were administered by a prefect (*nāgarika*) and a 'town council'.

These contacts with the representatives of central authority obviously enhanced the chief's reputation in the eyes of his fellow-citizens. He usually profited from this esteem by levying taxes of goods and produce, which proved acceptable benefits alongside the freedom from land-taxes which his own properties enjoyed. But his post was not inalienable, and the king had the right to dismiss him in favour of whomever he thought best. When a chief was at the head of an important group of villages and towns, he surrounded himself with a large staff and became an influential official. He might even become a petty tyrant; in such a case, the only recourse the villagers had against his exactions was an appeal to the king himself or, failing that, to the royal inspectors – so long as the inspectors were not circumvented by the *gāmabhojaka* on some pretext or another. However, such excesses were by no means the general rule but, rather, regrettable exceptions, and the village chief was most often the champion of his community's interests. He performed a whole variety of different functions, but his principal mission, as had been that of the *grāmaṇī* in Vedic days, was to defend the village against the incursions of bandits and 'savage' tribes, or against attack by enemy armies; it was by no means uncommon for village chiefs to lose their lives trying to protect their community's herds and flocks during raids of this nature. Isolated as they were from the capital, and far from the protection of the royal armies, they had to improvise the defence of their district with whatever means were available.

Apart from this occasionally heroic task, the *gāmabhojaka* was responsible for levying taxes (out of which he took an agreed share himself); these taxes were various and were sometimes unusual, ranging from the provision of jars of water and of boiled rice to the construction of sheds and warehouses, and including the delivery of grass, leaves, vegetables and fruits, flowers, milk, butter, curds and cream.[7] He was also charged with ensuring that, in accordance with the imperial edicts and the religious rules, animals protected by the law were not killed, and that the sale of alcoholic drinks was restricted, if not prohibited altogether. In addition, he had judicial powers, arbitrating quarrels and condemning the guilty to pay fines.

There existed, also, a privileged category of villages under royal protection. These were not only exempted from the usual taxes, either totally or partially; in addition, they enjoyed complete immunity, and royal officials themselves had no right to exercise their control in these localities, nor even to enter them.[8] Rocks were engraved with inscriptions, intended to perpetuate the observance of these villages' special status, and would-be offenders were warned that they would incur the royal wrath.

The village or town council was an institution that varied from place to place and from one age to another. The sources available to us differ considerably in their descriptions of their composition; they seem, at any rate, to have been better established in the southern regions. It is possible only to assert these general rules: they were composed of the most notable villagers or townsmen, and, in the capital, by the most influential guild chiefs (merchants, bankers, scribes and magistrates). Councils were apparently recruited from among the young people as well as from their seniors, members being entitled either 'elders' (*grāmavṛddha*) or 'prebendaries' (*bhojaka*).

Membership of such assemblies was entirely honorific and demanded an impeccable individual morality, under pain of exclusion; in such an eventuality the disgrace would involve the guilty person's whole family. Council meetings were held out of doors, or in the shade provided by the communal covered market which, in the villages, was composed of a thatched roof set on supporting pillars. The debates and deliberations were conducted with a certain effort at oratorical refinement; it was the ambition of every participant to sway his colleagues with the force and elegance of his arguments, but all decisions and sanctions were agreed in common.

The assembly's function was thus more or less analogous to that of the village chief, except that where the former system prevailed responsibility was assumed by the group and was no longer vested in one person. Nevertheless, in many provinces the council's advice was by no means considered to have the force of law; the *Jātakas* even mention a council all of whose members were put in prison because the people under their jurisdiction had refused collectively to pay their tax contributions, a fact which shows clearly that the central power was not always prepared to accept a council's decisions, however well-founded those might be in law. A few isolated regions still retained a vestige of the social structure of the old tribal republics which had existed before the arrival of the Āryans, in the shape of a more freely based type of administration, certain features of which still survived well into the fifth century AD.

Lacking contemporary statistics, we know neither the size of India's population at that time nor the proportional number of villages and towns throughout the country.[9] But we possess sufficient information to deduce that the India of that time remained, as it does today, essentially rural, large towns being rare in comparison with the number of villages and small towns. The villages formed basic unities, each one able to derive enough direct benefit from local agriculture and crafts to be self-sufficient and to exist independently of surrounding communities.

These conditions have existed throughout India right up to present times, and give Indian civilization its essential character. One may even be permitted to suggest that one of the most delicate problems facing the present government of the Indian Union is that of preserving and encouraging village autonomy while, at the same time, subordinating it to the distant authority of the central power.

In ancient times, this decentralization was made more complete by reason of the nature of the climate and the slowness of communications within the country's interior. But this state of affairs did not have the disadvantages which are apparent in the modern era: while today there may be some reason for fearing that village administration exercises a retrograde effect tending to paralyse the action of the central power, in those days its effect was salutary. The village unit was less liable than were large towns or the capital city to anarchic influences, and so constituted a stable element irrespective of dynastic changes; it assured continuity in the country's development, acting as a brake on misconceived ideas or dangerous experiments. We owe to it the long duration of usage and custom, the internal stability, the sustained morality of the people of India – and also the slowness of the reactions and of the general evolution of Indian civilization.

MINISTERS AND PUBLIC OFFICIALS

The importance accorded to ministers seems to indicate that they were expected to serve as a counterweight to the royal authority.

They formed a council of at least three members, sometimes eight or ten, occasionally rising to as many as thirty-seven. The essential elements of political policy were originated in this council, all decisions being elaborated during the course of secret deliberations and taken by majority decision. It played an important role. Under certain circumstances it could impose its point of view upon the king and, in any case, was authorized to act for him in his absence. And if the king showed himself to be too weak, it was the council of ministers – and consequently the prime minister – which took control of the State's destiny. Historical examples of this nature are not lacking, if one cares to read between the lines of official panegyrics.

The council had the duty of maintaining order, assuring the royal succession, preventing anarchy and, of course, ensuring the efficient functioning of the whole administrative organization. It made all minor decisions without consulting the king, but when important matters were involved, the king made the final decision. In the latter case, he made his will known through decrees called 'imperious edicts', prepared by his own chancellery; these decrees remained in force throughout his reign unless explicitly countermanded. It is not certain what form these edicts took: from Aśoka's time onwards, the most solemn edicts were engraved on stone, rock or copper, but their recommendations were so general that it seems most probable that there were also administrative texts, perhaps written on palm-leaves.

We lack precise information about the status of those appointed to ministerial posts, or about their exact functions. The council's composition varied according to the particular epoch and region, but they usually included princes of royal blood, military chiefs, eminent priests, wealthy representatives of the guilds and even, occasionally, chiefs from the inferior social classes; indeed, Buddhist legends contain many references to individuals of lowly origin who rose to high ministerial rank. Women were excluded from all such posts, being generally considered to be as talkative and flighty as parrots or *mainā* (a common bird in India whose powers of speech were, perhaps, rather overestimated in ancient times).

Although ministerial appointments soon became hereditary, the king or emperor still took the trouble to ratify the nomination of a new incumbent. This procedure was still in force during the Gupta dynasty and seems to have been designed to retain at least the semblance of a choice and thus avoid the principle of the automatic succession of members of a single family. The system remained unchanged during the Middle Ages, in the feudal kingdoms of central India, and a certain number of genealogies of these high officials have survived.

If one is to believe Kauṭilya, the recruitment of ministers was not left to the hazards of succession but was based, rather, on a series of tests to which the candidates were submitted; the requisite qualities are enumerated carefully and sometimes naïvely by various authors. In other words, individual virtue was supposed to confirm hereditary right: a wise and admirable principle which was, perhaps, never applied in actuality.

The functions of the various ministers remain obscure in most cases. Literary sources frequently mention the prime minister, who was the king's chief counsellor (*mahāmantrin*) and head of the council, and whose influence appears to have been paramount. In spiritual matters, the royal chaplain (*purohita*) had equally strong influence over the king but does not seem to have ranked as a minister. A minister 'of War and Peace' (whose title first appeared during the Gupta era) corresponded more or less to a minister of Foreign Affairs, concerning himself with political treaties and with diplomatic and cultural relations, as well as preparing reports on the gifts received by the king from foreign countries; he also accompanied the king on his military campaigns. A minister of Justice supervised the State revenues, sat by the side of the king during trial procedures, compiled reports of all important trials and received citizens' petitions for transmission to the king. Another minister had charge of the Treasury and the buildings housing the royal treasure. The arsenals and the army were under the control of the army commander. These diverse tasks do not seem to have called for any particular specialization (any more than today in the case of modern government ministers), and these officials were, in principle at least, interchangeable. However, evidence does show that some were 'counsellors' while others were 'executors'.

A body of secretaries and scribes, responsible to the ministers, was recruited largely from among the nobility; they wrote out all the Chancellery's reports, edicts and statements of law, the wording of which was then carefully re-read by several different officials to avoid any possibility of error. Special keepers of the archives were also appointed.

The official order of precedence placed the administrators immediately below the ministers, followed by the tax collectors, the superintendents and the royal officials who supervised the various branches of the economy. Here again, powers and functions are ill-defined, except as described by Kauṭilya, whose systematic exactitude is open to suspicion. According to him, two administrators divided between them the entire State apparatus. One of them concerned himself with the Budget and with the quest for fresh sources of revenue, and attempted to maintain the balance of the public finances, while at the same time assuming certain police and judicial functions in relation to crime; under his direction, local employees were responsible for preparing land surveys and taking censuses for fiscal purposes. The other administrator collected taxes and gifts, and looked after the goods in kind and the specie destined for the Treasury.

From the Maurya era onwards, superintendents were occasionally appointed for religious or secular missions such as tours of religious propaganda, or tours of inspection for a particular and limited purpose such as the suppression of some abuse. Chiefly, they were responsible for administering the royal donations made to religious establishments, and also for ensuring that particular police measures were duly applied. According to Kauṭilya, on the other hand, such functions were carried out by the State's head clerks and administrative assistants who, though inferior in grade to the ministers and other dignitaries, held the real reins of power in the administration because of the breadth and variety of their powers and functions, despite the fact that they derived less benefit from office and were also subject to severe punishment in case of misdemeanour.

Beneath these high dignitaries, a whole host of minor functionaries took some part or other in helping to promote the smooth progress of State affairs. The State seems to have had a complex structure; its multiple activities were placed beneath the control either of the central or the local administration, leaving little room for commercial or industrial autonomy. Everything was surveyed, measured, even managed by the State: cadastral registers and land-measurement, the produce of the royal farms and their outlying farm buildings, fields, herds, flocks, granaries; workshops, mills, monopolies; arsenals, military equipment, the proper upkeep of the different army corps; public finances, the money in circulation, market values, the standardization and stamping of gold, weights and measures, and work instruments. Road maintenance and road traffic, sea and river transportation all involved taxes, toll-charges, passports, sale permits and customs duties. A strict watch was kept on public slaughter-houses, gambling-dens, fermented drinks and hetaeras. Commerce was subject to quota restriction, and market prices were closely controlled. Measures of length and of time were constantly liable to official verification. There was a right of inspection of certain home industries such as those connected with weaving. Output and working conditions were supervised, in the country as well as in town, and regulations covered even the humblest tasks such as the gathering of dead wood and gleaning.

It may well be imagined that a considerable number of functionaries were needed to carry out these various duties, all the more because certain posts were doubtless more honorific than effective; on the other hand, there was no rule against combining several posts, and some military officials, for instance, held civilian positions as well. Especially from the Gupta dynasty onwards, all such officials were fond of adorning themselves with self-laudatory epithets. Apart from the important posts which we have already mentioned, there were many others of lesser importance: bards and heralds, bearers of the royal insignia, guardians of the Treasury and the State warehouses, overseers of the royal harem, charioteers and elephant-drivers, sentries, palace servants, armed female guards and so on. Among these assorted officials and employees should be included a rather strange category, that of the 'spies' (*cara*) charged with keeping a close eye on public opinion, and the behaviour of officials and even of ministers; others performed secret missions, gleaning information in foreign kingdoms, for example.

Most of these civil servants enjoyed certain privileges, one of the most advantageous of which was a guaranteed immunity against being sued for debt during the entire course of their professional activity. They also had the right to benefits in case of their own illness or that of their children.

This rather Utopian vision of a planned economy, and of a paternalism concerning itself with the kingdom's least activities may correspond to reality to some extent; it certainly corresponds to the ideal of codification so dear to the Indian temperament, which found a certain satisfaction (as, indeed, it still does today) in contemplating a well-established order, even if it remained in the world of theory – so long as that order agreed with tradition.

LAW AND JUSTICE, CRIME AND PUNISHMENT

If the king did not untiringly inflict punishment on those who deserve it, the powerful would roast the weak like fishes on a spit.

THE CODE OF MANU, VII.

The term *dharma*, used in ancient India to designate Law, covered a far wider field of meaning than the purely juridical. In Vedic times it meant the basic norm of religious life and ritual observance. It dealt with the cosmic and sacrificial order, and regulated the acts proceeding inevitably from this order of things; that is to say, public and private behaviour, social relations, customs, morals, the duties attaching to castes, and the hygienic prescriptions inherent in religious practice. But some time between the sixth and second centuries BC the instructions relating to these matters had become too obscure, and new texts were prepared which, though not repudiating Vedic conceptions, were more intelligible to those who used them. The base remained essentially religious. These revised texts attempted to codify tradition, and added a juridical element which reads sometimes like a technical treatise. Subsequently, the compilations were completed by the addition of commentaries which provided the equivalent of a science of law. Here again, we see a case of the transmission of traditional ideas originating in a still unknown prehistory and surviving through a very long period of Indian evolution.

In the form of *sūtras*, prose interspersed with maxims in verse, or *śāstras*, verse 'instructions', these books formed a huge body of work with close to seven thousand titles, though a great many of these are lost. The best known is certainly the *Mānava Dharma Śāstra*, more commonly called the 'Code of Manu', of which about a quarter is devoted to juridical questions. It must have been compiled before the second century AD, perhaps as early as the second century BC, or even earlier.

The king, as director of the kingdom and maintainer of the Law, was quite naturally responsible for applying Justice on pain of being deposed. It was his function, therefore, to judge and to punish, to chase evil 'as the hunter tracks a wounded deer by following the trail of blood' (the Code of Manu, VIII, 44), to seek out truth so as better to defend society. More than that, he was held responsible for any unpunished crime or unjust decision. It was theoretically he who presided over investigations and, according to Megasthenes, he spent part of his time each day listening to complaints and giving judgment; he himself brought civil action when there was no plaintiff. He does not appear to have played a personal role except in the most serious cases; usually he delegated his powers to carefully chosen magistrates (*dharmasthas*) whose principal qualities had to be a perfect knowledge of the articles of the law (there were about eight thousand!), a high moral sense and a character free of passion; in criminal matters, these judges were generally brāhmaṇs, whose posts were almost certainly hereditary; in civil affairs, they might be designated from among the notables. The court was sedentary but did occasionally transfer its activities to other places, as when following the armies during a campaign. Apart from the king and the *dharmastha* who served as his deputy, it consisted of judges or assessors, a clerk of the court, a scribe, and a guard or bailiff. According to Kauṭilya, a tribunal of three magistrates sat for each group of ten villages, while a high court sat in the district's or province's most important town. There was apparently no jury system, if we are to believe sources originating in the northern regions. A person found guilty was entitled to two, or sometimes several, appeals, but only the king was empowered to deliver a final judgment.

The guilds – whose importance we shall soon perceive (see pp. 102–6) – were subject to a special legislation applied by a conciliation board, the members of which were recruited both from among brāhmaṇs, and experts and technicians conversant with the matter under judgment. Each village had recourse to its advice in judging minor offences and arbitrating quarrels. The sentences passed by this council were fully binding and consisted of fines and penalties that included the power to order expulsion and excommunication, the fearful consequences of which have already been mentioned (see pp. 24–5).

Although the professional jurist obviously desired the exercise of justice to be rigid and free from all equivocation, Buddhist and secular literature speaks in a more realistic accent and often in satirical tones. In these tales the corruption of magistrates is a frequent subject, although the established rules were designed to make such a thing impossible, going so far as to recommend that judges should be spied upon by *agents provocateurs*. The judges had no easy task, if we are to believe the fourth-century author of *Mṛcchakaṭika* ('The Little Clay Cart'): they were often confronted with demands for justice based on unproven charges which subsequent investigation failed to justify; the plaintiffs exaggerated their grievances out of all proportion, refused to admit their own delinquencies, launched inflammatory accusations, and the rival parties exchanged insults in the heat of debate. The judge had to support successfully the rights of the poor and under-privileged, punish evil-doers and, at the same time, preserve himself from royal displeasure if he committed a professional fault, endure censure, and risk having his appointment – which appeared a sinecure – taken away from him altogether.

As far as we can gather from the various sources available to us, a trial proceeded in the following fashion. First of all, the plaintiff had between three and seven days in which to submit a summary of his case to the judge; to do this, he was recommended to seek the services of a scribe capable of drawing up the case according to the forms prescribed by tradition, and of establishing it 'upon the arguments and the facts'. Then he had to secure a maximum of three witnesses whom his opponent would not be able to challenge. These witnesses could not normally be chosen from among women, learned brāhmaṇs, officials, actors, minors, debtors, convicts or cripples.

On the day of the trial, the courtroom was swept and cleaned, and seats arranged by the bailiff for the use of the judges.[10] The court was led in by the bailiff; then, on the presiding judge's request, the plaintiffs were brought in. The clerk made notes of the declarations, and a summary of the complaint was inscribed in the ground or on a tablet; its gist could be altered by the plaintiff, right up to the last moment, by wiping out with his foot anything which seemed to him contrary to his statements. The defence was virtually in the hands of the witnesses, for professional advocates did not yet exist. These witnesses were required to attend court and were then questioned closely, but they were not under oath; a solemn adjuration was read to them, warning them of the corporal punishments which would be inflicted on them in the case of false evidence, penalties made more formidable by the prospect of additional punishment after death that would affect their future lives. Despite this warning, witnesses were still capable of using all sorts of ruses on behalf of the person whose case they had agreed to support, and consequently they were subjected to a careful scrutiny during their evidence. If a witness should show himself ill at ease or betray signs of apprehension, if his face became pale, or he suddenly broke out into a sweat, or if his mouth became so dry that he had to pass his tongue over his lips, then doubt would inevitably be cast on the truth of his statement. Other portents and omens were observed by the court, representing the will of the gods and deriving partly from magic.

If a heavy presumption of guilt rested on the accused and he continued to assert his innocence, he was put to the torture, the degree of which varied according to the individual and was milder for women; no torture at all might be inflicted on brāhmaṇs, children, pregnant women, old people, sick people or madmen. Another method of discovering the truth was the ordeal, although this was not usually employed except in grave cases where there was a great element of doubt; the most frequent forms were ordeal by fire or by immersion;[11] poison was also used; or the accused's tongue was pressed against a red-hot ploughshare; or the accused was weighed in a balance, and any differences in his weight during the course of the ordeal were interpreted as sure indications that he was guilty.

When judgment was finally given, a copy of the verdict, called a 'victory parchment', was handed to the winner of the proceedings. This, however, did not bring the course of justice to an end, for any fresh evidence discovered subsequently, any witness convicted *a posteriori* of perjury, might result in a reversal or amendment of the trial. Going to law was an expensive business for litigants, since the loser had to pay not only the legal costs but also the total amount of the wagers engaged by the adversaries on the outcome of the deliberations. When a defendant was found guilty at his trial, and then lost his appeal, he had to pay double this total amount; but if, by chance, he finally won the day, then the plaintiff was forced to pay the entire costs, and the judges themselves had to pay a fine.

Offences were of many different kinds. One of the most frequent was fraud or malpractice in commercial matters, and the conditions governing a bargain took this into account; the transaction was only considered finally binding after three full days had elapsed (ten days according to the Code of Manu). If the buyer returned the goods to the seller on the very day of the purchase, the agreement was considered cancelled; if he returned the goods on the following day he was bound to pay the seller a sum in compensation; on the day after that the indemnity was larger. But at least he had had the time to assure himself of the good or bad quality of the merchandise. When this so-called 'period of repentance' was up, the buyer was obliged to pay the whole of the price agreed for the transaction; if he failed to do so, he became liable to prosecution, only, however, if the transaction had resulted in an explicit bargain.

Fraud existed, too, when anyone acquired 'ownerless property', even if the good faith of both parties to the transaction could be proved. In such a case, the seller was accused of receiving and prosecuted as such, while the buyer was considered equally culpable. Property of this kind reverted rightfully to the king, who was considered its legal owner; he might either accept the entire property, or accept only one-sixth of it, and in the latter case he might hand over this portion to the discoverer of the hoard.

The importance of this piece of common law results from the custom that each family had of hiding a 'treasure' somewhere in the home or estate. The secret was handed down from father to son and the treasure was never removed from its hiding-place except in case of total ruin. If the heirs could not find the hoard, if their line became extinct, or if the domain was abandoned, the king had title to whatever was unearthed, however long a period might have elapsed since the family's last representative had vanished. Stolen property came within the provisions of the same laws. Fraud was, in fact, considered comparable to theft, and encompassed the falsification of weights and measures, of money, forgery of public or private documents, cheating at dice, and so on.

Fraud, in all its forms, was energetically fought by the administration. A special body of inspectors was charged with discovering and suppressing such activities, and to facilitate their task, they employed spies and even *agents provocateurs*. They also exercised supervision over the markets, to ensure that prices were not exorbitant. Overcharging was also made more difficult by the strict rules under which merchants and craftsmen operated.

But contemporary folk-tales, especially the *Jātakas*, are full of stories of far more serious crimes. Although most foreigners visiting India in ancient times agreed in claiming that crime in that country was very rare, Indian sources tell a very different story and seem to be, at least in part, authentic. First, there existed professional thieves, belonging to a special caste, who practised their 'art' as a religious duty – as the seventh-century Chinese Buddhist monk Hsüan-Ch'uang was the first to confirm. Secondly, fierce gangs of bandits roamed the forests, holding up caravans and ransoming solitary travellers. Villages and, more especially, towns and the capital were troubled with burglaries and house-breakings which the police were unable to put an end to entirely, despite sentinels, guards, watches and 'detectives'.

The stories of the *Jātakas* deal extensively with this banditry, and there is hardly a tale concerning the itinerary of a caravan from one point to another which does not mention the organized bands awaiting it along its route. While giving interesting details about their methods, the stories emphasize that these monstrous ruffians never shrank from any cruelty in order to get possession of travellers' belongings. But caravans faced less risk of attack than individuals travelling alone, especially if the caravan commander had taken the precaution of hiring a brave guide who was well acquainted with the dangerous passages.[12] When the brigands were dealing with only two fellow-travellers they did not hesitate to attack; in most cases, they kept one of the two prisoner and sent the other off to collect a substantial ransom, which did not prevent them sometimes from executing their prisoner and then killing the second unfortunate man when he returned, so that the site of their lair might remain secret.[13] They spared no one, not even a father with his son, a mother with her daughter, or a teacher with his pupil, despite the respect in which such individuals were habitually held. No more did they respect the priestly robe of such pilgrims as the Chinese monks Hsüan-Ch'uang and I-Tsing who both recount in their memoirs the distressing adventures of which they were the heroes in seventh-century India.[14] These two at least got away with their lives, but many were not so fortunate. Stripped of their clothing, beaten to death, the victims' corpses were left sprawling on the pathway at the mercy of beasts of prey; this was, from the orthodox Hindu and from the Buddhist viewpoint, the most ignominious death conceivable. The police could do little, for these outrages took place in isolated, uninhabited regions, and so the bandits along the highways were able to perpetrate their crimes with impunity. Sometimes, two rival bands of brigands clashed, fought a pitched battle and wiped each other out, a happy outcome which brought temporary peace to the region until fresh bands were formed.[15]

Burglars and thieves in the towns and villages showed themselves remarkably cunning and enterprising. Two very similar *Jātakas*[16] give spirited accounts of the nocturnal exploit of a thief who ransacked the shop of one of the village's richest tradesmen. The owner was woken by the noise, saw his bare shelves and dashed into the street crying 'Stop thief!' at the top of his voice. Immediately, the men of the village rushed out, torch in hand, to join in pursuit of the thief. They soon found his track: like the abject creature he was, he had not hesitated to defile himself (something no good Hindu would have dreamt of doing) by running along the village's sewage canal and then crossing the graveyard, a haunted spot which no one ever dared visit at night. The villagers halted their chase immediately, preferring to let him get away rather than risk defiling themselves.

However, in the capital the royal police showed themselves far less pusillanimous, as many stories make clear. Thieves were extraordinarily audacious, digging through the walls of houses, tunnelling[17] under the very eyes of the patrolling militia, scaling obstacles – and sowing terror among the population. They did not hesitate to attack innocent victims unable to defend themselves, or to engage in furious armed combat with whoever surprised them. Only rarely did anyone have the courage and the presence of mind to resist them and emerge unscathed from the encounter, and the example of a certain royal treasurer is all the more remarkable for that reason.[18] Alone in his home, in the middle of the night, surrounded by bandits armed to the teeth, he succeeded in putting them to flight by a clever stratagem: sparing no effort, he spent several hours blowing a trumpet, beating a drum, crying orders, talking, singing and laughing as though the house contained a crowd of servants and friends. The band of thieves gradually became convinced that they were dealing with superior forces, panicked, threw away their arms and fled.

Sometimes, after a furious chase,[19] the police succeeded in capturing one of these criminals. When that happened, his arms were tied behind his back, the necklace of red flowers reserved for those condemned to death was passed around his neck, and his skull was coated with brick-dust, the colour of which was doubtless symbolical of blood. Then, followed by an excited crowd rejoicing at this lucky capture, he was flogged at every crossroads, while a special drum was beaten so that the whole populace might know of his shameful career and fate. So progress was made towards the place of execution, which was usually to be found near the graveyard. There he was given a thousand strokes with thorny rods,[20] after which he was impaled alive, his head tied back so that his face was turned upwards to the sky. If indeed he was still alive at this juncture he would experience the additional agony of seeing the vultures and the carrion-crows gathering and wheeling overhead – and he would know what to expect: soon, the boldest of these birds of prey would alight on his head and peck out his eyes with their dagger-sharp beaks. . . .[21]

According to the *Smṛti* authors, corporal punishment is said not to have been inflicted during the Vedic age, but guilty parties were fined so many heads of cattle, a punishment which usually brought about the complete ruin of the culprit and his family. In later times, capital punishment was decreed for all murders (except in the case of brāhmaṇs), even when the death was caused through a duel; the extreme penalty was extended to various other crimes, including plots against the person of the king or the security of the State, breaking into the royal harem, burglary, looting, the theft of elephants or horses belonging to the king, etc. Impalement was the most usual form of execution, though there were many others. Sometimes the condemned man was buried in earth up to his neck, his hands tied behind his back; to scare off the birds of prey and the jackals, his only recourse was to shout and yell menacingly,[22] until exhaustion sealed his fate. Alternatively, he might be trampled to death by an elephant,[23] thrown head first down a precipice,[24] or abandoned, alone, in a boat headed down-river, after his hands, feet, nose and ears had been cut off.[25] In certain cases, the condemned person was burnt alive, torn apart by bullocks, or shot to death with arrows. Acts of banditry were punished by mutilation and imprisonment. Adultery was punished in several different ways, some of which are described in the Code of Manu. When a man was convicted of adultery he could be sentenced to imprisonment or banishment, or might even be impaled if he had been rash enough to become enamoured of one of the king's wives. Where he was suspected, but had not been caught in the act, the tribunal could force him to undergo the ordeal (see p. 54). The wife of a brāhmaṇ, caught in an adulterous liaison, was led through the streets astraddle a black donkey, facing the animal's tail, her body smeared with butter and her skull shaved; in this state she was exposed to the jeers and insults of the crowd. This was an infinitely degrading punishment, since the donkey was considered particularly despicable, a symbol of evil and lubricity.

It should be emphasized that the powerful influence of the humanitarian ideals spread by Buddhism led to a gradual disappearance of capital and corporal punishment, and it seems that under the Gupta empire these penalties scarcely existed any longer. Nevertheless, in the seventh century, under Harṣa, torture and imprisonment were still the most common forms of punishment, according to Hsüan-Ch'uang.

There was nothing to envy in the lot of prisoners, if we are to believe the descriptions contained in the *Jātakas*. The prison, under the direction of its chief jailer, was a fearsome establishment in which life was made unbearable for its inmates. Many prisoners died as a result of the tortures inflicted upon them and the privations they endured. They were left without food or water, suffering from the cold or the heat, lying helpless in their own excrement, usually sick, often leprous; their nails, hair and beard were never cut; their ankles were clamped into holes in a wooden frame and they wore handcuffs. They were beaten three times a day with whips, canes or bludgeons. Some were bound hand and foot, or chained to a wall, or thrown into a ditch where they were at the mercy of wolves, dogs, jackals, rats and cats, and soon met their death. Or a prisoner might be stretched out on his back, his jaws wrenched open forcibly and kept apart by the insertion of red-hot iron or copper wedges, and urine poured down his throat. Other instruments of torture were employed: cauldrons filled with burning and corrosive liquids, sharp swords, saws, razors, iron nails, needles, hatchets and pincers. These horrifying visions recall the torments of hell described in the Buddhist texts and illustrated in certain monuments, especially those of Barabuḍur in central Java (eighth or ninth century AD) and, later, at Angkor Vat in Cambodia (twelfth century).

The pathetic fate of these prisoners had become a matter of concern for the great Aśoka, despite the fact that his prisons had the reputation of never allowing a single one of their guests to emerge alive, and one of his inscriptions states:

> . . . Sometimes in the administration of justice a person will suffer imprisonment or torture. When this happens, he sometimes dies accidentally, and many other people suffer because of this. In such circumstances, you must try to follow the middle path (that is, justice or moderation). . . . This edict has been inscribed here to remind the judicial officers in this city to try at all times to avoid unjust imprisonment or unjust torture. . . . I have therefore decreed that henceforth prisoners who have been convicted and sentenced to death shall be granted a respite of three days. During this period their relatives may appeal to the officials for the prisoners' lives; or, if no one makes an appeal, the prisoners may prepare for the other world by distributing gifts or fasting.[26]

They had one single hope: whenever a new king was crowned, the gates of the prisons were opened and the prisoners released indiscriminately. But such amnesties were not so very magnanimous, for the prisons contained huge numbers of innocent people. Apart from the question of whether the condemned men were really guilty or not, it must be noted that, when convicted, their wives and all the immediate members of their families were incarcerated as well.

We may say, then, that during the period which concerns us

India was essentially a vast country whose political unification was extremely tentative, peopled by many different races (ranging from Āryans of the white race to partially subdued, often negroid tribes) speaking a great number of different languages. In this extremely diverse framework, administrative organization had consolidated itself as a guiding force, relying on penal codes to maintain order, order being personified in the figure of the king. But it was a kind of order which derived more from religious concepts than from social and moral obligations. Finally, the very existence of the entire country depended upon the economy of the State and so upon domestic and foreign trade, an aspect which we shall now proceed to examine before investigating more closely the conditions and realities of daily life.

CHAPTER FOUR

ECONOMICS AND DAILY LIFE

. . . *The merchants used to move about in the rivers as they wished, as if in tanks, in the forests as if in gardens and on mountains as if in their own houses. . . . As he [the King] used to protect the earth so she too gave him gems out of mines, corns from fields and elephants from forests.*

KĀLIDĀSA, *Raghu Vaṃśa*, XVII, 64, 66.

From ancient times, the importance of economics in Indian daily life has been emphasized in contemporary records, together with the question of how to maintain or raise the economic level. It was both an individual and a collective matter, and political control was applied as firmly in this field as it was in the realm of administrative practice.

The Indian State of those days was not a welfare State, and it was in its interest to allow private enterprise a degree of autonomy. But, at the same time, it needed substantial revenues to support its unwieldy administrative machine and provide backing for the military campaigns which every king longed to lead to success. Enormous sums were needed, too, to finance festivals, court luxuries, and the huge expenditure by the royal Treasury (which was not kept separate from the State Treasury). For all these reasons, the economic life of ancient India had, of necessity, to be highly developed. Since the entire country's economy was largely based on agriculture, the State ensured efficient operation by undertaking important irrigation schemes, supplying communities with water or seed where necessary, and supervising carefully the production of the crops, part of which would be set aside for the State granaries. Commerce was equally active, fed by local crafts, the caravans, and maritime and inland navigation. To facilitate the expansion of trade, and to maintain efficient communications, the emperors and kings all applied themselves to the task of creating routes and keeping them open.

In addition, they possessed a merchant marine. Finally, the State arrogated to itself a certain number of monopolies which provided it with revenue and, at the same time, allowed it to make use of a labour force unable to find work in private industry because of its social status. It was in these monopolies that the untouchables and those fallen from their caste were able to earn their living.

We shall examine these various fields in turn, and explain the regulations and methods governing each one.

AGRICULTURE AND STOCK FARMING

Agriculture was the corner-stone of ancient India's economy. Although we lack precise details and statistics, it seems certain that farming enterprises ranged from the cultivation of a single field, yielding scarcely enough to support a family, to great landed properties worked by a large number of hired hands.

The basic crop, even in that age, was rice; barley, wheat, millet and sugar-cane were also grown, as well as sesame and several different kinds of vegetable.

Great care was given to the question of irrigation, so vital for a high crop yield; indeed, this is still an urgent problem in a country that periodically experiences terrible droughts during which the earth cracks open and nothing grows. Consequently, the discovery of new sources of water supply was the subject for a special course of instruction.[1] From Vedic times, and perhaps earlier, Indians had learnt to sink wells in order to reach deep-flowing waters, to deflect the course of rivers so that they might supply canals, and to regulate the flow of these waters, or to make the canals overflow and so swamp the rice-fields.[2] The Maurya kings and their successors were all active in providing the country with reservoirs and wells, and in their inscriptions they frequently boasted of the works they had undertaken in this cause. If one flies, today, over India's vast stretches of cultivated land, one will immediately notice countless man-made irrigation systems, some of very ancient origin, for exactly the same methods have been used for millenniums: long, narrow channels bordered by small earth embankments. We are told that, in ancient times, these canals were kept full either 'by hand', that is with the aid of water-skins or a balance-pole (*tulā*), or else by transporting water on the backs of animals, or by using a bucket-chain. An ingenious system, still used in present times, was worked by oxen climbing up a gently sloping artificial ridge and descending it again time after time, in so doing hauling up from a well on each occasion a leather bucket filled with water which was emptied into a supply-canal.[3] The canals were excavated communally and served sometimes as demarcation lines between two neighbouring properties. It seems that the use of this commonly owned water often gave rise to keen disputes, and that it was not uncommon for the course to be diverted in the direction of one village's fields at the expense of another's. In such a case, violent quarrels resulted which developed occasionally into pitched battles between rival villagers,[4] and the disagreement had to be brought before the local council for adjudication.

While Indian farmers used irrigation to help their crops resist the subtropical sun, they also made full use of manures and fertilizers; for the former, they gathered animal dung and let it dry for ten months, while for the latter they made use of liquid manure and various animal and vegetable products. So as not to exhaust the soil, they practised crop rotation and the fallowing of land.

At the beginning of spring, they started ploughing the land, using a swing-plough drawn by two oxen. This draught was identical with that used today: made of two lengths of hard wood joined together at an obtuse angle, the plough was equipped with a handle on its upper part, while its pointed lower end was well sharpened, or reinforced with a strip of wrought iron. A curved pole was hinged into the body of this construction, ending in a yoke which rested on the necks of the oxen and was held in place both by the animals' humps and by an individual collar. The ploughman weighted the ploughshare by perching on top of it while gripping the plough-handle with one hand; with his other hand he urged the oxen forward with a whip. Some Jain texts state that there existed ploughs drawn by as many as twenty-four oxen, and that there were three different kinds of plough,[5] but pictures of ploughing scenes made during this period do not confirm these claims.

There were three principal sowings: first, rice, sown during the rainy season and reaped at the onset of winter; secondly, beans, peas, lentils and other leguminous plants (including sesame), which ripened during the cold season and could be gathered in spring; lastly, barley (*yava*), wheat, flax and hemp, mostly reaped during the spring or winter. Millet and sugar-cane, cut before the summer rains (except for the second growths which persisted until November), completed the list of staples. The fields were dotted with scarecrows fashioned from buffalo skeletons set up on poles.[6]

Of all these crops, rice was certainly the most important, wherever conditions allowed the ground to be sufficiently inundated. During the Vedic age, rice grew wild in certain terrains, as for instance on the banks of the Ganges, but was not yet cultivated; it was simply gathered in its wild state from the marshy hollows left by the river's periodical floods. Even before the Maurya dynasty, rice was not only harvested but improved by selection.

Three types of rice were grown, white, black and so-called 'rapid', this last ripening in two months. Rice-growing was a complicated process, involving a large labour force, since it was necessary to provide artificial flooding of the fields by means of a network of small canals. The cutting of the rice crop was followed by pricking out, a process carried out by hand, the body bent double for hours on end under the hot sun. The harvest was gathered just as autumn was turning into winter. To cut the rice, the peasants used wide-bladed sickles so curved sometimes that they were U-shaped.[7] After being cut, the rice was laid on the ground in bundles and threshed by hand; then it was winnowed. The grains were left to dry in the sun before being packed and carried to the village, where the rice was poured into large jars that were immediately sealed and stacked in rows in one of the granaries.[8]

The sugar-cane crop was watched over by overseers, whose motionless figures could be seen crouched down in the shadows of the high stalks.[9] After the crop was harvested it was kept in storage until it was required for processing, when it was pressed in a special machine to extract the sugar. The same method was used with sesame, which produced a widely used edible oil.

The making of cadastral surveys must have been an exceedingly complicated business in ancient times. The Buddha himself, contemplating a cultivated plain one day, compared it to a monk's patched cloak: the image was certainly well chosen. The little embankments bordering the narrow water-channels in which the muddy water sparkled, and the square or circular-shaped hedges and fences marking the boundaries of the fields all combined to give the land a fragmentary, patchwork look. The appearance of the Indian landscape is exactly similar today. A single parcel of land sometimes constituted one family's entire property, so that its produce had, almost impossibly, to feed the family as well as supporting it. Boundaries were established along the lines of natural obstacles and features, and also according to mysterious landmarks, knowledge of which was kept secret and handed down from father to son. Both principles were equally and fully valid, and those who attempted to displace or remove such landmarks rendered themselves liable to severe penalties at the hands of the local judicial council.

In the villages' immediate vicinity, the fields gave way to orchards, gardens growing vegetables or flowers, and sometimes plantations of jute or cotton. Fruits, flowers and vegetables were grown in abundance, including gourds and cucumbers, ginger, and spices such as pepper and saffron. Fruits were carefully ripened, wild varieties being picked and added to those grown domestically; both kinds were put to dry in special lofts, and the methods used to hasten the ripening process included covering them with straw, exposing them to the heat of a fire of dried dung, or mixing green and ripe fruit together. The yield was so abundant that whole cart-loads heaped high with various fruits were sent regularly to the nearest towns.

Cattle were of equal importance to crops in the village economy. Wealth was estimated on the basis of the number of heads of cattle in a herd, whether it belonged to a single individual or to the whole community. The herds were composed of bullocks and cows, buffaloes and cow-buffaloes, rams and sheep; swine, sometimes, and even dogs occasionally formed part of the herd, but horses only rarely, since they were not bred in India (see p. 86 regarding the importation of horses). Chronicles of the time list meticulously the material benefits to be derived from these animals: apart from dairy produce (for ordinary consumption and for use in religious ceremonies) they furnished skins, leathers, horns, hair from the manes and tails, and wool, all of these commodities being much in demand by the various crafts. A month or two after their birth, the animals were counted and marked with signs or emblems which made it possible to identify their owner; cows that had just calved were also counted and registered.[10] The care of the herds was entrusted to a communal cowherd or shepherd (*gopālaka*) who led them out to pasture each day. He whiled away the time by playing a bamboo flute whose melancholy sounds echoed through the countryside, as they still do today. But he had also to be capable of defending his charges against wild animals and thieves, and so was always armed with a bow. Classical authors devote much space to the quarrels which broke out constantly between the herdsmen of neighbouring villages, with each claiming superior quality for his own herd. At dusk, each *gopālaka* drove his animals back to his village and herded them into their special paddock, milch-cows being lodged in covered stalls. The *gopālaka* was held responsible for any harm caused to the herd while he was in charge of them, except when due to circumstances outside his control; his services were paid either in money or in kind, in the latter case it might be an entitlement to the milk of one cow out of every ten.[11]

Some of the means used to encourage breeding and milk-production were surprising: one recipe, for instance, recommended that draught-oxen should be fed on a mixture of meat, grass, hay, oil-cake, bran, salt, sour milk, barley, beans, fat and sugar, with liquor and ginger added, the purpose of the last ingredients doubtless being to 'ginger them up'. Horse-dealers certainly made use of stimulating drugs, administering them to their animals just before showing them to the would-be purchaser; but this was rightly considered a fraud and was condemned by the law.

Milch-cows were handled with particular care – but to little purpose, it seems, since milk yield remained extraordinarily low despite the fact that they were milked twice a day (except during the spring, when the milk was reserved for the young calves). To kill a cow was considered a grave crime, on a par with the murder of someone of high caste. To expiate such a crime, the guilty party was made to live among the herd for three months, his head shaved, clad in the skin of the slain animal; during the first month he was allowed to drink no liquid whatsoever except for a kind of barley-water. On top of this, he was fined ten cows and a bull, and if he was unable to furnish these he had to hand over every single asset he possessed.

Apart from cattle-farming, poultry was raised, but on a far smaller scale, and eggs were only a minor item in the general diet. This deficiency was largely made up for by the products of game-hunting and fishing (see pp. 98–102).

In ancient times, distinction was made between several different categories of farmers. There were those who cultivated their own land, those who had it cultivated by wage-earning labourers or serfs, and those who leased their land to 'métayers', farmers who paid rent in kind, in this case half the harvest and crop. There were few big landlords, and the largest estates nearly all belonged to the king, that is to say, to the State in fact. The temples, too, received vast properties as gifts and had them developed by hired labourers and staff. But these were exceptions, and most of the land was parcelled out in small lots, sometimes only big enough to feed a single family. Many small farmers, however, chose to work the land on the 'united family' basis, under the direction of a head of the family, pooling fields, cattle, agricultural implements, harvests, crops and grazing-grounds. Under this system, they avoided fragmentation of the family property and, to some extent, they guarded against risks and responsibilities.

Theirs was not an easy life. The vagaries of the climate often brought seasonal catastrophe: tornadoes devastated the fields, drought scorched the land, floods wiped out whole crops. Apart from these natural hazards, there was the problem of the laws of hospitality, which were rigorously applicable and cost the farmers dearly; the most onerous of these obligations involved the provision of food and fodder for the king and his suite during the course of their cross-country tours of inspection. On such occasions, the absolute right of the king and his dignitaries to provisions and stores from the local peasants might well reduce these communities to penury during a bad year, with no hope of replenishing their empty granaries before the following harvest.

To natural calamities and unavoidable obligations had to be added the burden of taxation. Taxes were numerous and were applied to collective enterprises as well as to individuals. The peasant had to pay not only a basic tax amounting to twenty-five or thirty per cent of the produce of his land at the moment when it was in full yield, but also a periodical (probably annual) contribution based upon his income. He had to pay his share of the general tax levied by the State on his village, as well as special taxes that were set against the services rendered by the State to the rural population – protection against theft in pasturages and fields, the cost of land-surveying, irrigation works, the upkeep and repair of canals. Fruit, herbage, honey and wood were all taxable. If the farmer was not the owner of the land he worked, he was liable to pay rentals or other concessionary fees in addition to the obligatory payment of communal dues and tolls. Under some reigns, tax and duty rates reached such heights that quite often villages would be abandoned by their entire peasant population, who preferred to risk bringing new land under cultivation in some other region rather than submit to such exorbitant demands.

But on the whole the State went out of its way to give agriculture favourable treatment and to avoid oppression of the peasantry, knowing how indispensable the peasants were to the whole country's prosperity. For this reason, the State recognized ownership of land after a period of five years if it had been brought into cultivation by the individual in question, or at the end of three generations (that is to say, a century) if the land had previously been worked. Similarly, chattels-personal, including cattle, became his property after ten years. Bringing new land into cultivation and the planting of trees and seeds were encouraged by the State through advances of money and loans of equipment to those breaking new ground. Despite these reliefs, the peasant was usually in debt. This state of affairs was by no means confined to this section of the community; most Indian families of the time were constantly in debt (see pp. 109–201).

COMMERCE

The importance of agriculture was equalled in ancient India by the great scale on which commerce was practised and by the essential role it played in the country's economic life, in large towns and small villages alike. It was supplied by local and craft production, by importation and by exportation, and was carried on by sea and by the great caravan routes. The whole Indian coast-line was dotted with ports, especially in Mahārāṣṭra, along the west coast, in the Tamil country, on the Malabār coast, and in Bengal. Through its geographical position, India profited from the communications established in two spheres, first, those between the Persian Gulf, East Africa and its own ports, which were regularly visited by Greek, Roman and (later) Arab ships; secondly, those connecting India with the countries of south-east Asia, where she possessed prosperous trading-posts established since the beginning of the Christian era. Chinese shipping, transporting fifty- or sixty-ton loads, sailed through the straits of Malacca to discharge their cargo in the gulf of Bengal. From about the eighth century onwards, Arab vessels were even bolder, rounding Cape Comorin at the southern tip of India for points as far distant as Yüan-Chow. The merchandise unloaded in the Indian ports was taken in charge by caravans, most of which converged upon the great international markets established in the regions of Peśāwar, Kābul and, further to the east, in the oases of Chinese Turkestān. In this way, Indian and foreign commodities were exported as far as Upper Asia, where the laden caravans reached the silk routes connecting the Syrian coast with western China.

For this huge traffic to proceed effectively and speedily, India needed, above all, well-planned, convenient routes and ports.

I. ROUTES AND CARAVANS

The emperors and kings of India found it greatly in their own interest to encourage this international trade, since the substantial taxes levied on all goods in transit helped to swell the Treasury's coffers and raise the general standard of living. From the Maurya epoch onwards, monarchs attached great importance to the construction of major routes, supervising such projects personally,[12] and in the fourth century Megasthenes[13] had already noted their excellence.[14] Their construction required the co-operation of a whole army of technicians, architects, engineers and carpenters, assisted by woodcutters, ropemakers, roadmenders, labourers and assorted hirelings.[15] First the soil was studied by experts. Then, armed with picks, axes and scythes, the workmen hacked out a path, cutting down creepers, undergrowth, bushes, thickets and trees, moving or flattening rocks, prising up tree-stumps, levelling slopes and humps, filling up holes and depressions. The final result was a flat, solid surface.

It seems that these roads were raised above the surface of the adjacent land, so that they would be usable even during the rainy season; at any rate, texts state that they were bordered by ditches backed with sand. Water-filled canals ran along the side of these roads, which were shaded from the sun by trees planted along their edges.[16] According to Megasthenes,[17] distance-posts were positioned every ten stadia (just over one mile). At road junctions, signposts gave directions.

Rest-houses for the use of travellers and pilgrims were set up at regular intervals; each of these halting-places was provided with a well and often with an artificial lake, such as one still sees throughout the Indian countryside, for use as a reservoir. The two major discomforts of long voyages in the Indian climate have always been heat and dust, and it must have been a real boon to the travellers of those days to be able to wash themselves, replenish their water-bottles and stretch out on a cool, smooth, well-swept wooden floor, safe from the wild animals prowling outside.

Once built, these highways remained a matter of great concern to the government. Their upkeep must have been an expensive business, soaked as they were for three or four months of each year by the heavy monsoon rains, and filled regularly with ruts and pot-holes from the weight of the constant traffic of herds, carts and caravans. Road maintenance was the responsibility of senior officials, known as *antapāla*, who were also in charge of the pilgrims' rest-houses, and had the additional task of pursuing and seizing robbers lying in wait for passers-by and caravans. All this cost a great deal, and the State covered its expenses by exacting a toll-payment from the merchants who found it necessary to make use of the imperial or royal highways. Although this tax constituted for them some kind of insurance against robbery, there were, nevertheless, cunning and unscrupulous merchants who attempted to defraud the revenue officials by taking to side-roads when approaching toll-points. But if their trickery was found out they were immediately thrown into prison. These tolls were payable to the octroi official of every village and town on the route, and amounted to a levy of a twentieth on grain, oil, sugar, pottery and cheap cloth, and from a fifteenth to a fifth on other merchandise. Confiscated consignments were sold by auction, with the Treasury and the community sharing the proceeds. The king was entitled to a nominal portion of each item disposed of in this way.

Commerce was supplied principally by the caravans which

threaded their way along the routes, picking up their loads in the few great coastal ports and transporting them up towards the north-western provinces where the caravan trails crossed the silk routes; these last formed an intercontinental network connecting Syria to China, crossing the mountain passes of what is now Afghānistān, traversing the Gobi desert and finally reaching the Tarim basin in Sinkiang by way of the series of oases which dotted the desert. Great markets had been held along the Indian frontiers ever since the third or second centuries BC (perhaps even earlier), and this international traffic continued to flourish until the tenth century AD. If we are to believe contemporary Buddhist texts it would seem that every merchant in India hoping to make a fortune had the ambition of organizing one or several caravans a year, risking his entire resources in the enterprise, or associating himself with other merchants if his own funds did not suffice. They were not prepared to leave the responsibilities of the voyage to a paid leader, and accompanied the convoy themselves, shrinking neither from the dangers nor the discomfort and fatigue of such a journey. Popular imagination appears to have derived particular pleasure from the evocation of these interminable marches through forest and across desert, and descriptions abound; in fact they are unduly repetitive, and the same details tend to appear again and again in different stories.

Every caravan possessed a leader, the *sārthavāha*, an important and knowledgeable individual who had had wide experience of this kind of expedition. The whole train's safety rested in his hands, as did the success of the voyage and the eventual profit to be realized from it; all those following the caravan were bound to obey him explicitly, whether they were caravaneers or simply unattached travellers who had joined on for safety and convenience after paying a reasonable fee for the privilege.

Preparations were long drawn out. It was necessary to assemble a great number of carts and wagons, to procure sufficient draught-animals, to load up the merchandise, and wood for the bivouacs, forage for the animals, rice and oil for the men,[18] jars for drinking water. The column formed up and began to move off before daybreak with a grinding of wooden wheels, stretching out in a long, thin line along the road and raising a thick, swirling cloud of dust that made the eyes smart and parched the throat. To preserve his full energies, the *sārthavāha* tried, as far as possible, to avoid the inevitable dust: if the wind was in their faces, he travelled at the head of the column, seated in his own wagon, surrounded by his officers; but when the wind was blowing in the same direction as their march, he let the convoy pass him and brought up the rear. Nightfall was the signal for the day's march to end. The carts were drawn up in several circles, the bullocks being penned in the centre of the circles. Camp-fires were lit all round the parked vehicles, both to heat the evening meal and to keep away wild animals. The men took it in turn to mount guard, with three reliefs during the course of the night, that is, every four hours. At daybreak the long procession started off once again, to the rhythm of the bullocks' slow tread.

When the caravan came to a river it was obliged to call a halt. None of these bodies of water had bridges, despite the fact that carpentry was a well-developed art in the country and bridges traversed the moats at the entrance to each town. Often the rivers could be forded; the cart-drivers knew the fordable stretches by heart and could guide their teams safely through the stony shallows. Otherwise, if the river was not too wide, the men would chop down a few trees and throw the trunks across the river-bed. But if the stream or river was too deep, rafts (*nāvatīrtha*) were constructed.[19]

Crossing jungles was not without its dangers, because of the presence of 'savage' tribes, naked except for a string of leaves around the hips, men and women equally expert at shooting poisoned arrows from their thin, light bows; they were likely to attack strangers with the aim of securing a human victim to sacrifice to their gods,[20] but they did not dare to pit themselves against a force as strong as that of a caravan. Greater danger for the caravans lurked, rather, in the forests and wooded country, where organized bands of brigands were quite bold enough to confront such large groups for the sake of the booty involved, and were experts at preparing careful ambushes (see pp. 56–7).

Desert crossings were the most feared of all. Sinister rumours circulated about the dangers to be met with in the wastelands: they had the reputation of being haunted by demons who devoured corpses, for instance. And there was always the risk of dying from hunger and thirst. The *sārthavāha* were well aware of the mistakes their companions might be tempted to make in an access of terror or privation, and they were in the habit of addressing admonishments to the assembled company before they set out through the sands, advising them to refrain from tasting anything unfamiliar, to eat no unknown root, leaf, flower or fruit without first showing it to the leaders, because innumerable poisonous plants grew in the regions they were about to traverse;[21] and if they were to taste such plants the leaders should be informed immediately, so that an emetic might be administered, otherwise they would surely die.[22] The *sārthavāha* also insisted that no one should stray away from the column, for fear of wild animals and quicksands.

Descriptions of desert crossings occur repeatedly in the *Jātakas*, and the precise and lively details make it seem probable that they were written from experience. These descriptions agree in most particulars. Before setting out over the sands, the caravan halted near the final well, which was always marked by a flag allowing it to be identified from a distance.[23] The caravaneers' water-bottles, and the jars stacked in the cart reserved for carrying water supplies, were filled with fresh water; this commodity was very strictly rationed throughout the crossing.[24] Travelling was done entirely by night, and the convoy started to get under way at sunset. Movement was impossible from the moment when the sun's rays first shone directly on the desert, heating the sand until it was soon red-hot, burning men's feet and animals' hooves alike. So the whole party set up camp at daylight and remained there throughout the day, seated or stretched out in the shade of the circles of parked carts, sleeping or gossiping. Then camp was struck once more with the usual bustle and commotion. As soon as the sand had cooled off slightly, the waiting caravan set off, each man and beast treading in the footsteps of those who had gone before.

The *sārthavāha* engaged a 'land-pilot' (*thalaniyyāmaka* in Pāli). Lying on a mattress in an open wagon at the head of the column, he would watch the stars and find his bearings from them;[25] behind him, the long procession stretched out of sight, sand swirling up from the cart-wheels and sinking under the men's feet. This hazardous march continued throughout the twelve hours of night, twelve hours during which they were all entirely in the pilot's hands. If he should happen to fall asleep, catastrophe resulted: the caravan wandered off course, went round in circles all night and, in daylight, if lucky, found itself at its original point of departure. More probably, the water and food rations were not sufficient to carry men and beasts safely back to fertile territory, and all perished unless the party was fortunate enough to stumble across a water-hole.[26] It was on such occasions that the demons appeared. First, they used all their wicked arts to lead the unfortunate wanderers further away from safety, then it was not long before they were gnawing the corpses and plundering the merchandise heaped in the carts; the bleached bones scattered alongside the various desert tracks seemed so many proofs of demoniacal activities. With the death of the men directly involved came absolute ruin for the merchants who had banked everything on the expedition's success.

II. MERCHANT SHIPPING AND PORT FACILITIES

Those who engaged in commerce by the sea routes ran even greater risks for themselves. Nevertheless, merchant shipping was very active in India and had, ever since Roman times, linked the Mediterranean world to China with great trading vessels (*nāva*), of which the Indian kings owned a fleet, though most of them belonged to wealthy individuals. These ships competed with the fleets of Greece and Rome, Iran and the Arab countries, as well as China's ocean-going vessels. Making use of the winds and the monsoon currents (a discovery attributed wrongly, it seems, to the Greek Hippalos), they had established, since the beginning of the Christian era, a regular service between Rome and the coast of Malabār, and between India and China. The voyage to the western lands took six months; on reaching their destination, the crews waited a year for the monsoon winds to blow in the opposite direction, then set off back again for another six-month voyage.

Merchant vessels are, unfortunately, rarely depicted in Indian art. One fresco in Ajantā does, however, give some details:[27] this particular ship carries three masts of equal height set with rectangular sails and with rigging; it also carries a curiously rigged jib, the upper tip attached to a sort of boom, and the opposite end fixed to a cross-beam set up on the deck. The ship is equipped, in addition, with steadying outriggers, secured between strong, bridged thole-pins on either side of the hull. The hull itself is high and massive, sweeping upwards at each end, the prow and the poop both decorated with pairs of eyes, as though the ship were some monstrous two-headed fish (these great eyes are still to be seen staring from the bows of fishing-boats and junks in several Asiatic countries today). Fore and aft, platforms project over the water, their purpose being presumably to allow the boat to be piloted by pole-soundings through shallow waters. On the aft-deck, jars are stacked together under a canvas canopy. The rather rudimentary pilot's bridge is situated aft of the mizzen-mast. So much for the particular vessel whose reproduction we have been able to study. This ship would also have had a rudder and an anchor. The anchor, when dropped, was able to hold a ship in a stormy sea, and to keep its keel steady in swells and cross-currents.[28] The rudder was strictly under the control of the pilot, and he sealed it whenever he went below decks, so that no one might touch it.[29] Some ships even had a launch slung on the deck to serve as a lifeboat.[30] Ship-building was the prerogative of the carpenters, a fact mentioned already in the *Ṛg Veda*,[31] which gives some indication of the long traditions of their craft. According to Pliny, they were capable of building ships 'of three thousand amphorae' (seventy-five tons burden). But Indian sources claimed even greater achievements for them, mentioning certain vessels large enough to hold from two hundred to seven hundred passengers and crewmen, plus a considerable cargo, cattle, provisions for the journey, abundant supplies of drinking water, and so on.[32]

The most important man on board was the pilot who, 'day and night, with unremitting zeal and sustained efforts',[33] directed the ship's course competently. He had to know all that it was possible to know about the sea, and how to steer by the stars and by watching the flight of birds. These last formed the subject of a special study: their habits were closely watched, and a pilot would often train some birds to fly towards the land but return if the distance was too great. These birds he would keep caged on deck, ready to release them whenever necessary.[34] Buddhist tradition makes great play with the cleverness of the pilots and mentions one who, having lost his sight after years of buffeting by salt spray, still insisted on returning to work and indeed succeeded in piloting his fishing-boat to a miraculous catch of precious stones.[35] The pilots were members of a guild presided over by an 'ancient' (*jeṭṭhaka* in Pāli), and, like the rest of the crew, were hired. The sailors were, it is claimed, fully aware of their inferior status, and were in duty bound to make every honest effort to be worthy of the clothing and food provided for them, and never to be idle.[36]

Long before the departure of an ocean-going vessel, would-be passengers started coming up to the owner or the captain to bargain for berths. Lengthy discussions ensued until the fare was finally agreed upon; this was always high, although no actual scale of charges existed. The passenger was also required to obtain a passport, for which he had to pay a special State tax, and which had also to be stamped with a seal (*agrihītamudrā*) without which the document lacked authority. Before the ship got under way, the crew and passengers made an offering of flowers to the gods and prayed to the divinities of the wind. Then they studied the omens, hoisted white flags to the mast-tops and brought out the oars. Finally, everyone climbed on board to the sound of drums.[37] The gangway of woven rattan was raised and the seven lines mooring the boat to the quayside were cast off. The parents and friends assembled to watch the departure cried out traditional phrases wishing a successful voyage, tears in their eyes. There now began for the travellers what must have been an unpleasant experience, for although no literary sources of that age mention the privations of an ocean crossing, later chronicles describe all the attendant discomforts. Yet many allowed themselves to be 'storm-tossed a long while on the dark seas' (I-Tsing).

The lack of space and comfort on board was nothing compared with the endless near-catastrophes that are described extensively in ancient texts in terms of awe that betray a perfectly legitimate fear. The travellers of those days had every reason to dread the waves 'which roar like thunder', the ocean 'immeasurable and infinite, with no coast in sight, shaken to its very depths, roaring with a great din, and filled with a profusion of fish, monsters and dragons of all kinds'.[38] The Chinese pilgrim I-tsing[39] expressed eloquently his terror when faced with the constant nearness of the abyss and the waves 'as high as mountains, damming the sea and stretching across the vast gulf. The billows rose into the sky like clouds.' The storms which occurred frequently along the Indian coasts at certain seasons made a deep impression on the popular imagination.

The ships underwent a tremendous battering at times. Hulls were often stove in by the waves' furious onslaught, or sprang leaks which gradually filled the hold with water and sent the ship to the bottom. The men on board, powerless to remedy this desperate situation, abandoned themselves to lamentations, tears and prayer. Their supplications were directed especially towards the goddess Maṇimekhalā,[40] assigned by the thirty-three gods the task of saving those of pure heart but, equally, of drowning sinners pitilessly. After a shipwreck, the sea grew red with the blood of the wretches devoured by man-eating fish or giant turtles. There were rarely any survivors.[41] Merchant ships ran the additional risk of being chased and boarded by the pirates and privateers who infested the Indian coastal waters, uncouth creatures existing on plunder and shrinking from no cruelty or outrage. To afford better protection against such attacks, ships often sailed in convoy.

But storms and pirates were not the only causes for fear: a dead calm could be just as menacing if it continued for a long time, and then the crew and passengers gradually exhausted their provisions as they lay becalmed under a leaden sun, eventually, perhaps, to die of thirst and hunger. Faced with such ominous possibilities, they had no remedy but to choose a sacrificial victim by ballot and abandon him in the middle of the ocean on a bamboo raft:[42] this offering would immediately induce the trade-winds to fill the sails once more.

Folk-tales were kept supplied with innumerable mythical or legendary episodes. One out of the many tells how a convoy of ships encountered a gigantic monster, the *timiṅgala*, which lived in the middle of the ocean and whose appetite was insatiable. Glaring with eyes that filled the crew with terror, it opened its gulf-like jaws so wide that the sea was sucked in, foaming and swirling. The ships were drawn irresistibly towards this maelstrom, quite unable to escape the current which pulled them inexorably into the monster's belly where they were ground to shreds.[43]

Despite such horrors, merchants continued to sail the seas in ever-increasing numbers. A famous legend[44] has as its hero the son of a wealthy Indian businessman, forced to confront the dangers of a shipwreck on the coast of Ceylon, at a point infested with ogresses. Possessing the magic gift of changing themselves into beautiful maidens, these repulsive creatures lured the castaways into their arms, then devoured them with sharp teeth. While his companions succumbed to their charms, the young merchant had the strength of spirit and the boldness to flee, thanks to the miraculous assistance of a horse sent by the gods; he duly returned at the head of an army to exterminate the ogresses and conquer the island, which thereafter knew a happy and peaceful existence. This is only a legend but it contains a grain of truth: Indian culture in overseas countries was indeed most often planted by merchants who had made the journey from their motherland, although, unlike the heroes of legend, they seldom used armed force to impose their presence, preferring simply to set up trading-posts.

They all ran great risks, but in point of fact most voyagers crossed the oceans without any misfortune ever befalling them;[45] many of them accomplished prolonged coastal navigations and returned safe and sound to the village of their birth to enjoy their hard-earned wealth. Orthodox brāhmaṇism condemned sea voyages, so most maritime enterprises originated in areas influenced by Buddhism. Indeed, brāhmaṇs who 'crossed the waters' were excluded from their caste, and we have already seen the tragic consequences of such a sanction (see pp. 24–5); members of other castes were denied funeral rites, a penalty equivalent to excommunication. There seems no doubt that the merchants belonged mostly to the moneyed *bourgeoisie* which had developed under the influence of Buddhism, where such prejudices had been abolished.

Commerce obeyed a series of rules which constituted the maritime law of the time. In most cases, the ships belonged not to the captain (who was the person most would-be passengers dealt with) but to an owner who fitted-out the ship and paid the captain to transport his cargo; it was the owner who eventually received the fares charged for passage. Sometimes, several merchants bought one or more parts of a boat from its owner and so became shareholders in it; they then shared in the profits to the extent of their financial participation, speculating both on a successful crossing and on the cargo being sold.[46] Since charges were extremely high, both for passengers and freight, the return was excellent, amounting sometimes to twenty per cent of the sum advanced for a single trip.[47] Loans were often made at exorbitant rates, and because of the enormous risks involved they sometimes carried as much as two hundred and forty per cent interest.

A complex code governed all sea and river traffic in India, which was supervised by a ministry (*nāvādhyakṣa*) whose authority extended equally to vessels on the high seas and the ferry-boats running services between opposite sides of the great rivers. This ministry was charged with suppressing acts of piracy; collecting harbour-dues, and taxes on fishing (a sixth of the actual haul); ensuring that assistance and repairs were provided for boats damaged by storms; and sending aid to shipwrecked sailors. All coastal villages and ports were obliged to organize a rescue service and to have at their disposal the necessary equipment; buoys, dinghies, barks, tree-trunks, rafts. Any refusal to lend aid was punishable by law. When goods were found to be spoiled through the effects of sea-water, the minister had the authority to fix a lower rate of taxation for the consignment in question.

It appears that the main ports were quite well equipped. In the approaches, towers were built, carrying lanterns that were lit at night as a guide for ships trying to enter harbour. But, usually, vessels berthed during the day, and one approaching harbour at nightfall would usually ride at anchor in deep water until sunrise. Docks were wide enough for ships to enter under almost full sail; dredging operations kept them open throughout the year and stone walls and breakwaters protected them against the action of the sea. A seaport would burst into frenzied activity when a merchant vessel arrived at the quayside and threw anchor.[48] Merchandise began to pile up on all sides: sacks of pepper, heaps of fresh or dried fish, mountains of rice, leather-covered bales, wax-stoppered jars, packages containing gold or precious stones. Covered boats ferried goods to the quayside from ships which had not found berthing space. The faint roar of the surf complemented the cries of the dockers as they hurried in every direction, bent double under their heavy loads. Near the quay stretched lines of warehouses, separated by streets which were also encumbered by piles of crates, bundles and bales.

A customs office was always to be found in the vicinity, and its activities continued throughout the day.

River traffic was equally active. Boats and ships were constructed solidly, dovetailing of the timbers being a usual practice. The rivers carried a great deal of traffic, and huge fleets of boats, belonging either to the State or to wealthy merchants, played a major part in transporting goods from one part of the country to another.

III. PRODUCTS, EXPORTS, IMPORTS

Thanks to the vigorous movement of goods throughout India, there was a constant interchange of all sorts of merchandise, ranging from the humblest commodity to the rarest luxury. The national product was supplemented by goods and materials conveyed through India in transit, the origin of which was not revealed to the consignee, so that the Indian merchants could retain exclusive sales rights. Apparently, exports exceeded imports by a large margin: India had the advantage of producing all its own essential commodities and, in addition, being able to provide many local products which were much in demand by its foreign customers as luxuries – ivory, fine woods, precious stones, perfumes and spices.

The market in ivory was particularly important. There was a constant demand from foreign countries, in addition to the needs of Indian high society, whose potentates made great use of this beautiful, easily workable and versatile substance. From it were fashioned bed and table legs, handles and knobs of everyday objects such as mirrors, flywhisks and sceptres, ornamentation for chairs, ceremonial carriages, the walls of elegant houses, sword hilts and scabbards, combs, brooches, hairpins, boxes and coffers, cages for rare birds, bindings for manuscripts, musical instruments, and so on. As can be seen, the country itself absorbed a great deal of the ivory that came on the market after being secured by elephant hunters (see pp. 99–101). Even so, India's ivory exports remained large enough to rival those of Africa in the international markets.

India was also famous for the quality of its precious stones and pearls, which were traded in several ports, particularly Barigaza (present-day Broach) near Bombay. The pearls came mostly from Ceylon, but large-scale pearl-fisheries existed on all parts of the Indian coast, in the Ganges estuary and in the southern areas alike. For these things, too, the Indian kings and princes were the primary customers; in fact it was a point of honour with the aristocracy to be perfect connoisseurs in the appreciation of gems (*ratnaparīkṣā*, a science developed some time before the sixth century).[49] Apart from these domestic buyers, a whole host of Iranian and Western merchants were constantly in India to buy gems and pearls for resale in their own countries. The sums paid were sometimes fantastically high, and settlement was often made in gold coinage, resulting in a serious drain on the resources of the Roman treasury in India's favour, during the era when Roman society was abandoning itself to wild extravagance (much to the disgust of the country's philosophers).

India continued to produce great amounts of precious and semi-precious stones whose quality remained superior to those from other sources, including diamonds, agates, onyxes, sards, chrysophrases, green or red jaspers, cats' eyes, purple amethysts, rock crystal, opals, rubies, sapphires, emeralds, beryls, blue or green aquamarines (the latter kind being the most in demand), zircons, tourmalins and turquoises (from Turkestan), etc. Indian jewellers made lavish use of all these gems in their designs, yet there remained plenty for exportation. At home, the jewellers led a most profitable existence despite the special government supervision to which they were subjected.

India also extracted from its own natural resources several products much in demand by foreign customers, particularly buffalo and rhinoceros horn and teeth, tortoiseshell (from the south), mother-of-pearl from oysters and certain other sea-shells, the flesh of giant lizards (preserved in brine) whose properties were much in demand by Western physicians, and even by cooks in search of novelty. One of the country's most flourishing industries concerned the extraction of a red dye and also the lac called shellac from the insect *Tachardia lacca*. Its own consumption was enormous, since this dye served both to colour fabrics – those worn in springtime by young women and symbolizing love – and to be applied on the body itself, especially the soles of the feet. At the same time, the export of this dye and shellac sometimes assumed an extraordinary importance, particularly when imperial Rome was in need of purple.

Apart from its native products, India specialized in transhipping certain commodities which the caravans brought as far as its ports; in this way, trading in skins and furs took place on Indian soil although these came principally from the Himalayan regions and Tibet. Indian ships carried westward magnificent tiger-skins, lion-skins and leopard-skins, as well as bales of skins of the marten and weasel from Tibet. Woollen fabrics, made of goat's hair or sheep's wool grown in Bhutan and Tibet, were woven in Kashmīr and transported from there to Iran and the Mediterranean countries, either by caravan or by sea. Silk was imported from China (where the secret of the animal origin of this material was successfully guarded for a long time) and transformed into luxurious fabrics, especially very fine gauzes. The Indians used a large proportion of these fine fabrics themselves, but still manufactured enough to export vast quantities. They also wove cotton (*Cossypium herbaceum*) which they grew themselves and made into fragile muslins that were then dyed in beautiful colours; this industry, in which they excelled, ensured the prosperity of many regions of India, but particularly Gujarāt, eastern Bengal (Dacca), and the entire south (Trichinopoly, Tanjore, Masulipatam, etc.). These fabrics, and also carded cotton intended for stuffing cushions and mattresses, were exported to Egypt, where the most important textile market was held, despite the fact that Indian cotton-goods were competing there with similar imports from the Near East.

Another valuable export was that of precious woods, which India produced in great quantities: teak (*Tectona grandis*), grown along the coast of Malabār in *kanara* country, in Travancore and Gujarāt, whose resistance to the action of salt water made it an ideal timber for constructional purposes; ebony (the *diospyros* of the Greeks), sent mostly to the Persian Gulf, where it had to compete with the Ethiopian production of that wood; various kinds of 'black wood' sold as ebony to unwary customers, a practice allowing genuine ebony to maintain its high price while still providing substantial profits from the sale of substitutes. Rosewood (*Dalbergia latifolia*) in its different varieties, in great demand for the construction of furniture, came from the coast of Coromandel and was sent to Broach for sale. Sandalwood (*candana* in Sanskrit, the *Santalum album*) grew in southern India (Mysore, Chimbatore and Salem) and was used for fashioning precious objects and for providing an essence used in making perfumes.

Perfumes and incense still have a tremendous importance, of course, in the East, where they are as essential for religious ceremonies as for private use. Apart from sandalwood, India exported gums and resins (myrrh, balsam, aloes, cinnabar, etc.)

which served also as colouring matters, condiments or medicaments; there was also an export trade in fragrant garlands made of various berries, flowers and leaves (laurel, rose, etc.), light metals, horn, coloured silks, all saturated in perfumed unguents, and plaited together with the aid of decorative gold thread. One of the most sought-after perfumes was musk, extremely popular in India itself among fashionable beauties and 'dandies' alike. Extracted from Chinese or Tibetan goats that were either caught in nets or else hunted with bow and arrow, it was transported in bladders placed inside tightly sealed vases; despite this protection, the humidity of the sea was apt to spoil it and the musk most in demand was that which had made the long journey from Tibet entirely by caravan.

The market in spices was equally lucrative. The most important of these were the various peppers (*Pipper nigrum*, *P. longus*, *P. officianarum*) harvested for the most part along the coast of Malabār and in Travancore, and exported chiefly to Alexandria for re-exportation to all the Mediterranean countries. The Arabs had long since secured for themselves a monopoly in the importation of India's crops of ginger (*Zingiber officinale*) which was transported in jars and served as a stomachic and as a medicament. The same applied to cinnamon (camphor as well as cinnamon-bark) whose resale was also in the hands of the Arabs. Cinnamon was considered a luxury commodity, and was used for many purposes, for condiments, for the protection of clothing against moths, for perfumery (incense) and for medicine. It was exported raw, the cinnamon barks and camphor leaves being packed separately. The oil-extracting process was carried out in Syria; the finished product was used to perfume wine and also formed an ingredient in the sauce accompanying oysters in Rome. Cardamom (*Elettaria cardamomum*), produced in southern India, was also highly prized and expensive. Costus-root (*Saussurea lappa*, *kuṣṭha* in Sanskrit) was, like cinnamon and cardamom, processed in Syria and was used for similar purposes.

Then came the different kinds of nard, of which spikenard was the most costly (*nalada* in Sanskrit), but which included *Cymbopogon schoenanthus*, *Andropogon muricatus* and many other varieties. Both their roots and their leaves were used in perfumery, in cooking and in medicine; the oil extracted from the plants was so precious that it was kept in small jars of alabaster or onyx.

South India had the competition of Ethiopia and southern Arabia in the preparation of this aromatic essence. Mention should also be made of cloves (*Caryophyllus aromaticus* or *Eugena caryophyllata*); sesame (*Sesamum indicum*); indigo – which was used not only for paints and dyes but also for the preparation of certain remedies; varieties of barberry, (*Berberis floribunda*, *B. aristata*, *B. lycium*); opium and rhubarb were perhaps exported. Sugar cane (*ikṣu* in Sanskrit) was exported in small quantities, as were rice (*vṛhi* in Sanskrit, *ariśi* in Tamil), millet and oats, these commodities being in demand only by Indian expeditions abroad. Ghee, a clarified butter (*ghṛta* in Sanskrit) was exported to East Africa, where this product of cow's or she-buffalo's milk was used as a medicine; in India itself it was a basic cooking ingredient and was also used in religious services. Finally, some fruits, such as coconuts, bananas, melons, peaches and apricots, and some varieties of cucumber and onion, reached the Mediterranean ports from India, but do not appear to have formed part of the cargoes made up specifically for regular exportation.

Many other commodities could be added to this already long list. India, for example, manufactured high-quality side-arms, for the country's smiths knew how to forge iron and even claimed to know the secret of steel.[50] The Indians made little effort to export weapons, and the arms traffic was mainly in the hands of the Arabs, Parthians and Syrians. But they did export metals, particularly brass, including a white brass resembling silver, and large quantities of good-quality gold obtained from the alluvial deposits of the Ganges and from the gold-bearing sands in southern regions (Mysore).

Other merchandise sent abroad consisted of animals: talking parrots, tame monkeys, pheasants, snakes and elephants, all of which found places in the private zoos of Western kings and emperors. Since sea-travel affected them adversely, they were usually transported by caravan.

Slaves, too, constituted a profitable international market, the major part of it under the control of the Arabs, who furnished 'Greek' women to the Indians, and 'Indian' women to the Greeks, the further the distance of their supposed place of origin the higher being the price to the buyer. Most of the women brought to India in this way were dancers or musicians, or else were imported specially to act as military guards in the royal harems.

India benefited also from the resale to her own customers, at substantial profits, of products imported from a third nation. China sent musk, tung oil, amber, cinnabar, raw and woven silk, hemp matting and cloth, all sorts of ceramic, lacquered and copper objects, wooden combs, paper, parasols, iron cooking vessels, sieves, needles and saddles. From the Khmer country, many valuable products were imported to supplement India's own output, particularly sandalwood, teak and aloes, cardamom, beeswax, kapok flock and kingfishers' feathers. Sumatra and Java furnished gold and musk. The Malay peninsula exported silver and tin (called 'white lead' in those times) from its well-developed mines; it also sold the finest nutmeg, logwood and ivory.

India imported horses for the use of her warrior-nobles and, in particular, the king. The cavalry was one of the four army corps, and the king traditionally acquired the finest horses available, sometimes for enormous prices.[51] One of the principal sources for these animals was Upper Asia, more precisely Khotān, whose horse-dealers undertook long and dangerous journeys during the dry season, driving before them five hundred or more head destined for the princely courts of India – and with the certainty of large profits awaiting them. The stablemen who had accompanied them were usually hired by the new owners to continue looking after the horses. The honesty of the dealers was suspect: among other things, they were accused of stealing, on their way back home, the best animals they had sold on the way out.[52]

During the entire period covered by the expansion of Rome, products of Mediterranean origin continued to come into India. These included red coral from Sicily, Sardinia and Corsica, the Balearic islands, Spain and North Africa; copper, tin, antimony, realgar, silver vessels and lamps, bronze containers; yellow amber, which came also from the Baltic and was usually exchanged for precious stones; Egyptian emeralds; glassware from Alexandria, Tyre and Sidon; and above all, the grape wine which India imported from various countries.[53] Along the south-east coast the wine came from Italy, notably Arezzo, as can be proved by the amphoras, cups and plates excavated at Virampatnam, all of which carry the marks of well-known potters;[54] similar amphoras have been recovered at Taxila (in present-day Pakistān). Along the west coast, wine imports provided the main traffic for the ports of Barigaza (Broach) and Muziris,[55] where they were exchanged for gold, pepper, spices and pearls. Wine was also brought in from Laodicea and Arabia,[56] and large supplies came from Iran and the regions under Persian influence such as Bactria,[57] Kāpiśa[58] and Kashmīr. Vines did exist in their wild state in some regions of India,[59] but it seems that the Indians had not learnt how to cultivate them, except in Kashmīr; the seventh-century Chinese pilgrim Hsüan-Ch'uang mentions vineyards in that region, and earlier Strabo[60] had referred to large jars with wax-sealed stoppers for storing wine.

When Rome collapsed, Iran took over a great part of her trade with eastern Asia, and India began to turn deliberately towards the countries of the southern seas. Western commodities became rare or disappeared from India's markets, but there was no slackening in their activity, and such goods were replaced by large quantities of spices amd many other products from the Pacific.

In the towns and villages, the tradesmen usually occupied a particular district whose streets were lined with covered stalls. These were very similar to those of today, lines of small shops with verandas that were raised slightly above street level. Opening right on to the street, they were crammed close together, separated by no more than the thickness of a post. The open fronts were closed at night with removable shutters. The merchant lived with his family on the floor above, in tiny rooms, or else in living quarters behind the shop on the other side of an inner courtyard.[61] Throughout the day, he sat cross-legged on the wooden floor, in the middle of his shop, scantily clad because of the heat and stuffiness prevailing in the cramped quarters, and usually bare-headed. The principal tradesmen, in town and village alike, were the milkman, the spice-merchant, the oil-merchant, the perfumer and the tavern-keeper.

The milkman was surrounded by containers of all shapes and sizes, and drew the curds from a deep pan with the aid of a long-handled ladle, pouring it into a small copper measuring vessel before selling it to his customers. The spice-seller's shop was encumbered with jars, dishes and pots, stacked in piles, while the walls were fitted with shelves holding more containers; boxes and bags dangled from poles within his reach.[62] The oil-merchant used a press which was set up in the back of his shop; it was subject to the tax levied upon professional tools and equipment.

Perfumers (*gandhika*) were credited with being capable of enumerating the different essences in a perfume by smelling it.[63] They sold sticks of sandalwood, myrrh and various kinds of incense; oils and perfumes with a base of sandalwood, musk or camphor, or extracted from roots, seeds or plants such as ginger, saffron, cinnamon, and so on; powders and pastes of sandalwood, pine, aloes or saffron, used to smear over the body after bathing, or indeed at any hour of the day or night, obtained by rasping the moistened wood or stem with a smooth stone; all of these commodities existed in numerous varieties and qualities, ranging from cheap and common products to the finest and costliest rarities. In addition, perfumers sold many different resins and gums extracted from the essences yielded by various aromatic trees and transformed into incense or paste for decorating and perfuming the body. Lac-dye – which must not be confused with lacquer, the resin of *Rhus venicifera* – was intended for staining the soles of the feet and the palms of the hands; its use was so fashionable that a whole industry sprang up to extract the colouring matter from the lac insect. Perfumers also had available for their customers, male as well as female, various eye-salves with an antimony base, as well as pills to cure bad breath, composed of camphor, saffron, musk, cardamom, cloves, all ground to powder, mixed with mango-juice and moulded into small balls. A combination of nard, gum benjamin, saffron, sandalwood, pine resin, camphor, myrrh, etc., all blended with honey and moulded into small discs or sticks, was used to perfume rooms and clothing by fumigation. To secure provisions for their stores, perfumers were assiduous clients of the caravans, thanks to which those products necessary to the production of perfumes, cosmetics and incenses circulated throughout the entire country. The extraction of lac-dye and resinous lacquer provided a means of living for a great number of peasants, because of the steadily increasing demand.

Tavern-keeping was a very different matter; although perfectly legal, this trade had a poor reputation. Every village had at least one tavern, identifiable by the flag it flew. The towns contained many taverns, grouped in the same district, but sufficiently spaced out to prevent them being side by side. They were often decorated and furnished in style, and contained several courtyards, rooms fitted with seats and couches, and also counters where perfumes, flowers and garlands could be bought. It was a lucrative business, for the sale of fermented and alcoholic drinks continued throughout the day and well into the night. The customers ate salt with their drinks to encourage their thirst; salt was an expensive commodity and under State control (see p. 109).[64] Most of the clientele were recruited from among the criminal classes, thieves, robbers and confidence tricksters; mingling with these characters were the king's spies, secret agents, and all those hoping to glean some news or information that might be passed on to interested parties in exchange for money. Quarrels were easily and quickly sparked, and the tavern-owner needed to be strong and firm enough to be able to eject any of his customers who became too boisterous. He was also obliged to pay an indemnity to anyone who was robbed while lying drunk in his establishment. The tavern was supplied by distillers, who extracted wines from palm, coconut and sugar cane. Despite religious interdictions, the consumption of intoxicating drinks was widespread among those of low caste, although wines and spirits were subject to heavy taxes.

To weigh their merchandise, tradesmen used scales (*tulā*) similar in form to the steelyard which is still used throughout India. The scales were composed of a single pan suspended by small chains from one end of a graduated arm. This arm was kept horizontal by means of a ring sliding along the notched stick, and moved along the notches until the arm's longer free section counterbalanced the shorter laden one. These standardized graduation marks guaranteed that the weight was true.[65] Usually, the seller weighed the merchandise first, then replaced it in the scale-pan by weights whose value he counted on his fingers, starting, in the Eastern manner, with the little finger; in this way, the buyer, too, could assure himself of the fairness of the price he had been asked to pay. In ancient times, the weights seem to have been made of stone. The size of the scales and the length of the tally varied according to the type of merchandise, the goldsmith's scales being smaller than the spice-merchant's. When heavy weights were involved, the public scales were used; these were of a different type, being suspended from a cross-beam by the centre of the balance-arm from each tip of which a pan dangled;[66] this more advanced form of scales seems to have appeared first in the sixth century.

Every four months, an inspector of weights and measures tested the accuracy of all scales and marked them with a stamp for which the tradesmen paid a tax. If the official discovered a falsification, he denounced the offender who was then prosecuted.

Payment was effected both in coins and in cowrie-shells (see p. 110), but merchandise was often bartered instead. Prices were fixed by a commissioner (*agghakāraka* in Pāli) on all common goods and on those goods under State monopoly. Traditionally, price commissioners negotiated bribes both from the king and from the merchants with a view to raising, lowering or maintaining price-levels, as the case might be. Haggling was as highly developed an art then as it is now, throughout the East, giving full rein to competition and to fraud but also making allowance for local tradition and custom. Bargaining was conducted in a rather unusual way: seller and buyer sat side by side, silently, touching each other's hands; particular pressures of the fingers according to a pre-arranged code allowed them to keep the amount of their transaction secret.[67] As soon as agreement was reached, the merchandise was delivered to the buyer's home, either by the merchant or by a porter. In the latter case, the buyer was responsible for indemnifying the porter if the latter suffered an accident on the way – unless, of course, negligence could be proved.

Besides the trades established on premises, there were, just as today, hordes of pedlars perambulating the villages and towns, crying their wares in nasal sing-song voices; they carried their goods on trays or in baskets balanced on top of their heads, or else suspended at the ends of a carrying-pole balanced on one shoulder, a method of porterage still in use today and very frequently represented in ancient iconography. Their improvised stands were made of rattan, and carried about with them until set up in a suitable spot. Some sold fragrant powders for the bath, colouring pastes for the body, incense and perfumes, cosmetics and flowers. Many posted themselves near bathing-pools, or along the banks of rivers where people came to bathe.[68] Others offered garlands and bouquets of flowers, ripe fruits, cakes and betel leaves. Often, licensed tradesmen hired these pedlars to hawk their merchandise, thus ensuring wider distribution and increased sales.

THE MANUAL CRAFTS

Commerce was supplied in great measure by the productions of local handicrafts. The practice of small crafts enabled most villages to exist in financial independence, without any need to seek outside assistance except in emergency. Nearly all craftsmen held shop on the same site as their workshop and could equally well be considered tradespeople.

Their social status varied considerably. Those who worked leather and skins, for instance, were particularly despised because they used the hides of dead animals – a defilement permitted only to an outcaste. Yet their occupation was of the greatest usefulness and importance: they fashioned shoes, and the thonged sandals which were the king's prerogative, and, in the countries of northern India, footgear for the warrior-nobles, hunters and grooms. They also furnished straps for various purposes, leather pouches for dredging water from wells, hunters' game-pouches,[69] the bindings for certain musical instruments, the skin-covered frames with which fruit in orchards was protected from dust,[70] and finally, leather garments, saddles, shields, etc.[71] Curriers used various sorts of leather, depending upon the objects being made; they tanned the skins of the cow, buffalo, goat and sheep, certain wild animals such as the tiger and hyena, and even the dog. Because they exercised a condemned craft they were liable to a supplementary tax.

On the other hand, carpenters were on a far higher social level because they constructed houses and wagons, and so were involved in ritual matters (see pp. 127–31). For their raw material, they went into the forests, which must have been far more extensive in those days. There they looked for the foresters whose arduous task consisted in chopping trees down, as well as caring for them on behalf of the State; if the foresters could not provide them with the wood they needed, the carpenters cut it themselves, following precise rules governing the type of wood to be used for a particular purpose. They sometimes used elephants specially trained to roll and carry logs and tree-trunks and to load them on the wagons.[72] They were careful not to chop a tree down before prudently warning the god who was presumed to live in it, and before offering him a sacrifice, they spoke to him in these words: 'May the god who lives in this tree leave it, and may the blame for dislodging him not fall on us.' After which, their consciences clear, they secured a thick rope around the trunk to direct its fall.[73] They sawed the logs and planks which they needed, numbering the segments carefully so that the timber-work commissioned from them could be finished and fitted as quickly as possible.[74] They then piled the lengths of wood into their wagons and took the load to the spot where the construction was to take place. There was never any lack of work: apart from buildings, they also constructed beds and chairs; wooden sandals inlaid with tinsel, or even with precious stones; chests and coffers; toys of all kinds, including spinning-tops. And they built ships, boats and vehicles of all kinds, including – if we are to credit the descriptions in rather later texts – flying machines![75] But their basic activity remained the construction of buildings.

Although their position in the social scale was rather more lowly, masons, stone-cutters and pavers were akin to the carpenters. Their bricks were often prepared and baked by the foresters; the stones were quarried, or recovered from abandoned villages[76] and reshaped by the stone-cutters for re-use. The bricks, stone blocks and paving-stones were loaded on to carts drawn by a pair of humped oxen; once arrived at the work-site, the animals were unyoked and, while a porter carried basket-loads on his head or shoulder between the cart and building-site, the pavers squatted on the ground, arranging the material on the prepared ground in regular patterns.[77]

Two other trades were indispensable to rural life, those of the blacksmith and the potter.

The blacksmith's anvil echoed all day long. Standing near his furnace which was filled with white-hot ore, he held iron bars over the fire with the aid of long pincers and then hammered, cut, twisted, drew out and shaped the glowing metal. It was claimed that some smiths knew how to turn iron into steel. Metallurgy had reached a remarkable state of development in ancient India: the iron column discovered at Dhārā (dating back to 321 AD), over forty feet high, and that of King Candragupta II in Delhī (fifth century) prove that in those eras the Indians already knew how to found far greater masses of iron than the European foundries attempted to handle prior to the second half of the nineteenth century. As for Indian steel, it was known to the Greeks and the Persians, and very probably to the Egyptians too.[78] Unfortunately, the technique is nowhere described; if one were to believe Kālidāsa (fifth century), the process consisted solely of beating the iron with a steel hammer![79] The blacksmith's trade was a good one, for it formed a basic adjunct to other professions indispensable to everyday existence. For the farmers he fashioned ploughshares, chains, spades, sickles and ox-goads. The carpenters came to him to buy axes,[80] hammers,[81] saws,[82] augers and bolts. The hunters were among his best customers, needing strong knives, hunting-spears and matchets for hacking out a path through the dense jungle. He supplied the barbers with razors[83] and the tailors with needles. His skill was sometimes so great that he was equally competent to make weapons and coats of mail, nail-scissors and surgical instruments, and cooking utensils of iron, tin, copper, zinc and lead.

The potter was at least as busy as the smith, since his products were in constant demand by townspeople and country folk alike. His equipment, although fairly rudimentary, was subject to tax. His technique was simple in the extreme.[84] He got blocks of clay from the shores of some nearby lake,[85] moulded the clay in water first of all, then mixed it with cinders and cow-dung. The paste thus formed was placed on a solid wheel whose hub revolved on a low axle standing on the ground.[86] The potter sat on the ground in the room specially reserved for this use (*kammasālā* in Pāli), and with great dexterity set the wheel turning by simple pressure of his foot against the shaft. He then began shaping the moist compound, while the wheel's rotation gradually endowed it with shape and symmetry. The pots were put to dry in an enclosure. The baking process was fairly primitive, kilns being unknown: the pottery was simply ranged along a shallow trench (*pacanasālā* in Pāli), alternating with piles of wood which were ignited, to complete the baking process already started by the sun's heat. There was no question of adding glaze or other refinements. Village pottery was restricted to a few more or less archaic types, decorated with very simple engraved or painted designs, but they were beautifully shaped and well proportioned, with no superfluous ornamentation.

When they were ready, they were lined up in a storeroom (*bhāṇḍasālā* in Pāli) while a first selection was exposed for sale in the shop (*paṇiyasālā* in Pāli). The potter was a familiar sight as he bent over his wheel, or, still smeared with clay, squatted on a pile of straw gulping down a soup in which a few balls of rice floated.[87] Or he could be seen perambulating the streets, almost invisible under his load of brand-new pots, crying: 'Water jars for sale.'[88] Among all the articles he fashioned for modest prices, only a few were designed for drinking and eating, for such utensils had to be broken after being used once only. The greater part of his output was of containers for carrying water and for storing household linen or grain, and consequently some of the pots and jars were very large. As excavations in the Pondicherry area have brought to light,[89] potters in some regions also executed large funeral jars and earthenware coffins (see p. 210). They also fashioned the earthenware dolls and playthings which were so widespread throughout ancient India,[90] sacred vases used in the sanctuaries and for religious ceremonies, as well as the begging-bowls used by mendicant monks.

The work of the basket-makers, too, provided articles that were basic necessities.[91] This work was often done by women, though the basket-makers had their place on the list of craft trades. They gathered their raw material from the sides of ponds, lakes and rivers[92] and produced a great variety of objects: sieves and brooms, used in every household, wealthy or humble;[93] boxes of all kinds, in which the mistress of the house kept her finery; countless types of hamper, basket and tray, whose shape and size varied according to the purpose for which they were required. With plaited grass (*darbha* or *muñja*), they made sacks, cords[94] and sandals (*muñjapādukā*). They also wove reed or rush matting whose uses were manifold: as roofing material, as separating walls inside houses, as garden fences, or as floor-covering for living-rooms. They wove umbrellas, very similar to those still used in south-east India, which gave protection equally well from the sun or the rain;[95] and light-weight fans to provide relief from the heat, in forms almost identical to those made in India today.[96] In addition, they constructed palanquins from bamboo slats; these had handles at each end and might be used to transport a holy man (*ācārya*), a child, or a gravely ill ascetic (*sādhu*).

Weaving and the clothing industries were highly developed.[97] Wool from the sheep and the goat, cotton, the bark of certain trees, the floss of the silk-cotton tree (*bombax*), hemp, flax, silk (which had been in regular use since the Vedic era),[98] antelope hair, and various grasses were all spun or woven. Cotton was carded with the aid of a bow, this work being carried out by women after they had first removed the seeds from the cotton-bolls. Indian weavers had a long tradition of dexterity in handling their looms (*veman*); they stretched out the warps of the cloth they were weaving with the aid of wooden pegs (*mayūkha*) and were famous for the speed with which they could make the shuttle (*tasara*) dart to and fro. Using the same means, they could create fabrics tough enough to serve as tent-cloth and others fragile enough to tremble in the least breath of wind,[99] gossamer-like muslins (Banāras), materials of staple fibre (Bengal, the Puṇḍra country, Assam), warm, soft woollens (Kashmīr); sometimes they wove blends of silk and gold thread. The dyers imparted beautiful colours to these fabrics, employing a great diversity of vegetable and mineral extracts.[100] Finally, embroiderers embellished the most luxurious of these fabrics. This entire industry was closely controlled by an 'overseer of threads', who had absolute authority over the spinning and weaving shops and over all such work undertaken at home; he regulated the output as well as working conditions. A tax was levied on all gear and equipment, especially the weaving-loom.

Laundrymen were sometimes dyers as well, and worked from shop premises (*rayagasālā*). They cleaned the materials entrusted to them by first moistening them with a preparation of soda, then warming them in front of a fire and rinsing them in fresh water. Laundering was done in the water of rivers or pools, the linen being beaten by slapping it hard against flat stones, brushing it and rubbing it, just as it is still done today. When he had finished, the laundryman would always perfume the linen before returning it to his customers. If he spoilt or ruined the material entrusted to him he had to pay compensation and damages, the amount depending on the extent of the damage.

The tailors also exercised a lucrative profession, despite the fact that everyday clothing was neither cut nor sewn, except for monks' habits, and the jackets and breeches of hunters and grooms. They cut their cloth, made alterations and sewed diligently, measuring the cloth with a graduated rule, sewing with needles bought from the blacksmith and kept safe in a bamboo case. Indeed, their competence was so great that they were generally regarded with some mistrust: unscrupulous tailors were known to give a new appearance to old garments by cunning piecing and patching, by rubbing the seams smooth with a round shell and then by dyeing the refashioned cloth brilliant but deceptive colours. At the first washing the fabric would invariably lose its freshness and turn into an unusable rag.[101]

Certain trades were connected directly with the arts, and these included sculptors in wood or ivory, goldsmiths and jewellers, makers of stringed and other musical instruments, and even those who fashioned garlands. Sculptors in wood usually worked in collaboration with carpenters. Sculptors in ivory were highly considered by their contemporaries, and justly so. They were equally adept at working in the mass and in bas-relief, cutting and engraving with a delicate and sure hand. They preferred to use ivory cut from living elephants rather than that acquired from dead animals.[102] Despite the tax on ivory, amounting to fifty per cent of its controlled price, they were always prepared to pay the highest rates for it, since their finished products were invariably sold immediately. They fashioned statues, bed and chair legs, handles for looking-glasses and flywhisks, game dice, and illustrated or ornamented plaques, either solid or perforated, designed as facings for furniture and coffers or even to cover the entire walls of great houses and palaces. Some magnificent specimens, going back to the first two centuries of the Christian era, have come down to us, thanks to the excavations undertaken in Afghānistān by Joseph and Ria Hackin during 1936–7 and 1939–40.[103] This discovery, the first of its kind, shows us that the art of the Indian workers in ivory was remarkable both as regards technique and aesthetic refinement. These craftsmen were also expert at carving horn,[104] shells and bone, particularly monkey's bones, used frequently for children's necklaces.[105]

The goldsmiths, also, handled substantial business. The gold they used was either mined from lodes in rocks or panned from the sandy shallows of rivers. All day long, gold beaters hammered the ingots into thin leaves. The goldsmiths tested their metals by fire, using little crucibles, specimens of which have been found in excavations; they knew the secrets of alloying, the techniques of gilding and silvering, the process of inlaying precious and semi-precious stones.[106] They could detect debased metals by testing the gold or silver against a touchstone. However, since their skilfulness also enabled them to fashion fake touchstones and artificial pearls, obtaining the latter by use of a mercury alloy, their honesty was not always entirely above suspicion, and for this reason the State exercised a strict control over their business. When a goldsmith was employed by a private client he worked in his patron's own house, an arrangement which allowed the client to keep a sharp eye on him.

A specifically Indian trade was that of the garland-makers (*mālākāra*), who were numerous and well regarded; they employed as a sales force hordes of down-and-outs who made a living of some sort out of peddling garlands. Each of these *mālākāras* owned a flower garden. After turning the soil and planting for the first time, he could expect to obtain a really fine selection of blooms after three or four years of constant attention.[107] Every evening, carrying two jars filled with water, he watered the plants;[108] throughout the year he tended them carefully. Every morning, he entered his garden accompanied by his daughters, to cut the flowers needed for that day's work; the cut flowers were placed in special baskets.[109] Together, they fashioned the garlands (*mālās*) in any one of the great variety of patterns and styles,[110] using for support *muñja* grass, reeds or cotton-plant stalks, and upon this central strand they built with consummate art – for it was indeed an art, included in the list of the 'sixty-four arts' (see p. 323, note 9). Apart from flowers, they worked into the garland peacock's feathers, horn and bone ornaments, shells, leaves, fruits and berries. It was a profitable occupation, for the *mālās* played a great part in Indian life: they festooned public buildings and gateways during feast days, they adorned the persons of elegant ladies and gentlemen every day, they served as offerings in holy places and as symbols of good fortune in ceremonies, especially the marriage ceremony. It is enough to say that the garland-weaver was never out of work, and if his profits were never enormous he nevertheless occupied an honourable place in society.

Craftsmen, like the merchants, were subject to heavy duties and taxes. Apparently they paid a tax on their shop premises; on top of that, every four months they paid a special stamping duty on the implements of their profession, and on their scales, weights and measures. Finally, goods and produce were taxed on the basis of a market price-list prepared regularly by a special superintendent. These taxes were payable in money or in kind, the amount ranging from four to fifty per cent, and were collected by an appointed official. In the case of imports and exports, or simply transit goods, toll charges and the tax on conveyance added to the prime cost of the merchandise, including those products under royal monopoly.

HUNTING AND FISHING

Other duly catalogued occupations existed, but it is difficult for our Western minds to accept them as falling within the category either of trade or of crafts. There were, for example, those who gathered sticks in the woods, carrying them in a basket slung over the back, to sell to housewives; those who collected leaves from trees, for which there were many different uses; grass-cutters armed with a sickle; collectors of honey who sought out this precious foodstuff by striking the trunks of trees so as to detect the hollows.[111] Among these humble callings, two categories stand out by reason of their greater importance: these are the hunters and fowlers, and the fishermen.

It may seem contradictory that hunting and fishing should have been included among the recognized professional activities, in a country where orthodoxy condemned the human consumption of fish, flesh or fowl. It is true that the killing of any living thing could only be considered with horror by the theoreticians of the transmigration of souls and of 'non-violence'. But India was essentially paradoxical, and beside a particular theory there was always room for some more or less specious explanation that made possible what was expressly forbidden. We have seen this already in connection with the fact of 'mixed' marriages. It was the same with the prohibition from consuming animal flesh: a Buddhist might well eat chicken so long as he had not killed it himself; and a fisherman was deemed to be only the indirect cause of the fish's death since the fish itself was responsible for swallowing the hook. . . . It should be made clear, in any case, that the prohibition of meat was less strict then than it is today, and even the brāhmaṇs themselves were permitted to eat it during certain festivals.

Professional hunters[112] usually lived near the jungle and forests, and undertook long expeditions to stock up with game. Many peasants also hunted game in the forests, imitating as well as they could the hunter's methods. The hunters sometimes took game-dogs with them, famished, savage creatures with short, yellowish coats and turned up tails, exactly like those that still prowl around Indian villages today.[113]

Armed with a bow or blow-pipe and a hunting-spear or javelin, they made use of many different kinds of trap and knew all sorts of ruses to kill animals or capture them alive. They built platforms in trees laden with ripe fruit, hid there and waited for hours, silent and motionless, until the antelopes whose tracks they had previously picked up came up to taste their favourite fruits; when the animals were within range they transfixed them with an arrow or poisoned dart.[114] Elsewhere, they laid traps. Some consisted of a bamboo stick stuck into the ground and bent forward, the free end carrying a running noose whose loop lay on the ground around a bait. If an animal tried to seize the bait the bamboo sprang up straight, tightening the noose around the animal and holding it firm.[115] Another trap, more complicated but applying the same principle, consisted of a bow concealed in the ground, strung with an arrow whose tip was extended by a noosed leather thong. An imprudent footstep released the arrow and hobbled the animal's legs with the noose.[116]

The hunters piled the carcasses in a cart and went into town to sell the skins and venison.[117] But they were also responsible for restocking the parks and hunting reserves maintained by the king and nobility, and then of course it was necessary to capture the animals not only alive but uninjured by traps. In such cases, they used a different method. After locating the regular trail of a wild antelope, they would spread honey on the grass where the animal came to graze; then they lay patiently in wait, hiding at first, then showing themselves increasingly so as to familiarize the animal with the sight and smell of man. After several days of this stratagem, during which the antelope had become gradually tamer, it became quite easy to seize it.[118] Monkeys were captured in the Himalāyas by using similar methods.[119]

Elephant hunting, with ivory as the object, of course, was a more dangerous occupation.[120] In some regions, herds of wild elephants caused great destruction, trampling down enclosures and houses; nevertheless, they were under official protection and vast reserves were proclaimed within which it was forbidden to hunt them. The elephant hunter (*pulinda*) was generally obliged to travel to a distant jungle and so had to mount a large-scale expedition for the purpose. The hunter chose a band of assistants and porters, who loaded several wagons with provisions and equipment. He would include in his expedition's equipment scythes to cut away undergrowth, knives to hack away branches and trailing vines, axes to cut down trees, a bamboo ladder for climbing over difficult terrain, planks to throw across marshy patches, and even a dinghy for crossing flooded areas. After they had beaten out a path for themselves to the foothills of the mountains, he had his assistants establish a base camp. Then he set out alone, scaling the rocky mountain-side with a dexterity which is worth recording in detail. Equipped with a rope and pitons (iron pegs), a hammer, a compass-saw, a bow and arrows, and a large leather bag, he first lassoed some rock projecting above him and climbed up, hoisting himself with the aid of his spear and by hammering pitons into the rock for footrests. These he recovered as he climbed by giving them a sharp tap. When he had reached the summit, he drove one more piton into the top of the mountain's opposite face, attached one end of his rope firmly to it, rolled the rest of it up and placed it inside the leather bag, in which he then sat among the rest of his equipment. After securing the rim of the bag around his body, he let himself drop over the cliff-edge, and started paying out the rope, looking like a fat spider at the end of its thread as he gradually lowered himself down the mountain-side.[121]

When he had finally reached the secret plateau in which the herd of elephants lived, he started looking for their regular drinking-place. When he had found it, he dug a square pit, shoring it up with stakes and stones, then covering it with lengths of wood upon which he strewed earth and greenery; he also excavated a tunnel leading underground to a side of the pit, with an opening into the pit large enough for him to be able to draw his bow. At nightfall, when the great pachyderms came to drink, one of them inevitably passed over the trap, which gave way under its weight. From his shelter, the hunter shot his poisoned arrows. While the rest of the herd thundered away in panic, the poison did its work and the hunter had only to saw off the animal's tusks. Tying them to the ends of a yoke which he carried over one shoulder, he rejoined the camp. Later, he could expect to reap a handsome reward when he sold the tusks to the ivory sculptors.

Like the hunters, the fowlers also lived in the country, usually on the fringes of some lake or pool. They trapped birds, or attracted them by imitating their calls, or by making use of decoys, according to whether they wanted to kill them or capture them alive, for they supplied both the tables and the aviaries of the rich. Concealed under a camouflage of leafy branches, they remained long hours in their hiding-place, waiting for a flock to alight. Then they used either large nets spread on the ground, whose corners they hastily drew together while the birds were still struggling in the meshes, or nets with long handles looking rather like tennis rackets. Or else they would set traps made of a stick carrying a thin cord of black horsehair terminating in a running knot like those used by hunters. Once the stick was firmly embedded in the river bottom, among the rushes along its banks, they had only to wait for some aquatic bird to get its foot caught in the noose.[122] They brought with them a basket or cage for carrying their haul. To kill birds in flight they used a bow or, sometimes, a falcon. Many of them gathered eggs, had them cooked and went to the nearest market to sell them. Finally, some specialized in training captured birds such as peacocks, cuckoos, partridges, parrots and blackbirds.[123]

As for the fishermen, they used hooks, nets and basket-traps. The Indian coastal waters were teeming with fish and the fishermen had no difficulty in filling their boats with the catch. They processed the fish themselves, gutting them, cleaning them, drying them, cooking them and selling them on the market. As well as fish they caught turtles, whose meat and eggs were highly esteemed.

Hunters, fowlers and fishermen had no additional expenses and so could count on a net profit, which was some recompense for the risks they undertook and the dangers to which they were often exposed.

Other professions were associated with these, but were exercised in the circle of the aristocracy and the royal family: these were the experts at training horses (*aśvādhyakṣas*) and elephants (*gajadhyakṣas*). The former were entrusted with the taming of horses still used to grazing freely. To make them manageable, they attached the animal to a post by a rope which was progressively shortened, meanwhile using a whip or goad on them, or beating them with a stick or cord, and forcing them to gallop in an ever decreasing circle. This method was calculated to break down the most recalcitrant animal's resistance, but it demanded on the part of the trainer a complete knowledge of the effects of the bridle and bit on the horse's mouth, nostrils, forehead and ears.[124]

Wild elephants were captured in the same manner as today, that is by using tame elephants to lure them into stockades where their training was undertaken. As soon as they were broken in, the trainers taught them all the manoeuvres and tricks they would be expected to carry out later on, on the battlefield or at the royal palace,[125] such as jumping over embankments and ditches (to avoid traps), sitting down and getting up on command, walking straight or in a zigzag, charging, and serving as a battering-ram against military fortifications.

THE GUILDS

A characteristic feature of craft and commercial organization in ancient India is to be found in professional classification by corporative groups (*śreṇis*). This is another aspect of the social structure, providing still further divisions within the basic division into castes and seemingly more important, in some ways, than the caste system itself. It is by no means uncommon to find stone inscriptions or Buddhist tales which mention a particular individual's calling but not his caste, that calling being synonymous with a fairly well-defined social class. This conception created very solid bonds that extended over the surface of a whole kingdom or an extensive region or even over the whole of India. It also constituted a powerful economic lever, since many *śreṇis* were able to build up large reserves of funds and could therefore exercise an indubitable influence in local and even State affairs. As a sign of its power, every guild possessed a special seal (*nāmamudrā*) made of bronze, copper, ivory, stone or terracotta, imitating in this the king, his ministers and his dignitaries.[126]

Traditionally, the number of guilds is supposed to have been eighteen, but one can compile a total of about thirty from the various sources available to us. Those we know most about are the cloth-weavers and silk-weavers, the dyers, the carpenters, the potters, the manufacturers of contraptions for raising and distributing water, pressers and sellers of oil, millers, gardeners and garland-makers, betel-quid sellers and sculptors in ivory. It is also probable that the thieves and professional beggars were grouped in guilds. And it seems certain, judging from the same sources, that no distinction was made between craft workers and merchants.

The *śreṇis* included artisans working alone as well as workmen forming part of a factory enterprise in which the project was executed in chain fashion, each workman making only a particular part of one object. Trades were nearly always hereditary and were followed by the entire family. Accounts do exist of cases where the same individual changed his profession several times or, on the other hand, where each member of a family followed a different trade, but these appear to have been exceptions. Specialization was further increased by the habit these families had of grouping themselves in whole villages; as in present-day Indian 'bazaars' particular trades are grouped in separate areas, so in ancient times they were concentrated in one living area to the exclusion of all other trades. This gave a particular character to ancient India's social organization: on the outskirts of woods would be found villages composed entirely of foresters,[127] or hunters, or fowlers; large towns were surrounded by clusters of villages whose inhabitants might be respectively blacksmiths, carpenters, weavers, dyers, potters and ivory sculptors. For this reason the guild system was often synonymous with the political structure in the villages and the local chief of the *śreṇi* would perform the same functions as the village head or *gāmabhojaka* (see p. 43).

Guild masters were nominated either by hereditary succession or by election, and it was not unknown for one to designate his successor himself when he felt himself unable to continue his functions effectively. Usually known as the 'Elder' (*jyeṣṭhaka*) or the 'Best' (*śreṣṭhin*) or even the 'Most Important' (*mahattama*), the master possessed a very real influence if his guild was prosperous, and might even become a counsellor to the king. He took part in the popular assemblies convoked by the king in certain circumstances, and, more frequently, in the regional councils. He, too, was entitled to a special seal which bracketed his name with his title of *śreṣṭhin*. He was assisted by executive agents and by a secretary (*kāyastha*). Normally, his function was to apply his guild's rules and see that its privileges were respected. He laid down working conditions and fixed salary scales. He maintained liaison with the masters of the other guilds with a view to raising or lowering prices, according to the circumstances. In many instances, he assumed the office of banker and managed the communal funds of the local branches of his guild, which remained collectively responsible for the delinquencies or failures of their individual members, including their chiefs, since the entire guild was liable to punishment by the royal court of justice in the case of breach of trust by a single group.

Apart from his administrative role, the guild master might be called upon to act as a magistrate, in order to expel a refractory or disloyal member, to inflict penalties or to arbitrate a conflict or a questionable deal. He could even become involved in social matters, since his authorization was necessary in certain cases, as for instance that of a wife desiring to leave her husband in order to become a nun. Also, he was head of the militia which every guild maintained to assure its own security and which was supported by guild funds (the king never intervened in questions of public order); in wartime, the militia of all the guilds were incorporated into the royal army and constituted one of its four official categories.

He was, then, an influential man. In theory, he owed his position solely to his professional capacities, having executed a 'masterpiece' after completing his apprenticeship. So, for instance, on a local level, a blacksmith capable of making a perfect needle which was both straight, fine, sharp, well-rounded, and carefully polished with emery would be judged to have passed as a master and might be chosen to succeed the head of the district's blacksmiths on the latter's death. [128] It is known that the members of each guild learned professional secrets which served as passwords to recognize each other.[129] Every guild possessed a banner and ceremonial flywhisks which were carried in procession during festivals; these had sometimes been conferred on them by royal charter. They probably all had at their disposal a headquarters or communal building whose rooms looked out over an inner courtyard containing a well.

The social undertakings of an individual *śreṇi* were considerable: it not only allowed its members the possibility of acquiring wealth and influential posts through the support it gave them, it also protected those who were unlucky or of limited talent. It played the role of local banker, accepting deposits, distributing dividends, receiving donations or subscriptions from which, with the donor's agreement, they set aside a certain percentage for the benefit of the community. It increased its funds further through the sums received in penalties and fines imposed on those who broke any of the guild's laws.

The merchants' *śreṇi* had the reputation of being among the wealthiest of all, and constituted a sort of moneyed *bourgeoisie* whose financial power seems often to have been considerable. Many of their members sponsored caravans and maintained fruitful commercial relations with their opposite numbers in the border regions, who assured them large profits on luxury products and on the goods and produce that constituted the basic necessities of life throughout the country.[130] With their profits, they acquired whole villages and cultivated estates, with an entitlement to a proportion of their income,[131] or herds and flocks together with their herdsmen and shepherds.[132] Others commissioned merchant ships and speculated on their cargoes, or contented themselves with subscribing a share. Several took up banking, the most enviable of all professions.

Craftsmen, too, often rose above the humble origin of their particular calling. One simple village potter, for example, who was doubtless blessed with a particular head for business, is described as having acquired five hundred workshops working solely for his firm, as well as a river fleet which he used to transport his production throughout the Ganges valley.

Several guilds were immensely prosperous. That of the ivory workers of Vidiśā (Bhīlsā, near Bhopāl) in the first century AD was in a position to offer one of the four monumental porticoes of the great *stūpa* of Sānchī, a magnificent work (still to be seen *in situ*) which is one of the masterpieces of ancient Indian sculpture (see p. 118). Similarly, in the fifth century the silk-weavers of Daśapura, who came originally from the Lāta country, were able to erect a temple of the Sun at their own expense and also pay for necessary repairs thirty-five years later.

Those parts of India where the Buddhist influence was greatest were also those where the guild system was most highly developed, and the most meritorious act did in fact consist in devoting one's fortune to pious foundations or the creation of almshouses. Donors traditionally supervised in person the daily distribution of aid, standing by the gate while the pathetic line of miserable creatures shuffled past in its quest for food, clothing and assistance.[133] These charitable activities by no means prevented wealthy merchants from bequeathing valuable properties to their sons. Others, on the other hand, cared little for the salvation of their soul, and succeeded in ruining themselves by abandoning themselves to a life of debauchery. Buddhist tales make frequent references to sons of families, brought up in luxury and indolence, who squandered their patrimony and so condemned themselves to a dreadful fate: maimed by the corporal punishments inflicted on them for their vices, reduced by their accumulated debts to begging, they were excluded from their *śreṇi* and went to swell the ranks of the paupers.

STATE RESOURCES AND MONOPOLIES

To compensate for its expenses, the State had to find substantial sources of revenue. These expenses were detailed in a traditional list of eighteen items, and there is no doubt that they were enormous. Among other things, it was necessary to provide funds to cover the costly functioning of a vast administrative apparatus; to meet the huge expenses incurred by popular or royal festivals; to cover the palace's household budget as well as the additional cost of royal banquets and pomp and ceremony in general; to pay for military campaigns, the upkeep of the army, royal hunting expeditions, the undertaking and upkeep of works of public interest, and so on. It was also necessary to take into account the loss to the Treasury occasioned by the exemptions enjoyed, in general, by brāhmaṇs, religious foundations,[134] women, minors, the sick, the elderly, students, men of letters, ascetics and, probably, much of the nobility. In addition, the State reduced taxes in the case of poor harvests, or as a reward to some military chieftain or diligent official; in fact such reductions were considered by many in these last two categories to be an inherent right.

By virtue of the conception – established by numerous literary sources – according to which the king was the true owner of the earth and the waters, the basic tax was, since time immemorial, levied on agricultural land, herds and flocks. This tax, called *bhāga*, represented the king's share. The rate, varying according to district and era, was calculated on gross production, taking into account the relative abundance of the harvests and the size of the herds of cattle, and ranged from a sixth to a third, a quarter being the most usual proportion. This tax was first paid in kind, grain in particular, but at some undetermined moment in history, probably contemporary with the first Buddhist writings (*c.* 400 BC), money replaced goods as the medium of payment. For cattle, tax demands are quoted as amounting to eight measures annually of ghee or one *paṇa* (see pp. 110–11) per head; another text mentions simply 'a fiftieth' without specifying the nature of the tribute. To these basic taxes was added an annual tax for the use of water coming from reservoirs or canals, which also 'belonged' to the king. All agricultural produce, and even the simplest commodities were taxable, including green vegetables, fruits, honey and firewood. On top of this, a collective tax was levied on every village, and the State charged fees for the provision of easements such as land-surveying, land demarcation, pasturage, irrigation, etc. The Treasury itself provided the allowances due to the community, as well as the manpower to which it might be entitled under the rules of statute labour.

In the field of commerce, the State levied tolls, octroi, customs duty, passport fees and taxes on the various forms of transport; taxes on shops, on 'industrial' tools and equipment and a fee for the official stamping of weights and measures; duty on intoxicating and alcoholic drinks (waived on holidays and feast days), and on produce and merchandise brought into town from the country (except that destined for religious ceremonies and observances).

An income tax seems to have existed at various different historical periods, applicable to the various trades and professions, especially those considered 'impure', such as curriers and butchers. Normally, the tax on professions varied from ten to twenty per cent, calculated on net earnings after allowing for general expenses and necessary risks and hazards involved. Even courtesans had to hand over two days' earnings every month.

These various sources of revenue were supplemented by those that the State derived from its own estates; these were administered by royal officials, and their produce went to stock the public granaries. Sufficient reserves were held back to force down prices when money was scarce, and to aid the population during food shortages. These crown lands were developed by tenant-farmers appointed by the royal administration.

Industrial enterprises, too, were operated on the king's behalf, and their profits went entirely to the Treasury; they consisted mainly of weaving and spinning mills, the workshops where gold and silver was worked and money struck,[135] arsenals and arms factories. The royal administrators employed male and female workers, recruited largely from among common law prisoners, paupers, cripples, orphans, prostitutes, and women abandoned by their husbands, whatever their caste. They were paid wages, and those women whose circumstances were honourable were protected by royal decree: the superintendents were strictly enjoined to authorize such women to work at home and allow them to bring along their completed work at dawn, so that no one might see them; furthermore the superintendents were forbidden to look these virtuous females in the face, or to speak to them except in connection with their appointed tasks.[136]

Megasthenes had already remarked on the richness of India's subsoil, and noted the many ways in which its products were used.[137] The working of mines constituted one of the State's monopolies and provided an important source of revenue. Two methods of operation were practised, some mines being under direct State supervision, while others were leased to concessionaries; but, in the latter case, the fees demanded by the State were so high, and the sale of finished products so burdened by export licences and a host of similar penalties that these concessions were as effectively under the control of the State as the other enterprises. By 'mines', Indian texts meant not only the extraction of metals and ore (gold, silver, copper, iron, red lead, mercury, manganese, mica) but also that of precious and semi-precious stones (diamonds, rubies, topazes, sapphires, emeralds, lapis-lazuli, rock crystal and various other crystals), and included pearl-fishing and fishing for coral, mother-of-pearl and shells. They also mention quarries where stone was cut for building or sculpting: sandstone, granite, crystalline rocks and marble, and those from which could be extracted unguents or cosmetics (realgar, in particular), colouring matters and ingredients used in medicine.

The production of salt in all forms was also a State monopoly. Contemporary texts list six different sources from which it was claimed salt could be obtained: the steppe (salt plain), the sea, natron (a soda found on lake-borders), alkalines, saltpetre (*sauvarcalā*) and rock-salt mines. Salt was considered a prime necessity and often featured in barter transactions, especially those conducted with the 'savage' tribes. It remained an expensive commodity, carrying a high rate of duty; of the six taxes applied to it, four had to be paid by the seller and two by the buyer.

The forests, also, were under State management, providing for the State's great benefit timber and precious woods which it used for its own purposes, sold to private contractors or exported. All the other forest products were its property, too: the animals, who provided skins, fur, horns, hair (yaks' tails, for example); the elephants, who were used for hunting and warfare, and whose tusks were, of course, valued for their ivory; the roots, wild fruits, vegetable essences, resin, honey, coconuts, and so on, all belonged to the State. Foresters were employed to look after the trees, supervise their growth, cut them down or replant them according to orders, and to produce the charcoal which was required in the operation of some industries.

The State extended its financial grip in other directions. It regulated gaming, levying a tax amounting to five per cent of the value of the premises where gaming took place, another tax on all stakes, and a third on dice. It appropriated the goods of deceased persons without heirs, and all discovered lost property and treasure in cases where the owner failed to appear or establish a claim within three years. Huge profits swelled the State coffers from a great number of taxes, confiscations, fines and penalties that varied according to the circumstances and the individuals involved. In wartime, taxpayers' rates were increased until they might even reach a level of fifty per cent of their property or their profits; war funds were further supplemented by 'voluntary' donations and by the results of public subscriptions, by the seizure of property belonging to 'heretics', guilds and religious establishments, and by private loans from wealthy individuals.

Generally speaking, the monarchs of ancient India appear to have exercised moderation (except when pressed by necessity) in imposing this all-embracing taxation system, thus following the counsels of prudence given by the lawgivers who recommended kings to imitate the gardener who picks only ripe fruit, or the leech which 'takes its food little by little' (the Code of Manu, VII, 129). They made every effort to build up reserves and so avoid special levies and taxes. They granted temporary tax relief or remission, and even loans of materials, to encourage new agricultural projects and the cultivation of virgin land. They were equally generous in the case of bad harvests or crops, or if a particular community had undertaken some project of benefit to the general public. They gave privileges to districts furnishing men for war service. To sum up: they tried to make the best use of the country's economic resources, allowed merchants and craftsmen to retain a reasonable profit level, and avoided imposing a crushing burden of taxation on the common people, except during exceptional circumstances when reasons of 'distress' authorized them to use every possible means to replenish the Treasury. Apart from the quite shameful privileges enjoyed by members of the ruling classes, the financial policy seems to have been perfectly sound.

MONEY, WAGES AND THE COST OF LIVING

In Vedic times, the unit of value appears to have been the cow, or sometimes the measure of rice; we have no precise knowledge of the exact epoch when gold and other precious materials were adopted as standard units for transactions. Money, properly so called, does not seem to have made an appearance before the time of the Buddha (sixth century BC). It then took the form of small bars of silver, the heaviest of which (*śatamāna*) weighed just over one and a half ounces (nearly fifty grams). This unit was subdivided into a half, a quarter and an eighth. Silver coins then appeared, weighing just under half an ounce (nearly twelve grams) and called *paṇas* or *kārṣāpaṇas*, composed of an alloy which included twenty-five per cent copper and five and a half per cent base metal. The small coinage was of copper and consisted of the *māṣa* (one-sixteenth of a *paṇa*) and the *kākiṇī* (a quarter of a *māṣa*). The lowest value, worth an eightieth of a *paṇa*, was a shell rather than a coin, the *kaparda* or *kaurī* (*Cypraea moneta*). Finally, a gold coin, carrying the borrowed Greco-Roman name of *dīnāra*, appeared early in the Christian era; according to contemporary authors it was equivalent to forty-eight *paṇas* (or sixteen pieces of silver of the Gupta dynasty). But these valuations are necessarily equivocal, since designations, values and weights change from one text to another. Each region, each dynasty, each king, each tribe, each temple and even each village used a different coinage; and it is very probable, also, that barter persisted as a practice long after currency had been introduced as a medium of purchase. Coins existed in a bewildering variety of shapes, dimensions and designs,[138] round or square, bearing emblems, divine or royal effigies, abbreviated inscriptions, etc.

It is, consequently, difficult to reconstruct the cost of living during this period of Indian civilization. It will be worth while reproducing the following table from Kauṭilya[139] if we take into account the fact that it is impossible to be sure whether or not it is quoting monthly wages and normal prices, nor whether these correspond to historical reality or rather to a theoretical scale based on the social hierarchy as envisaged in that era.

Fees and wages (monthly?)

48,000 *paṇas*

The chief priest
The king's spiritual master (*Ācārya*)
The prime minister (*mantrin*)
The royal chaplain (*purohita*)
The head of the armies (*senāpati*)
The crown prince (*yuvarāja* or *rājaputra*)
The queen mother
The chief queen

24,000 *paṇas*

The chief police officer
The guardian of the harem (*kañcukin*)
The chief of armoury and prisons (*praśāstṛ*)
The head of the revenue department (*samāhartṛ*)
The royal treasurer (*samnidhātṛ*)

12,000 *paṇas*

The princes and their mothers
The commander of an army (*nāyaka*)
The supervisor of manufactures
The twelve counsellors (*antri-pariśada*)

The superintendent general
The head of the border guard (*antapāla*)

8,000 *paṇas*
The guild masters (*śreṇīmukhya* or *śreṣṭhin*)
The regimental commanding officers of the army (*hastyaśvarathamukhya*)
The inspectors (*pradeṣṭri*)

4,000 *paṇas*
The chief supervisors

2,000 *paṇas*
The commanders of war-chariots
Physicians

1,000 *paṇas*
Fortune-tellers
Bards
Other supervisors
Professors of repute

Between 1,000 and 500 *paṇas*
Spies

500 *paṇas*
Trained infantry
Scribes and accountants
Cost price of a slave
Value of an elephant (*for fines*)

120 *paṇas*
Wages of craftsmen

60 *paṇas*
Servants
Medical assistants
Those performing statute labour

50 *paṇas*
Cost price of a female slave
Average cost of maintaining one man for a year

24 *paṇas*
Value of a horse (*for fines*)

12 *paṇas*
Value of an ox (*for fines*)

1¼ *paṇas*
Wages of a cowherd (or else the milk of one cow out of ten)

1 *paṇa*
Value of 123 *prasthas* of grain (about 400 lbs.)
Value of 300 *palas* of oil (about seven gallons) (*for fines*)

About ½ *paṇa*
Weekly expenditure of a workman

1 *māṣa* (1 of a *paṇa*)
Price of a truss of hay

1 *kākinī* (1/64 of a *paṇa*)
Calculation of the daily expenditure of a workman (under both Maurya and Gupta dynasties)

Part Two

INDIVIDUAL AND COLLECTIVE EXISTENCE

CHAPTER ONE

THE BACKGROUND TO DAILY LIFE

He saw the workshops thriving along the royal road, the river furrowed by boats, and maidens flirting with youths in the parks on the outskirts of town.

KĀLIDĀSA, *Raghu Vaṃśa*, XIV, 30.

THE CAPITAL, THE TOWNS AND THE VILLAGES

The descriptions of capital cities typical of ancient India's kingdoms all present a common feature: towns were built on a rational and well-conceived basis, in which the guiding factor was invariably a cosmological theory incorporating symbolistic concepts based on religious and popular traditions. The plans were fairly uniform and applied to secondary towns and villages as well, their essential principle being that the actual outline of the town was unimportant, and could equally well be square or rectangular, so long as its various components were identical in every case. Excavations and ancient depictions tend to confirm this quality of exact precision in town planning, though not with such strictness as theoreticians might wish for.

The site for the capital was chosen on the basis of the existing pattern of rivers: it was mandatory to establish it close beside one river, facing north not far from the right bank and sloping gently from west to east, following the land's natural declivity. Whether square or rectangular, it had to fit inside outer walls whose orientation was determined with the aid of a sundial, and each of whose four sides faced a cardinal point. The area covered was sometimes considerable; the ancient capital of the Maurya emperors, Pāṭaliputra, for instance, had a perimeter of about twenty-five miles.

During the Maurya epoch, the outer walls consisted of a colossal palisade made of huge tree-trunks embedded deep in the ground. Pāṭaliputra was fortified in this manner; fragments of its palisade are preserved today in the Patna museum, and their gigantic height and astonishing state of preservation are equally impressive.[1] During this same period, thick walls of sun-dried brick were also sometimes constructed, and at a later date burnt bricks were used, fitted together without mortar.[2] These ramparts were topped by serrated parapets along their entire length, as in Iran, backed by flights of steps and wall-walks, and punctuated at intervals by watch-towers perforated by loop-holes.[3] Each face of the fortified wall had its own huge gateway.

The ramparts were ringed by a series of moats serving as main sewers; lotuses floated on the surface and ducks paddled along, while housewives came to draw the dangerously polluted water for use in their kitchens. A bridge, bearing the picturesque title of 'elephant's nail' (*hastinakha*), crossed the moat before each entrance, though sometimes such bridges were replaced by plain earth-banks. In any case, they were preceded by one of those porticoes (*toraṇa*), so specifically Indian, made of two pillars leaning slightly towards each other and joined at their summit by one or several arched lintels. Erected as symbols of victory and of welcome, they were made of stone,[4] or wood, or even embellished with precious materials and ivory plaques. In the villages, they consisted simply of two thin poles stuck in the ground and joined at the top by festoons of greenery. On holidays, garlands of flowers and leaves were suspended from the lower lintel.

The town's main gateway was a building in itself, with massive towers flanking and overlooking the actual gates.[5] Resting on a base of cemented bricks or open stonework, the buildings were two or three storeys high, and constructed of wood, bamboo and clay daub. Inside were arranged various official apartments, including those of the toll-collectors; the windows of the offices were furnished with balconies and fitted with lattice-work or finely fretworked wooden screens. Interior stairways led to the upper storeys; the municipal granary was on the top floor and light was provided by gable-windows whose carved beams were decorated with paintings. The vaulted roofs were either thatched or covered with roughly baked curved tiles;[6] the joists were curved and painted; the crest of the roof was ornamented with a line of tapering, rounded projections fashioned from wood or terracotta; the doorway and fore-part of the building were embellished with statues. Near this imposing edifice, or sometimes on one of its roofs, was placed a bowl whose function was to 'bring rain' and which had, no doubt, a magical significance in relation to the foodstuffs stored in the granary.[7]

The main entrance was high enough to allow entry to elephants carrying palanquins, and throughout the day a never-ending throng of citizens streamed in and out. At night, the entrance was closed by heavy wooden door-leaves reinforced by iron bars. These leaves swung on thick stakes whose lower ends pivoted inside iron-reinforced sockets cut into the stone of the threshold, and when closed were checked by a central stone slab set into the ground.[8] They were kept fast by two removable thick iron bars which fitted into slots cut into the door-jambs.[9] But, to allow passage after closing time, a smaller door was built into one of the two door-leaves, secured on the inside by a sliding bolt chased with a design and made sometimes of silver. In this way, people could get in and out without there being any need to unbar the heavy main gates. The capital's security was an important matter and was meticulously organized at all times; at night-time or during wars, even the most innocent-seeming intrusions by unknown individuals or groups were considered suspect. A curfew was fixed for midnight. Secret passages, leading from points inside the town to concealed egresses far out in the country, were constructed, so that spies might ply their trade, and those in power make a quick getaway when necessity dictated.

Near the main gateway, facing east, there was always to be found a tall column standing by itself. It would be made of wood, stone or iron, and topped by a sculpted group or by a wheel resting on a bell-shaped capital, recalling similar columns in Persepolis. This was a most important monument in the eyes of the Indians, a symbol of victory and hospitality, endowed with both imperial and cosmological significance,[10] and forming part of the sovereign's 'regalia' (*ratna*).[11] Sometimes the sovereign had inscriptions engraved on these columns; the great emperor Aśoka made use of many of them to promulgate his edicts. They may also have served as sundials. The presence of such a column near a town, village or sanctuary was evidence that that place enjoyed royal protection[12] with all the privileges attendant upon such favour. This column was the object of popular veneration, being viewed as a theoretical centre of the earth and as the symbol of universal royalty. Men and women honoured it gladly and regularly by walking around it in a ritual procession called *pradakṣiṇā*; during this circumambulation, they touched its shaft with their right hand. The touch of the hands of countless generations has rubbed these columns smooth and made the surface concave at the height of a man's reach.[13]

The town itself, inside its ramparts, was encircled by a boulevard connected by a regular network of streets and lanes crossing each other at right angles. This basic concern with urban development implied a concern with symmetry and proportion which remained partially theoretical, since excavations have revealed more frequent whims of design and random modifications than the official documents and popular narratives of the time would lead one to expect. This accounts for the fact that the worthy traveller Hsüan-Ch'uang was able to emphasize the tortuous windings of the streets and lanes of the Indian towns he visited in the seventh century. The ideal plan, however, represented a quadrilateral divided by six main roads, three going from east to west, the other three from north to south. These formed extensions inside the town of the great communication routes which converged upon the capital. The traffic was tremendous, a panorama consisting of convoys of bullock-wagons, caravans, long files of porters, nobles and dignitaries with their trains, troops of cavalry, groups of pilgrims and countless pedestrians. This constant flow of humanity was supplemented by the ships, boats and rafts making their way along the adjoining river, some transporting merchandise, others carrying citizens on pleasure trips.

The main streets were paved with cobbles, and gutters ran alongside to carry off sewage water into the drainage trenches outside the town. These streets had to be wide enough to allow the passage of nobilities' carriages with their four-horse teams. The royal avenue, connecting the gates in the eastern and western walls, was the most impressive of these main arteries: it led straight to the centre of the city, where the royal palace's ramparts and beflagged roof-tops towered above the surrounding houses and could be seen from far away. The sixteen segments into which the town was thus divided were each, in their turn, cut by a series of smaller streets crossing each other at right angles and bordered by houses; off these streets ran narrow, filthy, dark and often winding lanes, which served as means of access to the meaner dwellings. These side passages were used by the members of the low castes and especially by the sweepers, who were so despised that it would have been considered intolerable to come face to face with one or to see one pass in front of the entrance-way to a good-class house. Hsüan-Ch'uang states that when members of these castes had legitimate occasion to use the main thoroughfares they were obliged to walk on the left-hand edge of the road.

In theory, each city interior should have been divided into eighty-one such blocks, but no doubt this was only an arbitrary figure for ritual purposes. It does seem, though, that the capital was in fact divided into a certain number of well-defined districts; texts even claim that each such district was surrounded by walls and enjoyed a certain degree of autonomy, possessing its own wells, its holy places, its sacred trees and its temples dedicated to local divinities. In such a scheme, each caste is supposed to have occupied a particular district, and similarly, an entire section of the city, consisting of both dwelling-houses and shops, was set aside for the trades and crafts. Every important town invariably had, too, a great expanse of ground reserved for the daily markets at which the peasants from the surrounding countryside sold their produce and products. The various guilds all possessed headquarters in the same district. The stalls lining the streets were separated from the living quarters by a courtyard, and were fronted by a veranda, as they still are today.[14]

Crowds of shoppers strolled along in front of the shelves piled high with green vegetables, fruits of all kinds, candied sugar, cooked rice and prepared foods ready for eating, whose pungent odours contrasted with the more delicate scents given off by the pyramids of incense sticks and sandalwood arranged on the perfumers' counters. Elsewhere, jewellers and goldsmiths cut and arranged precious stones, and polished different metals, while workmen fashioned bracelets of shell-work; tailors cut and stitched garments; smiths hammered out copper vessels; weavers worked their looms and sold materials. The garland-makers patiently built up their ephemeral works of art, threading heavy strings of stemless flowers interspersed with all the tinkling, brightly coloured accessories that set the blossoms off. Pedlars and hawkers sold their trumpery and trinkets from door to door. Here and there, the entrance of a tavern or gambling-den was surrounded by a knot of men of disreputable appearance.

The streets bustled with activity. Beautiful ladies, courtesans or nobles, were carried past in curtained palanquins as their servants battled a way through the crowd. Rich and poor, delivery-men and shoppers, hirelings and porters elbowed each other. The different costumes identified the wearers' rank or quality. The brown-skinned peasants wore loin-cloths and turbans, while their wives wore simple straight skirts and twisted their hair into a large coil worn on the neck. The young nobles, dawdling languidly, and ostentatiously adorned and perfumed, sheltered nonchalantly under a palm-leaf and bamboo umbrella. The brāhmaṇs were half naked, their hair gathered up in a knot on top of the head, the sacred thread across their chest, a bundle and a gourd hanging from one shoulder, holding a stick to ward off evil spirits; they wore sandals as a mark of precedence, and they, too, possessed an umbrella to emphasize their dignity; they sometimes led a fighting-ram or a trained monkey from whose antics they would make a little money. *Sādhus* (religious mendicants) were also to be seen, almost naked, their bodies smeared with ashes; and emaciated beggars bent double under the weight of some real or feigned misery; and snake-charmers and monkey-trainers in search of a generous audience; and sellers of tame mongooses. Sprightly young servants, neat-looking and carefully dressed, hurried past to deliver a private note or fetch a jar of perfumed wine from the nearest tavern. Buddhist monks with shaven skulls made bright patches in the crowd in their swaying yellow or garnet-red robes; they walked with downcast eyes for fear of meeting a woman's glance, forbidden to them by their rules. They went from door to door in search of their daily food, but since they were forbidden to cross the threshold they contented themselves with rattling the iron rings that dangled from the top of their pilgrim's staff; at this familiar noise, the charitable mistress of the house would hasten out and fill the monk's begging-bowl with rice. And everywhere there were housewives, carrying a young child astride one hip, buying provisions which were then placed in a basket with a handle carried on the arm, or a plain basket that was balanced on the head.

A few light carts (*pravahaṇa*) could be seen on the roads. These were two-wheeled vehicles, with roofs made of brightly coloured materials stretched over hoop-shaped ribs, furnished inside with soft carpets on which the driver and passengers squatted, and equipped with screens round the sides to protect the riders from the crowd's inquisitive glances. Drawn by two bullocks or horses,[15] they were used by the citizens for trips into the country and for town outings.[16] Occasionally, a parade elephant would pass, sounding with its knees the bells hanging from cords attached to its breast-strap, to warn people of its approach; or a two-wheeled chariot drawn by four horses abreast, a vehicle which fell out of fashion after the third century; or else a group of horsemen sitting comfortably astride hunting-saddles.

The curious and the idle leaned out of windows to contemplate the constant coming and going and hope for some unexpected diversion or excitement in the street scene: perhaps a suddenly enraged elephant would trample its mahout, a ram butt a passer-by,[17] a trained monkey escape from its owner, a hue and cry be raised after a thief, or a condemned man dragged along to his place of execution – all happenings well worth popular interest.

Further towards the centre of the capital were situated the residential districts. The buildings here were larger and better built; several storeys high (though never as high as the royal palace), they presented an even frontage of whitewashed wall along the sides of the avenues. At the back, they all possessed a garden with a well or a decorative pool. These houses were usually neither attached nor even adjacent, but separated by extensive stretches of greenery bordered by low walls with scalloped tops;[18] their entrance-ways were furnished with a portico similar to those preceding the city's outside gates. These same districts also contained many public buildings, recognizable by their more ornate architecture, which, like the private dwellings, all contained a domestic hearth. These buildings included those devoted to the town's health services, such as hospitals and maternity homes, and sanatoriums for aged and sick animals. Then there were alms-houses where charity was dispensed each day to the poor and to beggars, who were especially numerous in the largest towns, unfortunates who wandered abroad, living from hand to mouth, always on the verge of starvation. There were also rest-houses for the reception of voyagers and pilgrims. Other buildings housed educational establishments in which the masters (*ācārya*) were lodged.

In these residential areas might also be found several picture galleries (*citraśālā*)[19] open to the public and frequented by it particularly during the autumn. They were built with special care and skill, well lit in daytime by many windows or by open colonnades, and at night by masses of candles; they comprised several halls, stairways, and a refreshment-room with benches for the visitors. The paintings covered the walls of the main gallery (*vīthi*) and represented the celestial and divine world, illustrating the great epic poems or reproducing beneficent astrological symbols. These galleries belonged to wealthy private citizens, sometimes even to prosperous courtesans (who sometimes decorated the halls themselves),[20] but were not as magnificent as the king's own art gallery in his palace. The Indian people were so enthusiastic in their appreciation of painting and the plastic arts that there even existed mobile galleries mounted on wheels, which toured the countryside.[21]

In the vicinity of the royal palace one came to the areas set aside respectively for the courtesans, the professional musicians (who occupied a special category in the social scale), and the royal offices. Here were to be found the residence of the city administrator, the headquarters of the public scribe, the Treasury and all the other State secretariats. In these buildings were concentrated the administrative apparatus of the kingdom and the capital. Presided over by a commissioner and a 'municipal council', the latter was itself divided into administrative sectors each of which was in charge of an official called a *sthānika*; these sectors were subdivided into groups of families – from ten to forty – headed by junior officials, so-called 'cowherds' (*gopa*). The royal edicts and proclamations were announced by drummers as they were 'published' by means of inscriptions engraved on plaques of gold or copper fixed to bamboo posts.[22] Finally, public security and discipline were ensured by the 'spies' (*cara*) (whose complex role has already been touched upon), by the regular police force, by the guild militias and by the royal army itself, quartered near the ramparts. Indeed, the capital resembled a stronghold, and soldiers patrolled the parapets day and night, armed with bows and with lances.[23]

But this somewhat forbidding aspect was redeemed within the city by the existence, throughout the different districts, of many 'green zones' and a great number of canals, fountains, public bathing-pools, ponds, and natural or artificial lakes all covered with lotus blossoms. Pleasure gardens, squares and public parks alternated with alleys bordered by trees and mango groves, behind which private houses sheltered.

With its high surrounding walls, the capital gradually became overpopulated. Suburbs formed outside the fortifications, mostly poor and even slummy, inhabited by working people. These outer districts also contained the slaughter-houses (*suṇā*) and butchers' shops, the cemeteries and the execution grounds. An 'expansion committee' was occasionally set up by the city administration to study the problems caused by the necessity for building more houses; but the concepts dictated by ritual complicated the question seriously, since tradition forbade the development of plots existing between adjoining properties. The committee decided, in such cases, to authorize the construction of a town outside the city limits, to be designed in accord with a plan drawn up beforehand, and to populate it with the overflow of lower-class citizens who were cluttering up the capital. In this way, a whole ring of villages sprang up around the capital, each housing the members of one of the guilds upon whose products the city depended, especially the carpenters, sculptors and smiths.

Social activities were by no means confined within the city's walls; on the contrary. In the surrounding countryside, extensive stretches of land were set aside as sports arenas, where the people flocked to watch their favourite sport, fights between animals. Farther away, preferably in undulating country near the river running past the capital, the royal park was laid out: this covered a great surface, was planted with trees, bisected by a river, dotted with ponds and artificial lakes, and contained the king's 'country house', where he came to rest from the noise and activity of the court. This domain served both as a hunting reserve, where the deer could roam freely, and as a public park, where the citizens would stroll in family groups, and perhaps spend the whole day, taking with them a picnic meal; and where girls would go flirting with their suitors, travelling there in closed carriages. Halls and pavilions, flying standards, were reserved for courtiers wishing to relax and enjoy themselves. In the most isolated spots there were a few dwellings intended specially for monks seeking solitude far from the distractions of urban life.

No other town in the kingdom attempted to rival the capital

city in spaciousness or sumptuousness. The small towns and villages followed a simpler plan, but still obeyed generally the principal rules of the basic urban pattern. These villages were similarly surrounded by walls, with great gateways which were closed at night; but they possessed only two main avenues crossing each other at the centre, and it seems that the shoulders of these thoroughfares were usually rutted with dried mud. Instead of the large towns' system of open trenches, they usually had a lotus-covered pond or lake just outside the walls, where the housewives came to draw water with large copper vessels,[24] and where buffaloes wallowed voluptuously, only their heads and powerful horns emerging above the surface of the water.[25] All sorts of familiar fauna made their home in these bodies of water: soft-water crabs, fish, tortoises, cranes, water-birds, and the ever-present mosquitoes, all of which are frequently mentioned on one occasion or another in the fables and folk tales handed down by the *Jātakas*.

Village houses were lower and more modest than town ones; their outer walls were covered with a mixture of lime, earth and cow-dung, the last being considered a purificative agent.[26] The shops were more like street-stalls, and the crowd that passed by their displays were of more humble stock: farmers returning from the fields, pushing ahead of them a small flock of skinny sheep; ragged foragers, grey with chaff, a sickle stuck through their belt, carrying home trusses of hay tied around their hips;[27] women balancing on their heads large bundles of forage rolled inside a mat, to be used as animal fodder;[28] porters trotting along, laden with baskets suspended from each end of a pole carried across the shoulders. Then there were artisans in the process of delivering their merchandise, pedlars transporting their gimcrackery in a bag, strolling players looking for a suitable place to present their turns. Cattle mingled freely with the human throng. Heavy wagons drawn by bullocks (*grāmaśakaṭa* or *go-ratha*) rolled along the main streets;[29] these were (as they still are today) massive wooden constructions built by the village carpenter,[30] who followed time-honoured traditions in the matter of design. The body was relatively shallow, balanced on two large, heavy, creaking wheels with protruding hubs. A shaft with a yoke at its end was designed to harness a pair of hump-backed bullocks, the yoke resting on their necks between the nape and the dorsal hump; long wooden pegs, carefully carved and painted, were stuck through the yoke, one on each side of the beast's neck, enclosing it, with the additional means of a halter. In addition, their nostrils were pierced and a cord was passed through them, this being intended as a check on their fiery temperament. Their tails were carefully tied flat against their flanks, so that the swishing should not annoy the driver. The latter, squatting at the front of the wagon, his feet on the shaft, guided the team with the aid of a simple whip consisting of a stick and a plaited cord. These vehicles were surmounted by hooped ribs covered by matting, and were used particularly for transporting grain at harvest time;[31] the peasant's entire family, out in the fields, sought respite from the hot sun by sitting under its awning.

Apart from local and seasonal feast days (see pp. 144–8), rural existence offered only very rare distractions, and each day heralded the same repetitive rhythm of the farmer's routine. While the men worked in the fields, the housewives went about their daily chores and artisans followed their particular craft. Peace did not invariably reign between villagers, or even between villages, and Buddhist tales often mention the sometimes hilarious and bawdy quarrels[32] which provided the only relief from the monotony of daily life.

THE RITUALS OF CONSTRUCTION

The construction of a dwelling, that basic unit of Indian society, required great attention, necessitated the help of astrologers, priests and carpenters,[33] and involved the new owner in considerable expense. In principle, a house was built only on the occasion of a marriage, to found a new hearth which would shelter a new generation. But it was possible to buy one already built and even to own several houses.

A few weeks before actual construction work began, a suitable site for the proposed dwelling was sought, the chief task being to find a piece of land which could be readily irrigated. There were several possible solutions to this problem: perhaps a well could be dug, or else a spring might be diverted and a cistern set up on four stones; gutters would also be dug so that the drainage flow would be to the north of the house's bedroom.

Every home had to have some kind of water supply accessible in order to preserve its own autonomy.

The nature of the soil was carefully studied. If bitter or spiky grasses, or plants with milky sap, grew in it, it was considered unwise to build on it; but if it was covered with *darbha* grass (*Cynadon dactylon*), one would be sure to achieve saintliness of character there; tall, strong grasses would bestow physical strength on the future occupants. Climbing plants and annuals were the most promising, because – by sympathetic magic – the future household would know prosperity and would be ensured many descendants and an abundance of cattle.

Next, the soil's solidity was tested in several different ways, depending upon local tradition. Under the priests' guidance, the men would dig a hole of carefully calculated dimensions. If the quantity of earth removed from the hole could be packed back into it easily, the ground was considered propitious. If, on the other hand, the earth had swollen as a result of being shovelled out and back again, and left a mound above the surface after being replaced, the ground was declared unfit for building on. In another region of the country, a ditch would be dug and filled with water; if, after twenty-four hours, the liquid did not present certain well-defined characteristics, the priests recommended finding a different site. Sometimes a piece of ground was accepted or rejected according to whether a flame lowered to the bottom of the hole burned or went out.

One further criterion was required before the plot of land could be finally judged acceptable. The priest would examine a handful of earth and submit it to four successive tests: first, he crumbled it between his fingers to determine its consistency; secondly, he placed a little on his tongue and tasted its flavour; thirdly, he smelt it to identify its odour; lastly, he scrutinized it to define its colour. Each of these experiments was designed to be applicable to a particular caste; for instance, white earth was deemed suitable for the home of a brāhmaṇ, while red earth was appropriate for that of a *kṣatriya*, yellow for a free man, and black for an outcaste.

When all necessary conditions had been fulfilled, the priest solemnly assigned the land to its new owner during a ceremony, in the course of which a ditch was dug and an oblation poured into it to ensure that the ground remained firm and stable. Then he pronounced an adjuration designed to liberate the chosen plot from evil influences, in these words: 'May the spirits, gods and demons leave this place and find other abodes. From this moment, this place belongs to . . .', giving the new owner's name. The ceremony closed with offerings.

Now began the preparation of the soil. It was broken and turned several times; then it was watered, various different seeds were sown and certain plants, supposed to bring fortune, were put in. For the next three, five or seven days, the growth of the plants and the height of the young shoots was carefully observed. After any weeds had been pulled up, the earth was turned over once again, levelled off, and swept meticulously with a broom, so that it should be absolutely 'pure' and might become 'smooth as the surface of water' or 'smooth as a mirror'.

From this moment, the ground was ready for the construction work. The traditional plan and dimensions presented few problems. And, while the preparatory investigations were being carried out, the carpenters had been busy in the neighbouring forest cutting down the necessary number and kind of trees, and making beams and planks from the timber. These they had then numbered in sequence, according to their place and purpose in the building operation, so that they could be put together more quickly when the time came.[34] They had also taken into consideration the fact that many different varieties of wood had to be included symbolically in the framework at appropriate directional points, so as to avoid the possibility of dreadful calamities overtaking the future building: fire, death, occupation by the enemy, eye diseases and other such catastrophes.

For his part, the astrologer had been busy making calculations, and had finally announced a propitious day for construction work to begin, according to the horoscope he had been studying. Now that the date was decided on, the priest commenced a long preliminary ceremony, reciting various prayers and making offerings at one of the corners of the site. Soon after, some of the labourers dug a first hole at this point; when the cavity was knee-deep, the diggers moved off to a second corner, and the same ritual was repeated. These four holes were the positions for the house's corner posts; eight more holes were then dug, two on each side, and a ninth in the centre. A branch dipped in ghee was placed in each of these holes.

Now the carpenters came into action. They first brought up to the holes made in the ground facing east two pillars which were to constitute the doorposts of the house's main entrance, thrusting them into the holes already blessed by the priest, and fixing them firmly upright. The priest then sprinkled them with holy water. The pillars of the sides facing south, west and north were erected in succession. The central pillar, the last to be installed, required a longer ritual than the others, because it was the 'king pillar' (*sthaūṇārāja*), the one which was to support the roof's framework at its centre and would ensure the steadiness and strength of the whole building. The priest deposited an aquatic plant in the pit, then planted a few plant-seeds at the bottom which he sprinkled with water mixed with barley and rice: this offering was dedicated 'to he who is stable, to the deity of the habitat'. While the central pillar was being fixed in place, he intoned to it: 'Hold here firmly, o pillar, rich in horses and in cows; hold here in security, making the melted ghee drip down; hold here solidly in the earth, prosperous and long-lived in the midst of the prosperity of humans and animals.'[35]

The walls soon arose between the pillars, with the apertures for doors and windows gaping. These openings in the walls were carefully calculated so that none on opposite sides were in direct line; otherwise the house might be 'crossed by a glance'. The main door never faced westward, for this region belonged to the dead; it was furnished with a threshold made of a slab of stone, a symbol of stability, and its placing in position was accompanied by invocations. The leaves of the doors were fixed as soon as possible, to bar the way to evil spirits.

Once the walls were up, the superstructure was put in place, the framework being provided by bamboo cross-pieces lashed together by sisal cords. During the whole of this work, the priest continually chanted invocations appropriate to each particular operation. When the bamboos were secured to the pillars, he declaimed: 'Climb up the pillar, o bamboo serving as cross-piece.' And finally, when the ridge-piece was fixed in place he addressed the 'Lady Watching over the House', entreating her to grant the future inhabitants prosperity, fecundity and longevity, in these words: 'Take your place upon the pillar, mighty queen, keep our enemies at a distance, may your worshippers suffer no malice or hardship, o dwelling, and may we, in good health, live a hundred autumns.'[36]

Before covering the roof, mats were hung from the bamboo cross-pieces where appropriate, to divide the living space into separate compartments. The position of the ritual hearth was prepared, as were those of the altar where offerings were made, and the alcoves reserved for statues of the gods. Finally, the roofers covered the bamboo framework with thatch secured by plaited straw thongs, working outwards from the centre. In order to make the roof more waterproof, they reinforced the thatch with matting and plaits of reeds. There was no chimney, because cooking was done either in the open-air or under a separate lean-to roof.

When the building work was completed, it was still necessary to guard it against any future evil influences. For this purpose, a plait of reeds interwoven with special herbs and plants was hung above the doorway. Also a fence was put up round the house, made of mats tied together with cord; while the knots were untied, the priest declaimed: 'We untie that part of you, o house, which is knotted, we loosen your bonds and your knots.'

Now at last the house was ready. The owner made the rounds, touching the pillars one after the other, and addressing a brief invocation to each one; offerings were deposited at the foot of the central pillar, dedicated to the gods of the trees. The ceremony finished with prayers and with ritual aspersions designed to ensure happiness and prosperity to the new inhabitants; the master of the house sacrificed a goat and distributed gifts to all those who had taken part in the construction work.

THE HOME AND ITS FURNISHINGS

It seems probable that the kind of ritual just described took place prior to the construction of all dwellings, but these did, of course, vary tremendously in size and scale, according to whether their prospective owner was rich or of modest means, townsman or villager.

The village house was by far the most common type of dwelling, and came closest to the description given above; it consisted of one single ground floor only, the floor of beaten earth, mud walls, a single door, and rarely more than one window, the latter being narrow and covered with a wooden lattice. The roof was made of palm-leaves, reeds or matting, hemispherical in shape if the walls were round, or, if the walls were square, either semi-cylindrical or pointed and two-sided. Its bamboo framework, struts and wooden cross-pieces, and the dividing mats hanging from it were all particularly vulnerable to the fires which often ravaged the villages, under conditions where no effective counter-measures could be undertaken. The damage caused periodically by the rainy season to the roofs and walls necessitated extensive repairs as soon as dry weather returned. The plan was simple, and consisted mainly of the bedroom, facing north, the pantry, and the room in which the master received his guests.

The furniture was extremely sparse, and there were no seats of any kind, since everyone sat on the ground. The chief piece of furniture was a bed with a wooden or bamboo frame, set on four shaped legs, and a framework of diagonally crossed cords; this base was sometimes covered with matting or a piece of material.[37] Rattan stands shaped like sand-glasses, on which a tray was placed, took the place of tables and sideboards.[38] Domestic utensils[39] were restricted to pots of various shapes and sizes, used for storing the family provisions – oil, ghee, honey, pimentos and spices. Some were made of copper, others of earthenware. The largest were stacked on top of each other, the base of one fitting into the mouth of the one below, the one on top of the pyramid being capped by a conical lid or by abowl turned upside down.[40] The smaller pots were stored in nets that were hung from the ceiling's bamboo cross-pieces, to keep them free from impure contacts. None of these pots was used for the actual service of food, since ritual demanded that vessels from which one had eaten should be destroyed immediately the meal was finished. For this reason, thick, wide leaves – those of the banana tree, for instance – were used instead of plates, and disposed of after use.[41] When earthenware bowls were used, they were smashed after the meal, and consequently the village potter did a brisk trade in such receptacles.

While the common people lived in simple, even impoverished, domestic surroundings, city dwellers and families in easy circumstances possessed more extensive and better built houses.[42] Such houses were usually several storeys high, with two whitewashed façades, one opening on to a street or avenue by an entrance door furnished with a stone threshold and framed by two stone benches, while the other looked over a private garden containing various supplementary buildings. When the owner was an artisan or a merchant, the street frontage would also be provided with shop premises at ground level. Such a house was, in fact, a villa in the Roman sense of the word.

The main building consisted of several storeys whose height decreased progressively towards the top of the house. A veranda with columns shaded the ground floor and the others had balconies. The top storey, under the eaves, used for storing the family's valuables and reserve provisions, was lighted by gable-windows whose brightly painted wooden frames could be seen and admired from the street. These attic windows were called 'pigeon-cotes' (*kapotapālikā*), and birds were, in fact, often depicted on the roofs of houses, symbolizing the love uniting the couple living there. Then there was the custom of hanging from the windows gilded cages containing parakeets or parrots, brilliant in their multi-coloured plumage and loud with endless chatter. The roofs themselves might be thatched, tiled or shingled. Sometimes, they were terraced instead, and the family could then come up to enjoy the coolness of the night air and watch the stars. The windows were masked by lattice-work screens, by mats or by curtains decorated with geometrical patterns; the windows were also often fitted with solid shutters.[43]

The different floors were connected by fixed or removable interior stairways fitted with hand-rails; fixed staircases were made of brick, stone, marble or even (supposedly) rock crystal, while movable stairs were of wood inlaid with coloured stones.

A considerable proportion of the house space was set aside for private rooms, consisting of bedrooms, sitting-rooms, halls containing fireplaces, a refectory or dining-room, and reception rooms. Texts allude to the existence of a secret chamber,[44] or at least a secret compartment, situated usually in the anteroom, above the entrance passage. The family treasure was hidden there, to be made use of only in case of dire necessity. It might alternatively be buried in the ground, hidden in jars by the river bank, or simply confided to a friend. The hiding place was recorded on a gold or copper plaque handed down from generation to generation.

The house's different rooms were separated by mats or by tapestries made of widths of cloth in various patterns sewn together; hung from poles suspended about midway between ceiling and floor, they added their bright colours to those of the curtains that hung in front of the doors, kept parted by curtain-loops.[45] The floors were laid with polished tiles or mosaics. Precious carpets covered this surface. The walls sometimes had recesses built into them in which ivory or metal statues were placed. The rooms were kept fresh and humid by an ingenious method: goglets, long-necked vases filled with water, were hung from the ceiling; the porosity of the earthenware allowed the water to evaporate and helped to make the atmosphere less oppressive.[46] Every day, the rooms were perfumed by burning incense sticks in them, and by hanging up garlands of flowers and festoons of greenery.

Several annexes were to be found in the garden: a cloister, pavilions for physical exercises and games, another pavilion reserved for guests, one or more storerooms in which were kept the provisions necessary for everyday existence,[47] a wine storage room, a cellar and stables. A kitchen was arranged under a shelter, tiled and resting on poles.[48] There would also be an aviary, bird-keeping being a favourite family pastime. Finally, there were privies and, most important of all, steam-baths which were generally contained in a separate building. These bath-houses were to be found everywhere, even in Buddhist monasteries, and were highly prized by the Indians, who claimed, in fact, to be the inventors.[49] They were constructed of brick or stone and included a basement, a ground floor and a second floor reached by an indoor stairway. The outer walls were circled by a veranda or columns. Inside, the walls and ceilings were lined with plaster-coated animal hides. The amenities comprised an antechamber, then a room designed as a sudatorium, furnished with stone benches arranged around a fireplace, then finally a subterranean chamber surrounded by flowing water, in which the bathers came to relax and enjoy the refreshing coolness. Nearby was a swimming-pool. The bather first sat in the sudatorium, facing the fire whose heat soon made him sweat profusely; from time to time he was douched with warm water. Then he washed himself, and finished off by plunging into the pool. In default of such an installation, private houses boasting a certain degree of comfort possessed at least a room set aside for bathing, which guests were also invited to make use of, especially the physician when on a professional visit.

At night, lighting was provided by little lamps (a wick dipped in ghee) placed in wall-niches, or by lamps suspended in a frame made probably of metal,[50] or by torches held by servants.[51]

Business was carried on solely in the shop in front of the house, and guests never penetrated further into the home than the reception halls; even so, the family's private life tended to centre around the garden and its outbuildings, isolated from the city's surrounding bustle. The garden was looked after with great care; it contained a vegetable garden which the mistress of the house supervised personally and in which she grew the medicinal plants needed for treating the family's ailments. The rest of the garden was decorated with spreading trees, flowering shrubs and banana-plants. The general effect was enhanced by a few ornamental pools whose sparkling surfaces were half-hidden by pink lotus blossoms. A stream of water often ran along the bottom of the garden, permitting the daily ritual ablutions to be performed; and the garden itself was irrigated by a network of channels. Sometimes, during the hottest hours of the day, a revolving mechanism (*vāriyantra*) was set in motion which sent sprays of water out around it and so freshened the burning air.[52] A swing was fixed up in some shady spot, from a tree-branch or on a wooden dais, and adults as well as children disported themselves on it from springtime onwards.[53]

The gardens were enhanced by the beautiful display of colours of the flower-borders and flowering shrubs: the aśoka (*Saraca indica*), with a blazing orange or scarlet blossom, the pale blossoms of the *śirīṣa* (*Allizia leblek*), the sweet-scented *kadamba* (*Convolvulus repens*), the scarlet *kiṃśuka* (*Butea frondosa*), honey-scented jasmin, the white *atimukta* (*Hiptage madablota*), the *champaka* (*Michelia champaca*) with its sweet-smelling yellow flowers, hibiscus (*japā*), and many other varieties. Apart from the pleasant sight that they offered the eyes, they provided a constant source of supply of fresh garlands and other adornments for every member of the family.

Each household possessed its domestic animals: cats, often depicted in the act of stalking birds on the rooftops; peacocks, geese and parrots, whose cries served as an alarm signal when snakes appeared; and mongooses, trained by men of low caste, which performed the invaluable task of attacking snakes, fighting them bravely and killing them.

In these more luxurious homes, the furniture was more elegant and more varied than that to be found in rural houses. The bedroom of the master of the house contained a soft bed covered by a white bedspread, furnished with two pillows, one for the head and one for the feet, and surmounted by an elaborately decorated canopy. His room was large enough to contain, in addition, a divan and a small table on which were ranged unguents and cosmetics; on one side was a basket containing the garlands of flowers with which he bedecked himself each day; there were also containers of betel leaves and jars of perfume. These all had a part in his daily toilet. Near the divan, a cuspidor on the floor stood ready to receive the red expectoration caused by betel chewing. There was also another table, on which he could paint or draw, and wall-shelves contained books made of palm-leaves bound between two boards of carved or painted wood. A chessboard was in position near the bed, and a *vīṇā* (a stringed bow-harp) hung on the wall.[54] A bench, and a few cushions strewn over the ground, completed the room's furniture.

RELIGIOUS STRUCTURES AND SACRED SPOTS

The description of the background to daily life would be incomplete without reference being made to the innumerable religious edifices, attendance at which was an important feature of popular custom. During the preceding pages, we have alluded frequently to the religious basis of Indian society, and in the following chapter we shall describe the preponderant role that religious practices played in individual and collective existence. At this point, however, we shall consider simply the forms of holy places and shrines.

During the epoch with which we are concerned, a tremendous variety of such structures existed. Indeed, it is remarkable to what a degree mental and physical forms belonging to extremely different stages of evolution are to be found side by side; this fact demonstrates vividly the reluctance with which Indian tradition has ever consented to abandon archaic elements in favour of more recent formulas. For this reason, one witnesses a curious overlapping of disparate forms, some of which should logically belong to an extremely distant – even prehistoric – epoch, while others, on the contrary, denote an advanced stage of development, both in the field of beliefs and that of architecture. It would be wrong to imagine that the advanced forms characterize the mentality evolved in the large towns, while the primitive ones are typical of the more backward customs of rural society: in the capital as in the villages, the perennial nature of traditions permitted the most elementary form of sacred place and the most elaborately conceived religious edifice to exist side by side. This phenomenon is by no means restricted to ancient times; on the contrary, this same co-existence has been perpetuated right up to our own era, a fact which contributes greatly to the interest India presents to the historian of religions.

The idea of the sanctity of particular spots goes back to Vedism and beyond, expressing itself through natural elements such as knolls or rocks, a sacred tree, an upright stone, water in every aspect, or, in a more general manner, through a 'landscape' composed of these elements, so that their coming together characterizes the privileged place and transforms it into something quasi-divine. By a scarcely perceptible evolution, these essential elements were gradually transformed into a more abstract whole: the tree became the sacrificial stake, or even the royal column venerated at the entrance to all towns and villages; the upright stone gradually became metamorphosed into a phallus (*liṅga*) symbolizing the god Śiva, then into a statue erected on a plinth or altar, which was itself the evolved form of the rock in the ancient sacred 'landscape'. Water remained always supremely sacred in every aspect of worship; its fertilizing nature combined with properties considered purifying and even sanctifying. So as to protect the sacred spot or constituent parts of it against animals and evil spirits, they were surrounded, originally, by a wooden fence, then later by a stone wall, and eventually the latter became the temple's surrounding wall. In the same way, a shelter was constructed over the upright stone which later was transformed into the god's cella, and later still into a shrine. This logical process is generally that of all religious cults throughout the world; in India, its originality lies in the fact that all the stages persisted simultaneously.

As a result, it was possible to see in a single populated area a sacred tree surrounded by its fence, a domed monument of masonry (originating in the tumulus) called a *stūpa*, a pavilion containing the ritual fire or a live sacred serpent, and also one or several temples housing statues of divinities. In this way, manifestations of all the stages of evolution of the sacred place could be found grouped together, at the same point of time, irrespective of the antiquity of their respective origins, or even of the religion to which they had once belonged. The cult of sacred trees (see pp. 154–5), which evolved from a very ancient fertility cult, is a good example, in that it was adopted by Buddhism and became one of its fundamental themes: it was, in fact, while meditating under the shade of a certain fig-tree (the pipal or *Ficus religiosa*), growing in Bodh-gayā, that the historical Buddha received illumination (*bodhi*). This tree was the chief object of veneration for Buddhists throughout Asia, and the emperor Aśoka lavished great care and attention on it, first surrounding it with a wall surmounted by a wooden gallery, then, twenty-three years later, with yet another wall of brick and stone, so transforming the original sacred spot into a shrine. Bodh-gayā has remained to this day one of Buddhism's most holy places of pilgrimage. But it is significant that there is also a stone slab there, near the tree, called the 'diamond seat' (*vajrāsana*); this represents an evolved form of the stone or rock of the sacred landscape of ancient times, and still serves as an altar for offerings.[55] Not all sacred trees were honoured so ostentatiously, but even the humblest village possessed one, as did the capital city's main districts, so these great trees, on the branches of which villagers or city-dwellers came to hang garlands,[56] were, with their surrounding carved railings (*vedikā*), a familiar sight throughout the country.

Equally familiar were the small columned structures housing the sacred fire or else the image of a god;[57] and the altar-thrones, of which the *vajrāsana* of Bodh-gayā is the most famous example, upon which the god was supposed to take his rest, occasionally manifesting himself miraculously to some privileged devotee.[58] In addition, there were many temples and shrines whose taller timbered structures could be seen from far away.

The best known to us are the Buddhist shrines (*caitya*) whose smallest details can still be studied in the shape of the artificial caves, excavated for religious purposes, which still survive, and also the depictions on bas-reliefs and mural paintings. These cave temples were huge rectangular or apsidal constructions, containing a central nave resting on pillars, flanked by side-aisles. Their roofs were barrel-vaulted, and supported by an intricate scheme of curved ribs; light was provided by a high, wide entrance with a horseshoe-shaped gable-end, and also by dormer windows of the same type. The curved roofing, similar to that of communal granaries, was set off by a line of crest-tiles that had been turned on a lathe. These temples were built in exactly the same way as the private dwellings of the time. They were places where people met together and prayed, and where the faithful accomplished the ceremonial clockwise circumambulation (*pradakṣiṇā*) around a reliquary occupying the back of the central nave.

This reliquary was simply a small-scale version of the great monuments erected out of doors, called *stūpas* (*dāgäbas* in Sinhalese), which remain today the most venerated of all monuments in those countries practising the Buddhist religion. It is most probable that stūpas had a funerary origin, deriving from tumuli or even from the earlier Vedic tombs; later, they were set up over the ashes left by the cremation of the bodies of holy men or 'universal sovereigns', over relics having belonged to them, as a sacred trust, to commemorate a miracle, to mark a sacred spot, or simply to gain merit for the person who paid the cost of building it. Over a period of time, the stūpa retained the shape of a burial mound covered with a brick shell.[59] Then it evolved, but kept its essential nature of being a solid edifice which it was impossible to enter. The dome (*aṇḍa*) rested on a square or circular base, which became progressively higher in succeeding epochs; the flattened tip of the dome supported a square aedicule (*harmikā*) surrounded by a balustrade, from the centre of which rose the stone umbrella (*chattra*), symbol of dignity, which was itself surmounted by a 'rain pot' similar to those placed on the roofs of communal granaries.

The construction of a stūpa followed traditional rules. It began with the erection of four flights of steps, each of which was set steeply into one of the faces of the base wall. At the same time, the base was built up in three successive tiers. The dome was then constructed, of rough stones, rubble or pebbles bound with clay; it was often divided into sections demarcated by interior walls radiating around the centre like the segments of an orange. For more even distribution of the pressure of the construction materials, horizontal courses buttressed these divisions.

In the centre of the stūpa, at the heart of the masonry, a cavity lined with slabs of stone, like a box, communicated with the outside of the dome by a narrow tunnel. During the consecration ceremonies, the relics or the holy deposits were dropped into the cavity and the tunnel was then sealed up. Similarly, a sort of well was built into the centre of the *harmikā*, penetrating deep into the masonry of the flattened top of the dome and closed at its base by a large stone slab: this well was designed to receive the umbrella's heavy shaft made of iron or of hard wood. To hoist this to the summit of the stūpa, it was necessary first of all to construct four wooden 'towers', each topped by a winch and cables with which this great column could be raised up as high as the well's orifice and lowered into it until it was firmly held. Unfortunately, the iron pillar supporting the umbrella often fulfilled the function of lightning conductor, and many such structures were struck by lightning and destroyed. This is one of the main reasons why only a few of the ancient stūpas have survived.

Finally, the stūpa's stonework was overlayed, according to the region, by plaques of marble, schist or stone that were often sculptured, or else covered with a layer of stucco painted many different colours and gilded. A *vedikā* was put up around the base, and this usually had doors set into it that were either fitted with obstacles or screens to keep out animals and evil spirits – the latter were popularly supposed to be able to move only straight ahead.

The size of the stūpas varied a great deal, ranging from gigantic domes such as that of Amarāvatī (probably second century AD), which measured nearly one hundred and eighty feet around the base and was nearly fifty feet high, to tiny stūpas carved out of a single block of stone, erected piously by humble citizens. One of the most celebrated stūpas is that of Bhārhut (second century BC); its balustrade, most of which is preserved in the Calcutta Museum, carries splendid carvings on its pillars and handrail. Other famous examples are the stūpas at Sānchī in Bhopal (completed first century AD), still standing on their original site, in which the decoration is concentrated on the porticoes (*toraṇa*);[60]

and that of Amarāvatī, whose cap and base were covered with historiated bas-reliefs.

Behind the sacred nature of the stūpa, a symbolic meaning was gradually elaborated, according to which the actual body of the Buddha finally became identified with the monument; and the cosmological concepts current in ancient India, being grafted upon this tradition, ended up by identifying the stūpa as the symbolic microcosm of the universe.[61]

From about the fourth century onwards, these various religious edifices were supplemented by brāhmaṇic temples built of robust materials, although the old-style timbered buildings were by no means supplanted. These new temples, made of brick and stone, repeated the same formulas as those made of wood while adapting them to the new materials, thus initiating an architectural evolution which led to the gigantic achievements of the Middle Ages. In ancient times, the shrine remained comparatively small, occupying approximately the centre of a square or rectangular surrounding wall pierced with doors, one of which was considered the main entrance. Their orientation varied according to the divinity to whom the temple was dedicated, but was always most carefully calculated. Within the enclosure were arranged additional buildings, mostly made of wood and haphazard in arrangement; there was a hall for the staff, some secondary chapels, kitchens, stables for the sacred cattle, and a room set aside for sacred dances, dramatic performances and epic recitations. Ablutions were performed in a nearby pond or pool, and there was also a 'grove of penitence' where the inhabitants retired to meditate.

A brāhmaṇic temple was not frequented only by devout persons and by pilgrims; it also constituted a shelter for travellers and beggars, a refuge for condemned persons, and an asylum for the sick and the dying, who were brought there so that they might breathe their last in a holy place. Sometimes, indeed, it was the seat of a university: in that case it contained, in addition to the buildings already mentioned, a college, one or more hostels for students and teachers, and a hospital. Such a conglomeration was really a religious city, filled with activity and movement, thronged by the faithful and by pilgrims, by students, servants, priests, while hawkers of 'souvenirs' and garlands encumbered the cloisters where the visitors were resting and strolling. The courtyards had gravel surfaces, the doors were garnished with garlands of flowers and greenery, and the walls were marked by the imprint of hands dipped in sandalwood as a symbol of prophylactic magic and of veneration.[62] At the hours of the daily services and on the occasion of ceremonies and holidays, the sacred orchestra struck up its resonant music, just as it still does today. Gongs, clarinets, conches and cymbals, in a more or less discordant din which could be heard from far away, reminded all the faithful that a service was taking place.

This, then, was the extremely variegated background against which the religious existence of villagers and city dwellers unfolded, whatever their particular religion.

CHAPTER TWO

THE IMPORTANCE OF RELIGION IN DAILY LIFE

The shepherds disported themselves, taking pleasure in sprinkling and smearing each other with curds, milk, ghee, water and cream.
Bhāgavata Purāṇa, X, v.

In ancient India, the entire life of an individual was subordinated to religious concepts, to the customs imposed by these concepts and to the superstitions which insisted that each single act, however unimportant, must unavoidably entail a good or bad consequence. The religious mentality of the people was highly developed, and so this state of affairs was not only freely tolerated but even actively insisted on. The pre-eminent position of the priestly caste of brāhmaṇs encouraged this permissive attitude; but it is true to say, also, that the brāhmaṇs were frequently overwhelmed by the sheer strength of popular enthusiasms, which imposed on them, whether they liked it or not, a number of chthonic creeds which their love of dogmatic purity urged them to reject.

From the moment that he was conceived, an Indian belonged to a caste corresponding to a religious social structure. Furthermore, he belonged not only to a caste but also to a 'clan' (*gotra*), this tie of kindred being ratified by a sort of ritual communion (*śrāddha*). From birth to death, he received a whole sequence of sacraments: those of infancy, brāhmaṇic initiation, marriage or the eremitic state. Even after his death, ritual – which made him a 'father' (*pitṛ*) or ancestor – still bound him to his *gotra* and integrated him into the family's religious system.

Apart from these fundamental modalities, each person's daily life was lived within a framework of countless religious (and magical) acts, while the annual cycle of festivals provided the rhythm of collective life.

SEASONAL RITUALS AND FESTIVALS

Rural life was accompanied by rites, some of which were repeated at regular and close intervals, while others were only occasional or seasonal. The former were celebrated once a month, preferably on the afternoon of the day of the full moon, and took place in honour of the 'fathers' (*pitṛ*), that is to say each family's direct ancestors, all of whom were presumed to reside in the sky, or sometimes in the air or on a particular star, and who, in any case, ranked with the gods. So that they should not become hostile and would retain their nature as fathers, they were offered food to eat, rice-balls, meat-balls (*piṇḍa*) and cakes, placed on the ground on beds of rushes. This monthly rite was supplemented by other ceremonies, conducted at full moon and at new moon, which included the preparation and adornment of oblations, the enumeration of ancestors, and various offerings.

Apart from these specifically family rites, the peasant followed the rhythm of the seasons with their dependent festivals.

The new year began on a date which varied according to the particular region and, indeed, from one century to another, but usually coincided with the spring equinox. At this time of year, a 'spring-cleaning' was mandatory, and private homes were meticulously cleaned, washed, rubbed with oil and fumigated with a mixture of fragrant herbs. Several festivals were celebrated during this period, all popular occasions.

First of all, some time in February or March, there took place a kind of saturnalia (what is today called the *Holī*), the survival of a primitive fertility ritual, combining erotic games, 'comic operas' and folk-dancing. During the course of these festivities, men and women of every class chased each other through the streets and parks, armed with gold-painted syringes filled with water dyed red or orange, with which they squirted each other indiscriminately.[1] Large urns filled with coloured water were positioned at various points, to allow the participants to recharge their weapons.

During the same month, at nightfall, a ceremonial wagon dedicated to the spring sun was solemnly drawn through the town or village, its surface covered with iridescent and glittering fabrics and adorned with masses of flowers. Carrying flaming torches, the crowd pressed closely around it in a slowly moving procession, accompanying it with songs and rhythmic cries, pelting it with flowers, rice grains and incense, while an orchestra preceded it, beating drums and kettledrums loudly and blowing into conches with all their might.

While the king was ploughing the first furrow, amid great pomp and ceremony, on his own royal estates (see p. 39), the peasants propitiated their fields by sprinkling them with consecrated water; after doing this, they went through a pretence of sowing, then left the ploughshare lying on the fallow ground after sprinkling it, too, with water. On the following day, they made offerings of melted ghee to the furrow (*sītā*) and to its protective spirits, while reciting wishes of well-being and prosperity. As soon as the fields were ploughed, sowing took place to the accompaniment of certain rites, such as that of throwing broadcast three successive handfuls of grain that had been dipped in ghee. This ceremony provided the pretext for a feast on the eve of the sowing, after which the remains of the meal were added to the sacks of grain so as to assure, through imitative magic, the abundance and good quality of the crops.

Two weeks after the *Holī* spring festival, there took place the festival of the god of Love, Kāma, an occasion which demanded massed illuminations. And now, too, the swings which had been stored away the previous autumn at the onset of the monsoon were brought out again and set up in every garden. On the third clear day of the month of *Caitra* (March–April), girls and young women competed with each other on the swings in honour of the goddess Gauri; the higher they went, the bigger would grow the new shoots and the finer would be the harvest.[2] At the same time, in the brāhmaṇic temple the effigies of the gods were placed in cradles and swung to and fro, a process originating in a Vedic ritual in which the officiating priest (*hotṛ*) himself mounted the temple's swing to imitate the course of the sun.[3]

At the beginning of spring, too, effigies were constructed, from barley dough covered with wool, of a ram and a ewe, whose symbolic coupling would ensure that the herds flourished. Five oblations were also made, followed by six more on the first day of the first fortnight, and a votive rite on the sixth day of that fortnight. And during this period, a bull was consecrated and adorned, then let loose.

During May–June, at the time when the crops were ripening and the cows were calving, the festival of the 'mother of the spirits' (*bhūtamātṛ*) was celebrated. This lasted a whole fortnight and was more of an orgy than anything else. Men dressed as women, and women as men, for this 'mother of the spirits' was an androgyne who was supposed to live in the waters of the village's river. The whole population indulged in wild gesticulations, sang erotic songs and abandoned themselves to sensual debauchery.

There followed the processes of reaping, harvesting and threshing, each of which involved different ritual offerings, one to the 'cultivated field', another to the 'queen of the moles and mice', and so on. Insects and harmful animals were combatted by various magical incantations. Similar spells existed to ward off the storms that threatened the harvest. The marking of flocks and herds took place at this time, also in a ritualistic context. During July–August, new amulets, made mostly of shellac and special herbs, were fashioned and replaced the old ones in the prescribed spots.[4]

Finally, the eagerly awaited monsoon rains came. If their onset was delayed unduly, rain-making spells were chanted, or a twelve days' fast was undertaken, or a rainstorm was simulated by swirling stalks of grass in a jar of water. As soon as the rains seemed imminent, every household raised the height of the father's and mother's beds by placing additional supports under the legs; an offering of millet was made and, during a special ceremony, special fruits were cast on top of the other offerings, the whole constituting a rain-making spell. But the most vital precaution in this season was to avert the dangers arising from snakes, which became particularly aggressive as soon as they sensed the oncoming humidity; to this end, an oblation accompanied by incantations was repeated each day for four months, until the return of the dry season.

During this period (August–September–October), one or more festivals took place, devoted to Durgā; these comprised a procession headed by the ceremonial wagon in which the image of the goddess, sumptuously adorned, had been placed. The wagon itself was decorated with sparkling mirrors and with gaily tinkling little bells; it rumbled slowly through the rain-sodden streets, between the specially bedecked houses, while the women and girls covered the effigy with flowers, handfuls of grass, unhusked rice and water. In some regions, according to Jain sources, a 'house of flowers' was then constructed on the main road and decorated with magnificent garlands. Everywhere, in towns and villages alike, beautiful designs were made on flat stretches of ground, using grains of rice 'of five colours'.

At this time of year, the Buddhist monks emerged from the retreats to which they had retired at the beginning of the rainy season in order to give themselves up to meditation. Now they resumed their interrupted missions throughout the country, and their yellow robes could be seen once again in the streets.

During this same season, the festival of 'Indra's standard' was celebrated, at least vicariously, everywhere.[5] The presence of the king being mandatory, this festival was most brilliant and impressive in the capital itself. The 'standard' was a tree, carefully chosen in the surrounding forests.[6] After it had been cut down, and its branches lopped off, it was carried with great ceremony to the gaily bedecked town, where it was set up in the main square, then adorned with white banners, small bells, garlands, scarves of iridescent material, strings of bright trinkets and clusters of fruit of many different kinds. Its decoration was accomplished to the sound of drum-beats and the loud, welcoming cries of the crowd, and finally it was kept securely upright by ropes. It now became the focal point of popular celebrations, and dances, poetic songs, various kinds of juggling, and aspersions of camphorated water succeeded each other around it. On the seventh day, which coincided with the full moon, the 'standard' was lowered and carried to the river, where the current was allowed to sweep it away.[7]

When the rains had ceased, the beds in each household were replaced on the ground, and the master of the house sat down on the house's earth-floor, on strewn rushes, followed by his family, who arranged themselves by order of age; a rite in propitiation of the ground then confirmed this act of taking possession once more. During this season, an offering of bamboo shoots was also made.

At the beginning of autumn, sacrifices were performed to ensure the prosperity of the herds and flocks, and offerings of rice or millet were made at the same time. Then came the harvest-festivals. The farm-workers addressed their offerings to the two guardian spirits of the plough, and each category of worker carried out similarly appropriate rites. And a ceremony which was basically a ritual of death was performed at a crossroads:

in this, cakes were thrown up in the air and caught in either of two baskets hung from the opposite ends of a pole; there had to be as many cakes as there were members of the family, plus an additional cake which was subsequently buried in an ant-heap.

During October–November, the autumn-festival or Feast of Lamps (the modern *Divālī*) took place and provided a new pretext for public merry-making lasting three whole days. On the first day people bathed, purified themselves ritually and offered a libation in honour of the 'king of the dead', while temples and public places were illuminated. On the second day, a carnival was organized with music, dancing and games of chance; people drank alcohol to a point of drunkenness, and visited prostitutes. At midnight in the capital, the king emerged without any escort and mixed freely with the rejoicing throng. On the third day, the prostitutes went from house to house, wishing good luck to the inhabitants. At the same time, the king distributed presents. And the day ended with a cattle-fair and with fights between animals.

These combats were one of the favourite diversions of all classes of the population: oxen, buffaloes, horses, elephants and, in particular, goats, peacocks and cocks were trained to fight each other. The betting on the results involved large sums of money, and the owner of a successful animal or bird could expect to win a handsome amount. This festival was accompanied by 'drinking feasts',[8] bacchanalian revels during which the people were granted a temporary exemption from taxes on alcohol, and everyone was authorized to distil alcohol for his own personal use during the few days that the excesses lasted. The entire population was given free rein to abandon itself to an orgy of meat-eating and drunkenness. People were overtaken collectively by a wild gaiety, shouting, dancing – and, very often, quarrelling and coming to blows. The festival usually ended in disputes and more tragic events, resulting in innumerable broken arms and legs, ears torn off, and murders aplenty.

When the cool season returned with the winter solstice, there were fresh rejoicings, this particular celebration being accompanied by music, dances and a procession followed by immersion in the river, symbolic of fecundity.

Then the cycle recommenced.

In this manner, rural life was punctuated by rites and festivals occurring at regular intervals throughout the year, supplemented by superstitions and 'magical' experiments.

POPULAR CULTS, MAGIC AND SUPERSTITIONS

The invisible was as real as the visible to ordinary people. A great number of local and minor cults developed, some of which achieved such importance that they were eventually absorbed into the brāhmaṇic pantheon, and were even awarded a measure of recognition by Buddhism. The theory of the transmigration of souls, so firmly anchored in the Indian mentality, inevitably lent authority to the popular belief that there existed a whole category of supernatural beings, whose malevolent or benevolent activities exercised a constant influence on the life of individuals. The list was extensive: there were familiar spirits ranging the surface of the earth every night, devouring the putrefied flesh of corpses, vomiting fire and interfering with sacrifices; malicious, cruel goblins; vampires who loved to eat raw flesh; female demons and wizards, ogresses – the 'snatchers' who took possession of new-born babies and made them die; ghosts, too, who were all deceased persons that had succumbed to a violent death and had therefore turned into pernicious night-wanderers infesting the ground, the trees, the waters and the mountains. These fearful apparitions were opposed by a series of more or less well-disposed guardian spirits which lived everywhere – in the towns' and villages' outer gates, in springs, rivers and hills, in crossroads, stones and boundary-posts, in trees, in subterranean regions and caverns, cemeteries and cremation sites. Even the domestic hearth contained one.

The animal, vegetable and mineral worlds also formed part of this latent, mysterious life. Rare stones served as habitations for certain spirits, and such stones might themselves be the result of the coupling of certain genii. Plants, endowed with a dormant consciousness and some degree of knowledge, possessed magical powers and curative virtues, and featured largely in religious rites.

As for animals, they were akin to men, partly because, as a result of the laws of transmigration, they harboured a migratory soul, and partly because they were deemed to possess the same sensibility as men and the same capacity to express it. They often played a part in brāhmaṇic mythology and in Buddhist tales. Among them, the cow was already surrounded by great respect, though not yet the object of the cult which was later devoted to it; it was granted an important place in the semi-divine hierarchy because all its products (milk, curd, ghee, urine and dung) had a part in ritual. The bull Nandi, the god Śiva's mount, was one of the most august of all bovines and held divine status. Similarly, the horse was considered to be a sacred animal when it served as the king's mascot, and the god Viṣṇu incarnated himself in the form of a horse during the course of one of his 'descents' (*avatāra*) into the world of men; Buddhism also had its divine horse in the person of the *Bodhisattva* Balāha, whose mission consisted in saving travellers in distress.

The elephant was perhaps the noblest of all animals, for it was claimed that a cloud gave birth to it. Symbolizing strength and wisdom, stability and prudence, it had an illustrious representative in the brāhmaṇic pantheon in the person of Gaṇeśa, son of Śiva, elephant-headed and patron of intellectuals. Monkeys provided a constant theme for popular legend, in which they played the role of turbulent, empty-headed creatures, living in troops, commanded by brave chiefs, and committing various misdeeds which were, nevertheless, treated indulgently. They were also judged capable of prodigious feats. Several of them achieved lasting fame in brāhmaṇic mythology. One such was the virtuous Hanumant, son of the Wind, a solar hero and a messenger who flew like an arrow through space. Hanumant is celebrated by an epic poem in the Rāmāyaṇa; he was the object of a cult in which his image was represented by a vaguely anthropomorphic raised stone.

Some other four-legged animals were either feared or distrusted: the donkey's braying was baneful and it was itself the epitome of lubricity; the jackal was of ill omen; the dog was an impure and base creature, and a member of its species kept constant watch on the infernal regions governed by the god of the dead, Yama.

Birds were naturally assimilated into this supernatural world because their essential nature was believed to be celestial and solar. Wild ducks and migratory geese (*haṃsa*) symbolized souls journeying towards the moon. The crow, garrulous, inquisitive and greedy, was made responsible for transmitting love messages and also for delivering oracles. The cuckoo (*kokila*) awoke amorous desires with its languorous cries. The parrot, traditional confidant of young lovers, had the power to cure certain diseases, including jaundice, by transferring them magically to another object. And the partridge (*cakora*) had the reputation of feeding on the rays of the moon.

Certainly, this was a world of very minor deities. But it was still a vital entity in the popular imagination, so much so that it was often confused with the human world. At any rate, if we are to believe contemporary accounts, it was by no means rare to encounter a particular spirit materialized in human form,[9] its real origin being discoverable only by means of strange clues which constituted a sort of code of the supernatural. In addition, these fanciful beings often possessed the faculty of assuming human guise, marrying human beings and procreating a line of descendants that was half divine, half human.

Confusion reigned, and legends abound in the most astonishing misapprehensions. The most celebrated mistake of all concerns the life of the Buddha himself: he was seated beneath the tree of Enlightenment, after having just vanquished the dual assault of the demon Māra, when the holy woman of Buddhism, Sujatā, approached the sacred tree to deposit a food offering near its trunk, as she did every day. Seeing the Buddha, motionless, at the foot of the tree, in the attitude of meditation, the young woman thought that she was looking at the tree's guardian spirit and marvelled that she was able to contemplate it thus.[10] Undeceived by the Buddha, she realized the nature of the supreme being with whom she was confronted and served him joyfully. The fact remains that Sujatā was not otherwise surprised to encounter a guardian spirit of a sacred tree in human form. Doubt concerning the true nature of beings was, indeed, so commonplace that Buddhist monks were in the habit, before admitting a neophyte into the community, of asking him the curious question: 'Are you man or serpent (*nāga*)?' so that they might exclude him if he did not really belong to the human species.

Once the reality of this supernatural world had been admitted, the Indians' highly developed talent for classification set to work dividing the gods and guardian spirits into various categories. There were the *yakṣas*, who preferred to live in big trees, and the *nāgas*, who lived in caverns and subterranean waters; they are dealt with more fully in the following pages. There were also the *vidyādharas*, who had human form, were expert magicians and were specially adept at marrying any young woman whom they found sufficiently seductive. The *gandharvas* were celestial singers and musicians living in splendid cities, who wooed women (especially young, unmarried ones) and troubled the minds of men by urging them to indulge in wine, gaming and love-making. Their wives and lovers, called *apsarases*, were water nymphs whose beauty, created for the sensual delight of the gods, inspired passion in the hearts of all men who saw them, including ascetics, though they themselves preferred to choose their husbands from among warriors killed on the field of battle. It seems, though, that these nymphs were at the mercy of any man who was lucky enough to surprise one of them bathing in a river and succeeded in stealing her clothes.

Although each of these semi-divine categories possessed its own characteristics, these fanciful beings shared some common features: they all had a very long life-span but they were, nevertheless, mortal, vulnerable to certain wounds, and might even be captured by men through trickery.

They were able to make themselves invisible or to assume human shape, and they understood the language of animals as well as all mankind's dialects. However, they were endowed with only relatively limited magical powers, and most of them, for instance, were unable to divine the thoughts or plans of human beings unless these were spoken out aloud in their presence. They were organized in a fashion similar to human society, forming distinct peoples, possessing chieftains or even kings, living in towns and in palaces, making war and serving often as emissaries on behalf of their rulers both in the celestial and human worlds.[11]

The *yakṣas* were perhaps the best known of all these supernatural beings.[12] They were known by various epithets, 'those who are not men' (*amānuṣas*), 'marvellous and mysterious entities', or 'the hidden ones', and were sometimes confused with the 'cadastral gods'. They constituted a curious army – fairly low in the divine hierarchy – commanded by the obese Kubera, captain of Indra, king of the gods; their leader also had the tasks of distributing fortunes and protecting travellers.[13] Ancient painting and sculpture depicted the *yakṣas* under many different guises, including that of a horse's head on a human body;[14] but it seems, on the whole, that popular tradition had no very fixed ideas on the subject. In any case, they were polymorphous, like most of their celestial colleagues. But Buddhist tales provide a wealth of information on the mentality ascribed to them, and on their habits.

According to these accounts, they preferred to choose their home in large trees, either in forests or, more usually, in some lonely space on the outskirts of town or near the burial-grounds. Installing themselves in the fork formed by the conjunction of the tree's main limbs, or in the cavities of gnarled trunks, they settled down to found a family after marrying a dryad. Like ordinary mortals, they cherished their children and had friendly relations with other *yakṣas*, with whom they exchanged touching conversations.

But they also possessed enemies, chief among which were banyan trees and woodcutters. Banyans, the giants of the forest, spread their vast, rooting branches so widely that they condemned to certain death all neighbouring trees, deprived by the banyan's shade of the air and sunshine necessary for their own existence.[15] Woodcutters were equally treacherous: it was all very well for them to warn the *yakṣa* politely when they wanted to cut down 'his' tree – the fact remained that he still had no choice but to pack up and find another home. And this prospect seemed to affect the *yakṣas* deeply, not so much because of the trouble involved in moving to another tree (there were forests in abundance and, in any case, reforestation was an important ritual activity)[16] but rather because they were really an integral part of the tree of their choice; being identified with it, its loss was a personal and grievous blow. It is for this reason that they apparently preferred to inhabit the sacred trees to be found in every town and village, trees that could never be felled by woodcutters.

An added advantage for the *yakṣas* living in a sacred tree was that it provided an ideal observatory from which they could participate in everyday activities, and enabled them to indulge their fondness for admonishing and moralizing, and their penchant for making predictions. People frequently came to consult them; in an unearthly voice sounding like an echo, they gave their opinion, made comments and even acted as arbitrators. It was known occasionally for practical jokers to have the idea of imitating their supernatural voice so as to be able to make lying pronouncements. One of these pranksters paid dearly for his imposture: it is related that he climbed into the tree occupied by a *yakṣa* and got ready to be interrogated so that he could pronounce his false oracle; unfortunately, the interrogator began to suspect a hoax and, wanting to verify whether or not he was really dealing with a *yakṣa*, set fire to the tree, knowing that a genuine *yakṣa* would escape without harm – and the deceiver soon tumbled down from it, half roasted.[17]

The trees in cemeteries, peopled by vultures and carrion-crows, also harboured *yakṣas*. These contemplated the distressing scenes of burials and cremations, and witnessed the torturing of criminals, at the cost, sometimes, of seeing their finest branches lopped off to serve as stakes for impalement.[18]

The relationship between *yakṣas* and human beings was based on a sort of mutual blackmail from which both parties derived equal benefit: in exchange for appropriate offerings, they were more or less bound to grant what was asked of them. Their clients hoped to obtain from them honour, prosperity, longevity, all these being things that the *yakṣas* were supposedly in a position to obtain for them. In addition, the *yakṣis* (female *yakṣas*) had the particular mission of making barren women fertile;[19] but these dryads were not simply providers of children, for they were also ogresses who were just as capable of devouring children as of curing them of their childish ailments.

To gratify them, elaborate cults were built around them.[20] Their trees were surrounded by wooden or stone barriers, to guarantee them against all external attack, and an altar was built nearby. The earth around the tree-trunks was carefully cleaned and swept. The villagers, chiefly the women, came often to hang beautiful garlands on their branches, hoping to persuade the *yakṣas* to act in their favour. They sprinkled the trunk with sugared water, milk or honey, and smeared it with red-coloured powders and oils. Some made ritual lustrations by spurting water at the trunk from their mouths. Offerings of cakes were placed on its altar and between its roots, incense sticks were left to smoulder, and tiny lamps were lighted. Then the petitioners walked respectfully around the tree, keeping it to the right and occasionally stroking its bark with their right hand.[21]

In return for these attentions, the *yakṣas* were expected to render the services demanded, and if they got into the habit of accepting too many gifts without giving anything in exchange, the villagers did not hesitate to abandon them or, at least, hold aloof from them. On the other hand, it was dangerous to neglect them too greatly, since they often stood guard over treasure buried at the foot of their tree (and every individual hoped to possess it one day, with their consent); more important still, their very presence was a guarantee of the prosperity of the village in which they lived. Even so, it was considered perfectly normal to address them brusquely and demand immediate action. A discontented suppliant might very well speak to them in such terms as, 'If you do not grant me the favour I have asked of you, I shall have your tree cut down one week from now!', a threat which must inevitably fill the *yakṣas* or the *yakṣis* with anguish and prompt a spirit of compliance. On the other hand, if a satisfied customer promised them offerings, after having his wish granted, and failed to bring them, he could expect reprisals.[22]

In the daily life of countryfolk, cobras or *nāgas* also played an important part. In the days of Alexander the Great, the soldiers of the Greek army which had entered India had been mightily impressed by the country's serpents, which had terrified them with their sinister hissing at the mouths of caves and with their glittering eyes 'as large as Macedonian shields'.[23] The *nāgas* lived in the subterranean world and on the beds of rivers and lakes, forming a whole population with its own flourishing capital, Bhogavatī ('The-Rich-in-Pleasures'). Their sovereigns had the reputation of being very powerful and very noble-minded. Communication between their kingdom and the human world was established through the medium of caves and ant-hills, both of which occupied an important place in Indian popular tradition.

The *nāgas* were sacred beings whom it was forbidden to touch, and whose complex characters made them equally feared and adored. Their aggressive tendencies were proverbial, and their vengeful spirit made them quite capable, supposedly, of exterminating an entire population, either by exuding the fatal poison contained in their fangs, or by suffocating their victims in their coils. They were also capable of blinding people with their foul breath, or killing them with the fire of their glance: indeed, their gaze was so powerful that it could easily reduce a whole town to ashes. Yet, despite this, they were equally capable of coming to the aid of humans and could, like the *yakṣas*, make women fertile. They also guarded treasures buried in the ground, and awarded them to humans (but were equally capable of appropriating treasures themselves). They were adept at assuming human appearance, and many *nāgis* (female serpents) lived among men, arousing passions on account of their beauty; when night fell, however, they reassumed their snake-like shape, a transformation which must have demanded considerable skill in order not to betray their fearful origin.[24] The *nāgas* also had the reputation of 'giving rain', since they were chiefly to be seen prior to the rainy season, when the humidity regularly brought them out of their lairs. The skin they sloughed was supposed to have the power of granting invisibility to the one who picked it up, and to ensure him long life, or even immortality, since the process of sloughing off symbolized the soul liberating itself from evil and the cycle of rebirths.

They were, indeed, often considered as protectors of the domestic hearth, which, it was feared, might not survive if its tutelary serpent should disappear: consequently, food and drink were laid out for it assiduously. They sometimes assumed the role of 'presiding genius' in a particular village, in which case they were worshipped in daily ceremonies: the village built a small shrine for its tutelary serpent, in the shape of a pavilion,[25] with a well-sanded floor upon which the local people came to place offerings of milk (much appreciated by cobras), rice, fish, meat, liquid preparations and so on. And, every day, the master of each household made them an offering in his own home. Statues were raised to them, too, usually near the springs or pools of which they were the recognized protectors. Many of these sculptures can be counted among the masterpieces of ancient art; they represented them generally in the form of a man back to back with a coiled serpent sprouting a number of hooded heads, the man holding a ciborium filled with ambrosia in his left hand, and pointing with the outstretched forefinger of his right hand towards the sky, in a gesture of appeal for rain.[26] To conciliate them, the local inhabitants offered them water, a comb, perfumes or a mirror. Many spells and incantations existed, as well, some to attract their protection, others to guard against their attacks; a few privileged beings claimed to have obtained from the *nāgas* themselves certain magical formulas endowing them with extraordinary powers.

Charms and magical formulas did, in fact, cover the smallest contingencies of daily life. With the onset of a headache, the sufferer hastily transferred the pain to the hills and forests. A yawn or sneeze called for a wish to be quickly pronounced: 'May steadfastness and wisdom inhabit me!'[27] or 'Long life to such-and-such a person!'[28] – although such exclamations were perhaps as bereft of real meaning as when we say 'God bless you!' or 'The best of health!' When a drop of rain fell on one, it was a sign of good luck;[29] if it was a bird-dropping, it presaged happiness, but it was necessary to remove it without touching it with one's hand and then wash oneself with water.[30]

People also attempted to foretell the future. If, for example, the owner of a herd was anxious to know, during the breeding period, whether his animals were going to be fecund, he had to go outside the village in the small hours of the night, then, in the silence preceding dawn, yell three times at the top of his voice. If any animal other than a dog or a donkey answered him, he was assured of a good year; if it was a dog or a donkey, it was a bad sign; but if there was no answer at all, the experiment was invalid and had to be repeated the following year.

Dreams occupied an important place in everyday existence, and it was necessary to wash one's face carefully on arising, so as to ward off their potentially evil influence.[31] And, to regain tranquillity of mind it was indispensable to have the dream interpreted as soon as possible, either by a priest or a monk.[32] If the dream was judged baneful, the person who had dreamed it had to offer a sacrifice, make a libation of sesame oil, or even make a substantial gift to the brāhmaṇs. Bad omens might occur repeatedly during one single day: when a dove perched on the roof, it was certainly the harbinger of some misfortune. Bad luck was presaged also by the presence in the vicinity of the home of bees making honey or ants building their heaps;[33] and it was an unlucky sign when the right eyelid began to tremble nervously.[34]

The list of things that might disturb normal peace and quiet and destroy routine was almost limitless. To ward off these dangers, the inhabitants of ancient India had at their disposal an imposing series of magical practices which were infallible methods of keeping at a distance all the disquieting influences that lurked everywhere. The most effective measure was to murmur formulas (*mantras*), taken mostly from the domestic treatises (*Gṛhya Sūtras*) which provided long lists, classifying the spells according to the problem they were intended to solve. In addition, a great number of more or less harmless stratagems were in popular use when it was desired to grant blessings, to lay a curse or to compel someone to do something. And there were more or less complicated magical acts designed specifically to cure ailments, to induce the woman one loved to surrender to one, to ward off diseases of cattle, to bring success in a difficult enterprise, to win one's case in a law-suit or to come out top in a business bargain, and innumerable other objectives. Sometimes figures were moulded of clay, wax, wood or edible paste, representing a specific enemy, and then pierced with a sharp point, or burned, or eaten.

This, then, was the atmosphere in which daily life was conducted. These beliefs and practices were supplemented by the fundamental rites to which all had to conform each day, and by the sacred ceremonies which marked the important stages of existence.

CHAPTER THREE

THE INDIVIDUAL AND THE FAMILY

Wife, counsellor, companion in loneliness, beloved pupil in the arts of pleasure, whom pitiless death has taken away from me, only you could say how much more he has taken from me.

KĀLIDĀSA, *Raghu Vaṃśa*, VIII, 67.

The life of an individual – especially in the brāhmaṇic caste – was encompassed by three fundamental social structures: caste (*varṇa*), ancestry (*gotra*) and family (*kula*). We have already discussed that of caste (see pp. 23–32) and we shall deal with the family at some length later in this chapter. Ancestry was quite as important as caste, perhaps even more so, and the concept had some affinity with that of the clan, evoking perhaps the distant age when the Āryans had not yet totally lost their tribal character. The *gotra* claimed authentic or, more often, mythical ancestors, whose names were recited each day in the domestic ritual. To belong to a *gotra* was, to all intents and purposes, the prerogative of brāhmaṇs alone, and they believed firmly that they were the descendants of the saintly personages of Vedic times. The *kṣatriyas* and *vaiśyas* could hardly have the same pretensions; nevertheless, certain members of these castes did dare to assert an exalted lineage, braving the ironic amusement of blue-blooded brāhmaṇs. As for the low castes, they had no right whatsoever to any ascending line of this sort.

The theory of *gotra* followed the brāhmaṇ throughout his life: it was recalled to him not only each day as he recited piously the list of his paternal and maternal ancestors, but also each month, during the *śrāddha* rite commemorating these.[1] This rite was performed by the head of every family, accompanied by his sons, grandsons and great-grandsons. It consisted essentially in an offering of balls of rice or meat called *piṇḍa*, addressed to the family head's three direct ancestors, father, grandfather, great-grandfather, and, in a general sense, 'Fathers' (*pitṛ*) in general, in other words, the ancestors composing the family line. All the members of these past and present generations were *sapiṇḍas,* that is to say associated with the offering of the *piṇḍa.* The family's whole unity and its principle of mutual aid was based on this monthly rite, for a *sapiṇḍa* could be sure of receiving help in case of need from those belonging to the same *gotra* as himself.

It is certain that the concept of *gotra* played a very great part in the establishment of a family solidarity which might well extend to many blood relations and justify their presence being accepted in the common home, however great their faults or uselessness (see pp. 189–90).

This same idea of *gotra* assumed its full significance when a marriage was contracted: the woman left her own *gotra* for good, to belong thenceforward to that of her husband. It was no longer the names of her ancestors that she heard mentioned each morning, as had been the case while she lived with her parents, but those of her husband's family, of which she had become a part by virtue of the marriage sacrament.

Fidelity to the *gotra,* then, was the very foundation of family unity and hierarchy, and the protocol to be observed was a matter of ritual as much as of custom. The behaviour of parents and children flowed directly from it, and the reality of the family marked each member with an indelible imprint that he retained until the moment of renunciation, if he took holy orders, or of death if he remained within the mundane world.

Brāhmaṇism also propounded the theory that every man must, during the course of his life, traverse four successive and essential 'stages' (*āśramas*): first that of initiation, which marked the end of childhood. Until that moment (the age of initiation varied according to the caste) the child did not yet belong to the Āryan community, remaining outside society on its ritual plane and having simply the potentiality of being worthy of his ancestors. After the initiation which enabled him to enter into the life of ritual with the rank of student (*brahmacārin*), he attained, through the sacrament of marriage, the state of householder (*gṛhastha*), thanks to which he in his turn possessed a domestic hearth, founded a family and brought it up following sacred traditions. The third stage saw him renounce his worldly goods and withdraw into a hermitage of which he became a member (*vānaprastha*). Finally, by an ultimate renunciation, he had to sever all relations with society and become an itinerant monk (*saṃnyāsin*), heedless of all contingency, concerned solely with achieving his *karma* (see pp. 21–2) and so ameliorating his future rebirths.

This ideal theoretical path, which orthodox brāhmaṇs of ancient India sought earnestly and faithfully to tread, was complemented by a great number of personal sacraments (*saṃskāra*)[2] – forty or more – which accompanied the smallest events of an individual's life, from birth to death.

PREGNANCY AND BIRTH; INFANCY

From the moment of conception, the greatest care was taken of the mother-to-be who immediately became the most enviable of women and was entitled to be surrounded by respect and affectionate attentiveness. The awaited child was considered as a guest, and we shall see in later pages that the rites of hospitality were not dissimilar to those surrounding pregnancy (see pp. 197–8). Magic, of course, played its part too.[3]

The period of pregnancy gave rise to special attentions; the expectant mother was kept under observation by the family doctor, who had studied embryology and gynaecology (though purely in terms of their medical nature) as well as pediatry, all these being 'sciences' forming the subject of treatises and constituting part of classic Ayurvedic medicine.

The expectant mother was persuaded to take special precautions in sitting down, going to bed and sleeping; she was advised, in particular, to avoid standing up for too long or eating any dishes which were too hot or too cold, too sweet or too acid. Food was chosen for her that would make her well-disposed towards the child she was carrying. Anything that might possibly arouse regret or fear in her was carefully avoided, and, at the same time, she was forbidden to come near sick people. She dressed comfortably, perfumed herself with moderation and refrained from adorning herself with flowers whose scent was too heady.

At the end of the second or third month, she was traditionally supposed to develop an insatiable appetite, in which case everyone hastened to satisfy her least desires for fear that she might grow too thin, or lose her beauty, or become unhappy and fall sick. She was even authorized to eat meat if the fancy took her, and then a servant would run to the slaughterhouse or the butcher's shop.[4]

About this time, the expectant mother could try to divine the sex of her future child. One method, among many others, consisted in having herself touched by one of her youngest children, with his head turned away; if his finger pointed towards a member or organ on his mother's body that was designated by a word of masculine gender, it would be a boy (a good omen); in the opposite case it would be a girl.[5] It was also during the third month that the father undertook a ceremony which would ensure the birth of a son (*puṃsavana*). He bought the seeds and plants needed for the oblations in this ritual, while the wife prepared herself by washing herself from head to foot and donning a new robe that had never been laundered. An offering of herbs was made by crushing them in the household's millstone, taking care that the runner did not revolve in the wrong direction (from left to right). Then, standing behind his wife, the husband touched her right nostril with his right hand while reciting a ritual formula.[6]

At the onset of the fifth month of pregnancy, the future father offered his wife the 'five ambrosias' to eat, a mixture of sugar, honey, milk, ghee and curds that was the traditional offering to distinguished guests (see p. 197). Between the fourth and eighth month, the ceremony of parting the hair (*sīmantakaraṇa*) took place. This was the moment, according to the experts, when the child's members assumed their final form within the mother, when its heart became the seat of its understanding, and its conscience and sensibility appeared.[7] For this occasion, supposedly designed to ensure the child's security in the mother's womb, she once again performed a complete toilet. Her husband, standing behind her, tied around her neck a branch of *uḍumbara* (*Ficus glomerata*) laden with fruit that was still green: the symbology lay also in the fact that this tree is rich in sap. With the aid of a porcupine's quill marked with three white lines, the husband carefully divided his wife's tresses, three times in succession, by a very straight centre parting. After this, he prepared her a dish of boiled rice containing sesame and ghee, which she ate immediately, while the women of her caste sat around her, repeating interminably that they hoped she would become the mother of several sons.[8]

Towards the end of her pregnancy, she was expected to become completely languid; her physical weakness obliged her to discard most of her jewellery and other adornments,[9] and her body was rubbed with ghee to prevent a miscarriage. Twelve days or so before the expected date of birth, the father began to observe the rules of abstinence and purification. It was considered desirable that her labour-pains should start on a lucky date. On that day, the wife retired to an isolated, purified room to foil the wicked plans of the gods who stole children.[10] Meanwhile, the husband commenced the rites designed to favour her with a prompt and easy delivery: he filled a brand-new, shallow bowl with water, then emptied it in the same direction as the flow of the river at the bottom of his garden. He undid any knots he could discover inside the house. Then he visited his wife, placed a plant at her feet and a pot filled with water by her head. After this, he touched her belly and sprinkled water over her.

Meanwhile, a mixture of ghee, honey, water and curds was being hastily prepared, so that the lips of the new-born baby might be moistened with it. When the child appeared, and before the umbilical cord was cut, the father bent over him and breathed on him three times while invoking the Vedas. Then, in the presence of those assisting at the birth, he touched him and offered him, in a golden spoon, the honey mixture which had been specially prepared, wishing his son wisdom (*veda*), prosperity, long-life, intelligence, physical power, and the protection of the gods. Finally, he murmured low into his ear the secret name he had chosen for him in agreement with his wife, a name which would be revealed to the child only at the moment of his initiation and was known to no one apart from the parents (for the ten following days, the baby had no name at all and was referred to by round-about expressions).[11] The father's next action was to pronounce a formula to prevent the child from being ill, from crying and from suffering. The baby was then either sprinkled or bathed with consecrated water and placed on his mother's lap, while a talisman of resinous wood was tied around his neck and the umbilical cord was buried outside. The family astrologer made his calculations and announced the details of the horoscope to a scribe who carefully wrote down the predictions.

During the ten days following his birth, the child and his parents remained impure and none of them was permitted to take part in religious ceremonies. On the tenth or twelfth day, a religious ceremony took place in which the mother was readmitted to ritual existence and the baby was given a name for everyday use. The father repeated this name several times in his son's right ear, wished him, as he had done at birth, knowledge of the Vedas, intelligence and eloquence, then hung round his neck a gold coin threaded on a hempen cord. The husband and wife washed their heads and faces. The whole house was cleaned from top to bottom. Then, dressed in new clothing, as was the baby, they made offerings to the constellation under which the child was born, and to their own constellations. This last rite was repeated each month until the child's first birthday.

At four months, the child was taken for his first excursion outside the house, during the course of which the father had him look up at the sun and then carried him to the chapel of the tutelary divinity. Soon after, he was offered his first toys. When he was six months old he was given his first solid food (*anna-prāśana*). His father selected the ingredients, according to the qualities he wanted his son to possess: rice with ghee so that he should attain glory, ram's meat if he wanted him to be endowed with physical strength, partridge meat if he wished him to achieve saintliness, fish so that he should be gentle by nature. The father tasted the food, the child swallowed a few mouthfuls fed him by his father's fingers, and the mother ate what remained. The first baby gurgles, the first steps, the first intelligible words were all celebrated with joy and tenderness. His safety was carefully watched over, and a light burnt throughout the night by his side, a so-called 'lamp of jewels' (*ratnadīpa*) intended to protect him from evil influences. The lobes of his ears were pierced (*karṇavedhana*) to preserve him from sickness.

When he was three years old, if he was the child of a brāhmaṇ family, he was given a tonsure during the course of an important childhood sacrament called *cūḍākaraṇa*.[12] This ceremony was conducted with a good deal of solemnity. First, the child was carefully washed and then dressed in an undergarment and a top garment, neither of which had ever been laundered. A barber was summoned especially for the occasion, his reward being a jar filled with grain. He set out the necessary instruments – a copper razor, a mirror, some fresh ghee, and a cushion made of plaited grasses or a cake of dried cow-dung, the latter intended as a receptacle for the shorn locks of hair. While servants prepared dishes of rice, barley, sesame and beans, the mother sat the child on her lap. The father mixed hot and cold water together to the right temperature, and this water was used by the barber to wet the child's hair. Starting with the right-hand side of the child's head, after sprinkling a few leaves of *kuśa* grass over the damp hair and smearing ghee over it, the barber shaved off thc locks of hair together with the grass, while admonishing the razor, aloud, not to do any harm to its customer. The same procedure was followed with the left-hand side, and lastly the back of the head; of course he left a ritual topknot on the top of the shaved skull, arranging it according to the particular custom of the child's own *gotra*.[13] As he cut the hair, the barber handed each severed curl to the mother who placed them carefully on the cushion or cow-pat. The belief was held that the hair was the seat of a man's vigour, so, to prevent an ill-intentioned person fron gaining possession of it, the mother buried the collection of clippings in the fields, or in the stables, or in a river-bank.[14] The offering of a cow (or its equivalent value) brought this solemn rite to a close. Thenceforward, the young boy cherished this topknot which must never be cut off, since its removal would symbolize utter social disgrace (see pp. 24–5).

During their earliest years, children were looked after by the mother and were subject to no kind of discipline. The boys ran about naked, their skulls shaved around the braided topknot which was kept in place at the front of the head by being encased in a small egg-shaped bag; round their necks they wore a necklace of tiger's claws, or sometimes simply a cord from which dangled a single claw.[15] They built sand-castles,[16] whirled rattles[17] or beat two sticks together like clappers. As soon as they could walk, they pulled along little carts or animals made of clay, coloured and gilded, and mounted on wheels;[18] they also possessed windmills on sticks, hooters made of rolled leaves, drums made of earthenware, and suitably child-sized bows and arrows. They were fond of playing at dressing up. The girls, already wearing adult female garb, dandled wooden or ivory dolls, while the boys galloped around on broomstick steeds, pretending they were warriors.[19] Together, they threw and caught balls made of stuffed cloth,[20] played marbles, spun tops[21] and played at shop-keeping, paying for their 'purchases' with shells.

These children were petted and spoiled by their doting parents, who also looked after them very carefully, curing them of their childish ailments according to established rules (which were, indeed, more magical than scientific), administering vermifugal potions when necessary, and praying the dog-demons not to seize hold of their children by provoking epileptic fits.[22] However, the children of poor families experienced none of this idyllic upbringing, on the contrary: they were obliged to work from the moment they knew how to walk properly, participating in the daily activities of the adults; the boys accompanied their fathers to the fields and helped tend the herd, while the girls helped their mothers with domestic tasks. They were no less tenderly loved, for all classes of Indian society cherished their children. But, despite this fact, it remains true that, in very poor families, girls were not viewed with favour; indeed, baby girls were sometimes abandoned in some concealed spot, or even killed.[23]

When a boy reached the age of four or five, he had to leave aside his childish games and start learning the alphabet. This, too, was the occasion for a small family ceremony. For the next few years he was taught reading and elementary arithmetic, either by a tutor who gave him lessons at home (which was the case in brāhmaṇ families and in the families of averagely well-off *kṣatriyas*, or else by going to the village school or the local school in his town.

The school for giving elementary instruction was usually attached to the neighbouring brāhmaṇic temple, and consisted of a house built as a quadrilateral around a central courtyard planted with a few banana- and mango-trees; the house served also as a home for the teacher. The classes were held in the open air. The teacher, rod in hand, sat on a low stool, surrounded by groups of pupils squatting on the ground. Each child held on his knees a small board, on which he traced, with the aid of a reed pen and a little pot of ink by his side, the figures and letters which the teacher demonstrated. A cage containing a parrot would stand in one corner of the courtyard, and the teacher's *vīṇā* (see p. 314, note 54) hung on one of the walls. When the lesson was over, the boys had a recreation period during which they were taught wrestling and archery. This was followed by a rest period, when the children sat on stools and recited by heart whole passages from the texts that they had been taught earlier that day.[24]

But these were only preliminary exercises. As we have already mentioned, the child did not form part of the Āryan community prior to his brāhmaṇic initiation, and was not entitled to ritual instruction.

THE BRĀHMAṆIC INITIATION

This initiation[25] was restricted to the first three castes. The age at which it was undergone depended on the caste, being eight in the case of a brāhmaṇ, eleven for a *kṣatriya* and twelve for a *vaiśya*. It was a most important sacrament, called *upanayana* or 'second birth', and opened the way to the ritual instruction which was indispensable for a child if he was to become a *gṛhastha* eventually. This, then, was the beginning of an entirely new life and was considered a most solemn occasion.

It took place at various seasons, according to the caste: in spring for a brāhmaṇ, in summer for a *kṣatriya*, and in autumn for a *vaiśya*. In the same way, the ritual varied for the three castes, that involving the brāhmaṇs being the most comprehensive.

Since the day of the ceremony must necessarily be a lucky date, it was carefully fixed after astrological calculations. Early in the morning, the postulant completed a careful toilet. The barber shaved his skull smooth all round the ritual topknot. Then he was given a meal. After this he decked himself out with his finest ceremonial clothes and accessories.

During this time, his future spiritual teacher (*guru*) – who was due to officiate at the ceremony and supervise its successive stages – had arrived, accompanied by his assistants, all fellow-brāhmaṇs. He had already celebrated a morning service. Now, parents, servants and guests were grouped around the sacred fire to await the young boy's arrival. Near the hearth were arranged the objects necessary to his initiation: a stone (perhaps a millstone), a new garment, a black antelope skin, a sacred cord, a belt, and a cane made of *palāśa* wood (*Butea frondosa*) or *bilva* wood (*Aegle marmelos*). The guru had also ensured that there was a sufficient supply of logs for the sacred fire.

The postulant took his place next to his future teacher; they both stood side by side, their hands clasped, and the guru turned his face successively east and west. While murmuring appropriate formulas, he then invited the neophyte to mount the stone, stepping on to it with his right foot first, and pronounced the wish that the boy should remain as firm and stable as the stone beneath him. After this, the guru removed the garment that the boy was wearing and made him knot around his loins the new cloth that he had got ready beforehand, while using ritual phrases to wish him long life. Then he draped the sacred 'thread' (*yajñopavīta*) over the boy's left shoulder, and under his right arm. This cord consisted of three threads, each of nine twisted strands;[26] the new initiate was bound to wear it throughout his life, and never to remove it or break it, under pain of a severe penance. The guru now presented the boy with his belt, and knotted it three times successively around his waist. Finally, he placed over his new pupil's shoulders the antelope skin which was to serve him as a cloak and endow him symbolically with strength and valour.

Master and pupil then engaged in a dialogue, during which their future relationship was defined. Cupping his hands, the guru had them filled with water by one of his assistants, while the child said to him: 'I have come here to become a student (*brahmacārin*). Initiate me. I wish to be a student, under the inspiration of the god Savitṛ.' By way of reply, the guru asked him: 'What is your name?' 'I am called —' replied the pupil, pronouncing in public for the first time the secret name given him at birth. The guru continued: 'Do you descend from the *gotra* of the sage —?', mentioning the name of the line's supposedly original ancestor. 'I do descend from the *gotra* of that sage.' 'Do you declare that you are a *brahmacārin*?' 'I declare that I am a *brahmacārin*.' Then the guru sprinkled the water that he had been holding in his cupped hands over the boy's joined hands, three times, while pronouncing his new name and saying: 'I initiate you.' Immediately after this, he grasped the child's right hand between his own and murmured a series of *mantras* designed to commend his new pupil to the gods, so that they might bless his progeny, and endow him with strength, wealth, good health and mastery of the Vedic science. Then he made the boy turn round in a complete circle while looking up at the sun, thus

Town and Country

1 An Indian village with its sacred tree. The thatched roofs of the cottages can be seen in the background as women bring their offering of rice to the Buddha (*sujatā*)

2 A jungle hermitage. The circular bamboo huts seen on the right are roofed with leaves. The forest is crowded with animals and an elephant can be seen bathing in a pond. In the centre is a hunter with a bow and arrow, while next to him a woman brings back the fruit she has gathered

3 A besieged city. The armies include archers, cavalry, chariots and elephants. The brick wall of the city can be seen in the centre, near the enormous gate. On either side of the gate project several storied buildings: the upper floors, with balconies in front of the windows, were generally offices and the municipal granaries were at the very top

4 The worship of a *stūpa* by both earthly and aerial beings. The *stūpa* was, in essence, a dome surrounded by a fence rail. The interior usually contained a sacred relic and could never be entered

The Ruler

5 The initiation of a prince. An important part of this ceremony was the washing; here the prince sits on a throne (carved with goats) while two servants pour water over him from metal pitchers. Three females are in attendance – one with a flywhisk (*Mahājanaka-jātaka*)

6 A prince with his wife (holding the flywhisk) and their two small children (one holding a parasol) drive out of a capital city in the royal four-horse chariot. Behind them can be seen the king (right) and citizens watching them from the balconies

7 A *rājā* with attendants. Amongst the attendants, and indispensable to a king, are the carriers of the royal parasol (*left*) and the fly-whisk (*right*)

8–9 (*left*) These figures were probably intended to represent *yakṣīs*. However by the Kuṣāṇa period these women had taken on many of the attributes of attendants or even princesses of the great Kuṣāṇa kings

10 A snake charmer and his monkey

Religion

11 Life in a hermitage. One of the most important duties of the students there was tending the sacred fire. The figure on the right can be seen chopping wood, while the one on the left brings another log and others place faggots on the fire

12 The worship of a sacred tree. This was a remaining part of the ancient fertility cults, and while remaining common in that form, it also became an integral part of the Buddhist religion. Here the tree is being decked with garlands by the worshippers

13 Basketwork stands with plates of fruit and flowers. This is a scene concerning the birth of Buddha in which a brāhmaṇ casts the horoscope after a dream of Queen Maya

14 An ascetic in a classical yoga position

Cult

15 A terracotta cult image, probably a fertility goddess. She wears an elaborate headdress and huge earrings as does the image in fig. 18

16–17 Two *yakṣīs* from Mathurā

18 An image of a *yakṣī* from Bengal. It is possible that it represents a cult of a mother goddess

19 A *nāga* king. Like the objects of most cults, the nagas or serpents played a part in the Buddhist and Brāhmaṇ religions as well as in popular superstition. Here the *nāgarājā* is seen in a lotus-covered river, first (*centre*) as a five-headed cobra, then (*right*) with his wife and daughter and (*left*) paying homage to the holy tree of Buddha. In their human form the *nāgas* are characterized by the cobra heads on their turbans

Secular Life

20, 21 & 22 Highly refined and educated courtesans, such as the ones shown in these figures, played a large part in the life of the young noble, who was expected to have a mistress and to devote great skill to pleasing her

21

24 Children's toys of terracotta, such as this monkey, were extremely common

23 *Apsaras* with a *vīṇā* (bow-harp). Playing a harp of this kind, although originally restricted to women was, by the fourth century, an indispensable accomplishment for all nobles and even kings

25 A bronze water pot engraved with various scenes including a prince driving in a chariot

26 A detail from a medallion on a Buddhist rail pillar of a woman holding a mirror

27 (*right*) Travelling wrestlers, such as the ones shown here – as well as acrobats, conjurors and players – were a traditional form of entertainment at local festivals

28 A detail from a Buddhist rail pillar showing pavers at work

29 A caravan of wagons pulled by oxen

30 Four pilgrims (?)

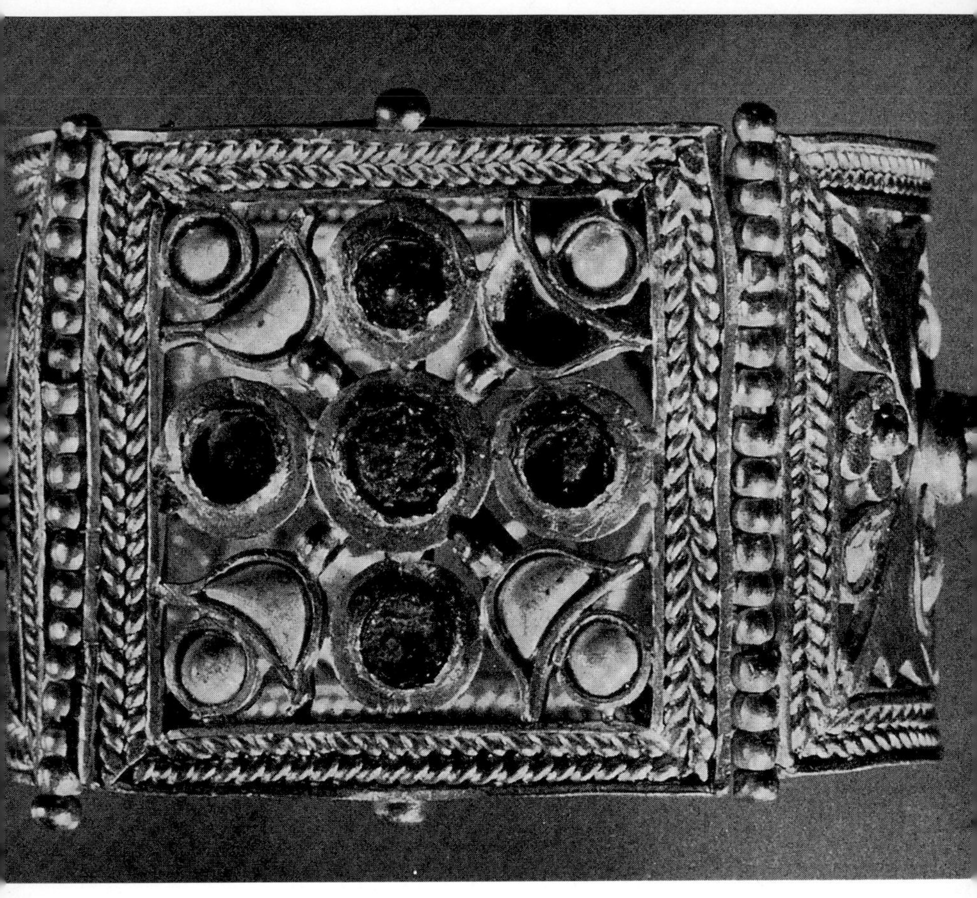

31 A gold bracelet, set with amber and white shells

repeating the ritual which the father had carried out soon after his birth. Next, he touched the boy over the heart, expressing the hope that his new pupil should feel affection for him and that their two natures might prove well-matched. Then he asked him: 'Whose *brahmacārin* are you?' 'Yours,' replied the child respectfully. 'I am your guru,' confirmed the master. The latter now walked silently around the ritual fire, with his pupil on his right, touched him over the heart once again, and repeated the circling of the fire. Finally, placing his hand on the young initiate's shoulder, he recited to him briefly a list of the duties he would be required to perform during the ensuing months: keeping the sacred fire alight, drinking only water, helping domestically in the hermitage, forgoing any sleep during the daytime, and remaining silent until he had replenished the supply of fuel for the fire.

The second part of the ceremony took place either immediately following the first part or, alternatively, one year later. In this, the initiate was taught the sacred formula (*Gāyatrī*) which he would later have to pronounce during each daily rite when he had become a master of the house. Seated by the side of his guru, the new initiate said to him: 'Recite, if you please.' The master contented himself with pronouncing the supremely sacred syllable which comprehends all the others: '*Ōm*.'[27] Following the pattern of the ritual, the pupil continued: 'Recite the *Savitṛ*.' And the guru chanted the formula of the daily service: 'Let us think on the lovely splendour of the god Savitṛ [the Sun], that he may inspire your minds.' To complete the ceremony, the master had his pupil swallow three mouthfuls of water, then handed his cane to him and walked alone round the fire while the pupil heaped logs on it.

The ceremony was over. While the guru was being presented with a cow (or its equivalent value), as well as the garment he had removed from his new pupil, the pupil himself had left the assembly, clad in the antelope skin and holding his cane high enough for its tip to be level with his nose. For the first time in his life, he was going to beg his food and that of his guru, a gesture which he would be repeating daily from then on. In actual fact, he went straight to his mother who was only too pleased to provide him with all the provisions he might require, but he still walked to the village afterwards in a symbolic quest for food. On returning, he reported to his guru what he had been able to collect in the way of offerings. Under the latter's supervision, he prepared their meal and, when given permission, ate. For the rest of the day he remained silent.

From now on, he belonged wholly to his guru. He had to follow him into his hermitage, serve him assiduously, and receive his teaching attentively. It amounted, in fact, to several years of austere existence consecrated to celibacy and a study of the sacred texts.

STUDENT LIFE AND TEACHING METHODS

The young boy who had just been initiated and had received the title of *brahmacārin* or 'brāhmaṇ student' had, as a result, left his family to go and live in a hermitage in company with his guru – his spiritual teacher – and, usually, several fellow-students.

Hermitages of this nature were usually situated at the verge of a forest, in some peaceful, isolated spot. They consisted of a few circular bamboo huts thatched with fronds, with a single door on a raised hearth, and lit sometimes by only a small square window.[28] In a suitable place, an area had been carefully weeded and covered with a surface of sand, to be fit to receive in its centre the ritual fire and the small pavilion on columns which served to shelter it.

The students were subject, here, to a rigorous discipline, within the framework of which they received religious and scientific instruction. They slept on a litter of rushes, arose before dawn, and had as their first duty that of greeting their guru reverently by touching his feet.[29] They were required to show total and prompt obedience towards him, standing upright with their hands pressed together whenever they addressed him. The guru was not a tyrant, and made every effort to teach his pupils the rules without ever misrepresenting the truth.

Outside the many hours devoted to study, the students' principal task was to cut the wood needed for the sacred fire, to chop the logs into equally proportioned faggots, to clean the emplacement with their hands, to water it, and to gather from the hearth the cinders which served to execute pious marks on the face and body. Twice a day, morning and evening, the wood-pile had to be replenished; and they, as well as their master, saluted the sun twice a day, as it rose and as it set. It fell to them, also, to go and beg their daily food, barefoot and clad in a dark-coloured tunic or an antelope skin. Their diet was simple and excluded both meat and honey; during periods of fast, they went without salt and spices, and slept on the bare ground. They ate only two meals a day, once in the morning and again in the afternoon. Their toilet was to be undertaken without complacency, and their hair was not shaved but allowed to grow, being rolled into a coil. Like many hermits, they often wore a skirt made from a sort of fibre (*valkala*) obtained by crushing the bark of certain trees between two stones.[30] They were trained to become physically tough: they did not shelter when it rained, and had only their antelope skin to protect them from cold and damp; when they swam across a river, they did not wipe their bodies dry afterwards, even in winter. The equipment in use at the hermitage was so simple as to be rudimentary, consisting almost entirely of ewers for drinking water, protected by filters to keep out insects, water-jugs for washing and cooking purposes, spoons for use in the sacramental rites, and a few axes for chopping wood.

The greater part of the day was set aside for study. At the beginning of his stay, the *brahmacārin* learned to accomplish the rites of the *saṃdhyā* which were celebrated at sunrise, at midday and in the evening (see p. 192); in the course of this first instruction, he learned not only to recite the sacred formulas correctly but also to control his breathing, to breathe in and out through a single nostril, to drink water in ritual fashion, to sprinkle holy water in the prescribed fashion and to pour libations into the ritual fire. After this, the guru taught him the Veda, proceeding from the point of instruction that he had reached in the little school he had attended as a small child. Each day the guru gathered his pupils around him to teach them the Veda. There might be as many as fifteen pupils, and the lessons continued for several hours at a time, while they sat on the ground, attentive to his every word. The method he used consisted in making them repeat correctly after him, word by word, whole passages of sacred script. To ensure that their memory remained perfect, he used mnemonic techniques: each word was repeated independently then together with the word preceding it, then in the reverse order – and each verse was repeated once again before the following one was tackled.[31] Thanks to these exercises, tradition was transmitted orally, and accurately, from one generation to another.

He taught them not only the Veda but also the contingent sciences necessary for a full understanding, that is to say, phonetics, etymology, grammar, prosody, literature, chemistry, astronomy and mathematics. These last three sciences were particularly highly developed in India during that epoch, and proportionately far in advance of the general state of knowledge prevailing in other ancient civilizations: by the sixth century AD, Indian scholars already knew how to extract square roots and cube roots in the classic manner still used today; algebra was in wide use, using sines, cosines and versines, as well as quadratic equations with unknown quantities.[32] Many other knowledges might also be communicated to the young students, including such arts as snake-charming, demonology and divination. The *kṣatriya* at the hermitage were, in addition, taught swordsmanship and archery, as well as the plastic arts, painting, music and dancing, all of these being activities normally forbidden to brāhmaṇs.

At the same time, the guru did his best to instil into his young disciples the moral rules of their respective caste, exhorting them to conquer within themselves all sensuality, anger, jealousy and greed. He preached sobriety to them, and forbade them to indulge in idle gossip, calumny, lying, frivolity or insults towards 'living people'. To this end, he taught them the principles which had been set forth for the use of *brahmacārin* from time immemorial, and encouraged them to apply these precepts by grading his charges in order of their intelligence and amenability. To undertake successfully the weighty task of moulding the character of these young people, it was of course indispensable that the guru himself should be endowed with a solid Vedic culture and a faultless moral sense. Being descended from a family where teaching was a hereditary occupation, and having been brought up in the same way as his own pupils, he usually possessed the necessary general qualities and took his role to heart. The means of discipline that he made use of were moral and persuasive rather than physical; he regarded corporal punishment as repugnant, and had recourse to it only as a last resort. Also, he refused to accept gifts of money or presents from his pupils, considering that it would be reprehensible for him to be beholden to those whose mentor he was. There did exist, nevertheless, bad masters who not only demanded cash fees but even showed favouritism towards those who paid them the largest amounts. On the other hand, a student was entitled to take legal proceedings against his guru, if he could prove that he had been maltreated. And, in any case, he was free to leave his master at any time.

It was, in fact, quite common for a *brahmacārin* not to stay with one guru for the whole of his student period, but to go from one to another, learning from each what he considered that particular guru was best qualified to teach. The duration of these studies varied considerably; theoretically, twelve years were allowed for each Veda – which would have meant that a comprehensive Vedic instruction would have lasted forty-eight years. Obviously, this period was, in practice, considerably less, although students in their thirties were by no means rare. In any case, these years were not continuous: the scholastic year lasted only five and a half months, or six months at the most, from July to January approximately, but even then the months of study were broken by numerous public holidays. And, in addition, any number of events provided sufficient reason for work to be suspended: thunder and lightning, eclipses, frost, sandstorms; or the birth of a child in the locality, a wrestling match, the death of the village chief; or any one of a series of seasonal festivals. If the most studious initiates regretted these interruptions, there was nothing to stop them pursuing their private studies during the vacation.

The hermitages were not the only centres of higher learning. There were, in addition, several well-known universities where young brāhmaṇs went to attend the lectures of India's most distinguished professors. The most celebrated universities were those of Taxila (in present-day Pakistan), Banāras, and Kāñchī in the south. These were real university cities, containing several clusters of colleges, most of which were subsidized by charitable foundations or royal donations. The number of students living in these university cities was very high: in Banāras, for instance, there were as many as five hundred in a single college. The form of teaching followed the same rules as those that applied in hermitages or with private tutors, and the students performed identical services for their particular professor.

Apart from these brāhmaṇic universities, there were others of equal importance, founded by Buddhists and Jains. The most famous was the university of Nālandā,[33] in the state of Bihār (see pp. 220–1), where novices desiring to enter the Buddhist order were trained, but which also taught the Veda, Hindu philosophy, logic, grammar and medicine. The most celebrated teachers of the time lectured there, and foreign scholars made long stays in the university, so adding to the ferment of intellectual activity. The monasteries and colleges covered a vast expanse of ground, each unit being enclosed within its own outer walls. And, for thirty or forty miles around, the countryside was dotted with hermitages in which several hundred students gathered each year, raising the total number of students in this whole great centre to some five thousand. Huge buildings and smaller pavilions served as residences, kitchens, refectories, store-rooms and cellars; there were also assembly halls and lecture rooms. Pools and artificial lakes had been constructed to provide for bathing and ritual ablutions. A whole population circulated in the streets of this great conglomeration: laics of all ages, women (for some students were married), and even children. The temples and sacred monuments which dominated the surrounding area with their splendour were also places of pilgrimage, where marriages were sometimes celebrated.

The termination of a young man's studies (*samāvartana*) was marked by a series of rites. There was no specific age at which his studies were considered completed; with the *kṣatriya* it was usually at the age of sixteen (but often later than that), since that was the age at which a young man supposedly started growing a beard. Repeating the ceremony of tonsure of his childhood, the student had his cheeks shaved for the first time in a ceremony with the evocative title of 'gift of a cow' (*godāna*) which was, equally, a sacrament.[34] Having proved himself and having completed the normal number of terms, the student asked permission from his guru to leave him and become a *snātaka*, 'one who has bathed'. Having obtained his agreement, he had then to make certain preparations and acquire all the objects that would be needed for the ceremony, for his master as well as for himself.[35] For each of them he obtained two sets of clothing, a turban, a pair of golden ear-rings, a necklace with a precious stone, a pair of wooden sandals,[36] an umbrella, a cane, as well as a garland threaded with seeds for massaging the body, unguents with a sandalwood base, pomade for the eyes, and a piece of wood from a 'pure' tree for the sacrificial fire. Then he bought a cow and assorted foodstuffs to distribute to the brāhmaṇs.

When these preparations were completed, the young man took a ritual bath which enabled him to assume the state of *snātaka*, made a ritual offering of water, and performed an adoration of the sun. The guru then invited him to sit down on a bullock's skin and proceeded to cut his hair and beard, his body hair and finger and toe nails, making a mound of these clippings which he confided to a person considered well-intentioned towards the young man who buried them in a stable or other appropriate place, as his mother had done on the occasion of the ceremony of tonsure when he was three years old.

The young man then cleaned his teeth and performed nasal ablutions so that his mouth and nose should be ritually purified. After he had sprinkled himself with holy water and had sanctified the objects which he would be using from then on, he put on two pieces of clothing, and the necklace which was to ensure him long life and health. Then he anointed his eyes, and put on his ear-rings, as a sign of double protection. After rubbing his hands with ointment, he passed them over his head to ward off headaches, then over his limbs; finally he looked at himself in a mirror. The guru now gave him the turban, the umbrella which would thenceforward symbolize his status as a *snātaka* because it was the symbol of the sky above his head, and, signalling to him to rise, a pair of sandals designed to lead him safely forward and protect him 'from all sides'. Finally he proffered him the bamboo cane which had the same protective character, especially against the wickedness of mankind and the rapacity of thieves. Thus equipped, the student placed on the sacred fire the log he had specially chosen beforehand. He spent the rest of the day meditating in solitude.

The moment of departure was approaching, but his first departure was only a pretence: he climbed into a bullock-cart after touching the yoke and praying that his own limbs would have the same force and vigour, and allowed himself to be carried to the home of a brāhmaṇ friend who had prepared a reception for him. He was received with all the honour due a distinguished guest (see pp. 197–8). After this, he returned to his professor's abode to take final leave of him. The guru required him to serve him a meal composed of his favourite dishes. The young man then offered him the presents he had got ready. Finally, he set off on the road leading to his own home and family, being careful to take his first step with the right foot.

As soon as he could see the roof of his home in the distance, he stopped and made obeisance. When passing through the door he paused to pronounce a formula of thanksgiving and to touch the two door-jambs. He saluted his parents with appropriate respect and greeted the other members of his family joyously. He was welcomed with honour and the village organized a splendid reception for him.

In the normal course of things, he would marry immediately on his return and, from being a *snātaka*, would become a *gṛhastha* (a 'master of the house').

BETROTHAL AND MARRIAGE

Fresh from the university, the 'twice born' was, in principle, expected to found a family in his turn without undue delay. All the principles with which he had been inculcated during his years of study combined to make him regard the future in the perspective of such a union. First, marriage (*vivāha*) was a sacrament and, as such, was a logical stage in the evolution of his life; secondly, it transformed the *snātaka* into a *gṛhastha*, representing the second stage of all normal lives. This new state would allow him to supplement the ritual fires with a new one (since marriage would authorize him to maintain one on his own account) and, consequently, to honour the gods to an even greater extent. This, at least, represents the mode of thought of the perfect brāhmaṇ, but there were exceptions to the rule, especially when the young man had an elder brother. The latter was bound to ensure their father's ritual succession, and had no choice but to take a wife as soon as he returned home; but his younger brothers, who were in any case not permitted to marry before him, had the opportunity of enjoying a greater freedom for some time to come and of leading a more frivolous existence, for, in the words of Kālidāsa, 'young people seek pleasures'.

Marriage was indissoluble, except in a few exceptional cases, where a woman's husband was demonstrably insane, impotent or fell into any other abnormal category. Divorce was permitted only in the lowest castes, and even then only during certain epochs of ancient times. Marriage being a ritual and sacramental union as much as a sexual union, it could be negotiated only when all necessary conditions were met on both sides: both spouses must be of the same caste and descended from equally honourable *gotra*; and the law of the 'clan' dictated, also, that there should be no common ancestor in the two families' genealogies, going back, in either case, seven generations on the paternal side and five on the maternal side.

Since these considerations were, ritually, of the greatest possible importance, it was logical for the parents to concern themselves very early on with the problem of securing suitable alliances for their children. Although girls and boys in Vedic times had been subject to few constraints and were free to indulge in amorous intrigues without being necessarily disgraced as a result, the evolution of moral attitudes since those times had resulted in a total prohibition of such relationships in the epoch which concerns us in the present study. Previous eras had accepted the idea of girls remaining single (with an undertone of irony provided by a few commentaries), but such a state of affairs was no longer tolerated except for the most peremptory reasons, such as an irresistible religious vocation. On the contrary, it was recommended that girls should be given away in marriage before they became nubile. The lawgivers viewed the feminine nature as being essentially perverse and ruled by instinct, and feared, therefore, that a nubile girl would not have the patience to await the legal ceremony before satisfying her desires; by evading her parents' watchful eyes she might well become enamoured of some disreputable young man and become pregnant – and a girl who had lost her virginity was completely unmarriageable.

The gossip of the day put out lurid suggestions that some girls lapsed into prostitution, others practised lesbian vices, and some even allowed abortions to be performed on them, a crime considered worse than murder. All such loose conduct could only lead, sooner or later, to a state of mendicancy. Faced with such a sombre picture, it was natural that parents should wish to marry off their daughters as early as possible; a further consideration was that, unlike boys, they were entirely dependent on the father and brought him no financial recompense. Nevertheless, it was usual to await their coming of age, although this varies considerably according to the author: sixteen, on an average, in the

Jātaka, but twelve according to Kauṭilya, and eight or twelve in the Codes of Manu. But, generally speaking, it was never below the age of six, and it would seem that child marriages were far rarer than they were subsequently, from the Middle Ages onwards.[37] Despite the supposed moral delinquencies of a certain number of young women, enumerated above, there is no doubt that these constituted a tiny minority, and that most young girls showed all the qualities that might be expected from the traditions in which they were brought up.

In fact, while the boys were with their guru, learning the Vedic science and solid principles for following a way of life based specifically on concepts of honour, the young girls were having an extensive literary culture implanted into them by pious tutors at home, or even by professors at a hermitage, where they might spend several years. They also learned various artistic accomplishments, such as painting, and playing the *vīṇā*. Their mothers taught them the domestic arts of managing servants, cooking according to the rules of ritual, weaving and embroidery, and the supervision of the family garden. They were brought up to believe that a woman was only fulfilled in motherhood, trained to show respect and obedience towards their father and husband, assured that their parents wanted only to see them happy: so, when the moment for marriage had arrived, they were ready to assume their new role. On the whole, they were virtuous and modest, intelligent and cultivated, capable of making their husbands happy; and one should, perhaps, not pay overmuch attention to the irascible pronouncements of certain misogynistic Buddhists who ascribed all the sins to womankind, claiming them to be mendacious, quarrelsome, greedy, inquisitive and capricious. . . .

Usually, two families started planning an alliance well ahead of time. The parents observed the niceties of convention throughout the protracted negotiations, disdaining to discuss the matter themselves, and calling upon intermediaries to act for them: these would be either friends or near relatives, or simply professional 'go-betweens' (*ghaṭaka*) whose services were paid.

The discussions dragged on. Both sides boasted of the qualities of the son or daughter they hoped to see married, their perfect education and irreproachable conduct, their respect and affection for their parents, and their healthy constitution, hampered by neither infirmity nor deformity (either of which would have rendered them unfit for marriage). Then came the consideration of the financial terms of the future contract. In the families of brāhmaṇs observing tradition faithfully, the provision of a dowry (*śulka*) was the responsibility of the girl's father; this often involved the liquidation of a considerable part of his patrimony, but he was anxious to furnish the agreed amount, for fear that he should be accused of selling his daughter.[38]

While negotiations continued between the two families, astrologers were given the task of studying the two young people's horoscopes, aided by lists of their personal characteristics that were supplied by the respective families. The examination of omens, the calculations resulting from the astral conjunction, and the study of the young couple's physical nature all provided prognostications which the astrologers made use of in order to fix the date of the marriage ceremony.[39] But, since several precautions were better than one, the betrothed submitted the girl to a test which was considered infallible for demonstrating the kind of domestic existence he might expect to enjoy, were she his wife. He had had eight small balls of earth prepared, each coming from different ground. According to the choice she made when he asked her to take one at random, he knew immediately whether, for example, his progeny would possess bountiful crops or extensive herds; or whether his wife would turn out to be an inveterate gambler, or make long voyages; or whether she would remain childless. If she chose the ball made of earth from a graveyard, she was destined to murder her husband. But if she picked the ball fashioned from some of the earth at the foot of the domestic altar, then they were both assured of a life 'of brāhmaṇic brilliance'. And if her finger pointed to the ball of earth taken from a pool which never dried up, this was a sign of abundance in all things.

When agreement had finally been reached, the young man decided to go and ask his future father-in-law officially for the hand of his daughter. He introduced himself by reciting his own names first, followed by the names of all the ancestors in his *gotra*, details of which, of course, had long since been provided to the girl's family. After the recital, he asked for the girl's hand in marriage, a request which the father granted without further comment. Both of them touched a vase filled with water, in which flowers, roasted seeds, fruits and even pieces of gold had been placed. The father blessed his daughter by resting the vase on her head and wishing her wealth and prosperity. Now that he was officially betrothed, the young man returned home, celebrated a religious service and made oblations.

From this moment, preparations for the forthcoming festivities were hurried forward. The astrologers delivered their verdict: the ceremony was to take place on a precise date, so that the days set aside for different rites should last exactly until the propitious day when the young married couple were able to cohabit and consummate their conjugal union for the first time. For his part, the bride's father began to build up the collection of jewellery which would constitute a considerable part of his daughter's dowry. The mother had the house cleaned from top to bottom; and she concerned herself with assembling everything that would be needed if the many relatives and guests who would be present on this occasion were to be received in a worthy manner. And all the members of the household would have new and sumptuous garments made for themselves, as well as appropriate adornments.

The young man's home was equally busy with preparations, as ceremonial robes were prepared, and presents for the bride and her family were chosen and set on one side. The bridegroom had already had a house built, within the precincts of the family property, which would be his home after marriage and where he would soon welcome his bride. And the bride's father had had an elegant pavilion erected in the courtyard of his own house, under the awning of which the young couple would stand and the marriage ritual take place.

The final preparations were in hand as the favourable conjunction of stars recommended by the astrologers approached, and on the day itself all was ready and the two families concentrated their attention on the betrothed couple.

The young man put himself in the hands of the women of his house. They rubbed perfumed ointment into his skin and applied cosmetics. They adorned him with a head-ornament, necklaces, ear-rings, and bracelets on his arms and wrists. They clothed him in a magnificent brocaded robe. And, last of all, they painted a caste mark in the centre of his forehead, and then handed him the mirror.

The young girl, also, was surrounded by women of her household, all helping to prepare her for the ceremony, but in her case they were all married women with living sons, for no widows were allowed among her assistants. Well before dawn, on the day of the ceremony, they had started bustling around her. First they rubbed her body with perfumed ointments and oil of sandalwood, adorned her with a garland of *dūrvā* grass, considered of especially lucky omen, and wrapped a beautiful silk skirt around her waist. In this state, she was led into the room where she was to be given a ritual bath. While a hidden group of musicians played soft music, the women poured perfumed water over her body from gold-plated jugs. Then they dried her with incense, and dressed her hair, dividing it into two tresses whose ends they tied with wool tassels, weaving sweet-smelling flowers into the tresses. After her bath, she was helped into a white costume. Then her face was made up with yellow and white pastes, her cheeks dotted with saffron, and her lips emphasized with red paste. The soles of her feet were coated with lac and her eyes rimmed thickly with black cosmetic. Finally, her jewellery was put on, necklaces, bracelets, ear-rings, gold-chased belt, while she admired herself in a mirror. Her mother personally painted on her daughter's forehead the golden mark which betokened marriage, and fastened around her right wrist the yellow-dyed woollen band or cord (*kautuka-sūtra*) which she was to wear for the next three days.

When she was ready, the bride walked to the domestic altar to pray to the family's tutelary deity; then she went to pay her respects to the women of the household, greeting each one of these older women in turn, starting with the oldest and so down the scale of age, while they in their turn overwhelmed her with good wishes, each one wishing her, in particular, that she should win her husband's undivided love. During this time, a vegetarian meal was served to these bridesmaids, who then performed four dances together, while food was presented to the brāhmaṇs.

By now, the bridegroom was ready at last, and had set out for his bride's house accompanied by his parents and a whole host of friends. This joyous yet solemn procession of people with their costumes of shot silk glinting in the sun, their sparkling jewels and their bright flowers, was accompanied by a band of musicians playing traditionally lucky airs. The bridegroom walked in an appropriately dignified manner, surrounded by companions who held a parasol over his head and manipulated flywhisks. The road leading from his father's house to that of his future father-in-law was gaily decorated: the houses were bedecked with flags, and vases filled with water were set before the doors; arches of foliage and flowers, framing brightly coloured paintings, had been set up along the way. The whole village was in a turmoil; children came running and women leaned out of windows or hastened to climb up to their balconies. Spectators threw flowers at the procession.

The bridegroom and his friends were met halfway by another procession advancing in the opposite direction, consisting of the bridesmaid's guests, and the two groups joined forces to make a massive collective appearance before the young girl's home. The bridegroom entered solemnly, to be received like a distinguished guest; a chair was offered him, water was produced so that he might refresh his feet, and the traditional drink of honey, rice and herbs was proffered.

The long-awaited moment had at last arrived. The bridegroom was led to the marriage pavilion which had been set up in the courtyard between the eastern door and the altar on which the nuptial fire would be kindled. A carpet had been stretched over the floor of the pavilion, and a curtain divided it into two crosswise. The bride arrived from the south, led by her father and her bridesmaids, while the bridegroom entered the pavilion from the north, and each sat on their respective side of the curtain without being able to see each other.

Those assisting at the ceremony clustered around. The officiating brāhmaṇs made a final check, to see that everything was ready and in place: to the west of the fire, a millstone and a sieve containing grains of roasted rice; to the north-east, a jar of water; a little farther off, the supply of wood for the hearth. The ceremony began with the sound of the prayers which the priest murmured as the curtain was drawn back. Even now, the betrothed couple were not permitted to glance at each other.

The father then approached his daughter and, standing over her as she remained seated, touched the top of her head with the point of a sword, in a ritual gesture of symbolically sexual significance. In a few words, he gave his daughter to her suitor without reservation, and then sprinkled a little water on his hands, the latter gesture being traditional in India in ratifying a gift. In reply, the bridegroom promised formally to be pious towards his wife throughout her life, to secure wealth and pleasure for her, and to form one single being with her.[40] This solemn promise bound the two for ever and made them man and wife from that moment on. They now received permission to look at each other, while the officiating brāhmaṇ hastened to state aloud, so as to ward off bad luck, that the young woman had no power to cast the evil eye upon her husband. To conclude this first part of the ritual, the father and his new son-in-law together made an offering of ghee and rice in the nuptial fire.

Then the husband approached his wife, who was still at the south-east corner of the carpet. Standing in front of her, he took her right hand between his own hands and murmured: 'I seize your hand for the love of happiness, so that you may live a long life with me, your husband. The gods have given you to me so that we may manage our household.' The spectators watched him carefully at this juncture, for, if he took hold of her thumb alone it would mean that he wanted a son; if he seized her other fingers but left the thumb free it meant that he wanted daughters; while if he clasped her whole hand within his own it meant that he would accept children of both sexes with equal joy.

The bride arose, and side by side the newly wedded couple approached the sacred fire. Lifting a corner of his garment, he knotted it to a corner of his wife's; then, joined in this way, they began to walk around the fire, keeping it to their right since it was a joyous ceremony. They circled it three times, and each time that they passed near the millstone lying to the west of the hearth, the husband made his wife touch it with her right foot, enjoining her ritually to be as firm as the millstone and always to confront enemies boldly. Now the husband pronounced the beautiful marriage formula: 'I am he, you are she, you are she, I am he; I am the sky, you are the earth; I am the song, you are the verse. Come, we shall marry and give children to the world! Loving, agreeable, joyful in heart, may we live for a hundred autumns!'

Holding a basket full of rice, the bride's father approached his daughter once again, while her attendants greased her hands with ghee, then poured some of the grains of roasted rice into her hands, as a symbol of prosperity and fecundity. Going up to the fire, she made four successive offerings with this rice, keeping her hands cupped; then she made a final offering, holding the sieve and throwing rice-grains into the flames.

The husband now unbraided his bride's hair; then they took seven steps together, right foot first, reciting together the following prayer: 'Take one step for food, two steps for strength, three for increasing wealth, four for good fortune, five for children, six for the seasons, and in seven steps be my friend! Be faithful to me, let us have many sons who shall attain a great age!' At each step, she scattered a little rice behind her, and the officiating priest sprinkled water in the marks left by her feet, using the water from the jar which had been standing to the north-west of the fire and which was now being carried on the shoulder of an assistant: this ritual evoked the idea of seed being sown and then made fertile by the rain. Then they stood still with their heads close together, and the priest sprinkled water over them both, thus consecrating their union finally for life, while the assistants threw rice and other cereal grains over them. The officiating brāhmaṇs were now presented with gifts: in principle a cow, but more probably its equivalent value.

But the sacrament was not yet complete, and the ceremony far from being over. In fact, the ceremony was about to continue elsewhere, for the moment had come when the young bride must leave her own family and join that of her husband. It is said that at this moment she frequently burst into tears at the prospect, and the author of the holy *Ṛg Veda* had been prescient enough to compose a ritual formula for the use of over-emotional young brides, which their husbands recited gently to them at that juncture: 'They [the eyes] weep for a living person [instead of for a dead person, as would be usual], they rejoice in sacrifice [the sacrifice accompanying the nuptial ceremony]. Glory to the Fathers [*pitṛ*] who have made that possible! Women are a joy to their husbands, so that their husbands may embrace them.' Thus consoled, she could devote her full attention to the wagon which was to take her away and which now required her presence to perform certain rituals. Two white bullocks were standing near the vehicle, waiting to be harnessed. She approached the wagon, smeared ghee over the pole and the two wheels, and then thrust fruit-laden branches through the empty sockets in the wheel-hubs. After she had done this, the pegs holding the wheels firm were replaced in the sockets, the animals were harnessed, and the inside of the wagon spread with fine cloths, ready to receive the married couple. The nuptial fire, which was to provide the foundation for their own domestic fire, was transferred carefully into the wagon, then the young couple climbed in and the vehicle moved off, followed by all the wedding guests.

If the way back to the husband's house was too short, the wedding party might well take a circuitous route, for the benefit of the local citizenry. In any case, the married couple had to pay special attention to road crossings, rivers, large trees and graveyards, and recite prayers asking protection for themselves against all obstacles and evil influences, each time one of these features came into view. In the streets, they looked at all the people who were watching their passage, whether from windows or at the side of the road, and asked them, in a loud voice, to wish them good luck. If, by chance, an accident happened, their first concern was to pile more logs on the nuptial fire and make an offering before proceeding on their way.

The bridal procession arrived at last at the house which the young man had recently had built to accommodate his new household. The brāhmaṇ women (those whose husbands and sons were all still alive) were grouped in front of the house waiting to welcome him. As soon as the bride and groom appeared, the officiating priest sang this hymn to the newly married couple: 'May all that is dear to you flourish here for you, thanks to your forbears: Watch over this home as mistress of the house, unite your body with this young husband here! When you are both ripe in years, may your speech and actions be wise!' He then invited the wife to enter the house, making sure that she stepped over the threshold with her right foot forward and without touching the door-step. The priest's next action was to set up the nuptial fire in the eastern part of the entrance hall and kindle it, after which he laid a bullock-skin to the west of the hearth and invited the couple to be seated on it. He applied a little ointment around the young woman's eyes, and she touched the ends of her plaits. Then a small boy was led in, a fine healthy child of brāhmaṇic caste, and placed in her lap. She gave him either roots or fruits to hold in each hand, then stood him on the ground again. Finally, while she touched her husband with her hand, he put a log on the fire and recited the names of his *gotra*, and the officiating brāhmaṇ anointed them over their hearts with ghee.

And now the marriage ceremony was really over. The bride remained seated and silent, with her husband beside her, until the stars came out, while the wedding guests chatted together gaily. Suddenly, one of the guests, scanning the sky as night fell, drew attention in a loud voice to the first star. After this, the husband pointed out the Pole Star to his wife and she broke her silence for the first time, wishing them both long life and many children and grandchildren. The husband offered six oblations, pouring a little of each over his wife's head, an action which was a symbolic assurance to her that he would remain faithful.

At this juncture they ate a meal which had to be 'neither bitter nor salted', boiled rice with curds. The husband first touched the foodstuffs with his right hand and then ate, giving the rest to his wife after he had finished. Morning and evening, they watched carefully over the domestic fire. For three successive nights they slept side by side, lying on the ground, without consummating the act of marriage. On the fourth day, the young woman untied from her right wrist the yellow band which her mother had attached, and so loosed the final knot tying her to her own family. They made further oblations and offerings together. That night he recited to her this beautiful formula: 'United are our souls, united our hearts, united our bodies. I pledge her my love; may our ties be indissoluble!' And, kissing her, he added: 'Be devoted to me, be my companion. . . . The bee's honey melts in my mouth, harmony dwells on my teeth.'

They now became truly man and wife, and prayed together that she should soon become pregnant. For ten days they did not leave the house. At the end of that period, their daily life resumed its normal rhythm, his as 'master of the house', hers as a future mother.

FAMILY LIFE AND ITS CONVENTIONS

The family (*kula*) represented the smallest, yet certainly the most important, social unit. Through the rules that governed it, the family exercised a direct influence on the individual and determined his behaviour, not only in the daily accomplishment of his duties but throughout his entire life. The *kula* maintained its ascendancy, in this way, from generation to generation, imposing durable ethical standards and a remarkable continuity of traditions.

Prepared, from childhood onwards, to fulfil their family role – the boys to be eventual *gṛhastha*, the girls to become mothers – most men and women followed quite naturally the path laid down for them by ritual, diligently performing all their personal tasks, and never transgressing the religious laws which were to guide them until they died. The exactitude to be observed in each rite being a primordial condition (and the smallest action being included in each rite), there resulted that a constant and unflagging attention to detail was demanded of the individuals concerned. This obligation provided a most effective protection against temptations or evil conduct, and a firm guarantee against any moral deterioration. Apparently, the moral rectitude thus imposed was not found too onerous, and people accepted so virtuous an existence with pious good will.

Before anything else, the family identified itself with the domestic fire, the fire which burnt on the nuptial hearth and had originally been kindled in the house when it was new and had just been occupied for the first time by the newly married couple. This fire was a constant source of care for the husband and wife for whom the flame burnt; they were bound to tend it carefully, aided by their eldest son as soon as he had been initiated, so that it should never go out. If, by ill chance, that happened, the *gṛhastha* was obliged to practise one of the 'expiations' (*prāya-ścitta*) designed for an accident of this kind, a proceeding which involved the carrying out of a long series of different expiatory rites, and necessitated the payment of fees to the priests charged with exorcizing this disastrous happening. Twice a day, shortly before the midday and evening meals, the family assembled in front of the fire's altar for the offerings which would be made by the head of the family (or, in his absence, by his wife) or by a priest attached to the household. In this way, the family affirmed each day the cohesion of all its members, reunited in a common ritual activity.

But the Indian family was often composed of a great number of individuals: far from consisting simply of a married couple and their children, it usually included, in addition, a whole group of relatives and connections, further augmented by servants and dependents, all of whom were considered to be solidary members of the family and were subject to the sole authority of its head. This formula, for what might be called a 'joint family', prevailed on every social level and represented perfectly the Indian way of life, based as it was on the ritual bonds of the *gotra*. It is still the rule in many Indian provinces.

A family of that nature constituted a genuine small-scale colony. A typical family would comprise the *gṛhastha*, his wife and their own children, of whom there were usually a large number; plus all the master's close relatives on the paternal side – his uncles and aunts, his male and female cousins, his nephews and nieces; plus the adopted children (who were to be found in many families), resident students (who were treated as children of the family), all the servants and slaves employed by the various adult members of these groups, and finally the whole horde of workmen and craftsmen living within the precincts and working for the entire household; in short, fifty people or more. This small army of individuals fully justified the architectural scheme of the family home, with its different buildings arranged within an encircling outer wall.

This miscellaneous collection of people was further augmented as a result of the practice of polygamy, as well as particular considerations resulting from alliances between different castes, and through remarriages. Remarriages were not as rare as one might imagine if one takes into account all the exceptions provided for in various texts.[41] Polygamy was permitted in all castes, but was practised mainly by the *kṣatriyas*, its main purpose being to ensure male descendants who would preserve the *gotra* intact, and so the continued existence of the *śrāddha* rite. Precedence was given the principal wife (the first bride, or the one of purest caste) and the second marriage was not undertaken, according to Kauṭilya, before a lapse of time varying between eight and twelve years, a period of time sufficient to convince the husband that his first wife was unable to give him a son. The matter could involve complications, when the order of succession was at issue (see pp. 212–14).

The children born from these different unions were admitted by society under certain conditions. With some exceptions, their position in the joint family was equal. Parentage presented quite a problem, in view of the communal existence of several households and the practice of polygamy, although those involved were not particularly concerned by such details: children called all their father's wives 'mother' indiscriminately, and in the same way cousins were referred to as 'brothers'. Domestic tranquillity was an absolute necessity in these private communities, and spells existed to ensure peace and to maintain it.[42]

We have seen the important place that children occupied in family life, and the extent to which parents cared for their health, education and behaviour. The eldest son played a pre-eminent part because he was directly associated with the family rite and that of the *gotra*: being the father's heir in terms of ritual law, he assumed the direction of the family when his father gave it up. The adopted or 'artificial' son (*kṛtaka*) had equal rights, in this respect, as a legitimate child, since a solemn ceremony had made him 'lose' his *gotra* and assume that of his second father. He had thus entered into the latter's ancestral line and was as worthy as a true son to celebrate the monthly office of the dead: the adopted son was, in fact, a substitute, 'a sort of magical creation of a real child' in the words of Louis Renou. Adoption was frequent, because the desire for a son became an absolute necessity in terms of ritual; even adults might be adopted – the primary consideration, in all cases of adoption, being the adoptive child's (or man's) caste and lineage.

The treatment of girls varied according to the epoch. In general, where a married couple's only child was a daughter, she could be treated as an eldest brother and enjoy the same rights so long as her descendants were still minors; however, her son was bound to the *gotra* of his maternal grandfather instead of continuing in his father's lineage, for which reason it was considered ill-advised to marry a girl (*putṛkā*) 'without brothers'. Although girls may sometimes have been considered as a sign of malediction in the lowest castes, and were seldom desired, this was not true of high caste families, who welcomed girls as joyfully as they did boys. In such families, a girl's future maternal role bestowed on her a quite definite importance.

Apart from children and close relatives, it was by no means rare for the joint family to act as host to some old uncle, usually a senile old sponger who was quite incapable of making himself useful in any way but lived in a corner of the house and profited from the relative comfort afforded by the community, without ever contributing much himself. This is a frequently recurring type in Indian literature, where he is depicted as a lazy creature of broken-down appearance, a good-for-nothing with an amiable character; he was treated with consideration and with the respect due to an aged relative, despite his obvious incapacity.

All the members of the family observed the same rules and obeyed a single authority, that of the *gṛhastha*. He was, at one and the same time, the father, administrator and guru of this community. He ruled the family in the same way that the king reigned over his kingdom: he exercised the same rights, submitted to the same restraints, and assumed the same responsibilities, only on the small scale of the family group.

Being the only one entitled to carry the *gotra*'s patronymic name, he represented the entire family. This obliged him to preserve intact a high personal morality which would redound to the credit of all around him; inversely, the honourable behaviour of each of his relatives rendered him even more respectable in the eyes of the social sphere in which he moved. For these reasons, he was bound to make every effort to be just and good, always careful not to allow feelings of selfish self-interest to develop in his heart, and to be a good father towards his own children and a good head of the whole family. In addition, his function as administrator of the family property extended to the property of all those living under his regime, and applied equally to the belongings of his wife, his sons and his other relatives, as well as to those of his servants and slaves. In fact he was considered a patriarch by all those in his family community and was treated with the greatest possible respect. Even so, he was enjoined from abusing his prerogatives. The times were already distant – if, indeed, they had ever existed – when he had supposedly possessed power of life and death over his children: law and custom combined to dissuade him from any such abuse. He held family councils to debate questions of common concern; but his eventual decision was final and irrevocable.

The mistress of the house, too, was an important figure, with considerable influence and standing in the family circle. She was the first to surround her husband with marks of respect and, when addressing him, always called him 'son of the venerable [father-in-law]' (*āryaputra*). She treated him as her master and tried to fulfil his every wish. In return, he treated her, simultaneously, as wife, mother, friend and adviser. As soon as she had borne him a son, it was the fact of her motherhood that was uppermost in the considerations of the whole 'clan', for now she incarnated the family hearth. The *gṛhastha* entrusted her with complete authority over all domestic affairs, including the flower garden, and the garden of medicinal herbs, which she supervised personally so that the household should never lack for herbal remedies. Despite everything, her authority was sometimes challenged when her mother-in-law lived under the same roof and had not yielded gracefully the domestic power she had wielded before her son assumed charge of the establishment. The respect accorded to the mother of the *gṛhastha* did not make things any easier for the wife. The best one can say is that sometimes the mother-in-law failed to live up to her unpleasing, age-old image, and then the young mistress of the house was able to devote herself peacefully and conscientiously to her domestic routine.

She seldom left the family compound, and when she did she was always chaperoned – less through constraint than by preference and tradition. The properly brought up Indian woman was timid and modest, and disliked showing herself in public unless enveloped in a voluminous shawl which turned her into a shapeless bulk, and with her face made invisible by a veil. Nevertheless, she took part willingly in the great celebrations to which she was invited with her husband (marriages, for example), as well as the tranquil country outings which the head of the family organized during the summer months.

Not all wives were so virtuous, it seems. Some committed all sorts of faults and were obliged, consequently, to pay fines to their husband, on a sliding tariff commensurate with the gravity of their misdeeds. The circumstances might involve a public reprimand, or even repudiation. Adultery, for example, was punished by the ignominious exposure of the delinquent wife on a donkey (see p. 59). The marriage might even be annulled in certain circumstances, and it appears that the initiative could, in some cases, be taken by the wife.

THE RITES AND CUSTOMS OF DAILY AND FAMILY LIFE

In his capacity as representative of the family, the *gṛhastha* assumed the greater part of the family ritual. His daily duties were burdensome, being divided between his religious obligations, his civic duties and his outside occupations. Each morning, he was obliged to wake up well before dawn so as to be ready before sunrise: if, by some mischance, he should still be asleep at that moment, he would have to remain standing for the rest of the day and stay silent.[43] As soon as he had woken up, he lit a little lamp standing in one of his room's alcoves, and began studying the Veda; seated on the ground, cross-legged, with an open book in front of him, he recited piously some passage from the holy writings. Then, wearing only a loin-cloth made of freshly laundered, thin, white material of some kind, he slid the door-bolt from its socket[44] and stepped out into the garden. The night was just giving way to day as he walked towards the river running along the edge of his property; he waded in and made an 'external' ablution first of all, while pronouncing an invocation to the waters; after this, he swallowed a few mouthfuls of water and then rinsed out his mouth, so as to accomplish the 'internal' ablution; finally, he splashed water over his head while repeating silently the holy verse (*Gāyatrī*) which had been taught him at the age of eight, on the occasion of his brāhmaṇic initiation: 'May I possess the lovely splendour of the god [naming his tutelary deity] that he may inspire my mind.' Then, turning towards the sun as it rose above the horizon, he adored it, bowing, with hands pressed together.

After emerging from the water, he refashioned his plait of hair into a coil and recited the *Gāyatrī* once more, this time aloud, while clasping a few leaves of *kuśa* grass (*Eragrotis cynosuroide*). He rinsed out his mouth three times, rubbed his hands together as though washing them, touched various parts of his body, performed an additional rinsing operation and began a meditation which he punctuated with breathing exercises: closing his left nostril with two fingers of his right hand, he breathed in vigorously through his right nostril; after holding his breath for as long as possible, closing the right nostril as well, with the thumb of the same hand, he opened the left nostril at last and expelled the air he had been keeping in. Before breathing in again, he repeated mentally a few sacred incantations (*mantras*); when he had performed this routine a certain number of times, he remained standing, with one foot planted against the ankle of his other leg. Then, facing the rising sun, his hands pressed flat together, he pronounced a few more mantras while making offerings of sesame, flowers, barley, water and sandalwood.

The morning rite, providing the link (*saṃdhyā*) between night and day, was now at an end, and he completed his ritual ablutions by dressing and adorning himself. Without indulging in unnecessary conceits, he completed all the details of his toilet carefully, put on a freshly laundered skirt, and perfumed himself. His final action, before attending to the business of the day, was to paint his caste-mark on his forehead.

Meanwhile, his wife, too, was devoting great care to the details of her own daily toilet – not for reasons of mere coquetry but because it was a ritual act and, also, because it was her duty to be pleasing to her husband. Each day, she bathed herself meticulously. Although the accessories ranged on her dressing-table may not have been as luxurious as those belonging to a court lady (see p. 269), they were still numerous enough: for her cosmetics, there were boxes made of ivory, horn, reed, bamboo, wood, lacquer, and various shells of animal and vegetable origin;[45] for dressing her hair she had wooden combs; and, unlike the poor who were content to look at their reflection in the surface of a bowl of water, she used a mirror made of burnished metal. To complete her toilet, she rimmed her eyes with lampblack (*añjana*), smeared her body with coloured and perfumed ointments, stained the soles of her feet with red lac, and placed a garland of freshly picked flowers around her neck.[46]

As soon as she was ready, she went to greet her husband, followed by her children. They saluted him respectfully, kneeling down in front of him to touch his feet, 'these feet which it is a favour to touch' (*Raghu Vaṃśa*, IV, 88). Then, while the father went about his business, his wife busied herself among the servants, supervising all their activities.

One of her essential tasks was to prepare her husband's food, however many servants the household might employ. This was because the ritual purity of the various ingredients had to be preserved, and consequently the husband could consume only food prepared by his wife, except when he was away on a voyage; in that case, he prepared his meals himself, or confided the task to some person of the same caste as himself. Even a king's daughter, if her mother was one of the royal slaves, was not fit to share his food in his presence.[47]

Before the midday meal, the *gṛhastha* made the first of the twice-daily offerings before the domestic fire, in the presence of the assembled family. He threw into the ritual fire, as an oblation, samples of the food that the household was about to eat, while murmuring prayers to various deities, to the spirits of the departed, to the Earth, Fire and other sacred entities. Then he made sure that portions of the food were reserved for the brāhmaṇs, and that food was thrown to the dogs, the insects and the birds, not forgetting the daily offering to the serpents. The ever-present crows, as hungry as always, swooped down to grab what they could from this feast. The *gṛhastha* had the added responsibility, when distinguished guests were staying in his villa, of supervising personally the meal which was to be served to them. It was only after accomplishing these various duties that he could start thinking of taking refreshment himself.

The same rites were repeated each evening.

The ritual of eating followed precise rules. Before the meal, the children washed their father's feet as a sign of respect, and then their mother's feet. The wife personally served her husband's meal, which he took alone, sitting on the ground or on a cushion. She filled a clean pot with water so that he could rinse his hands; after using it, he emptied it and placed the empty pot by his side.[48] A large banana leaf had been laid before him, and on this his wife heaped the different foodstuffs, one after the other. He carried the food to his lips with his right hand only, never even touching it with his left hand. After eating and drinking, he rinsed his mouth without swallowing the water.[49]

When he had finished, his wife ate in her turn, observing the same proprieties, and served by her children who only ate afterwards.

The diet was quite varied,[50] and although rice formed the main element, housewives were adept at cooking it in different ways and using it to the best advantage. Long-grained rice was made into a kind of gruel which was moistened with vegetable broth; medium-grained rice was boiled and served as the basic dish; small-grained rice was made into flour. Each day, the grains were husked by pounding them in a great wooden or stone mortar with the aid of a long, heavy pestle whose light, rhythmic blows echoed, as they still do today, throughout every household.[51] Then the grain was shaken in a winnowing-basket; sometimes, after the sieving, a hollow reed was used to extract the grains which had not emerged from their husks. The husks were collected and sold to the goldsmiths, who used them for polishing jewels.[52]

To cook the rice, a wood fire was lit over a few stones, with logs bought from the foresters who sold them at the gates of towns and villages. A cauldron was placed on the flames, filled with water in the proportion of three parts of water to one of rice. When the water boiled, the rice, which had been frequently rinsed beforehand, was added, and allowed to boil for fifteen minutes while the scum forming on the surface was skimmed off and the rice was stirred so that it should not stick to the bottom of the pot. When it was ready, the rice was drained, heaped on to a tray supported by a rattan stand and cooled with a little flag-shaped fan.[53] It was served with curds and with three spices, cinnamon, cardamom and mace, carefully ground, first of all, on a flat stone, with the aid of a small stone roller; or else it was served flavoured with ghee, mango juice or a sauce made of gram. When the rice was ground into flour and mixed with water, it formed a dough which was flattened with a rolling-pin and made into bread pancakes,[54] exactly similar to those eaten throughout India today under the name of *capāti*, and which, then as now, constituted the working-man's basic 'snack'.

Barley, wheat and beans were also part of the popular diet, eaten boiled or fried. Soups were made with the stock from boiled vegetables.

Because of the theory of non-violence (*ahiṃsā*) and the laws prohibiting the taking of life, meat and fish were forbidden in orthodox brāhmaṇic families, except on a few special occasions. Nevertheless, if one takes into account the legislation governing slaughterhouses, as well as the large number of hunters and fishermen mentioned in contemporary tales, it seems certain that these articles of food were eaten regularly by the *kṣatriyas*. But useful animals were never killed, nor were those which gave milk, except for gazelles.[55] When meats were boiled, they were flavoured with the juice of fruits or bitter herbs (*amlavarga*), such as lemon, orange, pomegranate (*dāḍima*), tamarind, sorrel (*cukra*), *Artocarpus lacoutcha*, *Spondias manifera*, and so on. During the banquets described in epic literature, the guests were offered 'whole animals roasted on the spit, such as young buffaloes, fat and fleshy, whose juicy meat was basted with melted ghee and served floating in a spicy sauce made of sour fruits and salt'.[56] Or meat was cut into slices and fried in ghee, sesame oil or mustard oil; sometimes, whole briskets, smeared all over with ghee and sprinkled with salt and pepper (*mārica*), were cooked in this manner. Birds were roasted, wrapped in bitter leaves and served with a thick sauce made of ghee, mango juice, salt and pepper. Succulent carps were also served at such meals.[57]

Meat dishes and vegetables (cooked in oil) were strongly seasoned with various combinations of curry ingredients, including chili pepper, cardamom, cloves, cummin and salt. Spices were handed around between courses to stimulate the palate and encourage thirst: roots, basil (*parṇāsa*), asafoetida (*hiṅgu*), ginger (*ārdraka*), andropogon (*bhūstṛṇa*), and so on. Garlic and onion were forbidden, and those who wished to eat these had to do so outside the town.[58]

In noble establishments, and at the king's table, a great variety of desserts were offered, including scented curds, creamy cheeses (*kilāṭa*), and balls of rice or wheat coated with sugar, thin slices of coconut and various spices, these last sweetmeats being either steam-boiled or fried in butter. Sweets were made of seeds fried in oil. Sugar-cane, refined and moulded into oval loaves, provided the base for sweet dishes (*modaka*) containing molasses, curds, ghee and pepper. These were followed by fruits, the favourite being mango (as it still is today), curds, whey and salted rice. Milk foods were very popular: for instance, sweetened milk flavoured with spices and camphor, and cooked with ripe bananas. Honey was usually reserved for great occasions.

The usual beverage which accompanied these rich, spicy dishes was simply water, milk or whey. But, here again, this depended on the social sphere and on particular circumstances. Despite the horror with which they were regarded by orthodox brāhmaṇs,[59] who contented themselves with mango syrup or lemon juice, fermented drinks were, nevertheless, widely consumed by all the other castes. The most popular drink was toddy, the fermented sap of the palmyra or coconut. Peasants were particularly fond of alcohols distilled from rice or barley, fermented juices of all kinds based on fruits or plants, and also a liqueur composed of raw sugar, pepper and distilled mango-juice. It seems that the *vaiśyas* preferred strong spirits, some of which were distilled from heavily scented flowers. In any case, people liked to perfume their drinks with mango blossoms or red *pāṭala* (*Stereospermum suaveolnes*).[60] The *kṣatriyas* drank wine distilled from sugar-cane and, if they were wealthy enough, grape wine. Wine made from grapes was the pre-eminently aristocratic drink, but was so rare and so expensive[61] that the king was usually the only person who could afford to drink it regularly (see pp. 86 and 275).

After dining, it was usual to chew quids made from the skins of *Citrus medica* or, better still, a betel-nut broken up, mixed with lime and other ingredients, and wrapped in a betel-pepper leaf fastened by a clove.[62] The pungency of the ingredients served to perfume the breath, and also, by increasing salivation, encouraged the digestion.

The Indians of that epoch were not in the habit of over-indulging in either food or drink, and reliable commentators of the time, such as the worthy fifth-century Chinese monk Fa-Hien, attest to the general sobriety of the people. Even so, drunken scenes, in which even women took part, were by no means uncommon, showing that there was some tendency to anticipate the 'drinking festivals' which were officially celebrated from time to time (see p. 148).

The *gṛhastha* was responsible, too, for performing the rites of hospitality to which distinguished guests were entitled. These rites went back to the Vedic age, and the gradually increasing emphasis on ritual codification made them ever more important as time went by.

When a guest was expected, the chair which was to be offered him was got ready, and a special beverage (*madhuparka*)[63] composed of sugar, ghee, curds, herbs and honey, was prepared. This was a sort of hydromel consumed on great occasions: women were given it to drink when five months pregnant, the eldest son's lips were moistened with it at the time of his birth, the student was offered it when he left his guru to become a *snātaka*, the suitor just before he went to ask for the hand of a girl in marriage, and the bridegroom when he arrived at the home of his future father-in-law on the morning of the wedding.

As soon as the guest appeared at the dwelling's main entrance gate, his host went out to meet him[64] and greeted him in an appropriate manner. A great number of different forms of salutation existed, depending on the exact relationship between the two parties: an inferior bowed his head before his superior; but in the case of venerable persons, such as his teacher, his father or mother, he touched their feet respectfully; the superior responded by reciting to him a formula of blessing.[65] When someone addressed a request to a superior, he joined his hands together in front of his chest. Brothers, and individuals of the same social status, embraced each other or shook hands.[66] In actual practice, a guest was automatically considered a superior and honoured accordingly.

As soon as he had been escorted inside the house, he was led to the cushion or rattan chair which had been set in position for him.[67] A servant brought him water to refresh his feet. Then he was offered water to drink. Finally, he was presented with a bowl containing hydromel. He was required to accept it with both hands and to place it by his side, on the ground, without drinking from it. Soon afterwards, he stirred the mixture three times in succession, by making a circular motion in the liquid with the thumb and index finger of his right hand, pressed together. He consumed the ritual drink in three mouthfuls (or in a single mouthful, according to other texts) and then drank a little water.[68]

If the guest was a brāhmaṇ or a king, the ceremony was completed by an important rite. He was led solemnly towards a cow (which was, of course, a sacred animal) and it was offered to him as a present. In the Vedic age, the animal was slaughtered in his honour, as the scapegoat for his sins, and ritual purification was thus achieved. In later times, the sacrifice became entirely symbolic; all that remained of the custom was that the *gṛhastha* held out a knife to his guest, who handed it back to him, reciting this formula: 'She is the mother of the Rudras, the daughter of the Vasus, the sister of the Ādityas, the womb of immortality. Do not kill the innocent cow; she is the very goddess of Earth. I say this to those who understand me.' Then he added: 'My sins have been slain. Let her go, let her drink water and graze.'

The reception ended with a meal that included meat, a food which was, as we have seen, rarely eaten by a brāhmaṇ, and the host supervised its preparation in person. The *gṛhastha* took leave of his guests by rising from his seat first, in their presence, following the code of courtesy that is still in use today.

Voyages were often necessary, and could be both long and dangerous. Many of those who undertook them fell ill and died; others were drowned attempting to ford some river, or disappeared over a precipice.[69] Before leaving on a voyage, the traveller made his obeisance to the domestic fire;[70] he placed a log on it as 'wood of good augury', and pronounced a formula appropriate to the purpose of the voyage. If, for instance, he was leaving on a business trip, he would say: 'The good is going towards the better.' And he accompanied this with a prayer for his own safety. Then he drank a specially consecrated beverage and took care to set off right foot first. If he was travelling in his own cart, he smeared it with ghee from the morning's ritual offerings. If he had to travel by water, he hung around his neck a boat-shaped amulet.

The whole time that he was away, his wife observed a mode of life resembling that of a widow: she no longer adorned or perfumed herself, wore neither jewellery nor flowers, and stopped making up her eyes with black cosmetic. She slept on the ground, beside the conjugal bed, never lying on the bed itself. And she counted the days which separated her from her husband's return.

When the returning husband first saw the roofs of his home in the distance, he made a gesture of salutation. And when passing through the door, he touched the two door-jambs and recited a prayer of thanksgiving.

THE CARES OF LIFE: DEBTS, SICKNESS

The various taxes to which the working classes were subject, and the heavy expenses resulting from ritual observances, donations and festivals often found the family budget inadequate and forced most Indians to contract debts. These were governed both by common law and statute law, and the whole business of borrowing and lending money was certainly an important and eternal factor in the conduct of daily life.

When a peasant borrowed money, he left as security with his creditor a chattel-personal in the shape of one or more heads of cattle. He pledged himself to repay the loan at an interest which was usually fixed at fifteen per cent per annum, apparently due monthly. It was not unusual for the borrower to be over-optimistic in his estimate of future income and so find himself unable to repay his debt. When this debt was in fact doubled by the accumulation of unpaid interest, and if it could be proved that the debtor was in good faith, the creditor was obliged to return to the debtor the security which he himself had been entitled to make use of up to that moment. When this situation occurred, the total debt could no longer be increased, unless it consisted of clothing, cattle, etc. In this case, the debt could be tripled or even quadrupled. Generally speaking, the debtor's principal hope was that the creditor should not be one of those usurers who were feared and despised in equal measure by the world, and condemned by the law.[71] Often, peasants were unable to liquidate their accumulated debts during their lifetime, a calamity which obliged them, according to their belief, to become the creditor's slave in their future lives. Apart from this problematical penalty, the hard fact also remained that the debtor's sons were obliged, in their turn, to assume responsibility for the loan. The unredeemed debt was extinguished only in the third generation, that is to say, after a hundred years.

It was not uncommon for a landowner or property owner to be so harassed by taxes and debts that he was obliged to sell all his possessions and become a wage-earner. He might also be involved with an intractable creditor who, after voluntarily renewing his promissory notes over a long period of time, suddenly confronted him, out of the blue, with a demand for repayment of the entire sum, including interest. The law authorized a creditor to use persuasion, legal proceedings, stratagems and even violence, and allowed him, if necessary, to have his debtor condemned to forced labour. An additional – and very curious – procedure open to the creditor permitted him to lay siege to the debtor's home, threatening to stay there and allow himself to starve to death, holding the debtor responsible if he died! A debtor was unfortunate indeed if he became the victim of this kind of blackmail: the creditor was, in fact, perfectly capable of carrying out his threat, and the debtor would have, on top of his other woes, the certainty of being found guilty of homicide and, what was worse, the consequent result that his *karma* would be so increased that he would have no hope at all any longer of improving the status of his future rebirths. The 'joint family' system palliated these severe disadvantages to some extent, since the family's solidarity provided a fund of strength in facing such adversities.

Sickness was another care which afflicted the individual as well as the entire community. It was often the direct cause of a family's ruin, either by keeping the householder from his work for a long period of time, and so building up fresh debts, or when it resulted in his death and thus led to the division of collective property and consequent hardship for the individuals involved. We possess no statistics that would give us any idea of the average age of death in those times, nor the proportion of infant and childhood mortality. What we do know is that India was ahead of most other ancient civilizations in possessing a highly developed science of medicine and surgery; and, although the people certainly resorted to magical practices in combating disease and sickness, they did benefit at the same time from a genuine body of medical knowledge, elaborated in treatises[72] and practised by professional physicians and surgeons.

There were two categories of physician (*vaidya*):[73] independent doctors called into consultation privately and responsible financially if convicted of error; and official practitioners in hospitals subsidized by pious or royal foundations, where medical assistance was free. Both categories underwent a long apprenticeship and received authority to exercise their profession only from the king. State physicians had their salaries stopped immediately if they committed professional errors or gave proof of scandalous conduct. In general, they were bound by the moral and professional rules instilled into them during the course of their studies: they were never to betray the sick under any pretext, even at the cost of their own life; nor, at any moment, allow their thought or speech to stray from the patient they were treating; nor reveal to a living soul what went on in the patient's home, or his private or family circumstances, or his physical defects, or the nature of the illness from which he was suffering.

When a sick person's condition necessitated the attentions of a physician, the head of the family sent for him in the name of the sick man, using an honourable member of the household as an intermediary. This approach to the physician had to be made at an auspicious moment, since the circumstances attending the arrival of the emissary at the physician's house could influence the way the ailment developed. After listening to his visitor's request for assistance, the physician had a servant carry bags filled with his medical and surgical instruments to the home of his new client, before appearing in person. He was received with deference, despite the fact that, in the eyes of the orthodox of high caste, he was impure: since he was in regular contact with sick people he was automatically excluded from ritual ceremonies. This impurity was enhanced by the fact that a direct relationship was established between sickness and sin, sin – whether voluntary or not – being considered a miasma whose malignant action could have repercussions on a person's health.

As soon as the physician had arrived at the sick man's home, he was invited to take a warm bath, surrounded with every attention and offered a meal of rice served in one of the dishes reserved for great occasions. He was then conducted to the patient and proceeded to a thorough physical examination, knowing that the smallest sign might provide him with valuable information. The establishment of a diagnosis was, in fact, recognized as being of primary importance, and physicians were taught to pay careful attention to all the symptoms that might prove useful to them: in particular, the patient's complexion, and the power and inflexions of his voice;[74] he also made him undergo certain tests to gauge any disturbance in his sense of taste or smell, deficiencies in his sense of touch, and his nervous and muscular reactions. But, since magic was (as it still remains) a powerful factor in Indian habits of thought, he also placed importance on the patient's recent dreams and hallucinations, since these possessed premonitory significance.[75] The physician made careful note of the various signs he had noticed as a result of his examination, linked them mentally with the groups of symptoms catalogued in the classical medical texts, and studied their pathology.

He now prescribed a regime and a course of treatment. He had at his disposal a considerable number of remedies, including plasters, ointments, rectal injections with oil, washing out the stomach, urethral injections, medicinal sprays, frictions and sudorific techniques. The various medicines were in the form of liquids, ointments or powders whose ingredients might comprise plants of different kinds (barks, roots, onion, leaves, seeds), animal and mineral products, water, ghee, oils acting as excipients, milk, juice of the sugar-cane, and spirits. Cow's or human urine (often that of the sick man himself) was considered a sovereign remedy in some cases. Chemical preparations were in use, such as concentrated lyes forming the base for infusions, decoctions and macerations which were used as vomitives, purgatives and caustics, and employed also in the form of potions, eye-washes, interior rinses, gargles, pills, and so on. But the physician considered it essential that his prescriptions should be accompanied by a special diet and also by rules of hygiene which he was himself the first to practise. He usually recommended the patient to eat meat and drink wine, and advised that he be given as much fresh air as possible, even exposed to the sun if necessary, for the curative powers of fresh air and sunshine were already recognized.

When the consultation was over, the physician was paid his fee and retired, accompanied by the respectful gestures of farewell of the entire family.

It would take too long, and be largely irrevelant to our purpose, to enumerate all the illnesses and the treatments applied to them. The best known, perhaps, were the fevers with the usual symptoms (headache, nausea, dry skin, shivering and leaden complexion), which were perfectly accurately classified as intermittent, quotidian, tertian, quartan and unintermitting fever. Leprosy was divided into seventeen different varieties and given various treatments, including frictions with a base of *chaulmugra* oil – a formula still used in the basic treatment of this disease. Pulmonary tuberculosis was considered incurable, although its successive phases had been carefully and accurately studied.

The important fact to remember about Indian medicine in that age is that it was founded simultaneously upon empiric knowledge and upon a magical tradition. Any discussion of the relationship between these two disparate approaches is outside the scope of the present work, but the scientific approach was epitomized by the advanced state of development of oto-rhino-laryngology, toxicology, ophthalmology (the most remarkably advanced of all the ancient medicines) and pharmacy. This last science benefited particularly from the extraordinary abundance of medicinal plants growing in India. Physicians knew the value of comprehensive tonics, and undertook the rejuvenation of clients through the administration of aphrodisiac drugs. At the same time, both minor and major surgery gave evidence of astonishingly bold development. Anatomical research – although contrary to ritual regulations – had been pursued since Vedic times, and practical studies were conducted on specially prepared corpses whose intestines had been removed, and which had then been wrapped in foliage, placed inside a cage, and immersed in running water for a week, so that its internal organs could be separated with an ordinary knife, rather than dissected, while fresh, with the aid of a scalpel. However, although many human organs were recognized and listed, there remained a good deal of confusion about their mutual relationship. Expert physicians were competent to lance an abscess, reduce a fracture, apply remedial bandages, cauterize a wound, apply leeches, bleed a patient, make cutaneous incisions, and perform surgical tappings and catheterisms. They were also able to extract foreign bodies and remove dead foetuses, perform abdominal and trepanning operations, and operate for stone (through the perineal tract) and cataract. Plastic surgery was one of the most advanced branches of Indian surgery, so that split lips or noses could be regrafted, and torn lobes reattached to ears – all services which were much appreciated by those wounded on the field of battle, or elsewhere.

A classic method of suturing wounds or surgical incisions consisted in making use of giant ants. The surgeon brought the ants' heads up to the lips of the wound and made them bite at regular intervals, cutting the body off immediately the jaws had clamped: the insects' pincers and heads remained firmly embedded in the flesh, and their presence was tolerated by the abdomen, whereas there was no thread known at that time that the body could resorb. Nevertheless, those operated on must have had only a dubious chance of survival, since the principle of asepsis was as yet unknown, and consequently antiseptics were not made use of.

Parallel with official medical science (or accompanying it, sometimes), magical practices remained very popular among the common people. Fevers were treated by sympathetic magic: for example, the sick person was sprinkled with water in which a red-hot axe-blade had been suddenly plunged, the hope being that the fever would be 'extinguished' just as this water had 'extinguished' the red-hot iron. Similarly, mental and nervous ailments, madness and epilepsy were more the concern of the sorcerer than the physician, since they were considered evidence of demonic possession. Amulets and spells were commonly used, too, in the case of wounds caused by poisoned arrows or the bites of venomous creatures. Even so, these very same cases were treated, in those days, by the administration of vomitives or of draughts containing antidotes, the application of appropriate plasters, the cauterizing of wounds, the extraction of blood by the use of pressure, and even the amputation of the affected limb.

DEATH AND FUNERAL CEREMONIES

The wise grieve neither over the dead nor the living.
Bhagavad Gītā, II.

When premonitory signs of death began to appear, the priest was summoned. The dying man called all his relatives to his bedside and, in conformity with tradition, spoke a few affectionate words to them, requesting them to share his possessions among themselves. Then he was lifted from his bed and laid out on the ground, so that he should die in the customary fashion, close to the earth.

After he had protected himself against impurity by reciting a prayer, the priest leaned over and whispered a verse of the Veda into the dying man's right ear, followed by a second verse whispered into the left ear. To the extent that his failing lucidity permitted, the dying man attempted to concentrate mentally on the two ways open before him: the one leading him towards the divine, the other condemning him to the process of rebirth. In a final effort, he tried to centre his thoughts upon the celebrated formula affirming the identity of the individual soul with the divine soul: 'What He is, that I am.' Then he died. One text[76] gives an impressive description: the fluid contained in the dying man's body 'absorbs strength from the earth'; a last convulsion seizes him and he collapses, muscles no longer functioning, while an odour of death begins to spread; next, the inner fire consumes the seats of breath and the vital points, 'burns the fluid which emanates from the orifices of the vessels'; under the action of this fire, the body burns up, the blood dries, and, with no fuel left to feel it, the inner fire flickers out; the five vital 'winds' no longer fulfil their respective functions and start rising up through the body, providing the sound of the final death-rattle before escaping to rejoin the universal wind; then begins the disintegration of the corpse.[77]

His widow, kneeling by his side, wept and lamented. Her grief was so great that she was not yet amenable to reason, to be persuaded that only common people gave themselves up to eternal sorrow,[78] and that 'what is born is assured of death, and what is dead is assured of life'.[79] Nothing could aid her in her present distress, and her loud lamentations were designed to prove how irreparable was the loss to her of her husband and life-long companion. 'My adornments are useless to me now,' she would cry,[80] 'my bed is quite deserted today. Pitiless death has taken you away from me, and so has taken everything away from me!'[81] The whole family echoed her grief.

Arrangements had to be put in hand without delay for the obsequies.[82] The *gṛhastha* summoned professional undertakers, who cut the dead man's hair, beard, body hair and nails, rubbed the body with perfumed oils, dressed it in a new garment, tied the thumbs together, and bedecked the corpse with garlands, before finally placing it on a bier. A group of professional female weepers had already been hired, and now surrounded the corpse and began exercising conscientiously their lugubrious art, beating their breasts, screaming, dancing around and tearing at their long dishevelled hair. All the family's relatives, even those living some distance away, had been forewarned of the event by the drummer whose rhythm continued to echo through the village, and they began to stream towards the house of death, all with their hair let down as a sign of their sorrow.

Meanwhile, the officiating priest was getting things ready for the ceremony; he obtained sacrificial herbs and ghee, ordered loads of wood for the incineration, selected a cow which was required for the ritual, and had the dead man's instruments of sacrifice brought to him.

When all was ready, a cortege was formed: at its head relatives carried the three ritual fires, and they were followed by the hand-bier supported on the shoulders of the oldest *sapiṇḍa*, both men and women, unless the litter had been placed in a cart drawn by cows. The other relatives brought up the train, in order of age, the oldest first.

The cremation ground, not far from the cemetery's wide

enclosure, was situated outside the village boundaries. The long file of pall-bearers and others in the funeral procession strung out along the path to the cremation site. The footsteps of those carrying the bier were effaced by a long, leafy branch fastened to the back end of the bier and trailing along the ground. The sacrificial cow, led by a male member of the family by a rope attached to its right foreleg, followed immediately behind the corpse.

A dais composed of poles with a roof of foliage had been erected above the funeral-pyre.[83] The officiating priest circled it three times, keeping it to his left (that is to say in the opposite direction to that observed in benefic rites), and sprinkled it by dipping a bough in the holy water, exorcizing the demons that inevitably haunted these impure grounds with these words: 'Be off, withdraw, leave this spot!' Then he placed the three sacrificial fires around the pyre, the first one to the north-west, and the other two to the south-west and south-east respectively. He distributed the cut herbs over the surface of the pyre's upper platform, and covered this with the skin of a black antelope, hairy side uppermost. The pall-bearers now approached, passed in front of the north-western fire and deposited the body on the antelope skin. The widow, still bathed in tears, was led up to the corpse from the north, and stretched herself out, weeping, by his side; she was then immediately helped to her feet again and made to descend from the pyre, unless she had decided to let herself be burnt alive there, like a 'true wife' (*satī*) (see pp. 211–12).

The officiating priest arranged on the corpse all the sacrificial objects that had belonged to the dead man: the libation spoons were placed in his hands, the wooden sword and the ladle by his sides, the great spoon on his chest, a dish on his head, the stones for pressing the *soma* on his mouth, small spoons on his nostrils, a small bowl over each ear, a basin, a cup and the cane on his stomach, a log on each thigh, the mortar and pestle on his legs and a basket on each foot. All the other instruments and containers, the millstone, the metal and earthenware utensils were either distributed among the heirs or else thrown away.

The time had now come for the officiating priest to sacrifice the cow. After killing it, he proceeded to cut up the carcass. When this was done, he placed the animal's kidneys, heart and various other parts on different points of the body, as prescribed by ritual.

The solemn moment had arrived: the officiating priest ordered the pyre to be ignited simultaneously with the three ritual fires. While the flames mounted towards the body, he recited hymns and prayers. The smoke thickened and swirled around the base of the dais until it was licked by flames. The priest watched the progress of the flames carefully, to draw portents from the way in which they spread: if the fire lit in the south-east reached the corpse first, it meant that the deceased had already been borne off on the smoke and had reached the celestial regions where prosperity was assured him; if the fire from the north-west was the first to touch the body, then the dead man had settled down in those dominions in the skies; but if the third flame had spread the fastest, then the deceased would be reborn among men. Lastly, if the flames from the three fires reached the corpse at the same moment, it was a sign of supreme good fortune.

While the funeral pyre burned furiously, the priest recited a new hymn, commencing with the words: 'These living beings have been separated from the dead.' When the flames had died down, the smoke had abated and the pyre had been reduced to a huge pile of smouldering ashes, the watching relatives prepared to leave the cremation grounds. Before doing so, they walked, in single file, three times around the pyre, keeping it to their left. Then they went away, still in single file, and taking care not to look back. Before re-entering the village they had to purify themselves, since their presence near the dead man had polluted them. With this aim in view, they walked towards the river and, when they had reached the bank, stripped themselves of all except a single undergarment and entered the water. Facing south, each made an offering of water to the dead man, repeating the name of the *gotra* and of the deceased himself. After emerging from the river, they put on a new garment, leaving the old one on the ground facing north.

Now they all sat down in a group, since they were not permitted yet to rejoin the living world of the village and had to wait until night-time, or at least until the last rays of the sun had disappeared over the horizon, before returning home. They whiled away the time by telling each other stories and exchanging gossip. As soon as the stars appeared, they re-formed their column, the youngest members of the party in the lead, and re-entered the village.

When they reached their respective homes, they touched objects of good omen before crossing the threshold: a stone, the domestic fire, a cow-pat, some roasted barley, sesame seeds or water. In the dead man's house, an earthenware jar was filled with a mixture of milk and water and left outside, uncovered, so that the dead man could come and bathe himself in it. An evening meal was served, consisting of saltless ingredients that had been bought or had been given as a gift by some friend, since the participants in the funeral were forbidden to prepare any food themselves on that particular evening. For the following ten days,[84] the relatives of the deceased might eat only saltless food, and were obliged to sleep on the ground and refrain from sexual relations. They might neither work nor permit anyone to perform work on their behalf, and they stopped studying the Veda and distributing gifts during this period. Every day, a fresh offering of food and water was placed outside for the dead man.

The eleventh day arrived at last. During the whole of this time, the dead man's partly calcined bones had remained among the ashes of the funeral-pyre: now that they were cold, and any unconsumed flesh had been picked off them by the birds of prey,[85] it was necessary to bury them, and the relatives made their way to the cemetery.[86] This consisted of a great expanse of ground enclosed by walls; it could be entered through any one of four porches (one designed for each caste, apparently) which were decorated with paintings and sacred sculptures. An altar stood in the centre of a large courtyard, as well as a chapel dedicated to the goddess of those species of tree whose wood was used in cremations. The surface of the ground was dotted with sacrificial stakes and many stone benches. It was a grassy spot, covered with undergrowth and many different varieties of bush and tree: spurge, hawthorn, the *bahera*, *andrachne*, the *alangi*, the *kānrai*, the jujube and other types of zizyphus, mimosa, *feronia* and *spigelia*. Tall verdant trees grew there, the kind of tree preferred by dryads, but also the trees from which stakes were cut when a criminal had been sentenced to be impaled (see p. 154). Here and there the pointed tops of funerary urns were to be seen, their red pottery standing out against the green grass; they provided perches for birds, 'the red-eared cock, the *poguval*, the impudent crow with his strong beak, the eagle-owl'. Channels of water ran through the grounds,[87] and pathways snaked through the copses. Domed funerary monuments, made of brick or stone, rose above the tangled undergrowth, and it is supposed that the Buddhists took these structures as a model when they began erecting stūpas.[88] Caretakers – who had, of necessity, to be *caṇḍāla* – lived in the grounds, in a few huts, and patrolled the area armed with sticks, a weapon being a most necessary precaution against demons, since the cemetery was haunted, as one may well imagine. In this desolate spot, howling and weeping and lamentation never ceased to echo through the groves: 'like the frenzy of the sea at high tide, these sad cries never stop', and, at night, they are joined by 'the dismal call of the long-snouted jackals, the voice of the eagle-owl calling the dead, the voice of the flesh-eating screech-owl'.

A large 'male' funerary urn with a pointed bottom had been ordered from the village potter; it was decorated only with a very simple design, executed by the potter with his finger-nails, around its neck, and had a few hooks jutting out from its waist, upon which garlands of flowers could be hung. The cover consisted of a sort of cup, pointed like the urn's base, and placed upside down over the orifice after the cremated bones had been introduced. For women, the potter fashioned 'female' urns.[89]

The officiating priest began by purifying the spot where the burial hole was to be dug;[90] he performed the same ritual as at the time of cremation, circling it three times and sprinkling it with the aid of a bough. Then he picked up the bones between his thumb and fourth finger and dropped them, one after the other, into the jar, beginning with the feet and finishing with the skull, after 'sifting' them with a sieve. When they were all inside, he purified them by sprinkling aromatics over them. The urn was then lowered into the hole and draped with garlands. The priest threw a little earth over it and the lid was placed over its mouth.

The ceremony was over. As they had done ten days before, the relatives left the cemetery without turning round. They bathed themselves once again, before offering the *piṇḍa* to the deceased. From that day, the *śrāddha* rite would be celebrated regularly each month by the dead man's eldest son.

The cemetery lay there, after the mourners had left, strewn with every kind of debris: 'cakes scattered among the undergrowth, empty hand-biers, cloths that had served as shrouds, discarded garlands, broken water-vases, the husked rice that had been thrown as offerings, were to be found everywhere in this vast scene of desolation.' The caretakers must have had a hard time keeping the place clean, if indeed this was among their responsibilities.

WIDOWHOOD, SATĪ

If the widower is seldom alluded to in ancient literature, it is for the good reason that he was expected to remarry as soon as possible, so that the daily ritual could be resumed; the fate of the widow, though, is frequently evoked, and for equally good reason.

Although condemned by the brāhmaṇic caste, suicide by a widow was becoming increasingly fashionable during the period which is the subject of the present study, especially among the *kṣatriyas*, where it was perhaps the consequence of polygamy. The first dated mention of this custom goes back to AD 510, when such an incident was commemorated by the erection of a stele (at Eran),[91] and the custom became widespread subsequently, especially in southern India. This voluntary sacrifice on the part of the widow was spectacular indeed: during the cremation of her husband's corpse, she climbed on to the blazing pyre and allowed herself to be burnt alive. This act was considered the supreme sign of conjugal fidelity, which is why a woman who performed it was named a *satī* or 'true wife'.[92]

The lot of the widow who survived her husband was far from enviable. The disappearance of her husband placed her in an inferior position, legally as well as socially. Not only might she no longer take part in the family's sacramental life, she had also to remain absent, thenceforward, from social reunions and ceremonies, where her presence would have struck a note of ill omen. She no longer wore jewellery or perfumes, her face was no longer made up, her hair was no longer hennaed or dressed or even combed.[93] Her fate was simply to live a chaste and austere life, sleeping on the ground, taking only a single meal each day, one without honey, meat, wine or salt, dividing her time between prayer and religious rites, and possessing only one hope: to be married to her husband again in a future life, and meanwhile to satisfy his soul by her faithfulness and good conduct until the moment of her own death. Furthermore, she was now subject to the direct authority of her eldest son in his capacity as head of the family. There was no question of her leaving her home and settling down elsewhere, for, by her marriage, she had become part of her husband's *gotra.* In the same way, she was strictly forbidden to remarry,[94] under pain of endangering the soul of the man to whom she had been indissolubly bound by the sacrament of marriage. In any case, a woman had to be a virgin in order to get married, so that the only possible grounds on which she might receive permission to remarry were if her union with her husband had remained unconsummated.

In general, she accepted unhesitatingly her new condition of life and the resulting austerities. Neither her temperament nor her education had conditioned her to envisage widowhood as a liberation which would have allowed her to live at last according to her own inclinations, after so many years spent following her husband's orders and advice.

The fate of young childless widows – sometimes scarcely nubile when married – was particularly cruel, for they were obliged to submit to exactly the same rules, and, consequently, normal life ceased to exist for them. They could look forward to one possible amelioration of their lot: the head of the family might 'enjoin' them to remarry, so as to ensure a male descendance; not with a man of their choice, certainly, but with their deceased husband's closest relative, usually his brother – even if he already had a wife.[95] This was remarriage 'by assignation' (*niyoga*), and was probably a survival of the ancient custom of compulsory marriage with a childless brother's widow (levirate), but by the sixth century it was already becoming a thing of the past.[96]

INHERITANCE AND RIGHTS OF SUCCESSION

Custom did not provide for any will to be drawn up; but a division of property was usually made by the owner during his lifetime, when he handed over the direction of his family to his eldest son before retiring to some monastery. In the event of his having been unable to take this decision before he died, his property was divided up after the question of allocation had been discussed in common, the decision of the head of the family being decisive. In the case of polygamy, the inheritance was distributed after taking into account the order of precedence of the mothers of the heirs, and their castes, since the *kṣatriyas* had the right to marry, in addition to a woman of their own caste (who became the legitimate wife), at least two other women of inferior caste.

Excepted from the inheritance were the dead man's clothing, the millstone, as well as all instruments and utensils of metal or earthenware that did not carry the personal mark of the deceased – those that were marked having been given to the eldest son at the time of the burial.

The same applied to the personal property originating in the widow's dowry (*śulka*) and belonging to her in her own right: this was all unassignable, and might equally well include jewellery and slaves. She enjoyed the same rights in respect of gifts (*yautaka*) received by her in a personal capacity, and any profits eventually realized by her own activities. Real estate was not treated as part of a woman's divisible property, and on the widow's death, such estate (*strīdhana*) was handed on in full and by priority to her daughters – or, lacking daughters, to her sons.

In joint families, real estate remained indivisible. There were, however, cases where such property was broken up at the demand of one or more sons who had attained their majority. But this division of landed property was condemned for both practical and moral reasons: first, it might well affect the family's budget adversely, and secondly it was considered an insulting decision directed against the head of the family's good management.

When the deceased was the *gṛhastha* himself, his entire property went to his sons, the eldest receiving an additional portion of the inheritance amounting to one-twentieth,[97] as a condition of which he agreed to assume from then on the duties of head of the family. Individuals afflicted with physical or mental deficiency were excluded from the partition. The father was perfectly entitled to favour a particular son by making him a personal gift, if he wished; for example, to encourage him to pursue religious studies, or to reward him for especially edifying conduct. In the case of polygamy, account was taken of the order of precedence of the different mothers, and consequently of their sons. If the deceased's only direct heir was a grandson issued from an only daughter, the grandson inherited his property, since he had entered his grandfather's *gotra*, not that of his father.

When the head of a family died without a son entitled to inherit, the inheritance went to his brothers and their descendants, evidently with the aim of preserving the family property intact. The theory of the *sapiṇḍa* retained its value in this connection, for these had priority of succession over the other members of the family, the *sakulya*, who could only inherit in default of relatives in direct line.

If the deceased was not the head of the joint family, but inhabited the domain, the division of his personal estate depended on the wishes of the *gṛhastha*, who could either retain it among the indivisible family estate, or leave it to the deceased's sons, or even deprive them of their inheritance in favour of his own sons.

In questions of succession, the adoptive son had the same rights in principle as though he had been legitimate, although his position often gave rise to discussion and argument. His case sometimes presented a curious feature: if his legitimate brothers had all died before him, he could inherit from his 'first' father and yet remained perfectly entitled to inherit also, eventually, from his adoptive father.

The position of the daughters was never well defined. In theory, they inherited only their mother's personal savings, and retained their rights over any objects bequeathed to them personally, but possessed only a life interest in any goods which might accrue to them from real estate. When their father died, it was customary for them to be maintained by their brothers, who were under the obligation to meet their wedding expenses and provide their dowries.

CHAPTER FOUR

MONASTIC AND ASCETIC LIFE

Children apply themselves to their studies; Young people go in search of pleasure; Old people practise asceticism; And in Yoga they bring their existence to a close.

KĀLIDĀSA, *Raghu Vaṃśa*, I, 8.

THE TWO FINAL STAGES OF LIFE

'Old people practise ascetism, and in Yoga they bring their existence to a close.' So wrote Kālidāsa. These were, in fact, the two final stages (see pp. 160–1) which a brāhmaṇic *gṛhastha* (householder) passed through before dying. As soon as his eldest son was married, and so in a position to perpetuate, in his turn, the ancestral rite, the head of the family could retire to a hermitage and hand over to his son the management of the family community. After making this decision, he distributed his possessions and, either accompanied by his wife or alone, went away to live on the fringe of society, first as a hermit (*vānaprastha*), then – this time without his wife – as a wandering monk (*saṃnyāsin*).

The decision to adopt a hermit's existence was not taken lightly, and certainly many *gṛhastha* must have decided against such a course. The husband's determination was often affected by the reactions of his wife, who might well express horror at the idea of sharing this new existence compounded of privations and frugality, or might even decide not to follow him in the path of renunciation. Heartbreaking scenes are recorded as being usual[1] when she first learned of her husband's decision; sometimes she fainted and lay unconscious on the ground while her attendants sprinkled water over her and fanned her with a palm-leaf in efforts to revive her. When she eventually came to, she had to be half-carried, weeping and lamenting, to relatives or intimate friends who could look after her and comfort her.

Life in the hermitage was exactly similar to the existence we have described in connection with the student (see p. 170 seq.), apart from the fact that the *gṛhastha* who became a hermit assumed the role of teacher rather than student. Even so, it was a frugal and retired existence, composed of meditation and renunciation, which was beyond the spiritual resources of many to accept voluntarily.

When the *gṛhastha* broke his first links with society by leaving the hermitage and becoming an anchorite, he required great force of character and determination to sustain his new existence: from now on he consecrated himself entirely to asceticism and contemplation, attaining thus the highest possible human estate on the spiritual plane, and achieving the most complete detachment, qualities that would ensure him deliverance from the contingencies of transmigration. This action made him a *saṃnyāsin* and automatically divorced him from society, to take his place among the 'outcastes' while still preserving unanimous respect. This was the ideal proposed by Brāhmaṇism to its best adepts, and many did their utmost to approach this ideal. Bāṇa has left a remarkable portrait of a typical recluse in his historical novel, the *Harṣacarita.*[2] In this account, he describes his emaciated and deeply wrinkled features, his hollow eye-sockets, the pupils of his eyes 'as red as drops of wine,' his aquiline nose, the distended lobes of his ears,[3] his prominent teeth and jutting jaws. He carried all his wordly possessions with him. The only outer garment he wore was a tattered old rag, coloured red, knotted around his chest; a red scarf hung from one shoulder or was draped around him. In one hand, he held a bamboo cane; with the other he balanced on his shoulder a yoke from the ends of which dangled multifarious objects tied together in a complicated manner by means of a cord made of woven hair. These included an instrument for scraping encrusted dirt from the skin, a bamboo-wood sieve, a spare loin-cloth, a begging-bowl carried inside a box made of *kharjūra* wood (*Phoenix silvestris*), a water pot held upright in a triangular-shaped framework of three sticks meeting at the top,[4] sandals, and a bundle of manuscripts tied together with a strong cord. Thus encumbered, the holy man wandered the length and breadth of the country, begging his daily food, and walking long distances to obtain a supply of salt.[5] During the rainy season, he withdrew to some retreat, and emerged again at its end to continue his never-ending pilgrimages and visits to holy places. The king sometimes invited a *saṃnyāsin* to attend his presence. And at other times they received visits from great public figures drawn by their reputation for wisdom and supernatural powers. Some *saṃnyāsins* put an end to their life by committing ritual suicide, often by submerging themselves in a sacred river and remaining under water until they died.[6]

BUDDHIST LAITY AND PRIESTHOOD; MONASTERIES

In the Buddhist world, the difference between monks (*bhikṣu*) and laymen (*upāsaka*) was, originally, very pronounced, both as regards the extent of their duties and rights, and as regards their way of life.[7] These differences tended to diminish as the ascendancy of the Great Vehicle became more pronounced, this later form of Buddhism being less exacting and offering more promises to the faithful. In ancient times, the layman, dressed in white, lived like a *gṛhastha*, sanctifying himself by giving alms to the monks; he was not forced to repudiate the religious practices prevailing in his social circle – a fact which explains the tenacious survival of popular cults and brāhmaṇic deities in Buddhist tales. But he was expected to observe the ethical rules forbidding murder, theft, lust (particularly adultery), falsehood and the consumption of fermented drinks. Generosity should, ideally, have been his chief virtue; learning and wisdom were expected of him in a lesser degree than if he was a monk, because he remained attached to mundane existence. He could, nevertheless, attain greater dignity if he enhanced the fundamental virtues by fasting six days every month, during which he took only one meal a day, before midday, and devoted these days to the recitation of the general rules of the fraternity, the reading of the holy scriptures and the preaching of sermons. In addition, he was expected to do without luxurious furniture, to eschew flowers and perfumes, and to refrain from singing, dancing and attending theatrical performances. If he desired even greater spiritual advance, he abstained from sexual relations with his wife or, if alone, remained celibate, fasted, and touched neither gold nor silver, following the practice of novices and monks. He might even leave home and abandon his family in order to follow religious vocation, as the Buddha himself had done. Exchanging his white garment for the monk's yellow robe, he renounced all his worldly possessions, determining to live in the future by begging. At the same time, he gave up any lucrative trade or profession that he had exercised hitherto, and swore never again to handle gold or silver.

He now entered into the Buddhist order,[8] the only bar being proof that he was a criminal or suffered from an incurable disease. He could be accepted from the age of eight onwards. On the other hand, he was free to quit the monastic state at any moment, and reassume the status of a layman. A teacher (*upādhyāya*) and a master (*ācārya*) undertook to instruct him. He shaved his beard and head, donned the yellow robe, and announced three times his wish to enter the community and learn the 'ten precepts' of Buddhism. Then he began his novitiate under the supervision of the master of the novices.

Ordination followed after an interval which varied in individual cases, and was conferred by a chapter of at least ten monks.[9] The novice asked to be admitted, three times in succession; if the chapter remained silent, the admission was granted, and the official in charge proclaimed it in public. The new monk was immediately informed of the four rules of monastic austerity which he would have to observe from that time onwards, as well as the four prohibitions, any breach of which would entail his exclusion.

Women entering the community had to wait two years for their ordination, during which period they were subject to six interdictions. They were ordained first by a chapter of nuns, then by a chapter of monks, before whom they presented themselves accompanied by their female teacher (*upādhyāyikā*) and monitress (*ācāryānī*). They were submitted to a harsher discipline than were monks.

Buddhist monks possessed nothing except their clothes. These consisted of an undergarment (*antaravāsaka*), an outer garment (*uttarāsaṅga*), a cloak (*saṃghāṭi*), a waist-cloth (*kusūlaka*) and a belt with a buckle (*saṃkakśikā*). These robes were coloured red or yellow, and were provided by the charity of the laity or else made by the monks themselves from discarded rags which they pieced together and dyed. They sometimes wore sandals, although this was considered a luxury, since they were entitled to nothing more than plain leather soles,[10] unless their footgear had already been worn by someone else.[11] Their equipment comprised a begging-bowl (*pātra*), a razor, tweezers for removing hair, clippers for cutting finger and toenails, an ear-pick, a tooth-pick, a piece of gauze for filtering drinking water, a needle, a pilgrim's walking-stick, and a bag filled with medicaments. And they were allowed an umbrella made of leaf-fronds for protection against the sun,[12] and a fan with which to cool themselves.

The monk arose early in the morning and spent some time in meditation. After this, he went off to beg his daily ration of food, begging-bowl in hand, silent, eyes downcast, never crossing the threshold of the houses he passed. His immediate object achieved, he returned to the monastery, washed his feet, retired to the shade and, shortly before midday, took his only meal of the day. His usual diet included rice and *capātī*, with plain water to drink; he was permitted to eat meat and fish if he was absolutely sure that the creature had not been killed especially for his benefit. Only the sick were allowed ghee, oil, honey or sugar. Under no circumstances might he consume onion or garlic. The monk also had the right to accept invitations to take his midday meal with laymen; but he was strictly forbidden to eat at any other time of the day, under pain of submitting to a severe penance. When he had finished his repast, he seated himself on the threshold of his cell and received his disciples or pupils. Then he withdrew to some lonely spot, sat at the foot of a tree, and passed the hot afternoon hours plunged in meditation unless, by unlucky chance, somnolence overcame him. At sunset, he took part in the public sessions which brought together laymen eager to instruct themselves, the curious and mere passers-by. In the cool of the evening, the monk bathed himself without indulging in the usual refinements; then he received his disciples once again and so initiated a series of edifying discussions which lasted well into the night.

Every other month he shaved his hair. He was never supposed to look in a mirror or into a bowl filled with water, except in case of illness. Adornments, cosmetics and perfumes were forbidden, as were profane music or song.

Monks forming part of a particular parish (*sīmā*), together with those who happened to be in the area at the time, were obliged to meet on the 8th, 14th or 15th of each month, at full moon and at new moon, to spend a whole day in fasting and in other more rigorous observances. On each alternative occasion, they confessed publicly before their brethren; this confession took place after nightfall, by the light of torches, under the direction of the dean, who first read out the whole list of faults and then interrogated each monk alone. Lying was forbidden by the rules of the order, so an admission of guilt was obligatory.[13]

In ancient times, the *bhikṣu* (the word is Sanskrit for 'beggar') had no fixed domicile. Some of these religious mendicants lived under a tree or in some natural grotto, though most of them settled near some village or town, living in a humble abode (*vihāra*), a thatched hut, a 'tower' (*prāsāda*), a house made of stones or a cave. Gradually, these recluses tended to group their *vihāra* together, and these agglomerations gave birth, in their turn, to monasteries (*saṃghārāma*) of varying size, built of brick or wood. These buildings were actually inhabited only during the monsoon period, since the rest of the year was devoted by the *bhikṣu* to pious peregrinations. These monasteries, some of which covered enormous areas of land, were subsidized by funds originating in royal or private generosity. Until the seventh or eighth century, some of them were established within rockbound circular depressions, the most celebrated of these being perhaps that of Ajantā. But many others were constructed in open spaces – and, doubtless, more comfortably furnished. Those of Nālandā in the state of Bihār, for example, which flourished until the twelfth century, have had extensive foundations revealed as a result of the excavations that have been undertaken on the sites.

As the Buddhist community increased in size, the monasteries expanded proportionately and ended up by housing a great number of individuals – monks and novices, itinerant brothers, servants of both sexes, slaves attached in perpetuity to the domain adjoining the principal buildings, transient visitors, and refugees. According to the accounts of the Chinese pilgrims of the time, the most prosperous monasteries harboured from three to five thousand souls.

The buildings were usually arranged in a great square whose sides sometimes measured as much as a hundred and thirty feet (see p. 174). They formed a cloister, with galleries about eight feet wide opening on to the cells and chapels, these latter rooms being about twelve feet wide. In the centre of the inner courtyard was to be found a stūpa (see pp. 139–41), or else a temple, which might be eighty or more feet high, was crowned with a cupola and adorned with little bells which tinkled in the wind. When it was necessary to expand the establishment, one or more supplementary quadrangles were built, adjoining the original monastery: Nālandā, for example, had at least eight such annexes.

The cells, clustered around the courtyards, contained rudimentary furnishings: a bed with a framework of stretched cords, resting on four short legs, a stool, a plank to serve as a back-board, a cuspidor, a few pieces of matting, some small cotton pillows and a bolster were the only authorized fittings. Any depiction of a human being or animal was prohibited on all utensils and seats. In some of the better-appointed monasteries, the monks' and nuns' living quarters were incorporated into multi-storeyed buildings shaped like pyramids and furnished with pillared verandas, or else they lived in cells insulated from the public gaze by screens or baffle doors. The chapels were to be found either in other courtyards or else arranged among the surrounding cells (preferably against the eastern wall), and contained a sculptured image. Access to the monastery was provided usually by only one door. A great number of halls and additional structures of various kinds were built up against the cloisters in a confusion of design resulting both from the lie of the land and the repeated modifications to which the original lay-out of the establishment had been subjected.

Apart from the cells and chapels, several additional premises served the monastery's practical needs, in particular a huge meeting hall anything from thirty feet in length, whose inside walls had niches for lamps set into them at regular intervals; in this hall the entire community gathered twice a month for collective prayers, and it provided the focal point for all the solemn acts of monastic life, from ordination onwards, including the expulsion of delinquents. It was also sometimes used as a refectory. A number of cells lay under the cloisters. A special chamber contained the domestic hearth. There was a pantry adjoining the kitchen, and a vestry where pieces of material, donated by the laity at certain festivals, especially that marking the end of the rains, were sewn together and made up into garments for the monks. Nearby were to be found granaries and storehouses for foodstuffs and medicaments. The monastery's treasures were kept safe in a special room. A covered well supplied drinking water, while a large tank met the needs of daily ablutions and provided the water needed for other domestic purposes. The prescribed rules of hygiene required the existence of clean, well-kept latrines, a rudimentary system of main-drainage, and, particularly, a bath-house. This last establishment resembled those to be found in well-appointed private houses (see p. 134), and included a room with hot baths, a steam-room, a room for cooling down, an anteroom where the water supplies were kept and a hall. The bathroom and the sudatorium were supplied with heat from fireplaces, with chimneys to carry the smoke away; they contained bamboo coat-stands, and benches. The bathers smeared their faces with clay before entering, as a protection against the tremendous heat.[14]

The material used in constructing such buildings depended on the natural resources of the particular region. Brick or stone was less usual than clay or cobwork, but since these last materials were not capable of withstanding permanently the fury of the monsoon rains, repair work was a frequent necessity, and they were often reinforced by wooden lathes covered with a kind of cement. The bath-house and the chamber containing the domestic hearth were carefully protected against the weather, and the inside surfaces of their walls were lined with a layer of brickwork. The other buildings were decorated inside with a coat of paint, red for the walls, black for the floor, and further ornamented by floral designs and garlands of fresh flowers.

The roofs were made of various materials: thatch, bricks, flat stones, cement, reeds or fronds. Those of certain buildings – the hall in which the monks' habits were pieced together, the cloisters, the steam-baths, and the well-covering – were of animal pelts covered with a lime mortar. A length of material was stretched under the roofs to prevent snakes and insects dropping into the rooms.

Whether these buildings were made of durable or perishable materials, their exteriors were usually richly decorated, so giving them an impressive appearance. The walls were usually set with a dazzling white lime mortar. Stone bas-reliefs covered the inside walls of the stūpas and temples. These were secured to the walls by various different methods: either by iron clamps, or by a mortise joint (as though the carvings had been of wood), or else by a thick layer of mortar in which long iron nails were embedded. The masons' marks which may be observed even now on still-standing walls prove that the bas-reliefs were prepared and installed separately. In certain monasteries, the stone reliefs were replaced by mural designs sculpted in the wall-plaster itself, so that the walls were covered with decorative designs and lively scenes featuring human figures, all on a large scale. These decorative schemes were enhanced by the application of bright colours and gilding to the surfaces. The brilliant effect was a source of wonder and delight to visiting pilgrims, some of whom were convinced that they were gazing at solid gold statues: the more knowledgeable realized that the stone or stucco had been coated with fine gold leaf, applied carefully to the contours of the reliefs.

The lively colours, the gold, and the whiteness of the limewash were broken here and there by all sorts of wooden constructions, which were particularly liable to destruction by fire: the pillars of the covered galleries, wicket-doors, the window's fretted screens, rafters and beams with carved ends, balconies and belvederes.

The general effect aroused the admiration of the Chinese pilgrims who recorded descriptions which have been partly corroborated by the excavations that have been conducted so far. Nālandā, for example, has been described minutely by I-Tsing:[15]

> Its buildings (of brick) are three storeys high, each storey being itself more than ten feet high. All the temples are laid out in a straight line and one may come and go at one's ease. The back wall of the edifice also forms the monastery's outer wall. The brickwork rises to a height of thirty or forty feet. As regards the monks' habitations, there are nine to each frontage; each such habitation has dimensions of about ten square feet. At the far end of the building, a window rises as high as the roof. At the very top of one of the corners of the edifice, a hanging walk has been built, allowing one to walk to and fro on the roof of the temple. At each of the four corners is a room constructed of bricks; learned and venerable monks occupy these.
>
> The door of the temple faces west; its top storey soars into the sky at a giddy height in space. On the door are engraved marvellous images whose beauty is supreme in the art of ornamentation. This door forms part of the surrounding structure. It was not originally built to stand out from its

background; but four columns have been set up two paces in front of it. Although this door is not, in fact, extremely high, even so the timber-work used for it and for the door-frame is very heavy and strong.

Inside the monastery, all areas more than thirty paces wide are paved with brick. For small areas measuring from five to ten feet, for all the ceilings of the rooms and for the roof surfaces, they make use of brick fragments the size of peaches or jujubes; they add a sticky paste and beat the surface with a wooden instrument. The surfaces of the enclosure walls are limed. They also make a mixture of hemp fibres to which they add oil with hemp residue and fragments of old pelts; this is kept moist for several days, and then the preparation is spread over the brick surface of a particular space; this is covered with fronds. After three days or so, it is examined to see whether it is dry. Then this surface is rubbed several times with polished stones; it is sprinkled with finely ground red earth or else a substance similar to cinnabar. Finally, the surface is polished with a greasy compound until it is as glassy as a mirror. The floors of all the great rooms and the steps of the stairways are made in this manner. When these operations have been carried out, passers-by may tread on this surface and cross it continuously for ten or twenty years without any fear that it will deteriorate or break.

There are no less than eight temples built in this way. . . . In truth, there are few places so perfect. . . .

The monasteries constructed within the circumference of rocky depressions were no less magnificent. Shrines and sanctuaries, there, were built into the rock, in great man-made grottoes decorated with sculptures and illustrative frescoes, their frontages featuring verandas resting on pillars, large windows occupying the whole of the gable-end, and doors. These sometimes constituted an impressive group: Ajantā, for example, had eventually at least thirty caves on its site, which was developed gradually between the first century BC and about the seventh century AD and continued to be used, perhaps, for some considerable time thereafter. These aggregations give us some idea, both of the importance of a Buddhist monastery during the period under study, and of its aesthetic perfection, for the beauty of the frescoes and sculptures is quite remarkable. This decoration had an essentially pedagogic purpose; the monks invited their visitors to admire the panoramas, armed, just like modern lecturers, with sticks, with which they pointed out the details of the scenes they were explaining. By no means all the rock-bound retreats covered as much ground as did Ajantā, and simple cavities or fissures often served as shelters for anchorites.

The life of the community varied with the seasons. Throughout the monsoon period (June–July to October–November) the monks were assembled in monasteries, having gone into retreat to devote themselves to the study of the holy scriptures and to meditation. To ensure the efficient functioning of these establishments, a few monks were entrusted with certain specific tasks, such as those of purveyor, building superintendent, cellarer, gardeners, tailors and dyers attached to the vestry, those in charge of stores and water supplies; and functionaries responsible for the equitable division of food supplies, the distribution of meal tickets, the supervision of voting slips, and so on. The monks all possessed equal rights, the only form of hierarchy being by virtue of seniority of ordination and the respect which such seniority demanded. In early times, the monasteries possessed no designated director, in obedience to the Buddha's express will that only the law which he had preached and the discipline which he had established should serve as guides. But the general practice developed of appointing a superior, who was always the senior member of the community in terms of age, without regard to his particular merits; he exercised authority over all aspects of the monastery's material existence, apart from administration and police matters, which were in the hands of special 'warders'. A layman was often appointed as a liaison officer between the community and the outside world.

Daily routine was regulated by the clepsydra or water-clock,[16] which was also in use in the royal palace and in wealthy private homes. This consisted of a metal basin placed on the ground and filled with water on the surface of which floated a copper cup (called a *kapāla yantra* or *ghaṭī*) with a small hole bored through its bottom, the diameter of the hole being calculated so that the cup would fill to the brim in exactly three-quarters of an hour. When it was full, the cup dropped to the bottom of the basin. The functioning of the mechanism was supervised by a continual relay of specially appointed servants or porters. The measuring of time commenced at 6 a.m., or approximately at sunrise; it divided the twenty-four hours into thirty-two sub-divisions of forty-five minutes each, and into eight divisions of three hours each. The divisions of time were announced in the following manner: when the cup sank for the first time, that is to say 6.45 a.m., the guardian – warned by the noise of the cup striking the bottom of the basin – beat a single stroke on a drum. Forty-five minutes later, at 7.30, he struck the drum twice; and at 8.15, three times. At 9 a.m., the last phase of the first division, he struck four blows, sounded the conch twice and executed a single drum-roll. The second division went through the same phases as the first, except that when it reached its last phase – corresponding to midday – the guardian struck four blows on the drum, blew a note on the conch, and struck the drum twice again. This was the moment when all the monks, without exception, should have finished their single meal of the day. The cycle then recommenced for the two following divisions, until the moment of sunset (6 p.m.). The four divisions of the night were signalled in exactly the same way as those of the day.

This, at least, was the method of measuring time at Nālandā, though I-Tsing records slight differences in procedure for the monasteries of Bodhgayā and Kuśinagarī. This way of counting hours was more satisfactory than that of the sundial because, obviously, it worked equally well at night or during overcast weather. Even so, it required the skill of a 'good mechanic', in I-Tsing's words, who was capable of calculating the diameter of the hole so that the cup should fill within precisely the required period of time. This technician had also to provide exact indications as to the level of water which should, on occasion, be allowed to rise in the cup, short of fullness, so as to allow for the slight seasonal variation in the duration of solar hours throughout the Indian latitude.

Such was monastic life during the four rainy months, in the best organized monasteries. But a reading of the third book of the *Mahāvagga* dealing with 'residence during the rainy season', gives one some idea of the difficulties of all sorts which confronted small religious communities and recluses; in 'cases of distress' (which were numerous), for fear of thieves, in time of famine, if one of the members fell ill, or for other equally serious reasons, the monks were authorized to interrupt their retreat and leave the monastery.

The return of the dry season was marked by solemn festivities forming a prelude to the dispersal of the preaching fraternity, after which the buildings continued to be occupied by only a few monks charged with the upkeep of the monastery. This festival (*pavāraṇā*)[17] consecrating the end of the annual retreat was marked by the presentation of gifts by the laymen to the assembled monks, by invitations to midday meals extended by the laity to the brethren, and by the participation of the former in the religious processions. The gifts consisted of pieces of raw cotton which would eventually be dyed, cut and sewn in the vestry.

The year's monotonous routine was broken, also, by other solemn festivals and councils, and, every five years, by special assemblies.

THE JAINS

Standing midway between the brāhmaṇs and the Buddhist monks, the Jains, too, possessed their own monastic order. Although 'heretical' in the eyes of the brāhmaṇs, their sect was guided – unlike the Buddhist order – by masters boasting of famous *gotras*. Both laymen and those in holy orders had to exercise the greatest care not to harm any living being. They were so strictly vegetarian that they covered their nose and mouth with a piece of gauze, to ensure that they would not inhale or swallow the tiniest living organism, even involuntarily; and they always filtered their drinking water. Their fundamental doctrine was based, mainly, on the principle of non-violence (*ahiṃsā*), to which, in our own time, Gandhi gave a political as well as a moral complexion. Followers of the Jain religion were originally, and have remained, extremely attached to their beliefs, showing an unshakeably fierce conservatism which has preserved their customs and ways of thought almost intact. The main difference today is that the quarrel which split their sect into two rival factions around the end of the first century AD has long since been healed. Those factions were the *Śvetāmbara* and the *Digambara*: the latter, 'space-clad', that is to say, practising complete nakedness, did not even possess a begging bowl; they are no longer to be met with in modern India. The rival faction authorized its followers to use begging-bowls, as well as certain numbers of objects and articles of clothing.

The Jain communities welcomed all men and women who had taken the decision to withdraw from the world, without distinction of class or caste (apart from a few exceptions).[18] No office might be held, within the order, by children, aged people, eunuchs, melancholics, the timid, the sick, thieves, enemies of the king, madmen, blind people, slaves, idiots, syphilitics, debtors, cripples, servants, pregnant women, young girls or those converted by force.

Those qualified for ordination required, first, their parents' consent. The community then assumed responsibility for the families' maintenance, even to the extent of awarding grants to the parents and to the masters thus deprived of disciples who would otherwise have continued to serve them.

A solemn ceremony marking their renunciation of the world was performed on some favourable day designated by the astrologers. A barber shaved the postulant's hair and beard, and the latter was then given a ceremonial bath and anointed. He clad himself in his finest garments and sat down beneath a dais, his mother on his right, his nurse on his left, the nurse holding a broom in one hand and an alms-bowl in the other. Now he was instructed in the principal monastic duties incumbent upon those donning the white costume of the Jains, and was welcomed formally into the order.

Like Buddhism, the Jain order comprised monks, nuns and laity of both sexes. The laity had the duty of subsidizing those who had taken the vow and of making substantial gifts to the temples to ensure their continued prosperity; in fact the upkeep of these religious communities depended almost entirely on the devotion of laymen and their faithfulness to the ancestral rites. The principles governing monastic life, similar to those of Buddhism, seem to have been applied more strictly.[19] The Jain monks begged their daily food and had to prepare it themselves (as did the brāhmaṇs) as well as preparing their own beverages. The smallest contravention of regulations entailed a punishment of some kind. Being inherently missionaries, they often led a wandering life during the course of which they were still obliged to submit to the rules of the order, never riding an animal or in a vehicle of any kind, and accepting all the innumerable dangers which faced a traveller in that age. They were permitted to break off their pious rounds in case of political disorders; and, if they were persecuted by the royal administration, they had the right to break the rules of the order, disguise themselves and ignore temporarily all interdictions and obligations. If they became seriously ill, members of the community carried them to the physician, procured the necessary medicines and cared for them to the best of their ability, whatever the cost might be and irrespective of monastic exigencies. Sexual relations with women – either nuns or prostitutes – were forbidden, unless resulting from uncontrollable desire. In similar fashion, they might break the code in any other 'case of distress', so long as they purified themselves subsequently, either by chanting magic formulas or by carrying out a sacrificial ceremony (*janna*) accompanied by the recitation of holy script.

Some Jain monks undertook an ascetic existence in lonely, remote hermitages. There they followed a typical anchorite's routine, sleeping on the bare ground, feeding on roots and grain, taking rapid baths, smearing their bodies with mud as a sign of penitence, remaining silent, and warding off all human contact by blowing a conch to signal their presence. They clothed themselves in skirts made of bark, lived in caves or simply under a tree, and drank only water. A few, it was claimed, lived as stylites.

Others taught and preached their doctrine by touring a particular locality, purifying their listeners by washing them with water and then smearing them with mud. These itinerant priests wore a robe and cloak, shoes on their feet, carried a stick made of three rods bound together, and travelled under the protection of an umbrella; they wore a brass ring and brass bangles. Their other personal possessions included a water-jug, a clay bowl, a teapot, a broom, a hook, a portable chair and a rosary.

All enjoyed a great reputation for their supposed magical science, and were presumed to be endowed with supernatural powers, thanks to incantations, charms, spells murmured aloud or pronounced mentally, and so on.

It may be interesting to note, finally, that the Buddhist and Jain monks often provided an example of ferocious rivalry – at least, if we are to credit the accounts of contemporary witnesses reported in ancient Indian writings.

Part Three

ROYAL AND ARISTOCRATIC EXISTENCE

CHAPTER ONE

CITY LIFE AND FASHIONABLE EXISTENCE

This morning, my friend, I heard a man singing, and his song reminded me of my lover,
And it reopened all the wounds which the Love-god's shafts had made in my heart.

Tamil poem.

If we are to believe the descriptions which abound in classic Indian literature, we must conclude that the austerity of family life practised by those of the brāhmaṇ caste, with its emphasis on ritual and its comparatively negative attitude to pleasures and comfort, was by no means shared by the *kṣatriyas*. In the capital, especially, the proximity of the royal palace was an added incentive to the inhabitants to lead a life which was not only more varied and ostentatious but also more dissolute. Festivals and diversions, in which the populace participated, succeeded each other, assuming a pattern with which rural life, with its routine of labour, harvesting and seasonal observances, could not compete. In addition, the *kṣatriyas* – who tended to live, when possible, in the vicinity of the royal court – enjoyed certain privileges unknown to the brāhmaṇs, so that the restrictions inherent in ritual observance were less severe and they were also able to indulge in gaming, sports and the arts. Wealthy businessmen, although belonging only to the middle classes, vied with the nobility in the forms of social display permitted to them: in fact, families often lived in a style of ostentatious luxury which was far above their means and involved them in heavy debts. For everyone, the king was the perfect example, and they all tried to imitate his mode of existence to the best of their abilities; indeed, it is often difficult to say in what respect a *kṣatriya* differed from the king himself.

THE DAILY ROUTINE OF A YOUNG MAN OF FASHION[1]

Waking up in a room similar to that described already on p. 136, the young man of good family anxious to be a 'dandy' (or what was called a *nāgaraka*, a 'city dweller', in the Gupta era) began his day with a carefully executed toilet, the multiple phases of which were almost ritualistic. After cleaning his teeth by rubbing them with a root, he bathed his mouth and eyes, applied a salve to his eyelids, and chewed a few betel-quids.

When these preliminaries were accomplished, he devoted all his attention to the bath which he took each morning either in a special room provided with water installed in the house itself, or else in the river that flowed by just outside the town. The slope leading down to the river was provided with couches and all sorts of equipment for the use of those who went there to bathe. He began by rubbing his body thoroughly with a sort of wooden hand coated with a scented powder. Then he poured oil over his hair and rubbed oil into his skin, before relaxing on a couch and having himself massaged. After the massage, he performed a series of exercises designed to keep his muscles supple. Finally, he stepped into the water and soaped himself (every other day, only) with a frothy preparation (*phenaka*). Once the washing procedures were over, he combed his hair carefully.

Back home once more, he continued the long process of his morning toilet. First, he smeared his whole body with a sweet-smelling unguent, powdered his chest with a camphorated talcum, painted a decorative mark on his forehead with red arsenic and drew designs on his arms with civet powder, symbolizing good fortune. He rimmed his eyes with black cosmetic and smeared some red lac over his lips. Every three days, he smeared lac over his whole body; every four days, he shaved his beard and moustache; every five days, or every ten days, he plucked out all his body hairs. When he had completed these lengthy preliminaries, he dressed himself in freshly laundered garments whose sweet smell was due to their having been fumigated in incense, adorned himself with jewellery, threaded flowers and strings of pearls into the coils of his hair, and, often, trimmed his nails. Finally, he looked at himself in the mirror to make sure that everything was in order.

Before leaving the house, he chewed a compound of mango,

camphor, cloves and other ingredients, to sweeten his breath, and hung a garland of flowers around his neck. He placed on his head a turban-like hat, armed himself with a parasol and a walking-stick, and strode off to attend to his business affairs. Since these required only the minimal presence expected of a wealthy scion, he was soon free to pass the rest of the day as he pleased. He took three meals, one in the morning, one at midday and one in the evening. Before the midday meal, he played a few rounds of some gambling game with his customers or cronies. After this meal, he took an afternoon nap; then he visited the parrots and *mainās* in his aviary to teach them new words. Later on, he found further entertainment in attending cock-fights, or fights between quails or pigeons, on which he betted enthusiastically.

After the evening meal, he received his friends in the reception-room of his home. He enjoyed playing host to society and, while waiting for his mistress to appear, passed the time agreeably in their company, listening to music, making pleasant conversation, and sipping alcoholic drinks. When he thought the moment opportune, he bade his guests farewell, following the traditional code of politeness, and as they left he handed them flowers and betel.

Once alone with his mistress, he initiated a love-play full of amorous propositions accompanied by delicate and tender caresses, to which she yielded willingly. After they had made love, each resumed a modest attitude. To end their evening together, they strolled out on to the terrace to gaze at the star-lit sky, nibbled at sweetmeats of all kinds and sipped gruel, coconut milk, sweetened mango and lemon juice, and fragrant wine. After she had retired, happy and still languid from love-making, he prepared for bed, rubbing a scented ointment over his face and crowning himself with a wreath of flowers before lying down to sleep until the morning in his elegant bedroom.

LOVE AND COURTESANS; PROSTITUTION AND THE CRIMINAL CLASSES

Amorous games played a great part in the life of the young *kṣatriya*[2] and Indian literature makes frequent mention of them. To conform to his traditional portrait, the young man must have been inordinately fond of feminine company. In any case, it would seem that he usually possessed a regular mistress, with whom he passed pleasant hours in shady gardens. They would sit side by side, sheltered by an arbour, near a cool sparkling stream, sipping heady liqueurs; or else, they would hide themselves from the public gaze in one of the summer-houses which were to be found in all well-appointed parks, listening to music played for them by the resident orchestra. In spring, the young man and his mistress played together on the swings which dangled from the branches of trees in the groves, and no doubt their proximity as they swung gently to and fro provided a new occasion for amorous conversation.

Their caresses, which have been minutely catalogued in the famous erotic treatise, the *Kāmasūtra* ('The Rules of Love') written by Vātsyāyana some time before the seventh century, ran the whole gamut from the most delicately tender kiss to the most advanced and complex erotic technique. The young women described in the *Kāmasūtra* were essentially flirts, consummate artists in disposing of their charms to the best advantage, feigning a modesty and timidity which only made them more seductive, displaying an entirely feminine inquisitiveness, delighting in finery and jewellery, expert at making themselves up and perfuming themselves to enhance their charms to the utmost, and equally expert at fluttering their eyelashes and moving their eyebrows in a way designed to arouse added excitement in the breasts of their lovers. These young women had a full command of all the resources required for the conduct of a love-affair: intoxicating wines and aphrodisiacs, tender words, languorous gazes, passionate embraces, quarrels, reconciliations, gifts, promises, fits of jealousy, sighs, tears and smiles, despair and ecstasy. They taught words of love to their parrots so that they could repeat them in the absence of their lover; they exchanged portraits with their lovers, and were consumed with anguish when they were apart. They were constantly plunged into misery or wafted on clouds of joy, and poets never grew tired of celebrating the beauty of their tear-filled eyes, their sulky silences, their angry outbursts, their anxious questions, their delicious enjoyment of shared love. And although, in India, the heart was considered as the seat of reason rather than of feeling, there seems no doubt that its young lovers of ancient times were as adept at expressing the sophistication of romance as any of our seventeenth-century European elegants and exquisites, fainting away just as often, and no less determinedly swooning with happiness or alarm.

The young man liked to hold his mistress against him tenderly, placing one protective arm around her smooth shoulder, knotting and unknotting her clothing, attaching her bracelets and necklaces, braiding her long tresses with garlands and with strings of jewellery, carefully making the central parting (*sīmanta*) which divided her hair, and personally painting between her eyebrows the mark (*tilaka*) which signified that her toilet was complete. He liked also to surprise her while she was sitting in front of her mirror, contemplating with fond satisfaction the nail-marks in her flesh left by his passionate love-gestures.[3]

This philandering was not necessarily reserved solely for a young man's concubines; it could perfectly well exist within the framework of a legitimate union. Polygamy enhanced the enjoyment derived by the man since it often resulted in favourites reigning side by side with the principal wife.

Even so, prostitution was a flourishing business, especially in the large towns and capital cities. The courtesans (*veśyā* or *gaṇikā*) formed a sort of guild headed by their most eminent member, who retained her position of authority until grave illness or death intervened.

There were all sorts and variety of prostitute, from the lowliest whore selling herself for a few coins, to the refined creature, boasting a careful and even brilliant education, possessing not only a complete knowledge of her profession but also artistic and intellectual talents. The reputation of the latter was as honourable as that of the former was vile, and their lot was equally different: while the common strumpet ended her days begging, or working in some State factory, the polished courtesan often achieved wealth and prosperity.

Rich or not, they were all subject to the control of a royal administrator charged specially with their protection, with the supervision of the brothels, and with the collection of the taxes for which they were liable: as we have already mentioned, they were obliged to hand over to the State treasury two days' wages per month.[4] In addition, they paid the instructors and experts who took a hand in perfecting their education; these teachers were, it seems, actively encouraged by the State, since those in authority considered prostitution to be an essential element in a smoothly functioning social mechanism.[5] Many prostitutes worked for pimps or bawds (*kuṭṭanī*); others who were more artful or more capable had themselves enrolled as spies in the secret services. They played a considerable role in society, too. They took part in country outings, inveigling the young man of good family into some garden or grotto; and they hired themselves out as musicians or dancers at private parties, for example the reception given for the birth of a child. Others, again, were attached to temples; these were called *devadāsī*, but they are rarely mentioned in ancient literature, and it would seem that temple prostitutes belonged mainly to a later epoch than that which concerns us in the present study.

There were several ways of making an assignation with a prostitute: she could either be accosted in the street, or visited in a brothel, or required to attend the client's home. Or else the customer visited her in her own home.[6] Many of them lived with their mother, or someone posing as their mother, and then the older woman looked after the business side of their activities, and concerned herself with their safety and health.[7] They displayed themselves to the gaze of passers-by, dressed in all their finery and heavily made up, close by the door of their house, 'like a precious object on a shelf'. In the brothels, the price was fixed in advance, as the client entered, varying according to the season, and the client's degree of affluence. Half the agreed sum was handed over to the designated or selected prostitute; the other half went into a fund which paid for the hire of costumes, and the purchase of scents and garlands which were distributed to a customer as soon as a bargain was agreed on, although the garments had, of course, to be returned by the customer before he left the establishment.[8] These appear to have been prosperous enterprises, profiting especially from the festivals which regularly gave all the towns (and the capital) an aura of feverish excitement, during which debauchery was legally permitted.

The young *kṣatriyas* chose their mistresses, as one may imagine, from among the most cultured courtesans. Some of these young women were as knowledgeable as they were beautiful, acquainted with each smallest detail of the rules of love-making, and excelling in the 'sixty-four arts':[9] which meant that they were perfectly instructed in every field of erotic, social, intellectual and artistic activity. Obviously, a courtesan endowed with such varied talents was much sought after, and was, one might say, worth her weight in gold. As a result, she was usually kept in style by some wealthy man, and her exquisite education justified the honourable place she held in society. She lived on a grand scale, attended by a host of servants, possessing a luxurious and elegantly decorated house, beautiful jewellery and adornments, a splendid selection of robes made from costly materials, several carriages, and even, perhaps, an art gallery, the supreme cachet of high social standing. She considered it important, too, to show generosity towards the brāhmaṇs at all times, making them frequent gifts and, if she was very rich, having a temple built for them at her own expense.

To establish her fortune, she had of necessity to remain on good terms with a whole number of different people, either because they were influential individuals, or because they were of use to her professionally. So she cultivated assiduously the friendship or goodwill of town watchmen, policemen, magistrates, astrologers, bankers and moneylenders; and, equally, that of the experts and practitioners of all the arts of embellishment upon which she depended so heavily: perfumers, florists, garland makers, hairdressers. Her importance was such that we are assured that the Buddha himself accepted the invitation to take his midday meal with a courtesan, rather than keep a previous appointment for the same time with a government dignitary. But the prostitutes' real friends were to be found, rather, on the fringes of society, among an assortment of miscreants including thieves, confidence tricksters, low-class magicians, cheats and inveterate gamblers. In any case, Indian moralists habitually emphasized that women of easy virtue must inevitably end up by associating with rogues and villains of this nature.

Ancient literature has described most tellingly the particular mentality of courtesans, bringing out its essential amorality. A prostitute seeking her fortune (in other words, the majority among her sorority) was careful to choose a man who would keep her luxuriously, rather than reserve her favours for a single lover. The man's financial status was, then, the primary consideration. And, when she had made her choice, she played the age-old gambit of making him fall in love with her, using all the resources of her accumulated knowledge, coquetry and cunning, reinforced, if necessary, by magical incantations and amulets, and not hesitating to assume an entirely false personality. But she was careful, as far as possible, not to become enamoured of any man whose fortune she desired more than his heart. The *Kāmasūtra* affirms that 'one never knows how deeply a woman is in love, even when one is her lover'.

The financial greed shown by courtesans in most of the classic tales is typified by the following anecdote. The son of a wealthy businessman had acquired the habit of visiting his mistress each evening, and presenting her on each occasion with a tidy sum for services rendered. Their liaison was long established, and the young man had always paid up punctually. He had even made her a generous gift on the death of his father, to compensate her for having had no share in the inheritance. And yet, one evening, when he had forgotten his purse, and promised to pay her the usual sum the following morning, his paramour did not hesitate to push him out on to the street, swearing that she would not allow him credit, even for a single evening.[10]

The sagacious courtesan was quite prepared to ruin her lovers: after all, did she not choose them so that their fortune should pass from their hands to hers? To achieve her end, she used all the tricks and subtleties she had learned by heart during her apprenticeship. When a liaison showed signs of being no longer profitable, nothing was simpler to her than to break off the relationship by using any one of a thousand stratagems; after which, she took a new lover who was at least as well off as the previous one, and congratulated herself on her increasing prosperity. If the first lover's financial affairs improved, she did not hesitate to return to him; but, in that case, the *Kāmasūtra* advised him to beware of possible vengeance, since the newly dethroned lover might well prove to him that the sincerity of his reconciled mistress was dubious, to say the least.

This may be the typical portrait of a courtesan of that era, but, even so, there were others who aspired to marriage, and even went so far as to renounce a comfortable existence in order to marry the man they loved – who was usually penniless – with the praiseworthy intention of founding a family line and becoming respectable women. When a legitimate union, even one involving financial disadvantage, was not possible, some other courtesans contented themselves with a semi-permanent or permanent liaison with a man, or even went to live with him, in which case they took great pains to behave in every respect as true wives.

Courtesans constituted dangerous competitors, in the eyes of many legitimate wives, despite the strict laws punishing adultery (see p. 59). The description of a married man taking a mistress is briefer but perceptive: from the moment he started deceiving his wife, he behaved with consummate hypocrisy, lied outrageously, made every effort to keep his illicit assignations secret, and tried to conduct his love-affair with prudent discretion. Even so, he ran many risks of being betrayed, since it was necessary to use the services of a 'messenger of love' (*dūtī*) and also to obtain the complicity of the servants. If they were caught *flagrante delicto*, his mistress was liable to even harsher penalties than himself.

Commerce with prostitutes was not, then, an entirely carefree process, and the hazards were aggravated by the annoying preference these young women displayed for the criminal element of society. We need no further proof than the story of the courtesan who fell in love with a thief, of which several versions are to be found in the *Jātakas*.[11] This particular courtesan had a wealthy lover who was entirely devoted to her, but whom she did not love. One day, when she was sitting at her window, she saw some policemen in the act of seizing a bandit whom they had been tracking across the town. No doubt he was good-looking, and seemed worthy of her interest. In any case, she decided on an impulse to save him from the fate of impalement which most certainly awaited him.

Without wasting a moment, therefore, the courtesan despatched a trustworthy woman-servant to the police commissioner, with the mission of bribing him. A typical Oriental bargaining session ensued, and the size of the sum offered soon conquered this high official's virtuous indignation. But he still had no intention of incurring the king's wrath: an execution had been proclaimed and an execution would have to be carried out, if not on the actual criminal then on someone else. This problem did not embarrass the courtesan in the least: why should not her lover, that rich love-sick numskull, finance the whole arrangement and become the involuntary victim as well? So, when he arrived, on his daily visit to his mistress, he found her in tears and not at all in the mood for their usual light-hearted banter. Pressed for an explanation she blurted out that the man condemned to death – about whom the whole town was talking – was, in fact, her own brother. This was the first that her lover had heard of the existence of a brother, for the good reason that she had only just invented him. However, he swallowed the tale, and was immediately persuaded to hasten to the commissioner, carrying the ransom which would free the prisoner. The gullible youth obtained the necessary funds, although the sum represented his entire personal savings, and hurried to the commissioner's office. The latter immediately carried out the plan he had agreed on secretly with the courtesan beforehand: as soon as the money was handed over, the thief was taken, in a covered carriage, to the courtesan's home, and the poor dupe was just as promptly conducted to the execution grounds. Night had already descended by this time, and the citizens were indoors when the betrayed lover was led past, so only the executioners themselves heard his sobs and his protestations of innocence.

That is not the end of this edifying story. The courtesan became hopelessly infatuated with the bandit whose life she had saved, but became his victim in her turn. Being justifiably suspicious of a woman who could so lightly dispose of other people's lives, he lured her into a lonely spot and strangled her. Then, faithful to his professional principles, he robbed her of everything she had with her, stripping her of every piece of jewellery she was wearing, despite his haste to escape the scene of his new crime. The narrator adds that the unhappy young woman, after lying unconscious, revived, and spent the rest of her life searching unsuccessfully for this villain, whom she had immediately forgiven and continued to love. But other versions claim, on the contrary, that it was she who killed him.

It should not necessarily be assumed from such lurid anecdotes that all prostitutes lived on the fringe of the law and associated habitually with criminals. Though these legends may well contain more than a grain of truth, it must be remembered that their intention was to illustrate the dangers of sin rather than to blacken deliberately the reputation of courtesans, whose existence was deemed necessary in a well-organized society. Indeed, many such women were mentioned specifically for their charitable instincts and their piety.

GAMES AND GAMING

Although games of chance were condemned by the brāhmaṇic code of conduct, they were played in all classes of society. And chess was enormously popular.

Chess (*caturaṅga*), one of India's most glorious inventions, designed originally as a means of working out military strategy, was played by four players who used two dice, four figures (king, elephant, horse, and chariot or ship) and four pawns, which symbolized the 'four corps' which traditionally constituted the army (see p. 284). Every day, the young nobles met together to play several sessions of the game.

Dicing existed in various different forms of play.[12] The dice were made of gilded shells, of wooden or ivory cubes,[13] or of the nut of the *vibhītaka* fruit (*Terminalia bellerica*), which was the size of a hazel-nut and had five facets. Chess was played on specially designed boards, or on a table whose surface had been inlaid with precious substances representing the requisite pattern, and dice were played, often, simply on the floor.

Two different dicing games are described in ancient texts. The favourite one appears to have been that called *vibhītaka*, the name being the same as that of the nut from which the dice were made. This game entailed taking a handful of dice from a heap of them and throwing those picked up on to the ground or board in any one of twenty-four permitted manners, at the same time announcing aloud the number of dice being thrown and the number remaining in the heap. The winner was the one who threw the number he had announced, at his first attempt; the rules demanding, in addition, that this number must be a multiple of four.

Another game, *pāśaka*, used three oblong dice with four scoring sides. These were thrown on the ground, and the points on the uppermost surface added up; to win, the total had to correspond with one out of the twenty-four combinations which had been agreed beforehand, as had been the amount of the stake. If each player won in succession, further rounds were thrown, and the stake at issue increased proportionately.

Dice also played a part in affairs of love, for the elegant *nāgaraka* used them to decide which young woman should be his companion for the night.

The passion for gambling was so great that many wealthy businessmen and nobles lost their entire fortunes. Although condemned by the brāhmaṇs, the habit became quite frenzied at times; reckless martingales were employed, and various spells and charms to ensure that the player won and his opponent lost were kept secret and used assiduously. Incantations for success were pronounced beforehand: 'I have beaten you, I have raked in all your stakes, I have pocketed your last penny. . . . My profits are here in my right hand, my skill in my left hand: may I win cows, horses, riches, gold.' The dice were also submitted to certain magical treatments – which probably included loading them. . . .

Poets have described eloquently the players' changing emotions, as they gasped with anguished expectancy while the dice were still rolling over the ground, became ecstatic at the sound of their clicking together, then desperate if it was a losing throw, but still ready to throw again, even if ruin stared them in the face, refusing ever to admit that they could possibly lose in the end. Gamblers inevitably fell prey to money-lenders, piling up huge debts and sometimes ending their lives tragically. But if social life was marked by terrible cases of ruination it was equally studded with cases of huge fortunes acquired through gambling; those who had gained wealth in this manner were labelled 'the black rich', as opposed to 'the white rich' who had earned their money wisely and honestly.

Gaming-dens seem to have abounded. They were subject to strict control by the State, and contributed large sums to the Treasury in the shape of taxes levied on stakes, the hiring of premises, and the dice themselves (see p. 109), since gamblers were not permitted to make or use their own dice. Cheats constituted something like a professional fraternity, although they were closely watched, and brought to book whenever possible, by a brigade of 'spies' appointed specially to supervise the way the gambling-dens carried on business.

FASHIONABLE ARTS, PLAYS, SPORTS AND DIVERSIONS

For the young *kṣatriya*, amorous pursuits alternated with various intellectual and artistic activities in which the aristocracy – with the king in the forefront – found plenty of time to indulge.

Music held a great place in the daily life of the nobility. They all learned to play the *vīṇā* or bow-harp, an instrument which was later replaced by a form of lute. This harp is one of India's most ancient musical instruments.[14] Originally, it was played only by women, but later it was played also by men, and the kings themselves became expert performers; in fact several kings, during the Gupta dynasty (fourth to fifth century AD), were so convinced of their prowess that they had themselves depicted on their coins clasping a *vīṇā*.[15] Members of the nobility always kept one close by, hanging it on their bedroom wall, taking it with them wherever they went, playing it sometimes as they strolled along – in which case it was slung from one shoulder with a strap. 'There are two things,' wrote Kālidāsa, 'which nestle on a lover's breast without ever leaving an empty space: a clear-toned lute, and a soft-voiced woman with beguiling eyes.'[16] Young lovers enjoyed teaching the technique of playing the *vīṇā* to their mistresses, and poets often evoke the grace of their supple hands running over the chords, meeting as if by accident and clasping tenderly.

Painting was another favourite pursuit, and held an important place in everyday existence. It served the purposes of religious propaganda, as when Buddhist monks explained the meaning of particular images with the aid of a pointer;[17] and it was sometimes used as the medium for conveying news, in the form of storied scrolls.[18] Painting was an essential adjunct of elegant love-life, since lovers were in the habit of exchanging specially executed portraits which they gazed at when they were apart. Among the nobility, young men and women possessed all the equipment required for artistic activity: 'pencils' for sketching, paint brushes of various dimensions with bristles made of animal hair, and shells or pots containing coloured powders, all arranged in a box whose outer surface was engraved with some design.[19] This apparatus constituted a highly appreciated gift when presented by a young gentleman to his betrothed.[20] The shapes of the pictures varied according to the subject, being rectangular for 'realistic' or 'pure' painting (*satya*), square for 'lyrical' or 'romantic' painting, circular for genre painting.[21] Religious themes were executed on long lengths of material with bamboo rollers at each end, which could be unwound or rewound at leisure, and on which the episodes were depicted in one uninterrupted panorama. Most ephemeral of all, pictures were designed on the ground itself, with the aid of coloured powders, especially on the occasion of marriages.[22] Every gentleman of taste possessed an art gallery, containing paintings which were sometimes his own work and which he enjoyed showing off to his friends. If he had learned sculpture, he would also set aside a room in a corner of his house where he could model in clay or carve wood.

The aristocracy devoted particular attention to the various forms of literary expression, and many noblemen composed poems or dramas in the elegant, sophisticated style in fashion at the royal court. The kings, too, devoted themselves to the arts of writing: the famous drama *Mṛcchakaṭika* ('The Little Clay Cart') has been attributed to Śūdraka (date unknown, possibly fourth century AD), while Harṣa (AD 606–47), King of Thāneśvar and Kanauj, wrote three interesting dramas. The Kings Samudragupta (AD 335–75) and Kumāragupta (AD *c.* 414–55) adorned themselves with the envied title of 'King among poets' (*Kavirāja*). Nobles and courtiers took part in literary functions which were held regularly in the open air, either in the public gardens or in specially organized 'clubs' (*goṣṭhī*) – an institution which the Indians invented long before the advent of the British![23] Competitions were arranged, presided over by some dignitary or even by the king himself, during which orators vied with each other in improvising on a given theme,[24] and the eventual winner received a prize, sometimes amounting to a huge sum of money or a valuable gift or, at the very least, an honorific title, 'master of knowledge', which firmly established his reputation. Some poets devoted themselves to a wandering life, travelling from one princely court to another, in order to increase their chances of success in such contests. These contests started with an open challenge being issued, those who refused to accept it for one reason or another being declared vanquished in advance. Then the actual competitors pitted their talents and virtuosity against each other, composing or solving riddles, phrases with a double meaning and puns, performing charades, improvising verses to set rhymes, composing erudite poems or declaiming long didactic or laudatory speeches. Feeling sometimes ran so high during these contests, that competitors were even known to use dishonest inducements, such as distributing secret bribes to members of the jury.

The theatre was at its peak of brilliance during the age which concerns us. The period between the first and eighth centuries AD saw the rise of India's greatest dramatic authors, some of them kings, others poets or brāhmaṇs, and the theatre received greater support and acclaim throughout India during that era than at any other time in the country's history.[25] Dramas were constructed according to the precise rules which were codified in various treatises,[26] and which made dramatic writing an art designed specifically for the intelligentsia, making no appeal at all outside the ranks of the nobility and the cultured classes. Actors depended entirely on the patronage of the king or of some wealthy individual, and it seems that there were no permanent theatrical companies except, perhaps, in a few particularly ostentatious courts. Like the acrobats, musicians, mountebanks and showmen of the time, actors were constantly on the road, seeking an engagement in some town. Theatrical performances generally took place only during religious or princely festivals, great pilgrimages, and public or private celebrations of some importance, such as marriages. In addition, it was usual at the 'spring festivals' (see pp. 144–5) to present for the first time new works which had, in most cases, been written specially for the occasion. Frequently, rival troupes competed, with their common audience as judge of their respective merits: the competition was not always above board, so great was the ambition to secure for one's company the honorific to which the winners were entitled.

Actors were recruited from the lowest castes, and so not even accepted as witnesses in law-suits. Despite their lowly status, a few of them benefited from the friendship of important people, so that they sometimes became the centre of jealous intrigue in court circles. They were often on very close terms with authors and poets, since their obligatory knowledge of Sanskrit automatically raised them to the latter's cultural level.

On the moral level, however, their reputation was deplorable, and their wives were generally considered to be over-generous in bestowing their favours. In the first century AD, the grammarian Patañjali, in his commentary the *Mahābhāśya*,[27] had already expressed the problem in these terms: 'When an actor's wife appears on the stage, ask her: "Whose are you? Whose are you?" She will always answer: "I am yours."' Their husbands were perfectly content to let them prostitute themselves and to pocket a share of the profits. In fact, the penalties laid down for adultery with an actress were far less severe than in other cases; actresses were, indeed, classified as being members of the courtesans' guild.

Even in those early times, actresses were fully aware of the importance of publicity, and their mothers (or supposed mothers) acted as their impresarios. The older woman's task was to help develop her protégée's charms and abilities as far as possible, to see that she retained a beautiful complexion, to increase her intelligence, to maintain her health by supervising her diet, and to perfect her education by having instruction given to her by teachers specializing in erotic art, dancing, singing, music, painting, handwriting and elocution. She was also given a rudimentary knowledge of grammar, logic and astronomy. On each festive occasion she was exhibited in public in all her finery, with an impressive retinue in attendance. When she actually appeared on the stage, her manager saw to it that a more or less discreet claque was present in the audience to applaud her. Influential personalities were persuaded to mention her name favourably in public, and her colleagues were bidden to praise, on every possible occasion, her talents, range of learning, beauty, virtuousness and charm.

Professionally, actors were classed according to competence, and those who graduated to leading roles were practically unbudgeable from their particular range of parts. Female roles were usually played by women, but also sometimes by men, so there seems to have been no firm rule in the matter. Casting did not present a great problem in view of the conservative nature of the Indian plays of that age: the male roles included, inevitably, a lover, a buffoon and a wit, while the female roles comprised lover and confidante. The minor parts were shared among the junior members of the company.

The troupe's manager was at the same time the theatre's chief stage-hand (he was called the 'rope-holder' or *sūtradhāra*), the producer, dramatic coach and star actor. His responsibilities were heavy and demanded of him qualities comparable to those demanded of a high functionary. The actress playing heroine to his hero was often his own wife, and she too had to spare time from the practice of her art to perform her domestic duties, such as preparing her husband's meals according to the appropriate ritual, and also to be conspicuous in doing charitable work.

And, like all members of the theatrical profession from time immemorial, she was bound to perform under all circumstances and conditions, whatever the difficulties or private griefs.

The manager had two assistants, a producer (*sthāpaka*) and a stage-manager (*pāripārśvaka*): the first conducted rehearsals, supervised the stage settings and acted as the manager's primary agent in all other aspects of the company's professional activities, while the second transmitted the manager's orders to the actors and actresses, conducted the choir, and played the stock minor parts.

There were no special theatre buildings[28] and actors used the halls reserved for dancing and music which were attached to most palaces and temples, or else they simply played in the temple itself, before the statue of the local god. Sometimes, improvised stages were erected, and in this case the manager observed the ritual presiding at all constructional work when he put up his temporary theatre.

The theatre formed a rectangle, with the stage occupying the end of one of the two narrow sides of the hall or room, and the spectators facing the stage in a mass, sometimes sitting on a platform supported by pillars. In principle, the spectators were seated according to caste or trade, and in any case the king and other distinguished guests obviously occupied the places of honour. Several categories of people were excluded from attending these performances, especially illiterates, foreigners, those of lowly extraction and 'heretics'.

The hall was decorated gaudily; long, narrow flags waved over its roof, while its gilded pillars sparkled with inlaid patterns of coloured stones and glass, and were bedecked with huge garlands of flowers interwoven with pearls and jewels.

The stage was made of wood, and its front was either tiled or decorated with stucco-work; the surface of the floor-boards was kept rough enough for there to be no risk of an actor slipping. The stage was decorated with paintings and bas-reliefs, and furnished with a painted back-cloth (*yavanikā*), in some soft material, whose colour varied according to the play's basic theme: it would, for instance, be white for an erotic story, yellow for a heroic saga, dull-coloured for a pathetic scene, multi-coloured for a farce, black for a tragedy or a gruesome scene, red for a story of violence, and so on. This back-cloth served also to conceal the wings, which opened on to the stage by two side-doors and were used as dressing-rooms. Two girls were specially employed to look after this cloth, drawing it aside or lifting it each time that an actor entered or left the stage, except on those occasions when the action called for the player to thrust it aside himself with a brusque gesture. A curtain hung down at the front of the stage; in the fourth century AD it was called a *samhartum*, indicating that it was rolled or unrolled according to the needs of the particular scene being enacted.[29]

No real scenery was used, but the actors had a stock of stage-props which they carried with them on their travels, and which must have been a burdensome part of their baggage since they included sham rocks and cliffs, carts and carriages, suits of armour, shields, an assortment of weapons, banners and animals modelled from clay. The time and scene of the action taking place on the stage were suggested by oral description, mime and music, while the gestures (*mudrā* and *hasta*) had already been codified, by then, into a silent language which tradition has passed down, untouched, to the present century. But the actors did enhance the characters they played with special costumes, appropriate adornments and make up. A light-coloured dress signified a feast or pious occasion; gaudy costumes were worn by kings, lovers, gods and guardian spirits; a dark costume indicated that the wearer was a madman, a traveller or an invalid. The system of make up was based on a colour symbolism which did not necessarily reflect natural appearances. The actors possessed a palette on which they mixed little heaps of colours, red brick, yellow arsenic, white, blue and lamp-black; while they blended these colours by hand, they recited propitiatory prayers, since this whole process assumed a religious character. Light tints indicated happy characters, kings and 'western' races; darker tints were used for characters coming from the south, barbarians, rival kings, and so on.

The performances probably began at sunrise. As soon as the audience was in its places, a roll of drums and a clash of cymbals heralded the start of the show. What we would consider as preliminary activities now got under way. First, a carpet was unrolled on the stage, watched by the still chattering audience, and the orchestra members filed on and took their places: facing east, the drums, and to their left the 'tambourines'; facing north, a singer flanked to his left by players of lutes, citharas (*vīṇās*) and flutes. The choir now appeared, with the assistant manager at their head. As they arranged themselves, the musicians busied themselves in tuning their instruments, and performing relaxing exercises with their fingers and lips after having purified their hands and mouths. Finally, the choir sang a song of welcome, the manager recited the opening blessing, and launched into the prologue, in which he always played the main role.

It was only after this that the play itself started. It presented several curious features. First, the drama combined recitation with mime and dance. Certain situations were never represented (for example, death, a calamity, a defeat, the downfall of a king or religious rites) but merely evoked in an introduction by a monologue or dialogue. Personalities were classified according to forty-eight different types, each corresponding to a particular character in the play. Only the hero had always to be noble and to remain unchangeable during the course of the action, conforming to the 'quality' which he incarnated. The relations of the various characters were governed by a series of rules of etiquette which were, no doubt, analogous to those prevailing in the society of the time: the names and titles given to the king, for example, varied according to the status of the character addressing him. Another interesting feature of these dramas is that the language spoken by the characters was not the same for all. Kings, brāhmaṇs and dignitaries, the principal queen, daughters of ministers, Buddhist nuns and courtesans spoke Sanskrit, except when wearing disguise in order to conceal their true status. Characters of lower rank and most female parts spoke one of the many Prākrits (vernacular languages and local dialects). This fact indicates that even though the Sanskrit language was the prerogative of the nobility, it was nevertheless understood by those who did not speak it.

Although dramatic performances provided the main entertainment at public festivals, there was no shortage of rival offerings. The news of some impending festivity drew an assortment of entertainers from far afield: conch-players,[30] drummers,[31] wrestlers, acrobats, conjurers, mountebanks of every kind, folk-dancers and folk-singers, all travelled long distances, if necessary, in the hopes of making substantial profits.

When a wrestling contest or some other spectacle was due to

take place, a tambourine-player perambulated the town a week beforehand to announce the event.[32] Wrestling matches usually took place before the entrance to the palace, in the enclosure set aside for games and shows, and provided a favourite diversion for the aristocracy and the common people alike. In fact, nobles quite often hired athletes themselves, and made them fight in public. The scene of action was gay with flags flapping in the breeze, and the citizenry quickly packed the rows of benches. When the wrestlers climbed into the arena, they strutted around, flexing their muscles, leaping in the air, crying out and clapping their hands. Then they grappled, holding each other tightly around the waist, their necks resting on each other's shoulder, their legs entwined, while each attempted to win a fall or break the hold.[33] The winner received a large cash prize from the hands of the king and was presented with a victory standard, the possession of which gave him national distinction.[34]

Acrobats showed off their extraordinary talents to the accompaniment of an orchestra whose big drums slung from cross-straps, sharp-toned flutes and piercing clarinets added their clamour to the cries of the mountebanks trying to attract a crowd. These acrobats built huge human pyramids by climbing on each other's shoulders. A bas-relief from Bhārhut, dating from the second century BC and now in the collection of the Allahābād museum,[35] represents a team of fourteen people: seven of them, with their hands raised above their heads, are supporting four others, who in their turn are gripping in their hands the ankles of two men, who are supporting a young boy in similar fashion. From the summit of this living pyramid he acknowledges the cheers of the crowd by raising his arms and waving the scarf which is the sign of his profession.

Other mountebanks specialized in performing dances with javelins, making the audience gasp with the skill and daring with which they manipulated four or five of these dangerous weapons.[36] Tight-rope dancers also excited the admiration of the crowd with their skill. And the equilibrists who balanced and walked at the top of a long T-shaped pole, held only by spikes attached to their shoes,[37] impressed the public equally, since a fall meant instant death.

It was perhaps the illusionists and conjurors, though, who knew the greatest success, even in the royal court. These pseudo-

'holy men', claiming to be as wise and skilled as the greatest yogis, exercised their powers of hypnosis over a whole audience. The most skilled hypnotists made use of a rope, and were helped by adroit confederates. Their usual trick consisted in first making a mango-tree grow from a fruit-stone which the master conjuror had already shown to the audience. Through the effects of his magic, the bush grew and grew until it had become a great tree. Then he threw his rope into the air and it appeared to fasten its top end round one of the tree's highest branches. One of his assistants climbed the rope up into the tree until he had disappeared from the sight of the awe-struck spectators. But the trick was not yet over. From the top of the tree, the confederate's severed limbs fell one by one on to the ground, where the magician put them together again and made a whole body out of them. He brought this to life by sprinkling it with water: the resuscitated assistant then donned a costume of flowers and began dancing to the acclamations of the crowd.[38]

Mime-dancers also appeared frequently at court. The star turn of their repertory was the so-called 'demi-motion' dance, in which the dancer moved only one foot, one hand, one eye, one nostril and one half of his mouth, while the other vertical half of his body remained as rigid as a rock. The effect was both comical and impressive, and provoked huge gales of laughter.[39]

Finally, sword-swallowers,[40] monkey- and mongoose-handlers, and snake-charmers also took part in festivals and celebrations: the snake-charmers kept their cobras in cylindrical bamboo baskets.[41] Other showmen exhibited pictures in some busy spot: they could be seen, surrounded by a throng of inquisitive children, with a painted canvas, stretched between sticks, held upright by their left hand, while with a rod held in the right hand they pointed to the figures and scenes depicted on the canvas and explained the story.[42]

Fights between animals provided a favourite pastime. Not only cocks, but peacocks, buffaloes, oxen, horses, elephants and rams were trained to fight. Large sums were gambled on the outcome of these contests, and the winning bird or animal could win huge profits for its owner.

Regattas were occasionally held, in which the king and his court participated. Then the surface of the river was covered with magnificently decorated boats, white sailed ships, galleys and barges, and small boats made of light wood, shaped to look like birds, fish or marine monsters. The regatta took place to the accompaniment of music, dances, songs and comic parodies. It also featured water-games, with teams of men and women trying to spray each other with syringes, as during the *Holī* festival[43] (see p. 144).

The pre-eminently aristocratic sport was archery. This art provided the theme for tournaments, on the occasion of princely marriages (*svayaṃvara*); the target was secured to the top of a long pole, near a pavilion built specially for the wedding ceremony. The winner of the series of contests of skill won the hand of the princess who was being offered in marriage.[44]

In this manner, from one festival to another, and from public entertainment to celebration, the aristocracy enjoyed its leisure, while the common people shared these pleasures to the extent that they were permitted to participate.

CHAPTER TWO

ROYAL EXISTENCE AND ITS ENVIRONMENT

These kings . . . have vanished. Those who came before, others beside them, and others still to come will vanish, as shall those who will succeed them. It seems as though the Earth is laughing, in the joyous outburst of her autumn flowers, to see these kings attempting (vainly) to undertake the conquest of themselves.

Viṣṇu Pūraṇa, Part IV, XXIV.

THE ROYAL PALACE AND ITS INHABITANTS

We have already shown, in our study (p. 38 seq.) of the king's functions and the kingdom's political structure, the important part the king played in every aspect of the country's existence. Predestined to royalty by open or hidden signs, incarnating the god Indra, 'Weather Maker' and compared to the Sun, ensuring his subjects' prosperity by force of his virtues and the justice of his rule, the king was also the ideal of the *kṣatriya*. For all these reasons, his person was surrounded by great respect and extraordinary pomp. The populace was always eager to catch a glimpse of him and he showed himself in public on numerous special occasions, including important festivals, pilgrimages, and before departing on a military or hunting expedition; sometimes he even mixed with his subjects incognito, leaving his palace by a concealed door.[1]

While the royal succession did not normally pose any problems, passing quite naturally into the hands of a crown prince who had had plenty of time to prepare himself for the responsibilities of being a ruler, there were cases where this procedure was not possible. It might happen, for example, that a king had no son, or was rumoured to be incapable of having one. It was then within his rights to have recourse to a particular solution -

generally disapproved of by the lawgivers – which consisted in calling upon one of his subjects, preferably a brāhmaṇ of high reputation, to have sexual relations with the queen; she was entitled to refuse her consent, except when the royal line was in danger of becoming extinct for want of a collateral heir.[2] In any case, the child born of such a union remained a bastard in the eyes of the lawgivers, although his right to rule was recognized.[3] Usually, however, the king had several sons, and if the eldest son was unable or ineligible to reign for any reason – if he was a gambler or a depraved personality, for instance – a younger brother could mount the throne. But it could also happen that the king died prematurely, in which case the queen (that is to say, his legitimate wife) assumed the regency, though this contingency, like the occupation of the throne by a very young child, was generally considered undesirable.[4] On the other hand, it was not necessary for the king to be dead before his successor was crowned; he might well follow custom in retiring to a hermitage, so as to end his life in an atmosphere of pious meditation. In addition, the reigning sovereign might even commit ritual suicide by drowning himself at some sacred river junction, by having himself burned alive on a pyre, or by practising the method of holding breath taught by ascetics.[5] But, in any of these cases, he would have come to his decision a long time ahead and abdicated only when the succession was assured.

The birth of a crown prince was the signal for tremendous celebrations which threw the whole city and palace into a cheerful uproar. From the moment that drummers announced the good news throughout the city, popular revelry began, and everyone danced, sang and drank together without distinction of caste. Congratulations and good wishes soon began to stream into the court, a general amnesty was proclaimed for prisoners in jail, and a delegation of citizens offered the king a sum of money representing the total collected from the people in a sort of voluntary tax, which was earmarked for the baby prince's welfare.[6] Many beautiful and valuable gifts were brought to the palace by delegates of neighbouring kings and vassals, by nobles and courtiers: garlands, camphorated delicacies, saffron for the bath in precious caskets, ivory boxes filled with aromatic betel-nuts dyed rose-red with powdered sandalwood, and so on.[7] During several days, the court was the scene of a succession of musical and dancing entertainments.

The childhood of the future king was, of course, spent in an atmosphere of special care and attention. He was brought up by nurses chosen specially by his father.[8] His everyday existence was interspersed with sacraments. As soon as he could toddle, his hair was dressed in the manner demanded by his caste, he wore a mustard-seed amulet on top of his head and, round his neck, a necklace of tiger's claws or coins.[9] His body was smeared with yellow oil so that it shone like gold. He started his studies from the age of three. When he was eleven, he started learning economics and politics. The military arts occupied an important place in his young life: his mornings were devoted to the theory and practice of arms, while his evenings were spent in learning difficult lessons. At fixed hours, the bards attached to the royal family recited epics to him. During this whole period he remained within the palace, far removed from the excitements and ostentations of the world around him, and observing a respectful obedience towards his masters. When these masters judged that he had acquired a sufficient fund of knowledge, he underwent a period of apprenticeship under the direction of a senior administrator; at the end of this practical training, the prince was assigned to a particular military service, then finally declared competent to assume a command. Usually, his father then sent him off to take part in some military campaign, after which he awarded him the governorship of a province or even the viceroyship itself.

His marriage, to a princess of his own caste, was celebrated with great pomp and in one of the six forms authorized for a *kṣatriya*. In former heroic eras, he 'won' his wife by emerging victorious from a tourney (*svayaṃvara*) involving an archery contest.[10] It was the occasion of a great celebration, to which all the empire's heads of state and vassals were invited. A pavilion was specially decorated for the occasion. Before the gathered assembly, the bride, holding a garland of white flowers, reviewed a procession of the suitors, then placed the garland around the neck of the winner; the marriage rites were celebrated in the presence of the defeated candidates. Like his father, the king, the crown prince had the right to possess numerous concubines, but only the princess wed by him in these solemn circumstances ranked as a legitimate wife.

It will be seen, then, that when the king abdicated or died and the crown prince had to assume power in his turn, the latter was mentally and physically equipped to direct the affairs of state. After his coronation, the solemn celebration of which deserves a more detailed description (see p. 277 seq.), he proceeded to live according to the great traditions of his ancestry, surrounded by a brilliant court comprising high dignitaries, ministers, governors, ambassadors, military chiefs, bankers and guild masters, together with courtiers of all kinds vying for his favour. A very strict etiquette governed their relations with the king, and any failure to observe this protocol was punished in exactly the same way as the minor faults condemned by the penal code.

The royal chaplain (*purohita*) held first place among the kingdom's great men. Even at the courts of the Buddhist kings, he was always a brāhmaṇ, reputed for his wisdom; his post was usually hereditary. Often, he had been the king's tutor when the latter was still a boy, and now served him as counsellor for both spiritual and temporal affairs. He was the king's favourite partner at chess and dice, supervised the efficient running of the palace in his absence, and did not hesitate to remonstrate with him if his moral conduct left something to be desired. The prime minister and his fellow ministers and councillors also had an influential relationship with the king, though they did not receive from him a comparable degree of respect or submissiveness.

An equally important personage was the field-marshal (*senāpati*) who, like the royal chaplain, enjoyed hereditary rights. The grand treasurer was another dignitary who figured largely in the court – a high-living millionaire whom Buddhist tales accuse frequently of sordid avarice. And until about the seventh century, perhaps, when war-chariots ceased to form part of the army's strength, a distinguished member of the court circle was the driver of the royal war-chariot, in olden times a valiant noble who was also a bard.[11] In those days, the king's safety, and sometimes his very life, depended on this man's courage and skill. The royal equerry, chosen from an aristocratic family, performed a similar function to that of a page in the Western courts during the Middle Ages; clad in a short tunic, he preceded the royal charger on all outings, holding in his hand a ring which may be identified as a *cakra*, a redoubtable throwing weapon and a symbol of royalty.[12]

Various dignitaries and officials of minor importance were employed in the personal service of the king and, for that very reason, were able to exercise a certain influence on him. His barber[13] was in a particularly favourable position because, although he was usually of low caste,[14] he had the supreme honour of shaving the king, cutting his hair, removing his body hair with the aid of golden tweezers and dressing his hair according to caste rules; he also enjoyed the custom of the other members of the royal family. He is traditionally supposed to have been very badly paid,[15] though there appear to have been exceptions to this rule.[16] But what is certain is that he acted as the king's confidant and, sometimes, go-between.

A whole host of servants hovered constantly around the king, performing different functions: those responsible for preparing his daily baths, those in charge of his extensive wardrobe,[17] who got ready for him the costume appropriate to a particular occasion, those who perfumed these clothes with the rarest essences, and the 'ornament makers' who designed his floral adornments and who selected the right jewellery to match the clothes he was wearing.

One should also mention the king's head cook: his job was no sinecure, if we are to believe the *Jātakas*. Apart from having to assure himself each day of the sufficiency and variety of the dishes destined for the royal table, he had also to endure the intolerable heat of the kitchen fires, before which he sat cross-legged, mixing the sauces with a ladle or a spoon,[18] his eyes streaming from the thick smoke, getting up from time to time to lean against the door and wipe off the sweat streaming down his face. Besides this, he had to defend his dishes against the impudent onslaughts of the ever-hungry crows,[19] whose nests were everywhere,[20] or against the voracious dogs which prowled around freely within the palace grounds.[21] And finally, although he commanded a whole army of scullions and servant-girls, he still had to endure with good grace the constant sampling of his preparations by the king's official food-taster, who was there to ensure that none of the dishes was poisoned. A similar official inspection procedure applied to medicines and to equipment used for massaging.

There were many other junior members of the royal household. Bearers of the royal insignia were entrusted with a great regalia which they carried behind the king whenever he moved from one place to another, and which included the white parasol (the essential symbol of royalty), the sword, the sandals (which 'ruled the kingdom' when the sovereign was absent), the flywhisks, the royal standard, and so on. Dwarf cup-bearers (who doubled as court-jesters), women in charge of the service of wines, wearing Greco-Iranian dress[22] modelled on the national costume of the country from which the wine came, male and female musicians, female dancers, artisans and technicians, and the whole band of minor adherents living in various parts of the palace, all had a precise and limited function, as Indian custom dictated.

But the king was not the only one who demanded special attention. Two animals, the royal elephant and the State horse, participated very closely in the life of the kingdom and were regarded as the palladia of the empire, being two of the 'seven jewels' (*saptaratna*) which consecrated the sovereignty of a universal king (*cakravartin*). The elephant destined to play this part was chosen for certain characteristics which were supposed to indicate a royal and holy origin, particularly a very light-grey hide (which was called white).[23] The king had the selected animal led around the capital in a solemn procession; then he consecrated it with a ritual aspersion and designated it expressly as the royal mount.[24] From that moment on, the elephant was lodged in a special stall, in which it received a daily visit from the king. Carefully chosen keepers looked after it, and a mahout was specially appointed as its rider. At festivals, the great beast was adorned sumptuously, its back covered by a fine striped or checkered carpet held secure by a girthband, clusters of jewels dangled from its ears, its bridle was set with gold and its head was crowned by a gold-chased tiara, a huge necklace encircled its neck and its legs were ringed by bangles of precious metals. Cords from which hung a large bell with a clapper or a row of small globular bells were tied above its knees, and the ringing or tinkling gave notice of its approach. The mahout, wearing a short tunic with sleeves, squatted on the elephant's neck, holding the royal standard in one hand and, in the other, a goad (*aṅkuśa*) inset with precious stones. The king mounted the animal by means of a 'golden' ladder[25] while it remained kneeling. Sometimes the king himself rode on the neck, in which case the mahout sat astride the rump, kept from slipping by a cord attached to the girthband on each side and passing round the small of his back.[26] The elephant of State was compared to Indra's mount, to Airāvata, and considered as a real personage, so that the courtiers spoke of it in human terms, praising its sagacity, prudence and intelligence.[27]

The horse of State was treated with similar honour and ceremony and its stable was hung with purple and gold draperies. For great occasions it was fitted with a saddle-cloth, a girthband, and sometimes even a hunting-saddle (a style affected by certain sovereigns, such as the Vākāṭaka kings of Ajantā in the fifth and sixth centuries AD), together with golden trappings, a browband sporting a plume, and its tail elegantly plaited and sometimes encased in a golden tube. The king visited it daily, and did not hesitate to dismiss any of the special grooms attached to its service if he did not consider them conscientious enough, despite the difficulty of obtaining trained personnel who were also endowed with the 'moral' qualities required for such an office.[28]

This mass of retainers and servants lived in the royal residences, moving from one to another according to the season, for the king usually possessed several palaces scattered throughout his empire, and sometimes more than one in the capital itself. In fact, the royal household was frequently on the move, since the king, accompanied by a 'portable palace', passed the hot months in the north of his empire, stayed somewhere dry during the rainy season, and returned south again as soon as cooler weather returned; alternatively, if the king was conducting a war he would establish camp on the frontier. This semi-nomadic existence was compensated by a theoretically immutable organization which re-created an identical atmosphere around the king, wherever he might be, while filling the daily needs of court life. Without doubt, there was also a sedentary staff in each royal residence to look after it during the court's absence.

The palace resembled a small-scale city, or, perhaps, a private villa of kingly dimensions. Wherever it might be, in the heart of the capital or elsewhere, it covered a great stretch of ground. Within surrounding moats, rose ramparts indented with triangular merlons, fortified by bastions and watchtowers from whose roofs standards fluttered in the breeze. Its vast gateways, facing the four cardinal points, were guarded night and day by mounted troops, while a garrison, quartered within the redoubt, patrolled the battlements. The chief gateway, ornamented with equestrian statues in ivory, sculptures 'faced with gold and silver' and plaques of engraved and carved ivory, faced the royal highway which ran through the capital from east to west.

The palace was divided into two distinct sections: one was public and accessible to all, the other was strictly private and housed the kingdom's chief political departments, the king's own residential quarters, and the harem. Both sections were divided into courtyards, paved with polished tiles, overlooked by elegantly designed buildings and connected by wide avenues along which carriages of all kinds circulated. The shape and style of the buildings varied according to their functions; there were long structures with barrel-vault roofs used as warehouses, pillared halls for public assemblies, and residential buildings comprising several storeys.

In the public section, the royal granaries were to be found situated above or flanking the gateway; here the busy supervisor watched closely while his functionaries weighed piles of rice and stuck an officially stamped marker into the top of each sackful.[29] Nearby, lay the alms-houses where the king came each day to distribute gifts to the religious mendicants and the needy. In the outer courts were situated the stables, cowsheds, elephant stalls, coach-houses where the royal carriages and palanquins were kept, and the aviary and zoo. The birds and animals housed in these various establishments were carefully selected specimens which were looked after carefully by a small army of grooms, stablemen and keepers, veterinaries and their assistants. Superintendents were in charge of the various sectors of this extensive area, making sure that the buildings were kept clean and the harnesses were in good repair, watching over the quality of the work performed by their juniors and paying them their wages. The horned cattle had their horns gilded and wore costly harnesses; the rams were trained for fighting, or else drew light traps.[30] Each day, the elephants were led to a place where they could take exercise; afterwards they bathed themselves, then remained indolent for the rest of the day. The royal stables contained riding-horses and also draw-horses for the war-chariots; these were all in the care of grooms clad like 'men of the North', that is to say, wearing long-sleeved jackets, tailored to fit, with a high collar open at the neck, and decorated with braid, plus breeches and leather sandals: a garb adapted by the Indians originally from the clothes worn by the foreign grooms who had accompanied the horses all the way from the plains of Upper Asia. Their usual stable duties included the preparation of the horses' fodder, which was usually a mixture of barley, peas and oats, although occasionally it consisted of root vegetables soaked in honey.[31] During the rainy season, the grooms needed to exercise particular vigilance in the care of their charges, since the hot, humid climate affected the horses adversely.

There were special sheds, in this same public area of the palace grounds, set aside for war-chariots and every variety of carriage. The chariots were modelled on two patterns, either the biga, with two horses, or the quadriga, with four horses abreast, similar to those of Etruria.[32] These chariots were armour-plated with iron covered by lion or tiger skin, and each carried a single driver. When due to leave on military duty, they were adorned with a banner, umbrella, flywhisks and bells, and equipped with appropriate arms and ammunition. Those designed to be displayed at festivals were especially carefully looked after, being made of wood of intricate pattern, painted in gay colours which were touched up periodically, and ornamented with ivory, gold or silver sculptures.

In the following courts were halls and pavilions surrounded by beautiful gardens which were open to the public. The halls were raised slightly above the ground, and access was provided by short flights of steps whose balustrades followed an S-shaped undulating line and were ornamented with heads of monsters. Their roofs were flat, and the ceilings were coffered with painted panels; dividing curtains were sometimes draped from the ceilings, as well as festoons of pearls. Their pillars, surfaced with blue or red lacquer, were decorated with circular gold-wrought motifs incorporating fashionable jewels, while their capitals were gilded. These buildings were reserved for public meetings and royal audiences; one, equipped with a full range of musical instruments, served as a hall for dances, concerts and theatrical performances. Others were set aside for games, and contained chessboards and chessmen, and boxes of dice. There were also reading-rooms, and a gallery containing the king's collection of paintings. Finally, somewhere in this area, or, alternatively, in the vicinity of the palace's temples and chapels, was to be found the royal gallery of portrait statuary (*devakula* or *gurv-āyatana*) containing the statues of former kings and royal gurus, which visitors came to honour and even venerate. An official (*devakulika*) was appointed to organize visits to this memorial, and act as a guide to the visitors, delivering little lectures on the qualities and great deeds of these heroes.[33]

Adjoining this public area lay the private sector of the palace, which could be entered only with the consent of the 'porter', a high-ranking official who was often the king's favourite[34] and commanded a large array of junior functionaries, his actual responsibilities being akin to those of a chamberlain or major-domo. Several departments of vital importance to the kingdom were situated in this private sector, including the arsenal and treasury.

The arsenal was both a State manufactory and an arms magazine. It was under the control of the war department,[35] and was directed by a superintendent who controlled the production of weapons, ensured that stocks were sufficient and maintained in good condition, held inventories, and imposed specifications for the shape, size and value of each type of weapon.[36] In some workshops, skilled men laboured throughout the day, straightening bent arrow-heads,[37] stamping the arrows with the names of their owners, repairing and refurbishing suits of armour, cleaning weapons affected by heat or cold and then laying them outdoors to benefit from the sun's rays. In other workshops, weapons were made and stored: bows and swords (emblems of the noble warrior, whose perfect model was the king), quivers and arrows, lances, pikes, shields, daggers and elephant goads; this establishment also manufactured the conches which served to rally soldiers and hunters and which were used also in the itinerant military bands that accompanied the armies; and protective armour for the soldiers and war animals, constructed from hard leather and well-toughened iron.

The treasury, of which the king was only the trustee, since it belonged to the State, comprised every valuable commodity of the era: that is to say, not only gold and jewels but also such things as incense, sandalwood and aloes-wood, which were all extremely costly items.[38] The treasury constituted a whole small district devoted to the crafts, with permanently accredited craftsmen 'examining, one by one, gems of all varieties, cats'-eyes, pearls, corals, topazes, sapphires, beryls, rubies and emeralds'. Jewellers at their benches mounted stones in gold settings, threaded pearls on red threads, rubbed cats'-eyes meticulously to make them lustrous, transformed conches into horns, or tested corals against the touchstone. Artists and designers, working specially for the king himself, produced new sets of finery and jewelled accessories which were then embellished by the goldsmiths; official valuers calculated the total worth of all the king's treasure, appraised the jewels that were brought daily by would-be sellers, and set a suitable price on the jewels the king wished to sell. It was here that buyers acquired their rarest gems, since the town's jewel merchants kept their finest specimens for the palace. In fact, the strong-rooms of the royal treasurer were piled high with magnificent objects worthy of a powerful monarch.

By penetrating further towards the palace's central structures, one came to the hall used for meetings of the king's council, which he attended each day, then to the pavilion 'reserved for flowers', then to the building specially designed for the royal ablutions, consisting of a sunk bath and a tiled room. It was in this area of the palace grounds that would be set up eventually the pavilion where the consecration of the new sovereign, when he succeeded his father, would be celebrated (see p. 277 seq.).

The catering department came next, with its storerooms stocked with food and drink supplies for the palace's entire population; they were filled with receptacles piled on top of each other, the base of the upper jar sealing the mouth of the one below it, and with individual jars stoppered with conical lids or inverted bowls. The king's cook operated in an annex formed of a few pillars covered by a tiled roof and containing one or more hearths made of flat stones. Sometimes, the cook hung a small basket up near the door to his kitchen, and kept a pigeon in it, tending it lovingly and feeding it with his own hands.[39]

Next came the part of the palace reserved for the king and his most distinguished guests. The pavilions here were even more luxuriously appointed than those in other parts of the palace, some of them possessing – so it was claimed – as many as seven or even eleven storeys. The authors of the time were more than usually prolix in describing these buildings: the most precious materials had been used in their construction; gold, silver and rare stones bordered the windows, which were surfaced with panes of sparkling crystal; whole rooms had walls lined entirely with sheets of ivory; wall niches contained massive gold statues. A secret door, concealed by paintings or sculpted panels, was built into a wall or pillar of one of these pavilions, and the operation of a concealed mechanism opened the way into a secret passage allowing the king to leave the palace, and even the capital, in case of danger. Various sources claim, also, that there existed one or more labyrinths.

Last of all, near the pavilion in which the king took his daily meals (see p. 275), stood his private dwelling which included a bedroom isolated effectively from all noise and bustle. It has been claimed that, during certain epochs, he never slept for two consecutive nights in the same place, so as to throw off the trail those who might be plotting to assassinate him during his sleep.[40]

The furniture in the king's private apartments was more varied and more richly decorated than that in the houses of his subjects. Couches, resting on detachable vase-shaped or bell-shaped supports, were covered with matting, or with a coverlet of woven goat-hair or silk, or with an animal pelt, printed with designs and figures. Hassocks of a kind were constructed entirely of reedwork and bamboo, woven in various patterns which often repeated arch-shaped or sinuous motifs; they were sometimes covered with a piece of material stretched over the whole framework or else fastened by large buttons, or alternatively they were draped with flounces and puffs, which gave them a strangely Louis-Philippe appearance.[41] Footstools, whose tops were sometimes caned, had stubby legs often shaped like animals' paws, and were covered with a saw-tooth patterned fabric or an antelope skin. Such apartments also contained chairs and armchairs, for which many different woods were employed, as well as precious materials such as gold, ivory and rare stones; these seats were usually accompanied by matching footstools. The furnishing scheme would be completed by a few tables and consoles, pedestal tables and wicker-work stands: all of these articles of furniture are reproduced in innumerable contemporary bas-reliefs and mural paintings.[42]

These various pavilions were constructed in the midst of great gardens looked after by a squad of gardeners in charge of a head gardener who is a familiar character in Buddhist tales. These spreading gardens were dotted with splendid trees of many different varieties, with thick foliage, and sturdy branches which sometimes served as supports for the ropes of a swing. The carefully designed flower-beds and groves were bright with thick clusters of flowers of all kinds, some brilliant, some pale and delicate, among which the orange-scarlet flower clusters of the aśoka tree (*Saraca indica*) stood up 'like sentinels'; the groves were set with flagstones, upon which strollers could lie down and relax. Artificial lakes and fish-ponds were frequented by swans and storks, and some of these ponds provided fish for the royal table; the surface of the water was covered with a profusion of rose-coloured or white lotuses and heavy-scented lilies. A summer-house, built on a little island in the centre of one of these lakes, was reserved specifically for amorous dalliance. Fountains and canals in various spots helped to keep the atmosphere cool and fresh. And the flatness of the ground was broken, here and there, by artificial hillocks. Dotted through the gardens were single columns, topped with a platform, to which peacocks were chained by one leg, and around which they strutted majestically, or, perched on top, spread their tails in a beautiful display; often their strutting and preening was accompanied by the discreet music of the royal orchestra playing in one of the park's shady retreats.

The central and most inaccessible part of the palace was that constituted by the buildings housing the royal harem.

LIFE IN THE ROYAL HAREM

It was usual, at least at certain epochs, for the king to be polygamous. Even so, one woman only was recognized as his legitimate wife and she lived in a special section of the harem and enjoyed the prerogatives accorded to queens; but the king continued to have what relations he pleased with his female favourites, concubines or even female servants. And though they accepted fully the priority granted the queen,[43] the women in the harem never tired of intriguing among themselves in the hopes of achieving favour in the king's heart. It could even happen that the king developed into a debauchee, neglecting his conjugal duties and the government of his kingdom, but in such cases amorous excesses led him ineluctably down a path of physical exhaustion which usually led to death.[44]

The royal harem was enclosed within its own ramparts and consisted of a cluster of pavilions around a few courtyards whose paving-stones were smooth and moist to the touch of bare feet, in the middle of beautiful gardens planted with aśoka trees whose lovely orange-scarlet flowers bloomed in springtime: their blossoms were symbols of love and played a part in seasonal ceremonies.[45] Apart from the king and the ancient guardian in charge of the harem, no man had the right to enter these premises. The entire personnel was female, including the little army which kept watch night and day upon the ramparts and at all the entrance-gates (see p. 33); armed with bows, lances or halberds, and sometimes wearing male costume, these female warriors were entirely in charge of the security of the women's quarters. The guardian (*kañcukin*) was recruited from among the eunuchs; he was a picturesque figure, well known in ancient literature and frequently depicted in the art of the time, always grumbling, complaining about his advanced age, his infirmities and the difficulties he encountered in carrying out his tasks. Cane in hand, clad in a white tunic, a cap disguising his baldness, he trudged through the different apartments and made a report to the king every morning.[46] The princesses were surrounded by a great number of female servants; and infants, too, were brought up within the harem precincts until they were old enough to be placed in the care of private tutors.

Far from the noise and tumult of the outside world, protected by a pleasant and luxurious environment, the king's wives lived for the moment when they would be honoured with a visit from their master, meanwhile devoting their days to the elaborate routine of their toilet, and to playing games and indulging in other agreeable diversions. The monotony of their daily life, spiced with intrigue, was broken also by group excursions, under the king's leadership, to the nearby river, where they all bathed in his company,[47] or to some place of pilgrimage, or to a festival; and they also undertook periodical voyages as the royal residence shifted seasonally from one location to another.

Their major preoccupation was their daily toilet, with the accompanying ritual of beauty treatment, which included hydrotherapy, massages, expertly applied ointments and perfumes, and the whole gamut of aesthetic devices which the extreme refinement of Indian civilization had accumulated in centuries of meticulous attention to such details.

By dawn, the serving-women were already in the process of attending to their own carefully executed toilets so that they should be ready to attend to the requirements of the princesses, as soon as they might require attention. Each maid had her specific task. The girl in charge of the betel box prepared quids composed of cloves, camphor and betel-nut rolled in the brilliant green leaf of the betel-tree; the boxes were round and made of ivory, and had to be kept filled, ready to be offered to their mistresses as soon as they awoke. The servant responsible for preparing ointments took a pride in her ability to concoct subtle blends based on secret recipes: she grated sandalwood on a soft, moistened stone, pounded the parings with a pestle in a small stemmed bowl,[48] blended the paste with oil, added flower petals and sweet-smelling leaves, then moulded them to form sticks. Other serving-women braided garlands, prepared the incense which would be set in each private room, and also lit sticks of incense over which they fumigated the clothing which the princesses would wear, holding each article for a long time over the fragrant smoke.[49] The bathing equipment was got together: razors and tweezers for removing body hair,[50] nail-cutters,[51] ear-picks,[52] roots and pastes intended for dental hygiene, instruments of massage in ebony, terracotta or bone,[53] ointment pots, and little containers of all kinds, made of precious substances[54] and designed to hold pastes and scented powders; and also flasks of perfume, scent-sprays whose bases were perforated with minute holes through which the essence could pass when the container was shaken while its mouth was kept sealed with the tip of one finger,[55] perfume-braziers in various forms, and the indispensable looking-glass; and yet again the small stick used to trace designs on the face and body,[56] the 'curlers' for certain styles of hair-dressing,[57] and the ivory combs with fine, close-set teeth, their surfaces embellished with delicate patterns;[58] and finally, the boxes and shelves containing finery and costume-jewellery, each item of which the wardrobe-attendants had to check carefully every day.

Meanwhile, the female musicians and dancers attached to the harem were also preparing themselves so that they should be ready to accompany the main phases of the princesses' toilet with their concert of music and dance.

Whenever they were to be near their mistress, the maids kept in their mouths a fragrant pill compounded of a quarter part each of lemon-yellow aloes and cinnamon to a half part of camphor.[59] When all was ready, the masseuses were the first to appear on the scene. During the hot season, a couch was set up in the leafy shade of the park; here the princess stretched out and, while the orchestra entertained her, her maids kneaded her flesh and rubbed her body with ointments and perfumed oils,[60] so as to make the skin supple and the muscles firm.[61] Her long tresses, dyed with henna, were smeared with an oil designed to promote the growth of the hair and preserve its glossy sheen.

After this, the princess took a bath; depending upon the season, she used the harem's bath-house, plunged into the river or the park's pool, or else stood under a waterfall.[62] If no running water was available, the perfumed contents of great pot-bellied vases (*kalaśa*) were poured over her, while other maids preserved her from indiscreet glances by holding up around her a pleated tapestry. She rubbed her body with a 'soap' preparation, then twisted her hair into a coil and massaged her gums with roots[63] and a paste composed of honey, fruit pulp, salt and oil. She bathed her eyes and rinsed her mouth with milk added to a decoction of various barks, and she repeated this process several times during the course of the day, to refresh herself as much as for hygienic reasons. When she had a headache, a few drops of oil were dripped into each of her ears. And she inhaled the fumes of a sweet-smelling liquid preparation with disinfectant properties.

Once out of her bath, her hair was dried and black incense brushed through it. The maid in charge of the betel presented her with a quid to chew,[64] while other maids clustered around her, busy with fans and flywhisks. Then they rubbed a paste of ground sandalwood into her body, smeared musk-scented saffron over her breasts and feet, and painted the soles of her feet with a diluted lac: now, a trail of red footprints on the floor-tiles would mark her leisurely movements.[65]

The next stage was the making up not only of her face but also of her body. With the aid of a small stick dipped into an oil of aloe-wood (*aguru*) possessing adhesive qualities, leaves cut and perforated to make decorative designs, and brown or red lac,[66] they executed patterns on her arms, breasts, shoulders, forehead, cheeks and chin;[67] these painted designs, black, red or white, interspersed with the bright green of the cut-out leaves,[68] stood out against her brown skin with its rosy hue resulting from the prior application of sandalwood paste and musk (*ālepa*).[69]

The eyes were rimmed heavily with a collyrium (*añjana*) of one kind or another, all of them known as khol[70] and used since very ancient times;[71] it was employed in the form of small sticks made of solidified paste, perfumed with sandalwood, and its use was so widespread that a regular rural industry, employing full-time trained women workers, existed to supply the demand.[72] But, in aristocratic circles, it was used in the form of a paste, so highly prized that it was kept in special little boxes made of precious materials,[73] and the eyelids were made up with the aid of a slender gold or silver stylet (*añjana-śalākā*).[74] The lips were painted with lac, then spread with an orange-coloured mineral powder (*aśmarāga*)[75] which made the whiteness of the teeth seem more brilliant by contrast. In winter, to prevent chapping, the lips were smeared with a wax-based solvent, moulded in pencils similar to our present-day lipsticks.

Before combing her mistress's hair, the maid took away from her the pet goose she liked to play with while her toilet was being attended to, its favourite game being to peck playfully at the ends of her tresses.[76] The hair parting (*sīmanta*) was traced with great care, and ran from the centre of the forehead back to the crown of the head; powdered sandalwood was sprinkled along it, and its outline was emphasized by a single strand of pearls ending in a pendant dangling at the middle of the forehead.[77] Interwoven with pearls or shells, the hair was plaited, braided or coiled, arranged in loose or tight plaits, set in small curls or a chignon, covered with a coif,[78] a huge turban,[79] or a delicate diadem of jewellery, or perhaps adorned with flowers, gold-chased pins, iridescent feathers or bows.[80] There were innumerable fashions in hair styling, depending on the individual's social status, the region and the epoch.

When the toilet was completed, the princess marked her forehead with a beauty-spot, the *tilaka*, made of a dark-coloured pigment;[81] then a maid held a looking-glass up, kneeling in front of her. This was a fairly large object composed of a metal disc, sometimes of gold,[82] one face of which was burnished while the other was furnished with a boss, in the Chinese style. This disc was framed and mounted on a handle which was more or less elaborately engraved and was usually of ivory.[83]

After putting on a light skirt, the colour of which varied according to the day, the hour and the occasion, the princess chose her dress accessories and jewellery. These were presented to her in baskets, and were of an astonishing variety: necklaces, long neck-chains, wide girdles, bangles, armlets and anklets, ear-pendants and rings, all exquisitely fashioned and worked;[84] these articles all had symbolic and even magical properties, protecting the wearer from evil spirits and from the baneful influence of certain planets. The anklets were so large and heavy that they were known to slip off the princess's feet;[85] they were hollow and filled with small pebbles, and the tinkling that accompanied her movements was so much associated with her that the sound has been celebrated unceasingly by Indian poets. The ear-pendants were sometimes very heavy. The lobes of her ears had been ritually pierced when she was still a baby, and the holes progressively enlarged by the insertion of increasingly thick cylinders cut from fish-bones;[86] this allowed her to wear heavy jewelled ear-rings or pass the stem of a fresh flower through the lobe.

Thus apparelled and adorned, the princess took her midday meal, while servants fanned her. After eating, she chewed a quid of betel, then took a siesta while fans continued to cool her and flywhisks ensured her an undisturbed rest. Afterwards, she amused herself by teaching her pet parrot tender words which it would repeat to the king on his next visit.[87] When the heat of the day had abated somewhat, the ladies of the harem made their way to the park, accompanied by their maids. There they strolled around,[88] picking flowers and imitating the strutting and preening of the peacocks, stamping on the ground so that their anklets tinkled.[89] Near the pool, they reclined under a shady arbour or sheltered from the sun in the pleasure pavilion, nibbling delicacies in company with their attendants[90] and feeding titbits to the ducks which came waddling up to them,[91] to their pet parakeet which they carried around in a gilded cage[92] and to the pet goose which followed them everywhere. They were served with red-hued, perfumed drinks[93] – perhaps mango and *pāṭala* juice[94] – poured from long, narrow vases into cups or bowls.[95]

They often bathed in the nearby pool; their maids helped them to undress and remove their adornments, packing the clothes and jewellery inside small chests placed at the water's edge – a wise precaution against thieves and monkeys, both of which were adcpt at taking advantage of a sleepy custodian and making off with her precious bundle[96] Sometimes, the king came to join them and plunged into the pool among them, admiring their 'firm young breasts' which made 'the lotuses tremble by creating ripples in the water'. They frolicked in the water until it grew red from the cosmetic which was washed off their faces and bodies, leaving their lips pale and dissolving the carefully traced designs on their skin.[97] Another favourite pastime was sitting in the swing that hung from the branch of a nearby tree, in the shade, and being pushed to and fro by two of their maids.[98] They also liked playing games with balls, throwing them with gestures designed specifically to show off to their best advantage the beauty of their arms and the firmness of their breasts.[99]

When they were finally back in the harem once more, they took their evening meal. Then they assembled in the hall reserved for dances, reclining in a gracious disorder while they awaited the king's arrival, passing the time by listening to a concert and watching the dancers.[100] A female dwarf (*vāmanikā*) circulated among them; it was considered good form to include one such dwarf among the palace staff, her main task being to divert the princesses by her antics as she strutted around in male costume.[101]

Daily life in the royal harem was, as can be seen, characterized by an agreeable and luxurious indolence, rhythmed by the king's visits and depending upon their master's humour and demands.

THE KING'S DAY

The king's daily routine was heavily filled and strictly organized. It has been frequently described in Indian literature,[102] and these accounts are supplemented by the historical evidence of two eye-witnesses, the Greek Megasthenes and the Chinese Hsüan-Ch'uang. It is in fact rather remarkable that the descriptions given by these foreigners, some nine centuries apart, confirm in their main outlines the Indian texts which, on the theoretical level, lay extreme emphasis on the establishment of an ideal programme. According to Hsüan-Ch'uang, who was for many years a guest of the emperor Harṣa of Kanauj (605–47), the emperor's 'entire day was not long enough' to permit him to complete all his daily tasks.

The king's day was divided into sixteen unequal parts according to the *Arthaśāstra*, but into three parts according to Hsüan-Ch'uang.

Like all Indians, he arose long before sunrise; each morning, at a precise hour, the palace orchestra awoke him from his slumbers. The *Arthaśāstra* recommended that his first action should be to 'reflect upon the conduct of politics' and urgent affairs of state, while Megasthenes states that the royal chaplain appeared at this moment to greet him.

After making a preliminary toilet, the king held a council with his ministers, hearing their reports, taking necessary decisions and deciding upon his secret agents' missions. Then, in the presence of his guru, the chaplain and the palace officials, he received the greetings and good wishes of his close kin. Next he saw the court physician, the chief cook, the head gardener (who brought him flowers and fruits), the keeper of the harem and the royal astrologer. Next he went into the public part of the palace, entering one of the first courtyards of the particular building where royal audiences were held. There he informed himself of the measures taken by his administrators to ensure the safety of the State, and received an account of public revenue and expenditure. After this, he devoted his attention to matters concerning town- and country-dwellers; while he listened to their complaints and claims, he often had himself massaged at the same time by the four experts employed for this purpose, thus saving an appreciable amount of time.

As soon as the public audience was over, he headed for his bathing-pool, or the bathroom in his private apartments, surrounded by a phalanx of menservants and female attendants. The bathroom consisted of a small pavilion with painted pillars, enclosed by bright-coloured tapestries; in its centre was a gilded tank, containing a seat which may possibly have been made of crystal. After undressing, he sat on it and his attendants poured over him the perfumed water which was contained in great jars standing around the rim of the tank.[103] After his bath, the king honoured the divinities, then returned to his apartments to complete his toilet and have himself dressed. His female attendants rubbed his body with a paste composed of ground sandalwood, musk, camphor and saffron. If any time was left to him before the midday meal, he relaxed by playing some game or other with his favourites or confidants, people who fulfilled the same role in his life as did the court jesters of our Middle Ages.

The pavilion set aside for the service of his meals was situated near the kitchens. He ate alone, as befitted a person of high caste, seated on a richly decorated chair in front of a low table; a tray on the table was covered with bowls and plates[104] whose contents, as we have already mentioned, were carefully tasted before being presented to him. During the royal repast, his orchestra played nearby, while female attendants manipulated fans and flywhisks around him. His diet was no different from that of the *kṣatriyas*. Indian kings were more or less vegetarian, and many observed the restrictions initiated by Aśoka, although the degree of adherence to his rules varied from one reign to another. Aśoka had repeatedly forbidden the mass slaughter of animals and poultry destined for the royal table. Instead of the killing of 'several hundred thousand' each day, he decreed that only three should be killed, two peacocks and one gazelle, and even that amount not every day. By the end of his long reign, this monarch had forbidden absolutely the killing of any living creature whatsoever.[105] His successors and emulators were not always so strict, but a certain sobriety was the general rule. On the other hand, wine was much in evidence in the palace; the king drank it from a goblet or gilded bowl, the wine being poured for him out of a flask or a slim ewer by a dwarf or a female 'Iranian'.

When his meal was over, he retired to his bedroom to take a siesta, stretching out on a mat strewn with cushions. Following his siesta, he granted an audience to his inspectors, gave them instructions and supervised the new deposits of gold being handled by the Treasury department. Then he presided over a further council of ministers and received the reports of his inquiry agents.

From then on, he was free to amuse himself as he wished. He practised archery with his nobles, or played dice with his chaplain, composed a painting, accompanied himself on the *vīṇā*, or listened to his bards while they recited the legendary epics and high adventures of his ancestors; or he might while away the time by teaching his parrots to talk, inspecting his gardens and aviaries or watching a fight between cocks, quails or pigeons. After the afternoon's fierce heat had given way to a slightly cooler temperature, he made his way to the palace's outer courtyard to visit his elephants, horses and war-chariots, and to review his men at arms.

As soon as the sun had gone down, he celebrated the evening rite. Then he saw his secret agents yet again. After this, he took a bath, usually with his wives, and ate dinner, to a musical accompaniment, with a few courtesans or favourite female companions, either in the palace or in the harem. The evening was spent agreeably in gossiping or playing games, or in listening to the orchestra and enjoying the dances. Later in the evening, he installed himself on a terrace, surrounded by his adoring women, to gaze at the stars.

Late at night, he finally returned to his own apartments, where his personal orchestra awaited him. After completing his nocturnal toilet, he lay down to sleep, so that he would be ready, only a few hours later, to start his daily routine over again. This routine might, however, be broken by any special occasion requiring his presence, such as a festival. Also, Indian kings enjoyed acting as host to foreign travellers, distinguished visitors and eminent religious personalities, and liked to talk with such guests at leisure.

In addition, the regular disposal of his time might well be disrupted by the unexpected arrival of one of his spies. In such an event, affairs of State took precedence over pleasure, and the king's day became even more heavily burdened than usual. But, on other occasions, he was able to escape temporarily from his duties and, with his ministers' consent, indulge in his favourite sport, hunting.[106] Then he went off on horseback, clad in a suitable hunting costume to protect his body, and followed by a few courtiers. Beaters armed with nets and traps, together with a pack of hunting-dogs, had the task of encircling the game, usually lion or wild boar, sometimes deer, but never peacocks or elephants.[107] The king attacked the wild game with bow and arrow, javelin, boar-spear or dagger, according to their species and his distance from them. He returned to his palace at the end of the day, healthily weary but prepared to resume his daily round of responsibilities in a few hours' time.

CHAPTER THREE

THE PUBLIC LIFE OF THE KING: IMPERIAL POMP

CONSECRATION

In whatever manner the new claimant to the throne might have acquired the right to rule, his investiture was invariably preceded by an act of consecration, this being an essential prelude to his existence as a sovereign. The ideal age at which the future monarch received consecration was twenty-four or twenty-five, that is to say eight or nine years after he had proved himself on his first field of battle and had started a career as viceroy or provincial governor. Normally, he would already have been married several years.

The choice of the date for the ceremony was left to the astrologers, whose calculations had to provide for a margin of about twelve days so that the preliminary rituals should be conducted during a propitious period. The council of ministers fixed all the details, following the instructions left by the preceding king, and laid down the rules of etiquette to be followed during the course of the succeeding ceremonials. At the same time, the citizens made their own preparations for this solemn occasion, putting up decorations throughout the capital, assembling the gifts which would later be carried to the palace, and going into debt, if necessary, so as to be suitably clothed and adorned for the event.

The kingdom's best architects erected a special pavilion for the royal consecration in one of the palace's outermost public courtyards. This pavilion consisted of a platform with an altar protected by a roof stretched between four corner pillars, and surpassed in splendour all the other buildings in the palace. In one part of the pavilion, the sacred fire burned near the spot where the royal treasure had been piled, a treasure consisting of the entire reserves of gold and other precious metals, jewels, golden vessels, regalias and the most valuable items from the royal armoury. In another part of the pavilion were heaped the offerings of the populace – plants of every kind, garlands, roast grain, milk and ghee, and new articles of clothing. The war-chariot was drawn up close by.

During the year preceding the consecration, the royal chaplain had made a series of offerings to the seasonal deities; now, twelve days before the initial ceremony, he started on a round of visits pertaining to State etiquette, during which he was closeted successively with the commander-in-chief of the armies, the crown prince, the queen, the governor of the capital, the chief administrator, the chancellor, the royal charioteer, the head artist, the court's superintendent of gaming and hunting, the minister of communications and, finally, one 'queen' symbolizing the entire harem. These visits, conducted in an atmosphere of appropriate protocol, probably had a ritual significance, associating the high dignitaries of State in advance with the activities which the new sovereign, with the considered approval of the brāhmaṇs, was about to undertake. In return for this ritual function, the chaplain received substantial gifts in the shape of oxen and cows, together with a bow, a leather-covered quiver and a red turban.

It was the chaplain's duty, also, to make a blend of sacred waters which would compose the lustral water to be used in the royal consecration: to accomplish this, he filled a wooden vase (made of *Ficus glomerata*) with water taken from the Ganges and all India's other sacred rivers, the ocean, springs, pools and wells. To this mixture he added honey and ghee and the genital fluid of a calving cow.

Shortly before the appointed day, the preparations were hurried forward. The city's and the palace's main gateways were decorated with fragrant garlands, and floral arches were erected. Banners and standards were hoisted on rooftops, along streets and over crossroads, on the terraces of houses, over temples, shrines, public buildings, shops and even from trees. Lengths of linen and silk, pearls and precious stones were hung from balconies and house frontages. Sweepers cleaned and sprinkled the royal road. Heaps of sandalwood and aloes were positioned at intervals along the route, to be ignited when the moment came so that their aromatic smouldering should perfume the air. Torches 'as great as trees' reared up along each side of the main avenues.

On the eve of the ceremony, the courtiers, in all their finery, surrounded the future king throughout the day, keeping a careful and respectful watch over him to ward off any evil influence. The royal chaplain paid him a visit in great pomp and style; the prince went out to meet the brāhmaṇ, as soon as his arrival was announced, as a mark of deference to his spiritual counsellor, who advised him officially to fast and abstain from pleasure during the coming night, then retired. The future king bathed before going to the temple, where he made an offering in the sacred fire and stayed for a few hours, lying on a bed composed of specially blessed grasses; on returning to his apartments, he gave his final orders for the conduct of the ceremony.

Long before daybreak, by the light of lamps and flares, the final touches were made to the public preparations: the avenues were swept one last time and sprinkled with sandalwood-perfumed water,[1] the piles of aromatic wood were lit, and the royal road was strewn with flowers. The populace invaded the streets:

> From the tumultuous waves of this joyous throng which fills the royal highway there rises a confused murmur like the noise of the sea. The inhabitants, including women and children, anticipate the royal consecration by watching for daybreak. All are eager to contemplate this great celebration which will make the populace rejoice and fill it with joy.[2]

Balconies, windows and gables were thronged with people awaiting the solemn hour.

Meanwhile, palace officials were setting up in the consecration pavilion the throne upon which the new king would shortly receive his investiture. This throne, made of fig-wood, was only provisional, since the dynastic throne was never moved from the hall where royal audiences were held. The vase containing the lustral water was placed close to the consecrational throne, as were all the objects due to be used during the course of the ceremony: a filter through which the lustral water would be passed, a whole tiger-skin on which the king would sit, four wooden vases in which equal shares of the water would be poured, a wooden sword, a bow and three arrows, a black antelope's horn, a branch cut from a fig-tree, and a large heap of dice; also, the garments that the king would put on, and bowls containing different offerings. The pavilion's periphery was decorated with golden vases filled with bouquets of blue lotus flowers. Further off, the gifts made for the occasion were piled high. Near the pavilion, the mahout had charge of the State elephant which was adorned with its most beautiful trappings, while a servant stood facing him, holding a white bull with gilded horns, a golden collar round its neck and bedecked with garlands.

The young palace retainers, armed with javelins and bows, waited in the adjacent courtyards. The ancient guardian of the harem, festooned with insignia, stood by its entrance door, while the musicians and female dancers assembled not far from the palace's eastern gateway. While the prince, clothed in brand-new linen, accomplished his matutinal religious duties, the brāhmaṇs were greeted respectfully at the gates of the town and conducted to the various shrines. The valorous warriors who had fought for the old king entered the palace's main quadrangle, robed in red, armed with long swords in scabbards made of precious metals and bows strung with red bowstrings.

Now that his ritual ablutions were completed and the sun had risen, the prince put on a sumptuous costume and seated himself on a gilded couch to await his chariot; when this arrived he took his place in it, flanked by two officials carrying the royal white parasol and the royal flywhisk respectively. The royal suite moved off, followed by the State elephant and the ladies of the harem; the procession made its way to the eastern gate of the capital, went out through it, then wheeled around so as to make a triumphal re-entry into town. Within the walls, a group of dignitaries which had been waiting to greet him saluted him respectfully and offered him their own good wishes and the congratulations of the populace which they represented collectively. The procession, headed by the orchestra, moved off in the direction of the palace. The chariot was surrounded by the brāhmaṇs and ministers, and followed by the municipal dignitaries; after these came men carrying insignia and trophies, and maidens with baskets of flowers and pastries. As the royal retinue proceeded up the avenue it was welcomed with loud cheers and blessings, prayers and choruses of praise. Women leaned out of windows, waving and applauding, while those lining the avenue strewed roasted grain, pieces of gold and flowers in front of the royal chariot.

Once inside the consecration pavilion, the prince was divested of his finery and dressed in the white garment of initiation in which he would participate in the ceremonial of making offerings and the rites preceding aspersion and enthronement.[3] The officiating priest made various offerings and poured the lustral water into the four special wooden vases, after which the future king took a ritual bath. Then the priest presented to him the bow and three arrows which symbolized victory in all four primary directions;[4] after this, the prince turned to face each cardinal point in succession, thus taking possession symbolically of the world and the cycle of the seasons, and so becoming regent of the entire year.

According to varying tradition, the enthronement might precede or follow the consecration with holy water. The throne was placed on the tiger-skin, facing east, and the king seated himself on it. Then the rite of lustration began, to the sound of music played by the royal orchestra: the brāhmaṇs, dignitaries, representatives of the people and the officiating priest (who was also the royal chaplain) filed past him, one by one, and sprinkled the king with water from a fig-wood cup or a conch-shell.[5] The priest used the black antelope's hollow horn to moisten carefully the king's whole body with the lustral water, and now he was finally and completely consecrated. With his dignitaries grouped around him, the new king was presented to the onlookers by the priest who had conducted the ritual.

But the ceremony was by no means over yet. During Vedic times, the king then climbed into his chariot, boar-skin sandals on his feet, and charged a herd of a hundred cows which he thus 'won'.[6] After this 'victory' he sat on the tiger-skin and played dice with his chaplain – a game whose ritual significance made it essential that he should win, in which royal feat he was aided by a little subtle chicanery.[7] Further rites succeeded these,[8] and new offerings were made by the officiating priest, of lotus, rice, cakes, ghee, roasted grain and milk. For their services in this most solemn of all ceremonies, the officiating priest and his assistants were awarded honorariums consisting of cows or pieces of gold supplemented by the gifts in kind which they had received during the year and on the day itself.

While the city echoed with the noise of popular celebration, the king, seated on a priceless ivory throne, allowed himself to be dressed and adorned once more. In his sumptuous attire, surrounded by his dignitaries and accompanied by his regalia-bearers, he walked to the throne-room and sat for the first time on the dynastic throne; this was a finely worked, gilded seat, upholstered with costly fabric, and featuring on its back a design incorporating animals, the symbolism of which was doubtless cosmological and affirmed the universal nature of the sovereigns who took their place on it.[9]

Mounted on his State elephant, preceded by the orchestra and followed by a long train of horsemen and people on foot, he now left the palace, progressed down the royal road, turned into the wide avenues that ringed the town, and circled his capital, imitating the path taken by the sun, in a solemn ceremony which symbolized his taking possession.

Once back in the palace, the king used, for the first time, his new golden seal, by stamping the first proclamation of his rule – an order liberating all prisoners, including those condemned to death. He also decreed that all draught animals should be unharnessed, all cages opened, and cows should not be milked on that day so that they might suckle their calves. During the ensuing fortnight, ritual ceremonies and festivities succeeded each other. For a whole year, the king refrained from shaving or having his hair cut, so that the hair might retain the vigour with which the lustral water had endowed it.

This was, at least theoretically, the procedure heralding each new reign.

ROYAL PROCESSIONS AND PILGRIMAGES

At regular intervals, the king participated in festivals and pilgrimages, appearing usually in great pomp and with an impressive retinue, a circumstance evoked frequently in literary descriptions and artistic depictions. The full resources of Eastern splendour were displayed in the dazzling spectacles provided by these royal processions that sparkled with colour as they made their stately way along streets and highways.

Preceded by his orchestra, with its bellowing conches and reverberating gongs, cymbals and drums, the king emerged from his palace, either on horseback or astride his elephant, the royal parasol held above his head. His close attendants and serving-maids clustered around his mount, including the young women carrying the royal sword, the sandals and the flywhisk. Gilded flag-staffs, flying gay-coloured bunting, waved in the breeze above their heads. A group of nobles on horseback, and a mass of followers on foot, composed the bulk of the train.

It was in such style that the king sallied forth to visit some brāhmaṇ reputed for his wisdom, a shrine, a monastery or a holy spot. For certain festivals, his wives accompanied him.

Centres of pilgrimage usually contained some source of sacred water (*tīrtha*) and attracted enormous crowds, as they still do today. The king, too, visited these holy places; their sacred character was of tremendous importance in Indian eyes,[10] and a pilgrimage could result in 'indulgences' and remission of faults, and even allow the pilgrim to leave confident of being hallowed for the rest of his days. Buddhists, Jains and Hindus all shared this same concept, and the custom, which has become more and more solidly established with the evolution of Indian thought, was already a most powerful force in ancient India.[11]

WAR AND VICTORY

The aim of a king in ancient India was not only to keep his territory intact but also to extend it by conquests, so that he might achieve the status of universal sovereign (*cakravartin*) by ruling over 'the whole earth'. Since the Indian king was a member of the *kṣatriya* caste and therefore a warrior by definition, he had of necessity to devote himself to the study of warfare, though it appears from the political treatises of the time that he resorted to war only after having exhausted the resources of diplomacy.[12]

Once he had ascended the throne, the king was expected to undertake a military expedition (*digvijaya*) which was, theoretically, a tour of his kingdom, progressing in the solar direction and during which he satisfied himself as to the loyalty of the vassals in the territories bordering his own. These vassals retained their own customs and even their own autonomous government, but were bound to render tribute and aid to the king.

The sovereign whose possessions were so extensive that he was competent to claim the envied title of 'great king of kings' (*mahārājādhirāja*) had his eldest son accomplish a rite which was both symbolic and martial, the sacrifice of a horse (*aśvamedha*). This rite, of Vedic origin, was later revived by the Gupta dynasty, and is described in the final section of this chapter.

Military campaigns were launched only after seasonal conditions had been taken into consideration, December being the preferred month when long marches were envisaged, or March and April if the target was nearby.

The army was composed traditionally of four divisions: war-chariots, elephants, cavalry and infantry. As we have already mentioned, war-chariots became obsolete during the seventh century AD, and perhaps even earlier, chiefly because their great weight made them difficult to manoeuvre and they were easily bogged down; but, up to that time, they provided the essential symbol of the king's participation in battle, the corps commander's chariot sporting a standard to which all the others rallied. These war-chariots performed both offensive and defensive functions, and were in the charge of an élite whose defeat entailed the certain defeat of the whole of the rest of the army. Each chariot was in charge of a driver and carried an archer accompanied by two subalterns. The driver, who sat on the shaft itself, had a perilous task, being exposed to the enemy's arrows without means of defence; he had also to be skilful enough to coax his horses and chariot into the twists and turns demanded by the developing battle strategy.

The war elephants were caparisoned in an armour consisting of metal plates;[13] they each carried three archers in addition to their mahout, and were sometimes guarded by three horsemen. The corps of elephants formed the advance unit of the army, forcing a passage, trampling down obstacles, and protecting the army's flanks by showing an unbroken front to enemy attacks. The cavalry was the army's most easily manoeuvrable element and was used for reconnaissance, surprise attacks, the pursuit of fleeing troops and the capturing of enemy reserves. The horses, like the elephants, were each known by their own name. It was customary to dope them before battle by giving them a draught of wine; the soldiers riding them were armed with a lance (or perhaps two lances)[14] or with a sword, or sometimes with a bow, and wore protective breast-plates. The foot-soldiers were armed with bow and quiver, sword and shield, and sometimes a spear or dagger: apart from their main task of fighting in open terrain and entrenchments, they were also responsible for setting up camp, and provided guards for the royal treasury, the arsenal and the military storehouses.

The army was followed by a long train of supply wagons, drawn by humped oxen, loaded with provisions of water, rations, medicaments and forage for both men and beasts, reserves of arms, spare parts and tools for repairing chariots, extra pieces of armour and shields, and so on. The baggage train was accompanied by a large assortment of civilians, including artisans, workmen, experts in digging trenches and constructing earthworks, carpenters, smiths, engineers, as well as surgeons and nurses. These were joined by the royal chaplain, astrologers, functionaries, courtiers and even some members of the royal harem. The progress of the army and its train was usually interrupted by fairly lengthy halts during which 'the soldiers drank juice distilled from the coco-palm, out of cups made from betel leaves, under awnings constructed by themselves',[15] and set out on 'joyous bathing expeditions to the river'.[16] But there were times, too, when forced marches had to be undertaken. Camp was mounted each evening, with look-outs and sentinels on duty.

Military tactics followed cast-iron rules. These laid down that an entrenched camp should be set up close to the fortress to be captured, which should then be besieged for a period of time long enough to force the beleaguered garrison to break out and give battle in open country. The camp was constructed like a town, on a quadrangular pattern with ditches, ramparts, and sentinels posted at all four gates; entrance was granted only to those people furnished with safe-conducts. Each of the four army corps occupied separate quarters, while the king occupied a site in the centre of the camp, in a state of constant preparedness, his arms by his side.

Battle was engaged only when the omens were favourable.[17] The day fixed for the clash was usually preceded by a week of prayers in which the king participated. On the eve of battle, he harangued the troops, drawn up in formation before him, then offered them a banquet. He slept that night in his chariot, his arms close by, and awoke before dawn to prepare himself; his chaplain helped him on with his breast-plate, while reciting hymns[18] designed to ensure him the protection of the gods. At daybreak, the army deployed in a theoretically immutable order, the royal standard (blessed with lustral water kept from the king's consecration) displayed in the van, followed immediately by the massive line of elephants plodding forward close together, providing cover for the infantry behind them. The front line of foot-soldiers consisted of archers, and the second of swordsmen, and they were themselves covered by a column of foot-soldiers at each side. Chariots were massed on each flank, with the cavalry immediately behind them. The king himself rode in the centre of the rearguard, and consequently the enemy's favourite tactics consisted in the execution of a pincer movement with the object of capturing him while avoiding the dangers of a frontal assault. The charge was sounded by conches, gongs and war-drums, a thick cloud of dust was raised by the chariot-wheels and horses' hooves, and the ground thundered with the noise of advancing elephants and infantry. War-cries were shouted by the milling throng, cries consisting of the name of their own leader, yelled at the top of their voice, the only way to distinguish their enemies from their own comrades. The dust-stained standards[19] fluttered above the heads of the soldiers, or fell to earth, pierced by arrows. Fighting stopped, by common consent, at nightfall and was resumed at daybreak, while during the entire engagement surgeons and nurses went among the wounded, giving aid, bandaging them or carrying them off towards their respective camps. Veterinarians cared for the elephants and horses. And meanwhile, batmen gathered up the used arrows from the field of battle, noticed the name of the particular owner stamped on them and, after dividing them into groups, straightened them or mended them according to need.

After the battle, the corpses were heaped on a series of funeral pyres, one for each caste among the slain, while vultures wheeled overhead and jackals prowled around, attracted by the smell of spilled blood. The close relatives and wives of the dead were authorized to assist in the cremation of their lost ones. In southern India, a stone was raised to commemorate their glorious end.

The victorious king's first concern was to recite a hymn of thanksgiving, to offer a divine service and to distribute offerings to the brāhmaṇs. He then supervised the distribution of booty, which included the defeated enemy's women: he usually took possession of his opponent's treasury and animals, reserving for his personal use one-sixth of the total. After this, he made the rounds of the wounded of both armies, offering them comfort, and also gave orders for the court martial of those soldiers accused of contravening the rules of war.[20] Finally, he made preparations for his entry into the surrendered fortress and, after marching in, restored the vanquished king to his throne on the condition that the latter declared himself his vassal. The fate of the prisoners was a matter for negotiation, but usually entailed their being deported for a limited period of time or being placed in slavery for one year in the service of the conqueror.

The king's return into his own capital was triumphal, and he was acclaimed enthusiastically and respectfully along the entire route. The city decorated itself in his honour, erecting floral arches and hoisting flags; when he made his glorious entry, all the women, young and old alike, threw grains of roasted barley under his feet. The entire kingdom celebrated the victory in a series of festivities which reflected the people's joy in their ruler's success. The king's comrades in arms were suitably honoured in their respective communities, and, once the initial glow of triumph had died down, these warriors doubtless waited impatiently for a new campaign which might further enhance their glory.

SOLEMN AND IMPERIAL RITES

The horse sacrifice called *aśvamedha*[21] added the final element to the king's consecration by conferring universal sovereignty upon him. This ritual went back to Vedic times and may even have been of Indo-Iranian origin; it was practised chiefly by the Śuṅga king Puṣyamitra (*c.* 176 BC) and by the Gupta emperors Samudragupta (*c.* AD 335–75), Kumāragupta (*c.* 414–55) and Ādityasenagupta (latter half of seventh century), the last recorded instance of its performance being in Orissā during the ninth century.[22]

This costly and onerous sacrifice, which spanned three days, constituted a royal and popular festival designed to secure prosperity for the kingdom and the entire population, and its preparation was spread over a period of one or even two years. It took place in February or March and rites to bring it to a final close took a further year.

The horse selected for this solemn sacrifice had to possess certain characteristics, apart from being a speedy and valuable charger. After a series of rites and offerings, the chosen horse was sprinkled with water from a pool, then let loose among a hundred geldings, being encouraged by those participating in the rite to gallop in a north-easterly direction. A squad of young *kṣatriyas*, including the crown prince, escorted the horse, their mission being to protect it, to prevent it from coupling with any mare, and to follow it during the whole year of its wanderings. The territories it traversed were considered as having been conquered by the king offering the sacrifice, and the youthful escort had sometimes to take up arms to ensure that the horse might go wherever it pleased. During this entire period, a daily ceremony took place at the palace, accompanied by anthems, music and offerings.

The horse invariably returned, eventually, to its point of departure, as a result of the assiduous attentions of its bodyguards, and then the preparations for the sacrifice were put in hand. A huge expanse of ground was cleared, levelled, swept and sprinkled with water, and on this flat surface was erected an altar, built with bricks and strewn with grass, together with sheds for the priests and the sacred chariots. To the east of the altar, twenty-one sacrificial stakes (*yūpas*) were put up and an equal number of animals were sacrificed to the god of fire, Agni. For three consecutive days an unending series of offerings was made to the sacred fire, during the course of which the officiating priest poured into it ghee, barley-meal and roasted grains of rice and barley.

The chosen horse was immolated on the second day. First, a number of mares were paraded before it, to make it whinny, the whinnying being regarded as the voice of the priest uplifted in song, identified with it ritualistically. Then it was harnessed, with three other horses, to the royal war-chariot, a chariot encrusted with gold ornamentation and carrying the king's white standard. To the sound of drums, the king, richly dressed and adorned and accompanied by his chief cantor (*adhvaryu*), climbed in; together, they drove to the sacred pool which lay to the east of the area appointed for the sacrifice. On their return, the queen and two other senior wives adorned the horse's mane and tail while chanting sacred phrases. Then the animals singled out for sacrifice were tied to the stakes and their throats cut (in one recorded instance, six hundred and nine victims, including twenty at the principal stake), except for the chosen horse which was untied, led to the northern edge of the sacrificial area and smothered, while a number of wild animals were released from captivity.

The king's wives were led to the scene of the holocaust, and up to the dead horse which they circled three times in each direction, murmuring ritual phrases of love to the carcass and fanning it with the skirts of their garments. The queen then lay down by the horse's side, while the priests and the king's other wives exchanged obscene remarks which formed part of the ritual, and the king and officiating priest engaged in a contest of asking and answering riddles. Finally the sacrificial victims were dismembered, the horse with a gold-inlaid knife, the other animals with copper or iron knives, and the horse's blood was offered in a thrice-repeated oblation at the sacrificial fire.

A mass of priests, nobles, dignitaries and guild chiefs took part in this impressive ceremony, which was attended also by the common people. The magnificence of this imperial sacrifice must have been awesome, with the endless series of offerings continuing late into the night, the dancing lights of the sacred fires and torches, the smell of roasting flesh and of spilled blood, the whispering of the priests, the ritual chants. . . .

The third day was consecrated to a solemn offering of *soma*, the sacred liquid, and was prolonged by a night vigil during which music was played and ritual recitations intoned. On the fourth day, all the participants purified themselves by bathing communally. Twenty-one sterile cows were sacrificed on this day, the brāhmaṇs were given numerous gifts, as on the preceding days, and among other gifts the king presented them with four of his wives or else their female retainers.

The *aśvamedha*, with its bloody rites rooted in protohistoric times, was essentially a symbolic performance which associated the entire population with the king offering the sacrifice. It acted at the same time as 'a victory spell, a charm to preserve sovereignty, a fertility spell and the acting out of a solar cult'.[23] The horse, in fact, symbolized the *kṣatriya* caste, and was offered to *Prajāpati*, the 'Lord of Beings' and 'Primeval Man', of whom it was the microcosmic representation.[24] Its course through the kingdom and beyond its frontiers, imitating that of the sun, conferred solemnly upon the king his character of regent of the year's span.

And the fertility rites which were a feature of the ceremonies were certainly intended to assure prosperity to the kingdom.

The reigning king reserved this triumphal consecration of his universal power for the end of his reign, and associated his eldest son closely with the proceedings, so that he might not only enthrone the latter but also transmit to him the glory that he had himself acquired. This was the apotheosis which heralded the close of an Indian emperor's public life, although, in addition he was sometimes prepared to renounce his royal pomp altogether and end his days in the serene peace of some pious retreat.

CONCLUSION

At the end of this survey of Indian life in ancient times, we must inevitably ask ourselves one question: to what extent can we accept this portrait of a civilization steeped in formalism, excessively attached to ritualism, veering between the gentleness and poetic charm of refined customs and manners and the cruelty of certain institutions imposed in the name of ritual?

It seems impossible to give a complete answer to this question, because we must remember that our research has to be conducted without benefit of factual reports covering particular circumstances. In fact, the surviving documentation of the age, although plentiful, never concerns itself with precise individuals, geographically located towns or identifiable palaces; these records invariably confine themselves to generalities, describing a desirable standard rather than the actual state of affairs, and never mentioning a single individual feature or outstanding point of interest. Sculpture and painting have transmitted to us only idealized portraits; chronicles and epigraphs consist invariably of grandiloquent panegyrics. And most of the evidence has long since disappeared: the luxurious private homes, all built from perishable materials, the even more ephemeral hovels of the poor, the sumptuous but impermanent military camps can be re-created only through the literature and art of the period. Nevertheless, the monasteries and shrines hollowed out of cliffs remain as living proofs of the reality and, indeed, perfection of India's architecture in ancient times, though it should be noted that none of these surviving man-made caves corresponds exactly to descriptive texts of the age. And though the Nālandā monasteries are an exception to this rule, we must remember that the meticulous description of them was made, not by an Indian author, but by a Chinese pilgrim.

Paradoxically, despite the fact that the 'name' (*nāma*) had a primordial importance in Indian life, being a ritually generative force, the entire field of Indian writing, with a very few exceptions, is anonymous; even when one knows the name of an author, one is not always sure of the epoch in which he lived and it is impossible to glean anything of his own personality. The individualistic philosophy of brāhmaṇic India, too, appeared to be in conflict with a fact of Indian life, which is peculiarly difficult for our Western mentality to comprehend – the fact that a great mass of humanity was distinguished solely by caste, lineage and clan.

In this maze of entirely theoretical descriptions, how are we to apprehend the reality of a living, suffering humanity? Our lack of resources on a formal level, which obliges us to rely on archaeological discovery, is supplemented by our difficulty on the psychological level where we are able to proceed only by deduction. Still, even though it may be beyond our power to correlate certain figures with historical fact or to discover whether or not the characters described in literary works existed beyond their legendary or fictional reality, the fact remains that the human essence of India shines through the great mass of stories, treatises and philosophical texts which her ancient civilization has handed down to us. Even the constantly reiterated preoccupation with the problem of defining an ideal norm and of integrating the whole of society into this theoretical structure symbolizes one of the most typical traits of the Indian mentality: a need for stability and established order, a framework which will perhaps simplify, and at least define, man's relationship with the cosmos and with his fellow-humans.

It is not our task in this work to pass judgment on the validity or the consequences of this attitude. We are concerned simply to make intelligible the need felt by the Indian people to conform to precise rules, a need that has become atavistic. These rules, established by lawgivers as well as by sages and thinkers, were based on a most careful observation of human nature and were unquestionably effective in calming the disquiet of the individual confronting the unknown or the inexplicable. A modern rationalistic mind may perhaps find it difficult to comprehend why so strict a spiritual regime was accepted, in the main, with such docility; but it must be remembered that the Indian does not share Western attitudes towards adversity. His innate fatalism tempers his reactions and, above all, his deep religious faith allows him to endure tranquilly the most tragic deprivation, especially when such misfortune is represented as being an ineluctable aspect of ritual and sacred concepts. A further important factor throughout the ages has been the Indian's faculty for renunciation, which has always expressed itself in every class of society as the final aim of a well-ordered life.

Even so, the very insistence with which the moralists stigmatized vices or mere defects of character and bad habits proves that, despite interdictions, punishments and harsh regulations, virtue did not always flourish in Indian society. Manu's lengthy enumeration, in his legal code, of delinquencies and their appropriate punishment shows well enough that contraventions must have been frequent. And it is easy to discover frequent contradictions between orthodox principles and common practice: for instance, a vegetarian diet was strictly laid down, yet hunters and fishermen continued to exercise their daily death-dealing profession; and a passion for gambling pervaded all classes despite the fact that it was strongly condemned by the law. In the social sphere, the prohibitions concerning marriages between members of different castes were so often ignored that a 'mixed' caste had eventually to be officially recognized. All this goes to show that a whole number of individual reactions were constantly at work behind the formalism advocated by priests and jurists.

If we study the lively anecdotes which abound in popular literature of the time we can derive a broader and lustier image of Indian society. A brāhmaṇ, for example, is deceived by his young wife, who persuades him through trickery to allow himself to be blindfolded and then promptly profits from his temporary lack of vision to take a lover. Or a woman incites her husband, who is too amorous to resist any suggestion of hers, to steal for her so that she may acquire a sari similar to those worn by ladies at court. Or inhabitants of neighbouring villages get involved in a quarrel which starts with mutual insults and scuffles, progresses through increasingly violent stages of threats and maledictions and finishes up with a pitched battle at the end of which most of the antagonists are maimed or injured. These are all just folk tales, of course, but there is no doubt that the characters involved were drawn from life.

But it would be unwise to regard such anecdotes as reflecting the psychology of ancient India more faithfully than the serious treatises and texts: there seems no reason to doubt that both visions of life are equally accurate and, indeed, complementary.

We need no further proof than the degree to which the present-day existence of orthodox families conforms to the rules established so many centuries ago. In a world in transformation, India is performing the dual feat today of exercising an increasing influence in world affairs despite innumerable difficulties and, at the same time, upholding the example of a living tradition expressing the spiritual yearnings of its people. Those who arise now to speak on India's behalf are not anonymous, as they once were; but, just as in olden days, they reflect the unique quality of their race and prolong effectively the lineage of those who, for millenniums, have never ceased to nourish and pass on to future generations the refinement, the brilliance, the sensitiveness of an incomparable civilization.

BIBLIOGRAPHY

Abbreviations Used

A.S.I.: *Archaeological Survey of India*, Delhi.
A.S.I.A.R.: *Archaeological Survey of India, Annual Reports.*
J.I.S.O.A.: *Journal of the Indian Society of Oriental Art*, Calcutta.
S.B.E.: *Sacred Books of the East*, Oxford.

Sanskrit And Pāli Texts In Translation

Artha-śāstra of Kauṭilya: rev. and ed. by Dr R. Shama Sastry, Mysore, 1929.

Atharva-veda saṁhita: tr. W. D. Whitney, *Harvard Oriental Series*, VII and VIII. Cambridge, Mass., 1905.

Bhagavad-gītā: tr. F. Edgerton, 2 vols. Cambridge, Mass., 1952.

Buddha-carita of Aśvaghoṣa: ed. and tr. E. B. Cowell, S.B.E., XLIX, 1894.

Bṛhat-saṃhitā of Varāhamihira: ed. and tr. M. S. Dvivedi. Banāras, 1895–7.

Culla-vagga: ed. F. Max Müller. S.B.E., XVII and XX, 1882, 1885.

Dīgha-nikāya: 'Dialogues of the Buddha', tr. from the Pāli by T. W. and C. A. F. Rhys Davids. 3 vols. London, 1899–1921.

Gṛhya-sūtra: The Grihya-sûtras, tr. H. Oldenburg and F. Max Müller. S.B.E., XXIX and XXX, 1886, 1892.

Hari-vaṃsá (suppl. to *Mahā-bhārata*): tr. into French by M. A. Langlois. 2 vols. London, 1834–5.

Harṣa-carita of Bāṇa: tr. E. B. Cowell and F. W. Thomas. Cambridge, 1897.

Jātaka: The Jātaka or Stories of the Buddha's former births, ed. E. B. Cowell with a commentary, and tr. 'by various hands'. 6 vols. Cambridge, 1895–1907.

Kādambarī of Bāṇa and Bhūṣaṇbhaṭṭa: tr. (abridged) C. M. Ridding. Royal Asiatic Society. London, 1896.

Kāma-sūtra of Vātsyāyana: tr. S. C. Upadhyaya. London, 1962.

Mahā-bhārata: The Mahabharata, tr. P. Roy. 10 vols. Calcutta, 1884–1896. *Mahābhārata* (selections) tr. C. Arnold. London, 1920.

Mahā-vagga: tr. from the Pāli by T. W. Rhys Davids and H. Oldenberg. S.B.E., XIII and XVII, 1881, 1882.

Mahā-vaṃsa of Mahānāma: tr. from the Pāli by W. Geiger. London, 1958 (reprint).

Maha-vastu. Mahâvastou, tr. into French by E. Senart. 3 vols. Paris, 1882.

Manu-smṛti (*Mānava-dharma-śāstra*): *The Laws of Manu*, tr. G. Bühler. S.B.E., XXV, 1886.
Milinda-pañhā: 'The Questions of King Milinda', tr. from the Pāli with intro. by T. W. Rhys Davids. S.B.E., XXV and XXVI, 2 vols., 1890–4.
Mṛcchakaṭika of Sūdraka: 'The Little Clay Cart, attributed to King Shūdraka', tr. A. W. Ryder. Cambridge, Mass., 1905.
Raghu-vaṃśa of Kālidāsa: *Raghu Vamsha*, tr. Sir Wm. Jones. Calcutta, 1901.
Rāmāyaṇa of Vālmīki: *The Rámáyan of Vâlmîki*, tr. T. H. Griffith. 5 vols. London, 1870–4.
Śakuntalā of Kālidāsa: ed. and tr. R. Pischel. London, 1877.
Viṣṇu-dharmottara: 'A Treatise on Indian Painting and Image-making' (Part III, a selection), tr. Stella Kramrisch. Calcutta, 1928.

Collections and Anthologies

Corpus Inscriptionum Indicarum: Inscriptions vol. I, ed. E. Hultzsch (*Aśoka*), London, 1925; vol. II, ed. S. Konow (*Kharoṣṭhī*), London, 1929; vol. III, ed. J. F. Fleet (*Early Gupta Kings*), London, 1888.
Epigraphia Indica: various editors (publ. as supplement to *Indian Antiquary* by Government of India). 27 vols. Calcutta and Delhī, 1892– (in progress).
Harvard Oriental Series: various editors and translators. Cambridge, Mass., 1895– (in progress).
Sacred Books of the East: publ. under the direction of F. Max Müller. 50 vols. Oxford, 1879–1900.
Renou, Louis. *Anthologie sanskrite*. Paris, 1947.

History and Civilization

Altekar, A. S. *State and Government in Ancient India*. Banāras, 1949.
Auboyer, J. 'L'Asie orientale', in *Histoire générale des civilisations* (dir. M. Crouzet): I, pp. 537–636, Paris, 1953; II, pp. 603–700, Paris, 1954; III, pp. 54–71, Paris, 1955.
Basham, A. L. *The Wonder that was India* (a survey of the culture of the Indian sub-continent before the coming of the Muslims). London, 1954; New York, 1954 and 1959.
Beal, S. (tr.). *Si Yu Ki. Buddhist Records of the Western World.* 2 vols. London, 1883.
Foucher, Alfred. *The Life of the Buddha*, tr. from the French by S. B. Boas. Middletown, Conn., 1963.
Grousset, R. *Sur les traces du Bouddha*. Paris, 1949.

Hutton, J. H. *Caste in India.* Cambridge, 1946.
Lamotte, E. *Histoire du Bouddhisme indien des origines à l'ère śaka.* Vol. I. Louvain, 1958.
Lamotte, E. *The Spirit of Ancient Buddhism.* Venice, 1962.
McCrindle, J. W. (tr.). *Ancient India as described by Megasthenes and Arrian.* 6 vols. Calcutta, 1877–1901.
Majumdār, R. C. and Altekar, A. S. *The Vākātaka–Gupta Age* (*c.* A.D. 200–550). Lahore, 1946.
Mookerjī, R. K. *Chandragupta and his Time.* Delhi and Bombay, 1952.
Munshi, K. M. *The Age of Imperial Unity* (vol. II of *The History and Culture of the Indian People*). Bombay, 1951.
Naudou, J. 'L'Inde', in *Histoire Universelle*, Encyclopédie de la Pléiade, Vol. I, pp. 1411–1519. Paris, 1956.
Nikam, N. A. and McKeon, R. (ed. and tr.). *The Edicts of Aśoka.* Chicago, 1959.
Nīlakanti Sāstrī, K. A. *The Age of the Nandas and Mauryas.* Banāras, 1952.
Przyluski, J. (tr.). *La légende de l'empereur Açoka* (*Açoka-Avadāna*). Annales du Musée Guimet. XXXII. Paris, 1923.
Rapson, E. J. *Ancient India* (vol. I of *Cambridge History of India*). Cambridge, 1922–37.
Rawlinson, H. G. *Intercourse between India and the Western World, from the Earliest Times to the Fall of Rome.* Cambridge, 1926 (2nd ed.).
Raychaudhurī, H. *Political History of Ancient India.* Calcutta, 1953 (6th ed.).
Renou, L. and Filliozat, J. *Classical India*, tr. P. Spratt. 3 vols. issued. Calcutta, 1957– (in progress).
Takakusu, J. *A Record of the Buddhist Religion as practised in India and the Malay Archipelago, by I-tsing.* Oxford, 1896.
Warmington, E. H. *Commerce between the Roman Empire and India.* Cambridge, 1928.
Watters, T. *On Yuan Chwang's Travels in India.* 2 vols. London, 1904–5.

Daily Life

Āchārya, P. K. 'Villages and Towns in Ancient India', *Law Volume* II (1946), pp. 275–84.
Agrawala, V. S. *India as Known to Pānini.* Lucknow, 1953.
Auboyer, J. 'Les jeux et les jouets', no. VI in series *La Vie publique et privée dans l'Inde ancienne.* Musée Guimet, Paris, 1955.
Auboyer, J. 'La Vie privée dans l'Inde ancienne d'après les ivoires de

Begrâm', *Mémoires de la délégation française en Afghanistan*, pp. 61–82. Paris, 1939–40.
Chandra, M. 'Cosmetics and Coiffure in Ancient India', *J.I.S.O.A.*, VIII, 1940, pp. 62–145.
Chandra, M. 'The History of Indian Costume from the First Century A.D. to the Beginning of the Fourth Century', *J.I.S.O.A.*, VIII, 1940, pp. 185–224.
Codrington, K. de B. 'The Culture of Mediaeval India as illustrated by the Ajanta Frescoes', *Indian Antiquary*, LIX, August 1930, p. 159 seq.; Sept. 1930, p. 169 seq.
Dīkshitar, V. R. R. *War in Ancient India*. 2nd ed. Madras, 1948.
Ganguly, K. K. 'Early Indian Jewellery', *Indian Historical Quarterly*, XVIII, 1 (March 1942), p. 46 seq., and XVIII, 2 (June 1942), p. 110 seq.
Gode, P. K. 'The Indian Bullock-Cart: its prehistoric and Vedic ancestors', *The Poona Orientalist*, V (1940), pp. 144–51.
Gode, P. K. 'The Role of the Courtesan in the Early History of Indian Painting', *Ann. Bhandarkar Inst.*, 1946, pp. 288–302.
Gode, P. K. 'Carriage-Manufacture in the Vedic Period and in Ancient China in 1121 B.C.', *Ann. Bhandarkar Inst.*, 1946, pp. 288–302.
Gurner, C. W. 'The Fortress Policy in Kautilya's Arthasāstra', *Indian Culture*, VIII (1941–2), p. 251 seq.
Jain, J. C. *Life in Ancient India as depicted in the Jain Canons*. Bombay, 1947.
Law, B. C. *India as described in Early Texts of Buddhism and Jainism*. London, 1941.
Majumdār, G. P. Series of essays in *Indian Culture:* 'Man's Indebtedness to Plants: Dress and other personal Requisites in Ancient India' (I, 2, Oct. 1934, pp. 191–208). 'Toilet' (I, 4, April 1935, pp. 651–66). 'Furniture' (II, 1, July 1935, pp. 67–76; and II, 2, Oct. 1935, pp. 271–6 and 277–90). 'Health and Hygiene' (II, 4, April 1936, pp. 653–4). 'Hearth and Home' (III, 1, July 1936, pp. 71–88; and III, 3, Jan. 1937, pp. 431–54). 'Domestic Rites and Rituals' (III, 4, April 1937, pp. 605–12).
Majumdār, R. C. *Corporate Life in Ancient India*. Poona, 1922.
Meile, P. 'Les Yavanas dans l'Inde tamoule', *Journal Asiatique*, 1940–1, 1, pp. 85–125.
Mehta, J. *Sexual Life in Ancient India*. London, 1953.
Mookerjī, P. K. 'Social and Economic Data in Asokan Inscriptions', *Indian Culture*, XI, 1945–6, p. 141–4.
Mookerjī, P. K. *Ancient Indian Education, Brahmanical and Buddhist*. London, 1947.
Mukerjee, R. K. *The Culture and Art of India*. London, 1959.

Naik, A. V. 'Studies in Nāgārjunakonda Sculptures', *Bull. Deccan Col.*, II, 1941, pp. 50–118, 263–300.

Pūrī, B. N. 'Toilet and Treatment of Hair in the Kuṣāṇa Period', *Indian Culture*, XII, 1945–6, p. 166 seq.

Saletore, R. N. *Life in the Gupta Age*. Bombay, 1943.

Sarkār, S. C. *Some Aspects of the Earliest Social History of India*. London, 1928.

Sengupta, P. *Everyday Life in Ancient India*. Bombay, 1955.

Sivāramamurtī, C. 'Samskāras in Sculpture', *Arts asiatiques*, II, 1955, 1, pp. 3–17.

Sivāramamurtī, C. 'Sanskrit Literature and Art, Mirrors of Indian Culture'. *A.S.I. Memoirs*, 73. Calcutta, 1955.

Upadhyaya, B. S. *India in Kālidāsa*. Allahābād, 1947.

General

Auboyer, J. 'Le Trône et son symbolisme dans l'Inde ancienne', *Annales du Musée Guimet*, LV. Paris, 1949.

Auboyer, J. *Arts et styles de l'Inde* (coll. 'Arts, Styles et Techniques', Larousse). Paris, 1951.

Coomāraswāmī, A. K. *Yaksas*. 2 vols. Washington, D.C., 1928–31.

Dumont, P. E. *L'Asvamedha, Description du sacrifice solennel du cheval dans le culte védique*. Paris, Louvain, 1927.

Fergusson, J. *Tree and Serpent Worship*. London, 1873.

Henry, V. *La Magie dans l'Inde antique*. Paris, 1904.

Keith, A. B. *The Sanskrit Drama and its Origin, Development, Theory and Practice*. Oxford, 1924.

Levi, S. *Le Théâtre indien*. Paris, 1890.

Marcel-Dubois, C. *Les Instruments de musique dans l'Inde ancienne*. Paris, 1941.

Renou, L. 'La Maison védique', *Journal asiatique*, CCXXXI, Oct.-Dec. 1939, p. 481 seq.

Shastri, D. 'Altars, diagrams, etc., in the ritual of ancestor worship', *J.I.S.O.A.*, VIII, pp. 166–73.

Viennot, O. 'Le Culte de l'arbre, dans l'Inde ancienne', *Annales du Musée Guimet*, LIX. Paris, 1954.

Vogel, J. P. *Indian Serpent-lore or the Nāgas in the Hindu Legend and Art*. London, 1926.

Archaeology: The Arts

Āchārya, P. K. 'Hindu Architecture and Sculpture', *Indian Culture*, VIII, 1941–2, 2–3, pp. 175–82; 369–72.

Barrett, D. *Sculptures from Amarāvatī in the British Museum*. London, 1954.

Coomāraswāmī, A. K. *History of Indian and Indonesian Art*. London, 1927.

Coomāraswāmī, A. K. 'Indian Architectural Terms', *Journal of Oriental Asiatic Society*, XLVIII, 3, pp. 250–75.

Coomāraswāmī, A. K. 'Early Indian Architecture', *Eastern Art*, III, 1930–1.

Cunningham, Sir A. *The Stūpa of Bharhut*. London, 1879.

Dīkshit, K. N. 'Excavations at Paharpur, Bengal', *A.S.I. Memoirs*, 55. Delhi, 1938.

Foucher, A. and Marshall, Sir J. *The Monuments of Sānchī*. 3 vols. Calcutta, 1940.

Griffiths, J. *The Paintings of the Buddhist Cave Temples of Ajantā*. London, 1896–7.

Hackin, J. and R. 'Recherches archéologiques à Begrām', *Mémoires de la Délégation archéologique française en Afghanistan*, IX. Paris, 1939.

Hackin, J., Carl, J. and Hamelin, P. 'Nouvelles recherches archéologiques à Begrām (ancienne Kāpiçī), 1939–40' followed by comparative studies by J. Auboyer, V. Elisseeff, O. Kurz, P. Stern, *Mémoires de la Délégation archéologique française en Afghanistan*, XI. 2 vols. Paris, 1954.

Kramrisch, S. *The Art of India: traditions of Indian Sculpture, Painting and Architecture*. London, 1954.

Kramrisch, S. *The Hindu Temple*. 2 vols. Calcutta, 1946.

Longhurst, A. H. 'The Buddhist Antiquities of Nāgārjunakonda, Madras Presidency', *A.S.I. Memoirs*, 54. Delhi, 1938.

Marshall, Sir J. 'Excavations at Bhītā', *A.S.I.A.R.*, 1911–12, p. 32 seq.

Rāmachāndran, I. N. 'Buddhist Sculptures from a stūpa near Goli Village, Guntur district', *Bull. Madras Gov. Museum*, new series, I, 1. Madras, 1929.

Rāmachāndran Rao, P. R. *The Art of Nāgārjunakonda*. Madras, 1956.

Sivāramamurtī, C. 'Amarāvatī Sculptures in the Madras Government', *Bull. Madras Gov. Museum*, new series, IV. Madras, 1942.

Smith, V. A. *History of Fine Art in India and Ceylon*. 2nd ed., revised by K. de B. Codrington. Oxford, 1930.

Vogel, J. P. *La Sculpture de Mathurā*, vol. XV of 'Ars Asiatica'. Paris, 1930.

Yazdānī, G. *Ajantā*. 3 vols. London, 1930.

CHRONOLOGICAL TABLE

DATES	HISTORICAL EVENTS	ART AND LITERATURE
c 3500–3000	Civilization of Balūchistān	
c 2500–2000	Civilization called that of the Indus	
before 1500	Invasion of the Panjāb by the Āryans	Composition of the Vedas The *Ṛg Veda*
c 1400		*Atharva Veda*
c 1300		'White' *Yajur Veda*
c 1000–800	The Āryans in the Doāb	Brāhmaṇism: *Śatapatha Brāhmaṇa*; the earliest *Upaniṣads*
c 558	Birth of the Buddha	Buddhism and Jainism
c 540	Birth of the *Jina*	
c 538	First kingdom in the Magadha	
518–5	Conquest of the Indus valley by Darius I	
c 478	Death of the Buddha	
c 468	Death of the *Jina*	
4th cent (?)		The grammarian Pāṇini
331	Alexander the Great of Macedonia defeats Darius III	
327–5	Campaign by Alexander. Defeats Porus, king of the Panjāb	
323	Death of Alexander	
322	The rise of Candragupta Maurya	
317–6	Defeat of the Greeks in the North-West	
313–2	Candragupta Maurya king of Magadha	Megasthenes at the court of Pāṭaliputra
305	Seleucus negotiates with Candragupta	
289	Accession of Bindusāra Maurya	
c 264	Accession of Aśoka	
c 260	Coronation of Aśoka	
c 251	Aśoka conquers the Kaliṅga	
c 250	Aśoka converted to Buddhism	Commemorative pillars and imperial edicts

DATES	HISTORICAL EVENTS	ART AND LITERATURE
c 227–6	Death of Aśoka	
c 189	Invasion of India by Demetrius	
c 176	Accession of the Śuṅga king Puṣyamitra (until *c* 140?)	
c 168	King Menander withdraws from the Magadha to the Panjāb (until *c* 145)	
c 150		The stūpas of Bhārhut and Sānchī The Buddhist philosopher Nāgasena The *Milindapañha* ('Questions of Milinda')
c 130	Invasion of Bactria by the Yüeh-chih tribe	
c 100		Column of Heliodorus at Besnagar
c 90–80	Invasion of the Śakas (Indo-Scythes) Collapse of the Greco-Bactrian kingdoms	
		The grammarian and philosopher Patañjali (author of the *Mahābhāṣya*)
c 70	Fall of the Śuṅga and Kāṇva dynasties. Rise of the Āndhra dynasty in the South	
		The *vedikā* of Bodh-gayā. Shrine and monastery of Bhājā
CHRISTIAN ERA		
c 30	Rise of the Kuṣāṇa dynasty	The *toraṇas* of Sānchī
78	The Śaka era. The Kuṣāṇas extend their power in India	
c 100		After the Buddhist schism, progress of the *Mahāyāna*

DATES	HISTORICAL EVENTS	ART AND LITERATURE
c 125	The Śātakarṇi (Āndhra) emperor Gautamīputra conquers the Satraps of the Mahārāṣṭra	Schools of Mathurā and Amarāvatī. Completion of the *Rāmāyaṇa* and compilation of the *Mahābhārata*. The Begram site in Kāpiśa. Drafting of the *Bhagavad Gītā*. The dramatist Aśvaghoṣa
c 144	Accession of the Kuṣāṇa king Kaniṣka	
c 185	Death of Kaniṣka	
before 200 (?)		The Buddhist philosopher Nāgārjuna
before 300 (?)		The sites of Nāgārjunakoṇḍa and Goli
c 320	Accession of the Gupta emperor Candragupta I	
c 335–75 (?)	Samudragupta In the Deccan: the Pallava king Viṣṇugopa	*Mṛcchakaṭika* ('The Little Clay Cart') of Śūdraka
c 375–*c* 414	Candragupta II. In the Mahārāṣṭra, his vassals the Vākāṭakas	The most splendid of the Ajantā caves The philosophers Asaṅga and Vasubandhu The poet and dramatist Kālidāsa
c 414–55	Kumāragupta I	
c 445–67 (?)	Skandagupta	
c 475–94 (?)	Budhagupta	
485	N. India devastated by the Hūṇas (Hephthalites). The Hūṇa king Toramāṇa	
c 490	Rise of the Valabhī kingdom	
c 500–40	The Hūṇa king Mihirakula in Magadhā (?)	
605–47	Harṣa of Kanauj	The poet Bāṇa The Chinese pilgrim Hsüan-Ch'uang (630–644) The site of Mahābalipuram

NOTES

PART ONE

CHAPTER ONE, THE GEOGRAPHICAL AND HISTORICAL BACKGROUND

1. *The Edicts of Aśoka*, transl. N. A. Nikam, R. McKeon, Univ. of Chicago Press, 1959, pp. 27–8

2. *Milindapañha* ('The Questions of Milinda', Pāli name of King Menander)

3. The dates of this sovereign are hypothetical. The most recent theory, due to Roman Ghirshman, ascribes to him the dates 144–85

CHAPTER TWO, THE SOCIAL STRUCTURE AND ITS RELIGIOUS PRINCIPLES

1. *Mātaṅga-jātaka*, no. 497, transl. Cowell and others, IV, p. 242

2. *Phandana-j*, no. 475, *ibid.*, IV, p. 130

3. They were also forbidden to sell fruits and medicinal herbs: *ibid.*, IV, p. 229, n. 1

4. A. Foucher, *Les Vies antérieures du Bouddha.*

5. *Citta-Sambhūta-j*, no. 498, IV, pp. 244–5

6. *Mātaṅga-j*, no. 497, IV, p. 236; *Citta-Sambhūta-j*, *loc. cit.*

7. *Setaketu-j*, no. 377, III, p. 154

8. *Citta-Sambhūta-j*, *loc. cit.*

9. *Satadhamma-j*, no. 179, II, p. 57. See also *Bhadda-sāla-j*, no. 465, IV, p. 92, where a king, who was the father of a daughter by a female slave, used a subterfuge to avoid eating in her company

10. This custom continued until the sixteenth century. These Amazon guardians are frequently represented in the paintings and sculptures of ancient times, especially in the work of the Amarāvatī school (second and third centuries AD). In the *Rāmāyaṇa*, II, vi, 9, they are described as 'the flower of womanhood, women of the highest distinction'. See A. Foucher, *L'Art gréco-bouddhique du Gandhāra*, II, p. 70

11. D. R. Chana, *L'Esclavage dans l'Inde ancienne*, Pondicherry, 1957. By the same author: 'The Ideological Aspect of Slavery in Ancient India', in *Journal of the Oriental Institute* (Baroda), VIII, 4, June 1959, pp. 389–98. Y. Bongert, 'Réflexions sur le problème de l'esclavage dans l'Inde ancienne, à propos de quelques ouvrages récents', *B.E.F.E.O.*, LI, 1, 1963, pp. 143–94

12. They could also be pledged: Renou, *La Civilisation de l'Inde ancienne*, par. 29, p. 110

CHAPTER THREE, THE POLITICAL AND ADMINISTRATIVE STRUCTURE

1. R. S. Hardy, *A Manual of Buddhism in its Modern Development*, London-Edinburgh, 1880, p. 153

2. *Mahāsupina-jātaka*, no. 77, I, p. 190

3. *The Edicts of Aśoka, op. cit.*, p. 53

4. *Ibid.*, pp. 37–8

5. *Dūta-j*, no. 260, II, p. 221

6. *Harṣacarita*, II (58), transl. Cowell and Thomas, Royal Asiatic Society, London, 1897, p. 41. It should be explained that these letters were strips of white cotton, sealed with red wax (after Hsüan-Ch'uang)

7. *Epigraphia Indica*, XXXI, Part I, p. 7

8. *Ibid.*

9. Imprecise details are given in various texts: when, for example, it is said that a certain village of carpenters contained 'a thousand families', what is meant is simply 'a large number'. See *Samudda-vāṇija-j*, no. 466, IV, p. 99

10. *Mṛcchakaṭika*, Act IX, transl. Ryder, Harvard Oriental Series, Lanman, IX, Cambridge (Mass.), 1905, p. 132 seq.

11. L. Renou, *Anthologie sanskrite*, p. 206 seq. Also *Cambridge History of India*, I, p. 247. The four ordeals (water, fire, weighing, poison) are also described by Hsüan-Ch'uang: see Beal, *Buddhist Records of the Western World*, I, p. 84

12. *Khurappa-j*, no. 265, I, p. 212

13. *Vedabha-j*, no. 48, I, p, 131 seq.; *Pānīya-j*, no. 459, IV., p. 72; *Samkha-dhamana-j*, no. 60, I, p. 147; *Bherivāda-j*, no. 59, I, p. 146

14. See René Grousset, *Sur les traces du Bouddha*, Paris, 1929, particularly p. 33 seq. and p. 260

15. *Vedabha-j*, *loc. cit.*

16. *Pucimanda-j*, no. 311, III, pp. 22–3; *Kanhādīpayana-j*, no. 444, IV, p. 18

17. *Mahilāmukha-j*, no. 26, I, p. 68

18. *Kālakaṇṇi-j*, no. 83, I, p. 210

19. *Kaṇavera-j*, no. 318, II, p. 40; *Sulāsa-j*, no. 419, III, p. 261

20. *Mūga-pakkha-j*, no. 538, VI, p. 3

21. *Puppharatta-j*, no. 147, I, p. 313; *Kāma-Vilāpa-j*, no. 297, II, pp. 302–3; *Sacchamkira-j*, no. 73, I, p. 177; *Kanhādipayana-j*, no. 444, IV, p. 18; *Mahā-Ummagga-j*, no. 546, VI, p. 197

22. *Mahāsīlava-j*, no. 51, I, p. 130

23. *Kulāvaka-j*, no. 31, I, p. 78

24. *Mahā-Paduma-j*, no. 472, IV, p. 120

25. *Culla-j*, no. 193, II, p. 82. Another torture is mentioned, that of 'straw and food', but it is not described: cf. *Sarabhaṅga-j*, no. 522, V, p. 65

26. *The Edicts of Aśoka, op. cit.*, pp. 61–3

CHAPTER FOUR, ECONOMICS AND DAILY LIFE

1. *Bṛhat-saṃhitā*, LIV

2. For details, see Louis Renou, *La Civilisation de L'Inde ancienne*, p. 197

3. A. Foucher, *La Vie du Bouddha*, p. 276 and fig. 4 (p. 376). Also *Cūllavagga*, V, 16, 2

4. *Kuṇāla-j*, no. 536, V, p. 219

5. J. C. Jain, *Life in Ancient India*, p. 90

6. *Harṣacarita*, transl. Cowell and Thomas, p. 228

7. Such sickles are reproduced in several stone carvings, a good example being at Sānchī, *stūpa* I, South gate: see Foucher and Marshall, *The Monuments of Sānchī*, vol. II, pl. XIX, d, 3. A fragment of this same portico, preserved in Sānchī's small museum, shows a person carrying a very curved sickle

8. Jain, *op. cit.*, p. 90

9. *Raghu Vaṃśa*, IV, 20

10. *Mahābhārata: ghoṣayātra*, III, 240

11. *Mānava Dharma Śāstra* (the Code of Manu), VIII, 230

12. We possess only fragmentary information about the network of routes in ancient times. See E. Lamotte, *Histoire du Bouddhisme indien*, I, p. 10

13. *Ancient India as described by Megasthenes*, transl. J. W. McCrindle, XXXIV

14. *Arthaśāstra*, I, 21; II, 4, etc. See the excellent passage in S. C. Sarkar, *Some Aspects of the Earliest Social History of India*, p. 15 seq.

15. *Rāmāyaṇa: Ayodhyākāṇḍa*, sarga lxxx, 1–2

16. *Ibid.*, lxxx, 5 seq.

17. *Megasthenes*, XXXIV, 5

18. *Vaṇṇupatha-j*, no. 2, I, p. 10

19. G. P. Majumdār, *Indian Culture*, II, 2, p. 280

20. Some representations of jungle dwellers are reproduced in K. N. Dikshit, 'Excavations at Paharpur, Bengal', in *Memoirs of the Archaeological Survey of India*, no. 55, pl. XLIX. See also G. Yazdānii, *Ajantā*, I, pl. XXXb. A detailed description of a young *śabara* ('savage') chieftain from the Vindhya mountains is given by Bāṇa in his *Harṣacarita*, *op. cit.*, pp. 231–2

21. *Phala-j*, no. 54, I, p. 135

22. *Phala-j*, *loc. cit.*, and *Gumbiya-j*, no. 366, III, p. 132; *Kimpatekka-j*, no. 85, I, p. 212

23. *Vaṇṇupatha-j*, no. 2, *loc. cit.*

24. *Apaṇṇaka-j*, I, p. 5

25. *Vaṇṇupatha-j*, *loc. cit.*

26. *Jarudapāna-j*, no. 256, II, p. 205

27. K. de B. Codrington, 'The Culture of Mediaeval India as Illustrated by the Ajaṇṭā Frescoes', in *Indian Antiquary*, LIX, August 1930, p. 159 seq.; and September 1930, p. 169 seq. See also the passages concerning Barabuḍur in A. L. Basham, *The Wonder that was India*, pp. 226–7

28. *Milindapañha*, VII, II, 11–12 (*Sacred Books of the East*, vol. XXXVI, p. 300)

29. *Ibid.*, VII, II, 16

30. *Ibid.*, VII, II, 16 (p. 301)

31. *Ṛg Veda*, I, 56, 2; I, 58, 3; I, 116, 5; I, 182, 5, etc.

32. H. G. Rawlinson, *Intercourse between India and the Western World*, p. 4

33. *Arthaśāstra*, IV, III

34. *Dîgha nikāya*, transl. Rhys-Davids, I, p. 222. See also *Kevaddha Sutta*, p. 15 seq. (Harvard Series, vol. 28)

35. *Suppāraka-j*, no. 463, IV, p. 87

36. *Milindapañha*, VII, II, 17

37. *Nāyādhammakahā* (cf. Jain, *op. cit.*, p. 118)

38. *Milindapañha*, VII, II, 9–10 (S.B.E., p. 298)

39. J. Takakusu, *A Record of the Buddhist Religion . . .*, Oxford, 1896, p. xxx

40. Cf. Sylvain Lévi, 'Manimekhalā, a Divinity of the Sea', in *Indian Historical Quarterly*, VI, 1930, p. 597 seq.

41. *Mahājanaka-j*, no. 539, VI, p. 222; *Sankha-j*, no. 442, IV, p. 9 seq. Jain, *op. cit.*, p. 118

42. *Losaka-j*, no. 41, I, p. 110

43. A. Foucher, *Les Vies antérieures du Bouddha*, p. 50

44. *Valāhassa-j*, no. 196, II, p. 89. See also E. Chavannes, *Cinq cent contes et apologues extraits du Tripiṭaka chinois*, no. 37; Foucher, *op. cit.*, p. 252 seq. This theme is reproduced most frequently in Mathurā: J. P. Vogel, *La Sculpture de Mathurā*, pl. XXb; and in Ajantā: Yazdānī, *op. cit.*, IV, pl. LI–LXV

45. *Suppāraka-j*, no. 463, IV, p. 87

46. *Cullaka-j*, no. 4, I, p. 20

47. *Mānava Dharma Śāstra* (the Code of Manu), VIII, 157, 406

48. Pierre Meile, 'Les Yavanas dans l'Inde tamoule', in *Journal asiatique*, 1940–1, fasc. 1, p. 85 seq.

49. Louis Finot, *Les Lapidaires indiens*, Paris, 1896

50. The allusions made to this technique are vague, however, and more fantastic than realistic. See *Mahā-ummagga-j*, no. 546, VI, p. 231 and fn. 6

51. *Jātaka*, no. 254, II, pp. 199–203

52. Foucher, *op. cit.*, p. 125

53. *Periplus of the Erythrean Sea*, para. 49, mentions the importation of wine into India. See Laufer, in *Sino-Iranica*, p. 220 seq. See also Herodotus, I, 133. For details of the above anonymous second-century work, see J. Pirenne in *Journal asiatique*, CCXLIX, 4, 1961, p. 441 seq. Also, L. Renou, *La Civilisation de L'Inde ancienne*, p. 196

54. For example, the name of Amurius (Caius), which has also been found in Palestine (Beisān), Alexandria and Athens; those of the Vibii and Vibieni, descendants of an ancient Etrurian family which had settled in Arezzo: see Sir Mortimer Wheeler, 'Arikamedu: an Indo-Roman Trading-station on the East Coast of India', in *Ancient India*, 2 (July, 1946), pp. 17–124

55. Meile, *op. cit.*, p. 103 seq.

56. *Periplus of the Erythrean Sea*, *loc. cit.*, para. 49

57. Since the second century

BC. Cf. P. Pelliot's Critical Bulletin in *T'ung pao*, 1921–2, XX, pp. 142–56

58. V. S. Agrawāla, 'Geographical Data in Pāṇini', in *Indian Historical Quarterly*, 1953, I, pp. 2, 30

59. Theophrastus, *Historia Plant*, IV, IV, 11. Vines are still to be found in the Nāsik and Pondicherry regions; they must have been more widespread in ancient times, since they figure, in a stylized form, on a number of bas-reliefs

60. *Geographica*, II, 1, 14, and IX, 10, 2

61. Sir John Marshall, 'Excavations at Bhītā', in *A.S.I., A.R.*, 1911–12, p. 32

62. Similar shops are reproduced in wall-paintings at Ajaṇṭā, cavern XVII: see Yazdānī, *op. cit.*, IV, pl. XXIII

63. *Jātaka*, I, p. 290; IV, p. 82, etc. See also *Divyāvadāna*, XXVI. Many interesting details are to be found in Moti Chandra, 'Cosmetics and Coiffures in Ancient India', in *Journal of Indian Society of Oriental Art*, VIII, 1940, pp. 62–145

64. *Vāruṇi-j*, no. 47, 1, p. 120

65. For reproductions of such scales see: for Mathurā, Vogel, *op. cit.*, pl. XXc; for Amarāvatī, D. Barrett, *Sculptures from Amarāvatī*, pl. XXVI; for Nāgārjunakoṇḍa, A. H. Longhurst, *The Buddhist Antiquities* . . . pl. XLIIa, XIXb, XLVa; for Ajaṇṭā, Yazdānī, *op. cit.*, IV, pl. XXIII

66. Yazdānī, *op. cit.*, I, pl. V

67. See Finot, *op. cit.*, p. v, referring to S. de Sacy, 'De la manière de compter . . .' in *Journal asiatique*, 1824, pp. 65–71

68. Moti Chandra, *op. cit.*, p. 100

69. *Śaddaṇṭa-j*, no. 514, V, p. 25

70. Jain, *op. cit.*, p. 103

71. *Jātaka*, no. 546, VI, p. 233. See Sarkār, *op. cit.*, pp. 57–8: garments fashioned from leather and skins were worn only by brāhmaṇs

72. *Alīnacitta-j*, no. 121, II, p. 14

73. *Kusanāḷi-j*, no. 121, I, p. 268

74. Foucher, *op. cit.*, p. 144. See also *Alīnacitta-j*, *loc. cit.*

75. According to the *Samarāṅgaṇa Sūtradhāra* attributed to King Bhoja (1018–55); fifth-century Buddhist literature contains allusions to flying machines: see G. P. Majumdār, 'Conveyances (Man's Indebtedness to Plants)', in *Indian Culture*, II, 2, October 1935, p. 288 seq. See also Baruā and Majumdār, 'Flying Machines in Ancient India', in *The Calcutta Review*, December 1933, p. 287 seq.; and P. Srīnivāsamurti, 'Aeronautics in Ancient India', in *Adyar Library Bulletin* (*Brahmavidyā*), XVI, 4

76. *Babbu-j*, no. 137, I, p. 295

77. A. K. Coomāraswāmy, *La Sculpture de Bhārhut*, Pl. XXVI, fig. 67. See also, by the same author, *La Sculpture de Bodhgayā*, pl. XIII and LI (2)

78. A. K. Coomāraswāmy, *Les Arts et Métiers de l'Inde et Ceylan*, pp. 113–14

79. Upādhyāya, *op. cit.*, p. 268, fn. 6

80. Called *kuthāra*: Bhārhut, Calcutta Museum, no. 337. See Coomāraswāmy, *La Sculpture de Bhārhut*, pl. XLIII, fig. 151

81. Called *mudgara.* See C. Sivarāmamurti, *Amarāvatī Sculptures*, pl. X, 12

82. These were hand-saws: Bhārhut, see Coomāraswāmy, *loc. cit.*, pl. XXVIII, no. 225 (72), Calcutta Museum, no. 291; Amarāvatī: see Sivarāmamurti, *loc. cit.*, pl. XXVI, 2c; Goli: see I. N. Rāmachandran in *Bull. Madras Gov. Museum*, I, part I, 1929, pl. I C

83. Longhurst, *op. cit.*, pl. XXXIV, b

84. Described by Jain, *op. cit.*, p. 101, following Jain texts. Still used today: solar cooking is hastened by plates of sheet-iron or zinc placed on top of the ditch. See also *Kusa-j*, no. 531, V, p. 151

85. *Kacchapa-j*, no. 108, III, p. 228

86. Yazdānī, *op. cit.*, IV, pl. VIa and p. 22. This technique is still used in several regions (Bombay, Pondicherry)

87. *Mahā-ummaga-j*, no. 546, VI, p. 156 seq.

88. *Serivāṇija-j*, no. 3, I, p. 10

89. J. M. Casal, *Site urbain et sites funéraires des environs de Pondichéry*

90. The most celebrated literary allusion to these toys is contained in the very title of *The Little Clay Cart* (*Mṛcchakaṭika*), a play attributed to King Sūdraka. See L. Renou and J. Filliozat, *L'Inde classique*, vol. II, § 1864, pp. 270–1. Many such clay toys have been found in excavations, and can also be seen depicted on ancient reliefs: see J. Auboyer, *La Vie publique et privée dans l'Inde ancienne*, fasc. VI, pl. I, 3 and 4

91. Jain, *op. cit.*, p. 102. *Kusa-j*, no. 531, V, p. 151

92. *Suruci-j*, no. 489, IV, pp. 200–1

93. The sieve was called a *śūrpa*, and can be seen, in particular, depicted at Sānchī I: see Foucher and Marshall, *op. cit.*, vol. II, pl. LII*a*. This was not only an indispensable domestic utensil but also an object used in religious ceremonies, and sometimes even considered a divine attribute; for example, the sieve carried by the goddess of small-pox, *Śītalā* or *Māriyammai*: see Auboyer and M.-T. de Mallmann, 'Śītalā la Froide' in *Artibus Asiae*, XIII, 1950, pp. 207–27

94. Reproduced at Bhārhut: Coomāraswāmy, *op. cit.*, pl. XLIV, fig. 164

95. Called *chattra* or *ātapatra.* Depictions of these are very frequent throughout ancient times. The most faithful reproductions are probably those at Bhārhut: Coomāraswāmy, *op. cit.*, pl. XLI, fig. 137; at Sānchī II: Foucher and Marshall, *op. cit.*, vol. III, pl. LXXXVII, 71*a*; at Sānchī I: *ibid.*, vol. II, pl. XVI; at Amarāvatī: Sivarāmamurti, *op. cit.*, pl. XXV, 1; at Nāgārjunakoṇḍa: Longhurst, *op. cit.*, pl. XX*b*; at

Goli: Rāmachandran, *op. cit.*, pl. VI F

96. Called *talavṛnta.* See also Sivarāmamurti, *Le Stūpa du Barabuḍur* (Publications du Musée Guimet, Recherches d'Art et d'Archéologie, VIII), Paris, 1960, pl. VII

97. Jain, *op. cit.*, p. 97. See also L. Renou, *La Civilisation de l'Inde ancienne*, § 80, p. 190

98. Although it seems that silk was mostly imported from China, the silkworm was bred in Bengāl and in Assam: see Basham, *op. cit.*, pp. 196–7. By the fifth century, silk weaving had become a well-developed industry (*ibid.*, p. 149, n. 19; and pp. 204–5). See also Sarkār, *op. cit.*, pp. 60–1

99. *Raghu Vaṃśa*, quoted by Upādhyāya, *op. cit.*, p. 258 seq. Interesting technical details are given by Sarkār, *op. cit.*, p. 61 seq.

100. Jain, *op. cit.*, pp. 102–3

101. *Baka-j*, no. 38, I, p. 95

102. *Sīlavanāga-j*, no. 72, I, p. 176

103. J. and R. Hackin and others, *Recherches archéologiques à Begrām* and *Nouvelles Recherches archéologiques à Begrām*, in Mémoires de la D.A.F.A., IX and XI

104. Mentioned in the *Ahiguṇḍika-j*, no. 365, III, p. 131

105. Jain, *op. cit.*, p. 100

106. Finot, *op. cit.*, *passim*

107. *Kummāsapiṇḍa-j*, no. 415, III, pp. 244–5

108. *Dhammaddhaja-j*, no. 220, II, p. 131; *Kummāsapiṇḍa-j*, *loc. cit.* See also Jain, *op. cit.*, pp. 103–4

109. *Somanassa-j*, no. 505, IV, pp. 277–8

110. *Kusa-j*, no. 531, V, p. 152

111. *Gumbiya-j*, no. 366, III, p. 132

112. *Rohantamiga-j*, no. 501, IV, p. 257

113. Hackin, *loc. cit.*; and, for Ajaṇṭā, Yazdānī, *op. cit.*, IV, pl. XXXIII*a*

114. *Kuruṅga-j*, no. 21, I, p. 57

115. Coomāraswāmy, *op. cit.*, pl. XXVIII, fig. 70

116. *Ibid.*, pl. XXIX, fig. 74

117. *Maṃsa-j*, no. 315, III, p. 33

118. *Vātamiga-j*, no. 14, I, p. 45

119. *Aṭṭhasadda-j*, no. 418, III, p. 204

120. Elephant hunting forms the theme of one of the most famous Buddhist tales, the *Śaddanta-j*, no. 514, V, p. 23 seq. This tale has very often been illustrated by different artists; it gives valuable details about the hunter's technique

121. The narrator adds that the hunter transformed his leather bag into a parachute and made the final part of his descent into the plateau by gliding like a bird

122. *Sammodamāna-j*, no. 33, I, p. 85; *Cullahaṃsa-j*, no. 533, V, p. 178; *Mahāhaṃsa-j*, no. 534, V, p. 187; *Sālikedāra-j*, no. 484, IV, p. 176. See also *Gijjha-j*, no. 399, in which vultures are captured: III, p. 204

123. Jain, *op. cit.*, p. 96

124. V. R. R. Dikshitar, *War in Ancient India*, p. 176

125. *Ibid.*, p. 168 seq.; Renou, *op. cit.*, § 84, pp. 198–9; *Arthaśāstra*, XXXII (transl. Sāstrī, pp. 137–9); *Saṁgāmāvacara-j*, no. 182, II, pp. 64–5

126. See Sir John Marshall, *A.S.I.*, *A.R.*, 1911–12, p. 45

127. *Khurappa-j*, no. 265, II, p. 232

128. *Sūci-j*, no. 387, III, p. 178

129. *Kāliṅga-j*, no. 479, IV, p. 145

130. *Akataññu-j*, no. 90, I, p. 220; *Apaṇṇa-j*, no. 1, I, p. 4

131. *Veri-j*, no. 103, I, p. 245

132. *Vissāsabhojana-j*, no. 93, I, p. 227

133. *Visayha-j*, no. 34, III, p. 85

134. Under some reigns, these did in fact pay taxes, but on a more modest scale than those to which the peasants were liable

135. Licences were sometimes granted to private individuals and to guilds, authorizing them to mint coins, after payment of duty of up to thirteen per cent

136. Basham, *op. cit.*, p. 180

137. J. W. McCrindle, *Ancient India as described by Megasthenes and Arrian*, pp. 31, 36–8

138. E. J. Rapson, *Indian Coins*, Strasburg, 1897; *Catalogues of Indian Coins in the British Museum*; V. C. Smith, *Catalogue of Coins in the Indian Museum, Calcutta*, Part One, Oxford, 1906; R. B. Whitehead, *Catalogue of Coins in the Panjāb Museum, Lahore*, Oxford, 1914; see also Renou, *op. cit.*, § 88, p. 203, seq., and Renou and Filliozat, *op. cit.*, vol. I, § 314 seq., p. 172, seq.

139. *Arthaśāstra*, V, 3. And see L. Renou, *op, cit.*, § 89, p. 205 seq.

PART TWO

CHAPTER ONE, THE BACKGROUND TO DAILY LIFE

1. *A.S.I.*, *A.R.*, 1912–13, p. 76

2. Sir John Marshall, 'Excavations at Bhītā', in *A.S.I.*, *A.R.*, 1911–12, p. 40. The outer wall was sometimes doubled by another wall, the space between them being made impassable by barricades of stones and by trenches

3. A. Foucher and Sir John Marshall, *The Monuments of Sānchī*, II, pl. LI*b*

4. The most celebrated stone *toraṇa* surviving are those of Sānchī. See C. Sivarāmamurti, *Sanskrit Literature and Art . . .*, p. 10. Also P. Stern in *N.R.A.B.*, p. 25 seq.; and J. Auboyer, *ibid*, p. 67

5. In a short article based on canonical and literary texts, 'Gopura "porte de ville" ', in *Journal asiatique*, CCXLVII (959), fasc. 2, pp. 251–5, M. Jean Filliozat makes a distinction between the gate and its 'towers': the reference is doubtless to the outjutting foreparts of the structure, depicted frequently in painting and sculpture

6. Tiles are found fairly often

in excavations. Described, in particular, by Marshall, *op. cit.*, p. 41

7. Named *amṛtakalaśa*, 'ambrosial vessel'. Also called *kalaśa-ghaṭa*, *kalaśa-kumbha*, *pūrṇa-kalaśa*, *varṣamāna*, *varṣasthala*, this vessel is imbued with a whole philosophical symbolism: see *Hōbōgirin* dictionary, article on 'byō', 2, p. 265 seq.; *Arthaśāstra*, II, 5, quoted by A. K. Coomāraswāmy, *Yakṣas*, II, pl. 64 seq.; Coomāraswāmy and Kershaw, *Artibus Asiae*, 1928–9; Roșu and Al-George, in *Arts asiatiques*, IV, 4, pp. 243–54, and VIII, p. 241 seq.

8. J. Auboyer, in *N.R.A.B.*, p. 68

9. *Ibid.*

10. See A. Foucher, *Études sur l'art bouddhique de l'Inde*, Tokyo, 1928; J. Przyluski, 'Le Symbolisme du Pilier de Sārnāth', in *Mélanges d'Orientalisme publiés par le Musée Guimet à la mémoire de Raymonde Linossier*, II, pp. 481–98; B. Majumdār, 'Symbology of the Aśoka Pillar, Sārnāth', in *Indian Culture*, II, 1, pp. 160–3; B. N. Sharmā, 'The Lion Capital of the Pillar of Aśoka at Sārnāth', in *The Poonā Orientalist*, I, 1936, pp. 2–6; J. Przyluski, 'The Solar Wheel at Sārnāth', in *J.I.S.O.A.*, IV, 1936, pp. 43–51; G. Coedes, 'Note on the Pillar at Sārnāth', in *J.I.S.O.A.*, V, 1937, pp. 40–1

11. The sovereign is frequently depicted on such wheel-capped columns, notably in the Amarāvatī school

12. *Raghu Vaṃśa*, I, 44: 'The villages founded by the king could be recognized by their sacred columns'

13. Concerning the various meanings of these columns, see J. N. Banerjea, 'Indian Votive and Memorial Columns', *J.I.S.O.A.*, 1937, pp. 13–20

14. Marshall, *op. cit.*, p. 32

15. Reproduction in Vogel, *La Sculpture de Mathurā*, pl. VIII *b* and LVII *a* and *b*. See also C. Sivarāmamurti, *Amarāvatī Sculptures*, p. 140

16. *Kaṇavera-j*, no. 318, Cowell, III, p. 41

17. A. K. Coomāraswāmy, *La Sculpture de Bhārhut*, pl. XLVI, fig. 194

18. This remains the typical layout of Indian private houses of any importance. See also Hsüan-Ch'uang in: S. L. Beal, *Buddhist Records . . .*, I, p. 74

19. See C. Sivarāmamurti, 'Citraśālā: Ancient Indian Art Galleries', in *Trivenī*, VII, Madras, 1934, pp. 169–85; and by the same author: *Sanskrit Literature and Art . . .*, p. 92 seq. See also Meyer, *Hindu Tales*, p. 174; Coomāraswāmy, *Indian Architectural Terms*, p. 255

20. J. C. Jain, *Life in Ancient India*, p. 164

21. Trivikrama Bhaṭṭa, *Nala-champū*, p. 195

22. *Mūga-j*, no. 538, VI, p. 17

23. Representations of these crenellated walls bristling with archers and spearsmen abound throughout ancient iconography, at Sānchī, at Amarāvatī and at many other sites

24. A sight that is still common;

it was frequently depicted in ancient iconography: see Foucher and Marshall, *op. cit.*, II, pl. LII *a*. See also a remarkable sculpture from Mathurā preserved in the Lakhnau Museum (no. B-86)

25. A theme often reproduced in ancient bas-reliefs: see Foucher and Marshall, *op. cit.*, II, pl. LXV *a*, 1

26. Hsüang-Ch'uang: Beal, *op. cit.*, I, p. 74

27. L. Renou, *La Civilisation de l'Inde ancienne*, p. 239 (*Harṣacarita*)

28. Depicted, for instance in a seventh-century bas relief in the Kṛṣṇa cavern at Mahābalipuram

29. The bullock-wagon is famous throughout ancient literature. Already mentioned in the Vedas (*Ṛg Veda*, *Atharva Veda*, *Aitareya Brāhmaṇa*, etc.), it still rumbles along the roadways of modern India. See G. P. Majumdār, *Indian Culture*, II, 2, p. 278 seq.; Sivarāmamurti, *Amarāvatī Sculptures*, p. 140. Many reproductions are available; see in particular: Coomāraswāmy, *op. cit.*, pl. XXVI, fig. 67 and pl. XXXI, fig. 84; Foucher and Marshall, *op. cit.* pl. XIX *c*, 3 (southern *toraṇa*, preserved in the Sanchī Museum); J. Hackin, *Recherches archéologiques à Begrām*, pl. XLV, fig. 105, and p. 70; Vogel, *La Sculpture de Mathurā*, pl. LVII *b*; Longhurst, *Nāgārjunakoṇḍa*, pl. XLVII *b*; Rāmachandran, *Goli*, pl. V, *c* and *d*

30. Who was called a *tvaṣṭṛ* in the Vedas, a *rathakara* in the *Jātakas*. The latter appellation also designated the shoemaker, since shoes were included in the general classification of vehicles

31. See, for example, pl. V *a* and VI *a* in Yazdānī, *Ajaṇṭā*, IV

32. *Ubhatobhaṭṭha-j*, no. 139, I, p. 299; and *Kuṇāla-j*, no. 536, V, p. 219

33. The following details are taken mainly from the following works: Louis Renou, 'La Maison védique', in *Journal asiatique*, CCXXXI, October-December 1939, p. 481 seq.; G. P. Majumdār, *Indian Culture*, III, 1, p. 71 seq.; O. Viennot, *Le Culte de l'arbre*, p. 66 seq.; S. Kramrisch, *The Hindu Temple*, 1, pp. 1–18

34. *Alīnacitta-j*, II, p. 14; H. L. Jain, 'Prefabricated Houses in Ancient India', in *Annual Bull. Nāgpur Univ. Hist. Soc.*, 4, 1949

35. Śaṅkha, *Gṛhya Sūtra*, III, 3, 1

36. *Atharva Veda*, III, 12, 5

37. These trestle-beds are to be seen reproduced on the ivories discovered in the Begrām of Kāpiśī around the first and second centuries AD: see J. Auboyer, in *N.R.A.B.*, p. 73. Usually they were covered by a cloth or a pelt, so the network of thongs is rarely visible

38. Called *bhojana phalaka* or *pattakaṇḍolikā* in Pāli, they are depicted frequently in ancient art. Good specimens may be seen in the following references: J. Auboyer, *loc. cit.*, pl. F, *j*, and fig. 30 *b*; Mathurā; Lakhnau Museum, no. J 533; School of Amarāvatī: National Museum of

New Delhi, no. 94, reprod. in Sivarāmamurti, *Sanskrit Literature and Art . . .*, pl. XVIII, 59. These supports are still in use today, either as an article of furniture, or by street traders who use them as the base for a tray displaying their wares

39. Various names are given to vessels used for cooking and eating. They are too numerous to be listed here. See Jain, *op. cit.*, p. 99; Coomāraswāmy and Kershaw, *loc. cit.*; K. de B. Codrington, in *Indian Antiquary*, LIX, August 1930, p. 171 and fig. F

40. Such stacking of vessels (*agghiya-panti*) is still the general practice throughout eastern and south-eastern Asia

41. This custom may be seen illustrated at Ajaṇṭā, cave XVII (fifth or sixth century): see Yazdānī, *Ajaṇṭā*, IV, pl. XIV *a*, in which skewered meat-balls are arranged on leaves serving as plates in front of each diner. This is still the ritual manner of taking food, and those who have dined in the brāhmaṇ restaurants of southern India will have eaten in this way

42. G. P. Majumdār, 'Hearth and Home', in *Indian Culture*, III, 3 (January 1937), p. 431 seq.

43. Yāzdanī, *op. cit.*, I, pl. XVI

44. The existence of secret chambers beneath the ground floor, also, has been confirmed by excavations: see *A.S.I.*, *A.R.*, 1911–12, p. 35

45. Yazdānī, *op. cit.*, IV, pl. XVII *a*, who traces a descent from these hangings to the *himrū* and *mashrū* fabrics still woven today in Aurangābād

46. G. P. Majumdār, *loc. cit.*

47. P. K. Acharya, 'Hindu Architecture and Sculpture', in *Indian Culture*, VIII, 2–3, p. 181

48. J. Griffiths, *The Paintings of the Buddhist Cave Temples of Ajaṇṭā*, pl. LXXXV

49. Acharya, *loc. cit.*

50. Bhārhut, Calcutta Museum, no. 184, reprod. in Coomāraswāmy, pl. XIII, fig. 33, and p. 53; also pl. XXIV, fig. 61; Foucher and Marshall, *op. cit.*, pl. LII *a*, 3; *N.R.A.B.*, fig. 96 (no. 55 *a*); P. Meile, 'Les Yavanas dans l'Inde tamoule', in *Journal asiatique*, 1940, p. 114; *Lalit Kalā*, no. 7, April 1960, pl. XXIV

51. Numerous references, especially Sivarāmamurti, *Amarāvatī Sculptures*, pl. V, fig. 32 and 33, and p. 142; D. Barrett, *Sculptures from Amarāvatī*, pl. VII; Mathurā: Lakhnau Museum, no. B-84 and J-532, etc.

52. *Raghu Vaṃśa*, XVI, 39

53. J. Auboyer, *La Vie publique et privée dans l'Inde ancienne*, p. 27 seq.

54. A bedroom of this type may be seen reproduced at Ajaṇṭā, cave XVI: see Yazdānī, *op. cit.*, III, pl. LXI (right). The *vīṇā*, during this epoch, was definitely a bow-harp; it was only after the sixth or seventh century that the term came to be used for a quite different type of musical instrument, i.e. a 'lute' made of a straight bamboo at each end of which is suspended a gourd, and garnished with one or more

strings. This last type initiated the contemporary *vīṇā*, a most elaborate instrument evolved through several centuries. See C. Marcel-Dubois, *Les instruments de musique dans l'Inde ancienne*, Paris, 1941, p. vi

55. J. Auboyer, *Le Trône et son symbolisme dans l'Inde ancienne*

56. This scene is frequently reproduced in ancient Buddhist art

57. For instance, at Māmallapuram, in the great bas-relief of the Descent of the Ganges

58. Coomāraswāmy, *Yakṣas*, I, p. 33 and n. 1

59. Illustrated in Foucher and Marshall, *op. cit.*, II, pl. LII *a*, 3

60. Apart from stūpa II, where the decoration is on the balustrade

61. Countless studies have been devoted to the stūpa; the most original work, now a classic, is that of Paul Mus, *Bārābuḍur, Esquisse d'une histoire du bouddhisme fondée sur la critique archéologique des textes*, 2 vol., Paris, Geuthner, 1935; also published *in extenso* in *B.E.F.E.O.*, XXXII (1932), 1, pp. 269–439, and XXXIV (1934), pp. 175–400. See also M. Benisti, 'Étude sur le Stoûpa dans l'Inde ancienne', *Bull. de l'Ecole Française de l'Extrême-Orient*, vol. L, fasc. 1 (1960), pp. 37–116

62. J. Auboyer, *op. cit.*, p. 11 seq.

CHAPTER TWO, THE IMPORTANCE OF RELIGION IN DAILY LIFE

1. *Raghu Vaṃśa*, XVI, 70. This festival does not seem to have been depicted in the art of the earliest epochs of ancient times, but frequent illustrations are to be found in Rājpūt miniatures from the sixteenth century onwards. It still takes place

2. J. Auboyer, *La Vie publique et privée . . .*, fasc. VI, p. 26 seq.

3. *Aitareya-āraṇyaka*, I, 2, 4, iv, 3

4. Victor Henry, *La Magie dans l'Inde antique*, pp. 42, 89 seq., etc.

5. L. Renou and J. Filliozat, *L'Inde classique*, vol. I, § 1213; J. C. Jain, *Life in Ancient India*, p. 216; O. Viennot, *Le Culte de l'arbre dans l'Inde ancienne*, Paris, 1954, pp. 94, 102

6. According to the *Bharata nāṭyaśāstra*, it was a bamboo: see Arnold Bake, '*Ein Indradhvajajotthāna in Nepāl*' in *Indologen-Tagung*, 1959 (dir Ernst Waldschmidt), Göttingen, 1960, pp. 116–21

7. This festival is still celebrated in many regions of India, particularly Orissa

8. *Surāpāna-j*, no. 81, Cowell, I, p. 208; *Pānīya-j*, no. 459, IV, p. 73

9. Reproduced in D. Barrett, *Sculptures from Amarāvatī in the British Museum*, pl. VII

10. This interpretation is even more precise in Cambodian, Siamese and Burmese tradition: cf. *Histoire générale des Religions*, 'Extrême-Orient', p. 414 and n. 164 (p. 537)

11. See, for example, *Hatthipāla-j*, no. 509, IV, p. 295

12. A. K. Coomāraswāmy, *Yakṣas*, 2 vol., Smithsonian, Washington, 1928–31

13. Kubera is also the half-brother of the giant Rāvaṇa, whose clashes with Rāma still hold breathless the readers of the epic poem the *Rāmāyaṇa*

14. C. Sivarāmamurti, *Amarāvatī Sculptures*, p. 75

15. *Palāsa-j*, no. 370, III, pp. 137–8

16. *Mahābhārata*, XIII, 58, 24; *Atharva Veda*, IV, 27, 4, 5

17. *Kūṭavāṇija-j*, no. 98, I, p. 240

18. *Pucimanda-j*, no. 311, III, p. 23

19. Sterility was considered as a malediction. Childless married couples sometimes had recourse to more or less coarse magical rituals, for descriptions of which see V. Henry, *La Magie dans l'Inde antique*, p. 132 seq. In many civilizations, up to and including the present century, tree-worship is in fact a fertility cult. The author of this present work has witnessed personally (in 1937) the persistence of this cult: in Egypt, women came to tie ribbons to the branches of certain trees in order to obtain children; and, in Rumania, the author has photographed stylized 'trees' that had been set up on the tombs of bachelors, so that they might find partners in the other world

20. *Rukkhadhamma-j*, no. 74, I, p. 75; and see Jain, *op. cit.*, p. 220 seq.

21. *Dummedha-j*, no. 50, I, p. 127; *Palāsa-j*, no. 307, III, p. 16. See also Coomāraswāmy, *La Sculpture de Bhārhut*, pl. XXII, XXIII, fig. 56–60; Barrett, *op. cit.*, pl. XXI *b*, XXV. For the leaving of handmarks (*pañcaṅgulika*) see J. Auboyer, *Le Trône eṭ son symbolisme dans l'Inde ancienne*, p. 11 seq.; and Sivarāmamurti, *Sanskrit Literature and Art*, p. 89. For this entire passage, see Viennot, *op. cit.*, *passim*

22. *Sulasā-j*, no. 419, III, pp. 261–2

23. J.-P. Vogel, *Indian Serpent-lore or the Nāgas in Hindu Legend and Art*, London, 1926; J. Fergusson, *Tree and Serpent Worship*, London, 1873; Jain, *op. cit.*, p. 219

24. Innumerable legends attest these beliefs, especially among the Khmers: J. Przyluski, 'La princesse à l'odeur de poisson et la Nāgī dans les traditions de l'Asie orientale', in *Études asiatiques*, pp. 265–84; V. Goloubew, 'Les légendes de la Nāgī et de l'Asparas', in *B.E.F.E.O.*, XXIV (1924), p. 501 seq.; E. Porée-Maspero, 'Nouvelle étude sur la Nāgī Somā', in *Journal asiatique*, 1950, pp. 237–68

25. The *nāga* cult appears to have inspired shrines of vast size as well, such as that discovered at Maniyār Math (Rājgir), which is probably a temple dedicated to Maninēga, already mentioned in the *Mahābhārata*: M. H. Kuraishī and A. Ghosh, *Rājgir*, Delhi-Calcutta, 1951, pp. 21–7

26. Represented particularly in the school of Mathurā: J. P. Vogel, *La Sculpture de Mathurā*, pl. XLI

27. Hiraṇyakeśin, *Gṛhya Sūtra*, I, 5, 16, 2

28. *Cullavagga*, V, 33, 3

29. Hiraṇyakeśin, *loc. cit.*, I, 5, 16, 6

30. *Ibid.*, I, 5, 17, 5

31. Renou and Filliozat, *op. cit.*, I, § 748

32. The importance ascribed to dreams was so great that a whole school of oneiromancy came into being. See Renou and Filliozat, *op. cit.*, I, § 1265; Jain, *op. cit.*, p. 148; *Mahāsuppina-j*, no. 77, I, p. 187. See also A. M. Esnoul, in *Les Songes et leur interprétation*, Paris, 1959, pp. 209–47

33. Hiraṇyakeśin, *op. cit.*, I, 5, 17, 5

34. *Raghu Vaṃśa*, XIV, 49–50

CHAPTER THREE, THE INDIVIDUAL AND THE FAMILY

1. Hiraṇyakeśin, *Gṛhya Sūtra*, II, 4, 10; 11; 12; 13

2. Illustrated in C. Sivarāmamurti, 'Saṃskāras in Sculpture', in *Arts asiatiques*, II (1955), fasc. 1, p. 3 seq.

3. V. Henry, *La Magie dans l'Inde antique*, pp. 81, 138, 144

4. J. C. Jain, *Life in Ancient India* . . ., p. 149

5. Henry, *op. cit.*, pp. 67–8

6. Gobhila, *Gṛhya Sūtra*, II, 6, *S.B.E.*, XXX, p. 301, n. 10

7. L. Renou and J. Filliozat, *L'Inde classique*, II, § 1656

8. The rite of *sīmanta* was observed only for the first-born. See Gobhila, *Gṛhya Sūtra*, II, 7

9. *Raghu Vaṃśa*, III, 2

10. *Gṛhya Sūtra*, *S.B.E.*, XXX, p. 302, n. 13

11. *Ibid.*, *loc. cit.*, n. 14

12. *Ibid.*, n. 18

13. He could leave him as many as five locks of hair, as was the case with the child-god Kṛṣṇa

14. Hiraṇyakeśin, *Gṛhya Sūtra*, I, 2, 9, 18; Āśvalāyana, *ibid.*, I, 17, 10; Śāṅkhāyana, *ibid.*, I, 28, 23

15. See M. T. de Mallmann, 'A propos d'une coiffure et d'un collier d'Avalokiteśvara', in *Oriental Art*, I (1949), 4, pp. 168–76. See also: *Kādambarī* (ed. Nirṇayasāgara Press, Bombay, 1912), p. 40; *Harṣacarita* (same ed., 1918), p. 134 or the version by Cowell and Thomas, pp. 115–16. Illustrated in J. and R. Hackin, *Recherches archéologiques à Begrām*, pl. LXIII, fig. 190, no. 330 (184 *b*); see also Foucher and Marshall, *The Monuments of Sānchī*, II, pl. XXXIV, *a*, 2

16. *Kālakaṇṇi-j*, no. 33, transl. Cowell and others, I, pp. 209–10

17. Illustrated in J. Auboyer, *La Vie publique et privée* . . ., pl. I. See also: *Trésors d'art de l'Inde*, Petit Palais, Paris, 1960, pl. 20, no. 117

18. Auboyer, *op. cit.*, pl. I, *3* and *4*; D. Barrett, *Sculptures from Amarāvatī*, pl. XXIX

19. Auboyer, *op. cit.*, pl. II, 2

20. *Kaṇhadīpāyana-j*, no. 444, IV, p. 19; *Mūga-j*, no. 538, VI, pp. 4, 9; *Vessantara-j*, no. 547, VI, p. 284

21. Auboyer, *op. cit.*, pl. II, *1*. The game of marbles is represented in cave II at Ajaṇṭā, right-hand shrine: G. Yazdānī, *Ajaṇṭā*, II, pl. XXXIII

22. Renou and Filliozat, *op. cit.*, II, § 1656; *The Cambridge History of India*, I, p. 237; Henry, *op. cit.*, p. 187 seq.

23. A. L. Basham, *The Wonder that was India*, p. 160

24. A. Foucher, *La Vie du Bouddha*, pp. 76–7. Illustrated in Yazdānī, *op. cit.*, III, pl. LXIII

25. *Gṛhya Sūtra*, *S.B.E.*, pp. 302–3, n. 20. I have in general followed the lessons of Śāṅkhāyana and Hiraṇyakeśin; as elsewhere, I have had to abridge the details to some extent

26. But hemp for the *kṣatriya*, and wool for the *vaiśya*

27. The Hindus attach prime importance to sound: to pronounce the names of the gods correctly, and to repeat them interminably in a litany ensures the total efficacity of the invocation and the rite. A great number of incantations (*mantra*) have been established in this way and transmitted ritually; the mantra is not only divine but is divinity itself, 'the material form of the god to a far higher degree than his image' (Filliozat). Such is the syllable *Ōm*

28. Very many representations of hermitages appear throughout ancient art and sculpture. See in particular: A. K. Coomāraswāmy, *La Sculpture de Bhārhut*, pl. XXXI, fig. 85; pl. XLIII, fig. 157; pl. XLV, fig. 176; pl. XLIX, fig. 233; pl. LI, figs. 247 and 253. Foucher and Marshall, *op. cit.*, II, pls. XXV, XXVII, XXIX, XXXIV, LII *a*, LXV *a*. J. Hackin, *N.R.A.B.*, fig. 97 (no. 55 *b*). J. P. Vogel, *La Sculpture de Mathurā*, pls. XVI *a*, LX *a*. Sivarāmamurti, *Amarāvatī Sculptures*, pl. XI, 14; LXIII, 5 *d*. A. H. Longhurst in *Memoirs of the A.S.I.*, no. 54, pl. XLV *b*, etc. Literary descriptions are equally frequent; one of the best known can be found in the *Rāmāyaṇa*, LVI

29. This is still the gesture of respect made today towards a venerable person

30. A. Foucher, '*Two jātaka*...' in *N.R.A.B.*, pl. IX *b*, and p. 128. There are numerous reproductions at Bhārhut and Sānchī

31. This form of instruction is still in use today

32. Renou and Filliozat, *op. cit.*, II, § 1687 seq.

33. J. A. Page, *A.S.I., A.R.*, 1926–7, pp. 127–34; S. Beal, *Life of Hiuen Tsiang*, 1924, p. 111; Watters, *On Yuan Chwang's Travels in India*, II, p. 164 seq.; *Mémoires de Yi-tsing*, transl. E. Chavannes, p. 84 seq.

34. *Gṛhya Sūtra*, *op. cit.*, p. 302, n. 19

35. *Ibid.*, p. 303, n. 20–21. Sometimes it was his relatives or friends who presented them: Hiraṇyakeśin, I, 2, 10, 4 seq.

36. Sandals of this type are

represented at Ajaṇṭā, cave XVII, left-hand wall of the entrance-way

37. The 1949 constitution prohibited these absolutely

38. Brāhmaṇic theory admits of eight forms of marriage, of which the first four are considered regular: the 'brāhmaṇic' type, the most noble of them, is the one described above; the marriage 'of the gods', in which the girl is given to the officiating priest; that called 'of *Prajāpati*', without contract or dowry; that of 'the Wise Men', in which the bridegroom makes a payment in kind to the bride's father, which is a disguised purchase. Then come the irregular forms: that 'of the *Āsura*', in which the girl is bought for money, a form of marriage considered extremely reprehensible by the religious lawgivers; that 'of the *Gāndharva*', a secret union by mutual consent; that 'of the *Rākṣasa*', characterized by an abduction followed by a combat; finally, that 'of the *Paiśācas*', which is, simply, rape. A ninth form, that 'of the *svayaṃvara*', in which the bride was won during the course of a tourney, was practised by the *kṣatriyas*

39. For a fuller description, see *Gṛhya Sūtra*, *op. cit.*, pp. 300–1, n. 9

40. *Ṛg Veda*, X, 85, 36; *Atharva Veda*, XIV, 1, 50–1

41. L. Renou, *La Civilisation de l'Inde ancienne*, p. 95 (§ 20)

42. Henry, *op. cit.*, p. 94 seq.

43. Hiraṇyakeśin, *Gṛhya Sūtra*, I, 5, 16, 14

44. *Kusa-j*, no. 531, V, p. 153; *Cullavagga*, VI, 2, 1

45. *Mahāvagga*, VI, 12, 1–4; *Cullavagga*, V, 28, 2

46. M. Chandra, 'Cosmetics and Coiffure in Ancient India', in *J.I.S.O.A.*, VIII, 1940, pp. 80, 105, 124, 132

47. *Bhaddha-sāla-j*, no. 465, IV, p. 92

48. *Mahā-ummagga-j*, no. 546, V, pp. 183–4

49. *Ibid.*

50. Renou, *op. cit.*, § 109; Renou and Filliozat, *op. cit.*, I, § 1204; Basham, *op. cit.*, pp. 213–215; B. S. Upādhyāya, *India in Kālidāsa*, p. 196; Jain, *op. cit.*, p. 123 seq.

51. Culinary occupations are depicted frequently at Sānchī and Ajaṇṭā: see Foucher and Marshall, *op. cit.*, II, pl. LII *a*; Yazdānī, *op. cit.*, I, pl. XII, and IV, pls. XXXVI and LXX

52. Foucher, *Les Vies antérieures du Bouddha*, p. 185

53. Illustrated in Sivarāmamurti, *Amarāvatī Sculptures*, pl. XLVI, 2 *b*

54. *Maha-ummagga-j*, *loc. cit.*

55. According to Hsüan-Ch'uang, the forbidden meats were those of the ox, donkey, elephant, horse, pig, dog, fox, wolf (?), lion and monkey: Beal, *op. cit.*, I, p. 89

56. *Harivaṃśa*, transl. Langlois, II, p. 104

57. Monnier-Williams, in Notes to *Śakuntalā* of Kālidāsa

58. Hsüan-Ch'uang: Beal, *op. cit.*, I, p. 88

59. Prohibitions from consuming alcoholic drinks abound throughout all classical writings

on ritual matters. See, among others: *Vāsiṣtha Dharma Śastra*, XX, 44; XXI, 11; *Baudhāyana*, I, 5, 10; IX, 3; XIX, 18; *Mānava Dharma Śāstra*, V, 89–90; VII, 47; IX, 13, 80, 84, 225, 237; XI, 68; XII, 56

60. Upādhyāya, *op. cit.*, pp. 196–7

61. E. H. Warmington, *Commerce between the Roman Empire and India*, p. 265; Renou, *op. cit.*, § 110; Upādhyāya, *op. cit.*, pp. 196–7; Jain, *op. cit.*, p. 124 seq. This is the actual *pān*

62. Upādhyāya, *loc. cit.* This same mixture is still consumed throughout India today

63. Upādhyāya, *op. cit.*, p. 211

64. *Raghu Vaṃśa*, V, 2

65. This is still current practice. Hsüan-Ch'uang (Beal, *op. cit.*, I, p. 85) mentions nine different forms of salutation

66. Upādhyāya, *op. cit.*, pp. 209–10

67. Renou and Filliozat, *op. cit.*, I, § 1209, p. 589. In Vedic times, the cushion was a heap of grass

68. Similar rites are still practised in the Japanese tea ceremony. Before the guest is handed the bowl containing a little green tea (which he must accept with both hands), the person offering it to him revolves the bowl three times, in an anti-clockwise direction

69. Beal, *op. cit.*, I, p. 107

70. Henry, *op. cit.*, p. 111 seq. The ritual was much longer and more complicated, according to *Harṣacarita*, II, 63 seq. (transl. Cowell and Thomas, p. 44 seq.)

71. *Vāsiṣtha Dharma Śāstra*, II, 40; *The Code of Manu*, transl. Buhler, X, 117

72. Principally, the *Āyurveda* and the classic treatises of Suśruta and Caraka, written originally in Sanskrit, but whose fame spread so far afield that they were translated into Pāli, Bengali and Nepāli, and partially inspired the treatises of southern India written in Tamil. Outside India, translations are known in Kuča dialect, Khotanese, Tibetan, Mongolian, Chinese and Arabic. Numerous commentaries were appended to the original texts in these different regions. Indian medicine was developed earlier than Greek medicine, and so gave the West the principal names in its pharmacopoeia and the corresponding prescriptions

73. Renou and Filliozat, *op. cit.*, II, § 1619–81; Renou, *op. cit.*, p. 184; Upādhyāya, *op. cit.*, p. 290 seq.; Jain, *op. cit.*, p. 178 seq.; Henry, *op. cit.*, pp. 165 seq., 179 seq., 187, 190, 197, 205; Basham, *op. cit.*, p. 498 seq

74. See the description of a dying man in *Harṣacarita*, transl. Cowell and Thomas, p. 140 seq.

75. A. M. Esnoul, *Les Songes et leur Interprétation*, pp. 223–6

76. The *Vaikhānasa Gṛhya Sūtra*, V, 1, transl. Renou, *Anthologie sanskrite*, pp. 53–4

77. This description conforms with the belief, accepted equally in medicine and in philosophy, which established an analogy between the cosmos and the human body, both being com-

posed of the same elements: empty space, wind, fire, water and earth. Wind, fire and water combine in the body to create and maintain life: any disorder in their relationship produces humours (*doṣa*) leading to death

78. *Raghu Vaṃśa*, VIII, 90

79. *Bhagavad Gītā*, transl. Edgerton, II, 1–28

80. She was even supposed to smash them, as an irremediable sign of her state of mourning

81. *Raghu Vaṃśa*, VIII, 66–7

82. For further details of this procedure, see the following *Gṛhya Sūtras*: Aśvalāyana, IV, 1–6, and Pāraskara, III, 10. Also Renou and Filliozat, *op. cit.*, I, § 740–2 and 1196 seq.; Jain, *op. cit.*, p. 241 seq.; J. M. and G. Casal, *Site urbain et sites funéraires des environs de Pondichéry*, 1956, p. 19 seq., 27, 29, 50 seq.

83. Casal, *op. cit.*, p. 29

84. Ten days for a *sapiṇḍa*; the period varied according to the degree of relationship or the social status of the deceased (but three days at the very least)

85. A charnel-house is mentioned by Cowell in his edition of the *Jātaka*, I, p. 215, and n. 2

86. According to the description of the cemetery of Kāveripatnam taken from the *Maṇimegalai*, VI, 36–96, transl. Léon Saint-Jean of Kārikāl, and publ. by Casal, *op. cit.*, p. 51 seq.

87. Aśvalāyana, *Gṛhya Sūtra*, IV, 1, 15

88. S. C. Sarkar, *Some Aspects of the Earliest Social History of India*, p. 39 seq. See also *Harṣacarita*, p. 164

89. The sex of funeral urns is specified in the *Gṛhya Sūtra* by Aśvalāyana, IV, 5, 2. It is of interest to note that three of the urns unearthed at Muttrapaleon by J. M. and G. Casal (those numbered IV, XIV and XV) presented the special feature of being 'flanked on their upper part by two small twin-shaped urns in the form of breasts, jutting out at each side (pl. XVIII)'. Although such interpretations must be approached cautiously, it does seem that the female symbolism detected by these authors may well correspond with the injunctions of the *Gṛhya Sūtra* of Aśvalāyana mentioned above

It is also of interest to note that the urns recovered from funeral sites in southern India contained bones that had been gnawed clean (by beasts of prey) and showed no signs of calcination, contrary to the true brāhmaṇic cremation ritual

Sarcophagi, made of earthenware, were unearthed in relatively large numbers during the excavations at Sanur: see *Ancient India*, no. 15 (1959), pp. 10–20, referring to the 1950 and 1952 excavations of a layer dated approximately 200 BC–AD 50

90. Aśvalāyana, IV, 5, 1 seq.

91. *Corpus Inscriptionum Indicarum*, III, p. 92

92. Sarkar, *op. cit.*, pp. 82–3 and 186–7; Upādhyāya, *op. cit.*, p. 189; *The Cambridge History*

of *India*, I, pp. 292–3 and 414–15 seq.; Sivarāmamurti, *Sanskrit Literature and Art*, p. 89 seq.; Renou, *op. cit.*, § 22

93. Upādhyāya, *op. cit.*, p. 204

94. Many social reformers, including Gandhi, preached the remarriage of widows, which has since been authorized by the constitution

95. For further details, see Renou, *op. cit.*, § 23

96. *Ibid.*, p. 98

97. *Ibid.*, § 12–15 and 24; *idem*, *Anthologie sanskrite*, pp. 208–9

CHAPTER FOUR, MONASTIC AND ASCETIC LIFE

1. *Nāyādhammakahā*, ed. N. V. Vaidya, Poona, 1940, I, p. 25 seq. Also *Uttarādhyahana*, 19; and Jain, *Life in Ancient India*, p. 105 and n. 235

2. Transl. Cowell and Thomas, III, 12: this description is completed by appendix A, p. 263 seq.

3. A fact due to the heavy jewellery which they wore during their previous social existence, often characterized by gaudy ostentation, and which they now renounced. The distended lobes became a symbol of wisdom

4. Frequently reproduced, especially at Ajaṇṭā, cave XXVI (*parinirvāṇa*). See G. Yazdānī, *Ajaṇṭā*, IV, pl. LXXX

5. *Asaṁkiya-j*, no. 76, transl. Cowell, I, p. 186

6. Hsüan-Ch'uang mentions such suicides: see S. Beal, *Buddhist Records of the Western World*, I, p. 86

7. For this whole passage, see E. Lamotte, *Histoire du Bouddhisme indien des origines à l'ère çaka*, Louvain, 1958, p. 59 seq., 71 seq., 330, 546, 686

8. The *Mahāvagga*, part I is devoted entirely to the subject of admission into the order of *Bhikṣu*

9. In no case could it take place during the rainy season

10. *Mahāvagga*, V, 1, 28

11. *Brahmadatta-j*, no. 323, III, p. 53

12. *Ibid.*, p. 54

13. *Mahāvagga*, II

14. M. Chandra, 'Cosmetics and Coiffure in Ancient India', in *J.I.S.O.A.*, VIII, 1940, p. 76 (following the *Cullavagga*, V, 14, 2–5; VII, 8, 2; VIII, 8, 2; X, 27, 4; etc.)

15. *Mémoires sur les religieux éminents*, transl. E. Chavannes, p. 85 seq. See also: H. D. Sankalia, *The University of Nālandā*, Madras, 1934

16. *Sūrya siddhānta* (*c* AD 350), XIII, 21 seq., and XI, 8 (transl. B. Deva, *Bibliotheca Indica*, pp. 90–1 and 211). See also: I-Tsing, *A Record of the Buddhist Religion as practised in India and the Malay Archipelago* (AD 671–695), transl. J. Takakusu, p. 144 seq.

17. *Mahāvagga*, IV

18. Various reasons, often misanthropic or pessimistic, are listed in the Jain canons: see J. C. Jain, *op. cit.*, p. 193

19. See *S.B.E.*, vol. XXII, p. XXII seq.

PART THREE

CHAPTER ONE, CITY LIFE AND FASHIONABLE EXISTENCE

1. *Kāmasūtra* of Vātsyāyana, I, 4, 8 seq. Suśruta, XXIV (*Cikitsāsthāna*). See also M. Chandra, 'Cosmetics and Coiffure in Ancient India', in *J.I.S.O.A.*, pp. 75, 97 seq., 122

2. See, primarily, the *Kāmasūtra*, transl. S. C. Upādhyāya with foreword by M. Chandra, London, 1962. See also C. Sivarāmamurti, *Sanskrit Literature and Art, Mirrors of Indian Culture*, p. 13 seq.; and O. Gangoly, 'The Mithuna in Indian Art', in *Rūpam*, nos. 22–3, 1925, p. 54 seq.

3. Theme represented from the third or fourth century AD onwards, especially at Nāgārjunakoṇḍā. See *Raghu Vaṃśa*, XIX, 28

4. The *Arthaśāstra* of Kauṭilya, II, 27

5. The *Kāmasūtra* in particular; but Renou, *La Civilisation de l'Inde ancienne*, § 77, thinks that this should not be taken too literally

6. *Vaṭṭaka-j*, no. 118, transl. Cowell, I, p. 261

7. *Ibid, loc. cit.*

8. *Takkāriya-j*, no. 481, IV, p. 157

9. The list of the sixty-four arts is given in the *Kāmasūtra*. It is somewhat surprising in its diversity, but it represents everything which a cultivated man or woman should know. It ranges from the fine arts to pharmacy, mineralogy, the exploitation of quarries and mines, by way of magical practices and charms, disguises, conjuring, the preparation of sweetmeats and sherbets, that of cosmetics and perfumes, the composition of charades and enigmas, etc.

10. *Aṭṭhāna-j*, no. 425, III, p. 282 seq.

11. Kaṇavera-j, no. 318, II, p. 40; *Sulasā-j*, no. 419, III, p. 261

12. J. Auboyer, *La Vie publique et privée dans l'Inde ancienne*, fasc. VI, p. 21 seq. Illustrated in Cunningham, *The Stūpa of Bhārhut*, pl. XLV, 9; G. Yazdānī, *Ajaṇṭā*, II, pl. 38. Later, numerous examples exist of the divine couple, Śiva and Pārvatī, playing dice: Elephantā (sixth century AD), Ellorā (seventh-eighth centuries AD)

13. Many ivory dice have been found in excavations of sites from the Mohenjo Dāro epoch onwards

14. See C. Marcel-Dubois, *Les Instruments de Musique de l'Inde ancienne*; bow-harp: p. 80 seq.

15. Frequently reproduced. See, for instance, Sivarāmamurti, *op. cit.*, pl. XXIV, 80

16. *Raghu Vaṃśa*, XIX, 13

17. From the era of the Kuṣāṇa dynasty: *Aśokavadāna*, VII

18. It is supposed to have been in this manner that King Ajātaśatru learned the news of the Buddha's *parinirvāṇa*

19. *Kāmasūtra*. Also *Harṣacarita*, transl. Cowell and Thomas, p. 214

20. *Kāmasūtra*

21. *Viṣṇudharmottaram*, transl. P. Shah, Baroda, 1958

22. *Śilparatna* of Śrīkumāra: see also *Harṣacarita*, *op. cit.*, p. 123

23. This was a group of aesthetes (*rāsikas*) who met together for literary recitations and discussions. The *goṣṭhīs* still exist

24. On 27th July 1960, a deputy of the Indian Congress improvised his speech in verse . . .

25. S. Lévi, *Le Théâtre indien*, Paris, 1890; A. B. Keith, *The Sanskrit Drama in its Origin, Development, Theory and Practice*, Oxford, 1924. The most recent critical synthesis is in L. Renou, *L'Inde classique*, II, §§ 1845–1903

26. In particular, the *Bharatanātyaśāstra*

27. *Mahābhāṣya*, VI, 1, 13

28. J. C. Jain, *Life in Ancient India as depicted in the Jain Canons*, p. 188, describes one, but following belated sources and in redundant style

29. B. S. Upādhyāya, *India in Kālidāsa*, p. 224

30. *Saṁkhadhamana-j*, no. 60, I., p. 147

31. *Bherivāda-j*, no. 59, I, p. 146

32. *Ghata-j*, no. 454, IV, p. 53

33. Illustrated in Cunningham, *op. cit.*, pl. XXXV, 2. See also Auboyer, *op. cit.*, pl. 3 and p. 4. A medallion recently discovered at Nāgārjunakoṇḍa represents two wrestlers very much like those of Bhārhut

34. Jain, *op. cit.*, p. 240

35. Illustrated in S. Kramrisch, *The Art of India*, pl. XVII

36. *Dubbhaca-j*, no. 116, I, p. 259

37. Jain, *op. cit.*, p. 241

38. This turn is still performed today. The illusion is so perfect that photographers have attempted—unsuccessfully, of course—to record the scene on film. Described in the *Suruci-j*, no. 489, IV, p. 204

39. *Ibid.* See also A. Foucher, *Les Vies antérieures du Bouddha*, p. 202

40. *Dasaṇṇaka-j*, no. 401, III, p. 208

41. Illustrated in D. Barrett, *Sculptures from Amarāvatī*, pl. XXVII; Yazdānī, *op. cit.*, II, pl. X b

42. *Harṣacarita*, *op. cit.*, V, 170

43. *Harivaṃśa*, transl. M. A. Langlois, II, p. 93 seq.

44. Auboyer, *op. cit.*, p. 9

CHAPTER TWO, ROYAL EXISTENCE AND ITS ENVIRONMENT

1. However, *Raghu Vaṃśa*, XIX, 7, mentions a small circular open window out of which the king allowed one of his feet to dangle, this being the only part of him visible to his courtiers, and duly venerated by them

2. *Bṛhad Purāṇa*, III, 74. The *Raghu Vaṃśa*, I, 35, recommends that a king afflicted with im-

potence should make a retreat in a hermitage, subjecting himself to fasts and a milk diet. For the prostitution of queens, see *Kāliṅgabodhi-jātaka*, no. 479, Cowell, IV, p. 142

3. Manu, IX, 65

4. *Mahābhārata*, Udyoga Parva, 38, 43. And *Rāmāyaṇa*, Ayodhyā, ch. 68–9

5. These methods of suicide, especially the first, were undertaken by several Indian monarchs in certain eras, especially during the Middle Ages in central India

6. *Suruci-j*, no. 489, IV, p. 203; *Sarabhanga-j*, no. 522, VI, p. 66

7. *Harṣacarita*, IV (143), transl. Cowell and Thomas, pp. 111–12

8. E. Senart, *Essai sur la légende du Bouddha*, p. 300 and n.

9. *Vessantara-j*, no. 547, VI, p. 251

10. Senart, *loc. cit.*, p. 300 and fn.

11. *Rāmāyaṇa*, *loc. cit.*, 59

12. See J. Auboyer, 'Quelques réflexions à propos du cakra comme arme de guerre', *Arts asiatiques*, XI, 1 (1965)

13. Motī Chandra, 'Cosmetics and Coiffure in Ancient India', in *J.I.S.O.A.*, VIII, 1940, p. 73, citing the *Jātaka*; and R. Fick, *Die soziale Gliederung . . .*, pp. 287–8. See also, *Gaṅgamāla-j*, no. 42, III, p. 269; *Sigāla-j*, no. 152, II, p. 4; *Illīsa-j*, no. 78, I, p. 200

14. *Gaṅgamāla-j*, *loc. cit.*

15. *Suppāraka-j*, no. 463, IV, p. 87

16. *Makhādeva-j*, no. 9, I, p. 31

17. It contained furs and pelts from the Himālayas, fabrics and woollen blankets from Nepāl and other regions, 'as smooth as the surface of a polished stone', fine cloths woven in Banāras, silk imported from China and very light cotton stuffs from all the chief Indian weaving centres. See Chandra, *op. cit.*, p. 81

18. A. Foucher, *Les Vies antérieures du Bouddha*, p. 104 seq.

19. G. Yazdānī, *Ajaṇṭā*, IV, pl. V

20. *Jātaka* no. 418, III, p. 258

21. *Jātaka* no. 537, cited by Foucher, *op. cit.*, p. 287

22. Illustrated in Yazdānī, *op. cit.*, III, pl. LXVI

23. It may be noted that this is still the case in Thailand and Laos

24. *Alīnacitta-j*, II, p. 16

25. *Mahājanaka-j*, no. 539, VI, p. 27

26. Frequently portrayed at Bhājā, Bhārhut, Sānchī, etc.

27. The entire literature of ancient India emphasizes the importance accorded to the State elephant

28. *Giridaṇṭa-j*, no. 184, II, pp. 67–8. See also Foucher, 'Deux jātaka sur ivoire', in *India Antiqua*, 1947; Hackin, *Nouvelles recherches archéologiques à Begram . . .*, p. 84

29. *Kurudhamma-j*, no. 276, II, p. 258

30. See the Catalogue of the Exhibition of Indian Art in London, 1947–8, pl. XIX (no. 111)

31. Foucher, *loc. cit.*

32. Portrayed at Bhārhut, Bodhgayā, Sānchī, etc.

33. A custom known in the Kuṣāṇa epoch, at Māt near Mathurā, in the Gupta epoch, and perpetuated by the Rājpūts. See Luders in *Epigraphia Indica*, XXIV, p. 194 seq., and Bhandārkar, *ibid*., XXI, p. 4 seq.; V. S. Agrawāla, Mathurā Museum Catalogue, III, pp. 38–45; C. Sivarāmamurti, *Sanskrit Literature and Art*, p. 90 seq.

34. *Harṣacarita*, II (68), p. 49

35. *Arthaśāstra*, II, 18

36. V. Dikshitar, *War in Ancient India*, p. 16 seq., and pp. 214–15

37. A bas-relief at Bhārhut depicts an artisan busy straightening an arrow-head: see A. Coomāraswāmy, *La Sculpture de Bhārhut*, pl. XLVII, fig. 200

38. *Arthaśāstra*, II, 11. See Chandra, *op. cit*., p. 82 seq.

39. Foucher, *op. cit*., p. 104. Illustrated in Sir A. Cunningham, *The Stūpa of Bhārhut*, pl. XLV, 7

40. *Ancient India as described by Megasthenes* . . ., transl. J. W. McCrindle, pp. 71–2

41. Frequently depicted until the end of the Gupta epoch, but not afterwards. See J. Auboyer in Hackin, *op. cit*., p. 73

42. For the different types of seat, see Auboyer, *Le Trône et son symbolisme dans l'Inde ancienne*, pp. 9–45

43. *Raghu Vaṃśa*, XIX, 4–36

44. *Ibid*., 48–54

45. In springtime, women went into the gardens and touched the trunk of the aśoka tree with their right foot to make it blossom. This is a frequent theme in both literature and art

46. *Śakuntalā*, act V, scene III. See Sivarāmamurti, *Amarāvatī Sculptures* . . ., p. 100 and pl. VII, fig. 14

47. *Raghu Vaṃśa*, XVI

48. Depicted at Ajaṇṭā, cave XVII: see Yazdānī, IV, pl. X

49. *Mahābhārata*, IV, 8, 16; *Saundarānanda*, IV, 26

50. Razor (*kṣura*), see *Atharva Veda*, VI, 68; Tweezers (*sandāsaga*), see J. C. Jain, *Life in Ancient India* . . .

51. Nail-cutters (*nakhacchedana*), see *Cullavagga*, V, 27, 2. Special attention was paid to nail-care by both men and women: the nails, especially those of the left hand, were allowed to grow long, and had to be well looked-after, polished, shining and meticulously clean. Buddhist monastic rules laid down that it was forbidden to clean the nails with the nails of the other hand oɪ with the teeth, to pare them by rubbing them against a wall or to polish them

52. Ear-pick (*kannamalaharanī*), see *Cullavagga*, V, 27, 6. One of these instruments, in bronze, was unearthed during excavations at Sirkap (Taxilā): see *A.S.I.*, *A.R.*, 1914–15, p. 17, pl. XXIV, 34, and p. 23, pl. XXIV, 28

53. A terracotta massage instrument was also unearthed during excavations at Sirkap: *op. cit*., 1915–16, p. 15, pl. VIII. Others made of ox-bone, are mentioned in *Cullavagga*, X, 10, 2

54. Sometimes shaped like

fruits: see *A.S.I.*, *A.R.*, 1902–3, p. 184

55. One such scent-spray was unearthed at Sirkap: *op. cit.*, 1928–9, p. 52; and another at Bālāhisār: *ibid.*, 1902–3, p. 184

56. Called *patrāṅguli*: see *Saundarānanda*, IV, 13–16

57. A small instrument unearthed at Sirkap is probably identifiable as a hair-curler: see *A.S.I.*, *A.R.*, 1914–15, p. 20, pl. XXIV, 29

58. Combs (*phaṇiha*, *prasādhanī*) were made of ivory, wood, metal or horn. One, of ivory, was unearthed at Sirkap: see *A.S.I.*, *A.R.*, 1926–7, p. 119; another at Taxilā: *op. cit.*, 1928–9, p. 51, pl. XXI, 13–14. See also G. P. Majumdār in *Indian Culture*, I, 4, p. 663; and Sivarāmamurti, *Amarāvatī Sculptures*, p. 120

59. *Agni Purāṇa*, CXXIV, 41

60. The composition is given in *Agni Pūrāṇa*, CCXXII, 33

61. Suśruta, *Saṃhitā* (quoted by Chandra, *op. cit.*)

62. Portrayed at Mathurā, col. of Lakhnau Museum (no. J 278), see catalogue of London exhibition 1947–8, pl. VIII, no. 53

63. Suśruta, *Saṃhitā*, XXIV, 4

64. Sivarāmamurti, *Amarāvatī Sculptures*, p. 139

65. *Raghu Vaṃśa*, VII, 7. See also B. S. Upādhyāya, *India in Kālidāsa*, p. 207 and n. 2

66. Together with white *agallochum*, saffron, crocoite, etc.

67. These designs, called *viśeṣaka* and *bhakti*, are frequently described in Indian texts. See Chandra, *op. cit.*, *passim.* This custom has persisted in certain regions (Rājputāna and Mathurā) on the occasion of marriage ceremonies

68. A decoration of this kind (frequently mentioned in texts) may be seen depicted in the statuary of Bhārhut: see Coomāraswāmy, *op. cit.*, pl. XXI; and Upādhyāya, *op. cit.*, p. 206 and n. 21. The designs were of many kinds, representing the sun, the moon, a star, a trident, an elephant hook, flowers, stylized foliage, various symbols, or simply patterns of dots

69. This paste, used to enhance the brightness of the eyes, to give the face a gracious contour and to make the complexion like the colour of a lotus blossom, was also supposed to be good for the skin, prevention of itching and eruptions and removing its imperfections: see Suśruta, pp. 40–1

70. Five categories of khol are listed: *kālāñjana* (black), *rāsāñjana*, *sota-añjana*, *geruka* (yellow), *kājjala* (lamp-black): see Chandra, *op. cit.*, p. 77

71. See Chandra, *op. cit.*, pp. 104–5

72. *Ibid.*, p. 78

73. Called *añjnī*: see Jain, *op. cit.*, p. 105 and no. 235

74. *Mahāvagga*, VI, 2, 1

75. *Bharata Nāṭyaśāstra*, XXIII, 28–33. A small box which had contained red lip-paste was unearthed at Sirkap: see *A.S.I.*, *A.R.*, 1928–9, p. 52

76. This scene is frequently reproduced, especially in the bas-reliefs of the Mathurā school and

the ivories of Begrām: see Hackin, *Recherches archéologiques à Begrām*, pl. VIII, no. 53

77. A detail to be found already at Mathurā and seen frequently at Ajaṇṭā

78. As, for instance, at Bhārhut and Sānchī

79. Adorned with aśoka branches: see Auboyer in Hackin, *Nouvelles recherches archéologiques à Begrām* . . ., p. 64, pl. C (f)

80. Sivarāmamurti, *Sanskrit Literature and Art* . . ., pp. 30–35, *Amarāvatī Sculptures*, pp. 106–7. Each variation of these elaborate coiffures bears a particular and often evocative name

81. The composition of this paste varied considerably

82. Looking-glass: *mukura*, *ādamsaga* or *ādasa* in Pāli. For one of gold, see *Raghu Vaṃśa*, XVII, 26. See also: Upādhyāya, *op. cit.*, p. 207; G. Rao, *Elements of Hindu Iconography*, I, 1, p. 12; K. de B. Codrington, 'The Minor Arts of India', in *Indian Art*, p. 177, and *Indian Antiquary*, LIX, August 1930. Those unearthed in excavations are of copper and furnished with a hafted tenon: see *A.S.I.*, *A.R.*, 1915–16, pl. IX, 3 and 101 (pp. 16–17) and pl. XV (p. 20)

83. Such as those at Sirkap. One such looking-glass has been discovered in the ruins of Pompeii: see A. Maiuri, 'Statuetta eburnea di arte indiana a Pompeii', in *Le Arti*, I, 2, pp. 111–15 (Florence, 1939); see also Hackin, *op. cit.*, pp. 41–2

84. Sivarāmamurti, *Amarāvatī Sculptures*, pp. 107–16; K. K. Gānguly, 'Early Indian Jewellery', in *Indian Hist. Quart.*, XVIII, 1 (March 1942), p. 110 seq; G. P. Majumdār, *Indian Culture*, I, 1, p. 664; Upādhyāya, *op. cit.*, p. 203. Many details are provided in *Śukra Nītisāra*

85. *Raghu Vaṃśa*, XIII, 23

86. J. M. Casal, *Fouilles de Virampatnam-Arikamedu*, pl. XIII A, and p. 29

87. *Raghu Vaṃśa*, V, 74

88. A theme which has inspired many poetic descriptions throughout epic and classical Indian literature

89. Hackin, *op. cit.*, fig. 30 b; Upādhyāya, *op. cit.*, p. 254

90. Hackin, *op. cit.*, fig. 667

91. *Ibid.*, figs. 22, 25, 659, 660

92. J. P. Vogel, *La Sculpture de Mathurā*, pl. XIXa; Hackin, *loc. cit.*, fig. 667

93. Hackin, *op. cit.*, p. 70

94. *Stereospernum suaveolens* (Bignonia). See *Raghu Vaṃśa*, XIX, 46

95. Hackin, *op. cit.*, p. 79 (pl. E, fig. *f* and *j*)

96. *Mahāsāra-j*, no. 92, I, p. 225

97. *Raghu Vaṃśa*, XIX, 9 and 10; XVI, 56 and 66

98. Hackin, *op. cit.*, fig. 140

99. Called *kandukakrīdā*: see Sivarāmamurti, *Sanskrit Literature* . . ., p. 42; Auboyer, *La Vie publique et privée* . . ., VI, pp. 4–5 and pl. III, 2; *Raghu Vaṃśa*, XVI, 83; *Nalinikā-j*, no. 526, V, p. 102 (this concerns a painted ball attached to a string)

100. C. Marcel-Dubois, *Les*

Instruments de musique de l'Inde ancienne, pl. XXXIX, 1

101. Hackin, *op. cit.*, p. 62 and n. 10. See also: *Buddhacarita*, III, 12; *Ratnāvalī*, act II, 3; Sivarāmamurti, *Amarāvatī Sculptures*, p. 100

102. Kauṭilya, I, 19; *Daśakumāra*, VIII; Manu, VIII, 145 seq., 216 seq.; *Mahābhārata*, XV, 5; *Yogayātrā*, II, 17 seq., etc.

103. Chandra, *op. cit.*, p. 121, citing Bāṇa's *Kādambarī*

104. A. H. Longhurst, *Nāgārjunakoṇḍa*, pl. XXXVI, b

105. Yet one tale even refers to a cannibal king; see Foucher, *op. cit.*, pp. 284–7. *Jātaka*, no. 220, II, p. 136, n.

106. Kings were not all in favour of the prohibition of hunting, as the great emperor Aśoka and a few others had been. Their status as *kṣatriyas* made it almost obligatory for them to practise arms, whether for war or simply for hunting. And, in general, the ideal image of a king was that of a warrior and brave hunter

107. *Raghu Vaṃśa*, V, 50; IX, 49–53, 60, 65, 67, etc.

CHAPTER THREE, THE PUBLIC LIFE OF THE KING: IMPERIAL POMP

1. *Divyāvadāna*, II, 27–9
2. *Rāmāyaṇa*, II, 3, 1 seq.
3. We have abridged this proceeding somewhat
4. J. Auboyer, 'L'Arc et la Flèche dans l'iconographie ancienne de l'Inde', in *Artibus Asiae*, XIX, 3–4, 1956, pp. 173–85
5. This lustration is well illustrated in the Khmer lintel from Vat Eng Khnà now in the collection of the Phnom Peñh museum: reproduced in *Histoire des Religions*, 1960, II, p. 289
6. This hunt must have been shammed, although it may originally have been a genuine *corrida* giving the king a patrimony composed of the community's herds. It has been viewed as the symbol of the king's suzerainty over his subjects' possessions
7. Auboyer, *La Vie publique et privée dans l'Inde ancienne*, p. 25
8. The king handed a wooden sword to his brother, who gave it to the governor, who passed it on to the police commissioner; the latter entrusted it to a man from the same tribe as the king. Then a libation took place, during the course of which the ten men taking part each drank simultaneously from a separate cup
9. Auboyer, *Le Trône et son symbolisme dans l'Inde ancienne*, p. 153 seq.
10. See *Agni Purāṇa*, CIX; L. Renou and J. Filliozat, *L'Inde classique*, I, §§ 1114–15 (p. 341); Pavitrānanda, 'Pilgrimages and Fairs: their bearing on Indian Life', in *The Cultural Heritage of India*, III, p. 153 seq.
11. It may be noted that these

pilgrimages inspired a thriving industry producing votive offerings which are evident, in excavations, from a very early period

12. V. R. R. Dikshitar, *War in Ancient India*, pp. 201 seq., 217 seq., 300 seq., 337 seq.; Renou, *La Civilisation de l'Inde ancienne*, §§ 53, 63, 69

13. *Arthaśāstra*, II, 32

14. Arrian in *Ancient India as Described by Megasthenes and Arrian* (transl. J. W. McCrindle), XVI

15. *Raghu Vaṃśa*, IV, 42

16. *Ibid.*, IV, 45

17. A rainbow, for instance

18. *Atharva Veda*, XIX, 20

19. *Raghu Vaṃśa*, V, 42

20. See Dikshitar, *op. cit.*, p. 67 seq. and p. 91

21. P. E. Dumont, *L'Aśvamedha*, 1927

22. A. L. Basham, in *Journal of the Andhra Historical Research Society*, X, p. 14

23. Dumont, *op. cit.*, p. x

24. Auboyer, *Le Trône et son symbolisme . . .*, p. 136 and n. 2

INDEX

Daily Life of the Aztecs

JACQUES SOUSTELLE

A vivid account of the fierce, honourable, death-obsessed, profoundly religious Aztecs on the eve of the Spanish conquest. Even in the darkest symbolism of their blood-drenched worship they appear as people with whom we can sympathise. "It is, without question, the most brilliant, the clearest and most readable portrayal of Aztec life available in any language" *Observer*

Paperback
UK: £12.99 352pp + 24pp b/w 1 84212 508 7
USA: $19.95
CAN: $29.95

Daily Life of the Etruscans

JACQUES HEURGON

On the evidence of their brilliantly evocative wall paintings, terracottas, bronzes and jewellery, the Etruscans appear to have had a tremendous zest for life with a fondness for dancing, horse-racing, every form of musical activity and sooth saying. ". . . the high literary intelligence informing it makes the book a most desirable companion to the more purely archaeological works which have been appearing of late" *Sunday Times*. "The best popular book yet published about those mysterious people" *New Yorker*

Paperback
UK: £12.99 352pp + 24pp b/w 1 84212 592 3
USA: $19.95
CAN: $29.95

Life and Leisure in Ancient Rome

J.P.V.D. BALSDON

What did a Roman citizen do between getting up in the morning and going to bed at night? Dr Balsdon uses a wide variety of sources to answer this and many other questions about what life was like in Ancient Rome. "Precise, detailed, and reliable, and informed throughout with a genuine sense of what it all felt like . . . By far the best single volume on its subject" *Guardian*

Paperback
UK: £12.99 464pp + 16pp b/w 1 84212 593 1
USA: $19.95
CAN: $29.95